THE LIFE AND LETTERS

OF

SAMUEL WELLS WILLIAMS, LL.D.

MISSIONARY, DIPLOMATIST, SINOLOGUE

BY HIS SON

FREDERICK WELLS WILLIAMS

Scholarly Resources Inc.
Wilmington, Delaware

SCHOLARLY RESOURCES, INC.
1508 Pennsylvania Avenue
Wilmington, Delaware 19806

Reprint edition published in 1972
First published in 1889 by G. P. Putnam's Sons,
    New York and London

Library of Congress Catalog Card Number: 72-79841
ISBN: 0-8420-1355-5

Manufactured in the United States of America

CONTENTS.

CHAPTER I.
1812–1833.

PAGE

The family of Williams in America—William Williams of Utica—Sophia Williams—Birth and boyhood of Samuel Wells Williams—Early influences—Schools—He attends the Rensselaer Institute at Troy—Proposal from the American Board to go to China as missionary printer—He completes the course at Troy—Prepares as printer in Utica—Sails from New York in the *Morrison* . . 1

CHAPTER II.
1833–1837.

Canton and the factories before the Opium War—Relations with the mandarins—Difficulties in the way of mission work—Elijah C. Bridgman — The *Chinese Repository*—Missionary occupations—Death of Robert Morrison—Withdrawal of the East India Company—Dr. Parker and the beginning of hospital work—Mr. Olyphant—Mission press removed to Macao—Life in Macao—Tract-giving with G. T. Lay—Death of Edwin Stevens—The *Morrison's* trip to Japan—Her repulse and return—The Japanese sailors . 54

CHAPTER III.
1837–1845.

Commissioner Lin and the opium—The "Chinese Chrestomathy"—Rev. S. R. Brown and the Morrison Education Society—Trouble in Canton—The Opium War—Difficulties of foreign residence—The war ended and ports opened to foreigners—The "Easy Lessons in Chinese "—" English and Chinese Vocabulary "—" Commercial Guide "—Caleb Cushing and the treaty of Wanghia—Efforts to raise a Chinese metallic type fund — Mr. Williams leaves China—The journey through India and Egypt—Palestine—Italy and Paris—London—Movable Oriental types—Arrival in New York 101

CHAPTER IV.

1845-1852.

Lectures for the type fund—Mr. Williams settles in New York and compiles "The Middle Kingdom"—His engagement—Life in New York—Marriage—" The Middle Kingdom " published—He obtains the degree of LL.D.—Sails for China with his wife—The Term controversy—Literary work—Private and public life—" Tonic Dictionary" commenced—Death of William Williams—The *Chinese Repository* concluded—Life and occupations in Canton 146

CHAPTER V.

1852-1854.

Arrival of Com. Perry's expedition in China—Mr. Williams engaged as interpreter—The expedition reaches Lewchew—Napa—The Bonin Islands—The squadron in Yedo Bay—Meeting at Gorihama—Perry returns to winter at Macao—The Tai-ping insurrection—Illness and work—Preparations for the second expedition to Japan. 183

CHAPTER VI.

1854-1855.

Journal of the expedition—Lewchew again—The ships in the Bay of Yedo — A treaty proposed — Negotiations—Japanese timidity—Perry's conduct—Visit to Hakodadi—Simoda—Reflections on the expedition—Return to Lewchew and China—Commodore Perry's letters to Mr. Williams—The Perry medal 206

CHAPTER VII.

1855-1858.

Appointment as United States Secretary and Interpreter in China—Mr. Williams' reluctance to accept—The " Tonic Dictionary " completed—The second war with China—The mission press destroyed with the factories—Resignation sent to the American Board—W. B. Reed, United States Minister Plenipotentiary—War opens with Yeh's capture—Mr. Williams' family sent to America . . 234

CHAPTER VIII.

1858-1859.

The Allies at the Peiho—Negotiations with Tan—Capture of the Taku Forts—The foreigners at Tientsin—Kweiliang and Hwashana—

Treaty-making — Kiying — The Toleration Clause—The treaty signed—The Americans return to Shanghai—The Legation visits Nagasaki — Death of Olyphant — Scenes in Shanghai — Tariff treaty arranged—Mr. Reed's departure 254

CHAPTER IX.

1859.

Second expedition to the Peiho—Repulse of the English at Taku—The Americans at Pehtang—They are escorted to Peking—The audience discussed—Entertainments—Death of Aitcheson—Return of the Legation to Shanghai—The coolie trade—Return to America 297

CHAPTER X.

1860–1867.

Sentiments regarding the war—China again—Death of Walworth; of Dr. Bridgman—The "Commercial Guide" rewritten—To Peking with Mr. Burlingame—Scenes in Peking—Diplomatic and missionary interests—Mr. Williams brings his family to Peking—Living in the capital—Letter in defence of missions—The co-operative policy—Letter on a mission to Kiukiang—Building a United States Legation—Botany about Peking—A trip to Mongolia—Mr. Burlingame's mission to the treaty powers . . . 327

CHAPTER XI.

1868–1876.

Letters from Peking—Family sent home again—A medal from the king of Sweden—Mr. Burlingame's death—Wm. H. Seward in Peking—The dictionary finished—Mr. Williams superintends its printing in Shanghai—A third visit in Yedo Bay—Return with family to Peking—The "Syllabic Dictionary" published—Audience with the Emperor—Through Europe to America again—He returns to Peking and resigns—Farewell to Peking—Testimonials from missionaries and friends 373

CHAPTER XII.

1877–1884.

At home in New Haven—The professorship of Chinese in Yale College—Persecution of Chinese in America—Essay on Chinese immigration—Petition to President Hayes—The great famine of

1878—Paper on the Term question—Rewriting " The Middle Kingdom "—Death of Mrs. Williams—American Bible Society presidency—American Oriental Society elect Mr. Williams president—Compliments from Professor Ko of Harvard—Accident and illness—The revised " Middle Kingdom "—Death—Reminiscences and characteristics 421

INDEX 483

LIFE AND LETTERS

OF

DR. S. WELLS WILLIAMS.

CHAPTER I.

THE American branch of that numerous family from which the subject of this biography descended, was founded by Robert Williams, a Puritan probably of Welsh origin, who emigrated from Norwich, England, in 1637, and became one of the earliest settlers and leaders in the town of Roxbury, now a suburb of Boston. Two facts may be recorded of him: one, that he lived to his hundredth year; the second, that he became the ancestor of more ministers—and more long-lived ministers—than probably any other man in this country. An oft-told legend of the family relates that while he was urging his timid and reluctant wife to endure with him the hardships of a passage to the new country, she had a dream foreshadowing that from her loins should come a line of pious and illustrious preachers, whose sturdy voices should sound the truth to millions in that land. "I cheerfully prepare," she said, "for the journey to such a glorious future"; and though the day of fulfilment began after her death, she being dead has spoken loudly to posterity from scores and hundreds of pulpits, and transmitted something, perhaps, of her goodness and dignity to thousands who bear her name.

To his youngest son, Stephen, the centenarian left the more valuable part of his estates; " nor would I have the others think hardly of me for so doing "—he observes apologetically in his will,—" for he lives under the same roof with me, and thereby hath been more helpful and comfortable unto me than the other sons have." It is not recorded that any other member of the family attained to the extraordinary age of its founder, but the heritage of long life seems to have remained with his progeny through many successive generations. The offspring of the favored son Stephen continued to occupy the ancestral farm until the fifth and sixth remove from Robert of Roxbury, a line of godly and upright men and women, who maintained the name with honor and respectability, but appear never to have reached positions of great distinction or command.

In the year 1780, Thomas and Ezekiel, two brothers of the fifth generation, established a tannery in Framingham, Mass., where, for ten years, they struggled in vain, against the exhaustion following the Revolutionary war, to make their business a profitable one. Disaster at length fell upon them; they were compelled to make what peace they could with their creditors, and in 1790 they emigrated to the settlement of New Hartford, in Whitestown, N. Y. Here they recommenced the business of tanning, and at the end of a few years of untiring industry and economy, succeeded in saving enough to return to Massachusetts and pay off their debts. The spectacle of this resolute twain plodding through winter snows, in order to satisfy to the utmost farthing the last of their creditors in Framingham, is of itself sufficient to confirm their honest as well as direct Puritan descent, the spirit of whose moral code they were doggedly determined to preserve. After this we are not surprised to learn that these brothers were both eminent for piety, deacons in the church, and charitable to the extreme limit of their means.

Deacon Thomas Williams, the elder of the two brothers, brought four children from Massachusetts, the youngest of whom, William, was baptized and usually known among his contemporaries as Billy Williams. He was, when a boy, apprenticed to Wm. McLean, of New Hartford, the pioneer of printing in Central New York; about the year 1800 he joined the printing establishment of Asahel Seward (who afterwards married an elder sister), and upon coming of age young Williams entered with him into a partnership under the firm name of Seward & Williams. The energy and ability of both these men were such as to make their business a profitable one, and their house soon became the most important publishing concern and bookstore west of Albany. The character of the works issued from their press savors of the time : N. Webster's Spelling Book, the sole right of which in Western New York was most advantageous to the firm; "Watts' Divine Songs," with Doddridge's "Principles of Christian Religion"; Murray's "English Reader"; an abundance of school books and primers; nine or ten stereotyped editions of the New Testament. The presence of Thomas Hastings in the village afforded Mr. Williams not only his warm friendship, but the valuable copyright of his "Musica Sacra" and his "Spiritual Songs," both commanding large sales. A more ambitious undertaking was the reprinting of the Edinburgh Encyclopedia, in connection with a Philadelphia publisher. Lack of means retarded the enterprise, which seventy years ago was at best a precarious venture for the United States, and at the end of twenty years from its commencement, after the death or disappearance of most of the subscribers, the last volume of the encyclopedia appeared simultaneously with the downfall of its allied publishers. This catastrophe occurred some years after the withdrawal of Mr. Seward, who, in 1824, left his brother-in-law to carry on the business under the latter's name. Mr. Williams, who curiously enough was an indefatigable anti-mason, while his partner was a member of the village lodge, became in 1830 publisher of the *Elucidator*, a paper designed to counteract the increasing influence of masonic organizations. As newspaper publisher he had previously engaged in issuing the *Utica Patriot* and its successors the *Patriot and Patrol*, and the *Utica Sentinel*, down to the year 1824. But his newspapers were pecuniarily less profitable than his other enterprises, and brought him eventually into a lawsuit.

Mr. Williams obtained the title of colonel during the war of 1812, his stern sense of patriotism holding it to be the duty of every citizen to volunteer in time of danger. "In February, 1813," writes Thurlow Weed, who was at that period an apprentice in his printing-office, "when an attack on Sackett's Harbor was threatened and expected, and volunteers were called for, Mr. Williams was the first and most active man in Utica in raising a company. So prompt indeed were his movements that in thirty hours after the requisition was received, we were on our way in sleighs for the Harbor. Then when the danger seemed imminent men did not cavil about rank. Col. Seward, of New Hartford, self-raised to a captaincy, took command of our company, while Mr. Williams, who held the rank of major, acted as sergeant. And here, as in a subsequent campaign, when he was on the lines in the staff of Gen. Collins, Col. Williams was highly valued as a soldier, as he was through life esteemed as a citizen."

Identified in one way or another with nearly every new movement in the village, Col. Williams occupied in the community the position of one whose well-known energy and experience were called upon as a matter of course in any undertaking accounted a public enterprise. In this relation his name naturally appears as first among the list of chief engineers in the fire company of Utica at the time of its reorganization in 1828. To protect its four hundred buildings, the village had, as early as 1805, purchased a fire-pump and apparatus, manned by some dozen men and attached by lines of bucket-men (and women) to the town pump or the river at times of conflagration. A score of years later this organization developed into a volunteer fire department, and in 1831 it had increased to six companies; among the members of "Engine No. 4" we find the names of Col. Williams (who withdrew from the post of engineer in 1830), and of his two eldest sons, Wells and Dwight. While not a man of strong physique, he possessed the best elements of leadership in his coolness, self-control, good judgment, and a persuasiveness of manner that made sternness unnecessary. He was appropriately called "the busy man" by one who remembers him : " Colonel in the militia, elder in the church, foreman of the fire company, editor of the leading newspaper, he was probably one of the most popular men of his time." " As a friend and benefactor," relates Dr. Bagg,* " he was wise and helpful ; as a citizen, public-spirited beyond his means ; his counsels, his exertions, and his purse were ever at the service of individual want, and proffered in the promotion of every enterprise calculated to benefit the place. In short, in every relation Mr. Williams ranked high for his purity and integrity, his cheerfulness and equable temper, his self-sacrificing spirit, and his practically useful life."

Col. Williams' house, after the practice of that time, was the home of most of the young men employed by him, and to the stirring Christian influence of this surrounding they frequently ascribed their subsequent successes in life. Their number in the course of twenty years was considerable, and a noticeable proportion of them acquired more than local reputations. Thurlow Weed, already referred to, joined this office and household in 1812, and there as a journeyman printer commenced his notable career and first wielded his vigorous pen. Henry Ivison, who emigrated as a lad to America from Scotland in 1829, was taken in charge by Mr. Williams, after his parents' return to Scotland, as much from an impulse of pity for the boy's lonely state as from a conviction that his intelligence and manly character could be turned to some account. The fine qualities of head and heart of the great publisher, as well as his almost paternal interest manifested in those under his employ, may be

* " Pioneers of Utica," p. 166.

fairly traced to his eight years spent under the roof of Mr. Williams. Others apprenticed in the same way were George S. Wilson, a devout and supremely benevolent character, whose noble, cheerful, and elevating influence upon the youths of Utica appears to have been something akin to magnetic, and who eventually, by dint of a self-acquired education, entered the ministry, and continued his useful career in Sacketts Harbor; Alfred North, afterwards a missionary to the North American Indians; Stephen Wells, George Hatch, Chauncey Dutton, and R. B. Shepard. The latter, through a long and prosperous lifetime, has attributed to Mr. Williams and his wife much of his success and all his spiritual happiness in life; by means of the latter's influence he was persuaded to become a teacher in the Sunday-school while still unconverted, and by her side afterwards, " agonizing in prayer for his spiritual deliverance, he gave his heart to God and found peace."

Mrs. Sophia Williams was an excellent example of what was highest, noblest, and best in the Puritan stock. Like her husband's parents, her father, Samuel Wells, had come from New England among the early settlers in New Hartford. Foremost in piety, diligent in his affairs, the impress of his character appears clearly enough upon that of his daughter in her maturity, though his death took place too early in her life for us to consider her development as due directly to his moulding influence. He died when she was twelve years old, and while she was at school in his birthplace, Hartford, Connecticut. As the oldest of his six children, Sophia Wells was brought by this unexpected and overwhelming affliction to her mother's side, and to the care of the younger children, thereby causing a sudden and entire alteration in her life, which had the natural effect of maturing her mind and sobering her disposition far beyond her years. This trait of sobriety, joined to the habits of untiring diligence and thrift acquired under her mother's watchful influence, seems to have been a cardinal characteristic noticed and remembered by all who knew her; to her brothers and sisters her example was the way of wisdom, her advice law; to her companions in the village and church she was at once a pattern and a favorite, a girl whose natural impulse was forever towards the right, whose sympathy was alert in behalf of the unfortunate or the sorrowful.

Her conversion and union with the church took place when, about a year after her marriage, she gave birth to her first child. A severe and alarming illness ensued, from which indeed she never wholly recovered; but during its course the awakening was complete, and by the sound and kindly counsel of her husband was the means of turning her from mere earthly goodness to an entire holiness of living, to a spiritual life of rare beauty and consistency. One of her closest friends was Mrs. Whittlesey, the founder and editor of *The Mother's Magazine*, with whose ideas and projects toward quickening mothers as a class to the mighty importance and responsibilities of their position she warmly sympathized. In return, Mrs. Whittlesey felt for her the most ardent admiration, as for one who was at once a model and a standard-bearer of her profession. "Her watchful care by night and day" (she says of her in the *Magazine*), "was unremitting. On the subject of training them while young to habits of industry, Mrs. Williams' example furnished a model for every mother. The ten children who survived her, nine of whom were sons, were kept while young *constantly employed by their mother*. She was no less attentive to the best good of the young men in her husband's printing establishment, many of whom became pious, and are now filling stations of usefulness. Nor were her servants forgotten. Many of them still revere her memory as one that cared for their souls. Nor was she inattentive to their temporal comfort and happiness. She encouraged them to fidelity by superintending every part of her house herself, when not absolutely confined to her room; and she also assisted with her own hands in every departmentment of labor." She joined the Maternal Association in 1825. " Previous to this time she had never raised her voice in prayer in the presence of others, not even with her children. Such was her extreme diffidence that it was not till her soul became exceedingly burdened by the spiritual necessities of her children that she could be persuaded to pray even with her Christian sisters. But no sooner did she take up this cross than she became a distinguished member of the association. It was here too that her last social prayer was offered up. The diffusiveness and fervor of that prayer will not soon fade from the recollection of those that heard it; it was even at the time suggested to the minds of some present that they should hear her voice no more, so earnestly did she labor for an assurance that every child and mother belonging to the Association might meet in heaven."

With her, prayer, precept, and practice went hand in

hand; from a kindly word of counsel to her children or their playmates, she turned to succor the beggar at her door; from the religious meeting to the bedside of some sufferer; from her own kitchen, laden with nourishing food for the starving, we hear of her as ever actively on the pathway of love and good works. This was before the days of hospitals, refuges for the destitute and fallen, homes for the needy and aged, and to such as this veritable mother in Israel the poor had learned to turn for relief, medicine, and food, for sympathy in distress, even for warm clothing in winter and employment at all times. The Sabbath-school she regarded with especial interest and affection, both from her husband's responsibility in it and her own delight in laboring for the souls of little children. Though feeble in health, she never omitted a single preparation on Saturday evening for attending Sunday-school on the morrow with her entire flock, and this with absolute promptness; their clothes in order, their lessons learned, their books and bibles gathered, her household went forth—teachers, children, apprentices, and servants—and trudged behind the good dame to church, a brave array; and when they had taken their places in the school, there was no question among the others but that the time had come to begin.

Chiefest of all, however, her interest was aroused in the cause of missions; from this her attention never strayed; it seemed as though, after the change in her own spiritual life, she thought no effort too severe if it led to the salvation of a single soul. In such work her love and influence upon others were supreme. Mr. James Garritt, the first missionary from Oneida County, was not only fitted out by her own hands, but owed his conversion and much of his religious education to Mrs. Williams. Her last efforts of this kind were in behalf of Loring S. Williams, a missionary to the Choctaws. It is related that upon one occasion when in church, after listening to a warm appeal from the pulpit on behalf of the charity nearest to her heart, she found herself without the means of contributing to the collection which was being made; but drawing from a mother's holiest treasure, "I give two of my sons," she wrote, putting the paper into the basket with a prayer that was answered after her death by the lives of two of her sons, devoted no less sincerely than herself to the regeneration of the heathen.

SAMUEL WELLS, the oldest of the fourteen children of William and Sophia Williams, was born in Utica, September 22, 1812. The ill-health of his mother made it necessary that his early infancy should be spent away from home, and for some years he was put in charge of his mother's aunt, Miss Dana. That excellent woman once capsized the sleigh, while driving with him on a stormy day from New Hartford to visit his parents; after picking herself and her conveyance out of the snow-drift, she hurried on, when with the recollection of her errand came the discovery that her muff and the baby stowed within it were lost. "Shall I go back?" she queried. "Yes, for God may have something for him to do; moreover, I cannot spare the muff." The nurseling lived to thank his grand-aunt for many favors besides this, and treasured to the end of his life kindly memories alike of her nurture and admonition.

His early boyhood was passed without many companions in his grandmother's house, a farm near New Hartford. "Here I spent some of the happiest days of my childhood," he observes in one of his letters, "running at large over orchards, woods, and meadows, catching fish with pin-hooks and butterflies with straw-hats, scratching my hands in quest of blackberries and bruising my shins in endeavors after apples, riding horses to water and trying to milk cows, who I used to think half-laughed at my vain attempts." The same gracious dame who had moulded the sterling character of his mother had an influence hardly less marked upon him. "I have associations about Grandma Wells' old house [he writes again] that are as ineffaceable as petrifactions—indeed, my mind was in the formative state when I used to ramble there, and she of all its attractions was brightest and best." It was while living on the farm with his mother's family that the boy came to be called by his middle name to distinguish him from her youngest brother Samuel.

When old enough to be of some use and less care in the house of his father, Wells came to Utica to live. The village is described in Spaffords' "New York Gazetteer" of that time as a "flourishing incorporated postvillage, the commercial capital of the great western district of this State, where are many mills, factories, machine shops, and a vast many buildings other than those enumerated. Several printing offices and large book-stores, where weekly papers are published, which are widely circulated through the surrounding country. The hotel, which is an elegant establishment, and the many fine private mansions of gentlemen of taste and opulence, give Utica a character in this respect worthy a great commercial town." This greatness would have been generously estimated by its five or six thousand inhabitants, but to a stranger its three or four muddy streets with tan-bark sidewalks, its few hundred wooden houses huddled between the Mohawk River and the newly cut canal intimated less of a commercial capital than existed in the minds and hopes of the enterprising Uticans. In those days the eager rivalry between them and the people of the older settlement of Whitestown had not yet subsided, and the struggle for supremacy was entered into with delight by the boys of both places. With them it meant, of course, regular pitched battles, in which Col. Williams' boys hurried to the fray with the same impulse that had sent their father to fight the invaders from across the lake. On one Saturday afternoon the vanquished from Utica were dragged under a dripping aqueduct near the battle-ground and sent home to concoct plans of revenge upon their adversaries, while frightened mothers dried their sodden clothes. It is not recorded what they did in return.

The completion of the Erie Canal, however, settled all questions of emulation and pushed Utica at once to a foremost place among the towns of the State. Great was the enthusiasm when Gen. La Fayette, the nation's guest, reached Utica upon the partly finished canal in June, 1825, and received an ovation from the delighted and patriotic citizens. The unbuilt, miry road, which had recently been laid out in front of the house where Wells was born, received the name of the popular Frenchman whom it commemorates to this day. Greater even than this occasion was the opening of the canal some four months later, when the lad of thirteen listened all day long with his impatient mates for the booming of the cannon that from hill-top to hill-top across the length of the State announced the inrush of the lake water into the channel which brought it to the ocean; and when on the following Sunday the triumphant Governor Clinton, descending from Lake Erie to Sandy Hook, reached Utica with his flotilla, and with formal reverence attended divine service at the Presbyterian Church, the boy's eyes seemed to see greatness for the first time, and gave to his mind an indelible impress of the scene.

His life at home was a busy one; the children of honest parents in such a community knew no other. In some respects the serious and occupied household must have sorely weighed upon this eager and restless spirit. " How I used to wish, when I was a boy," he said once, " that my father would sit down and talk with me about what was instructive and new ; but business and cares prevented me from enjoying any such intercourse. Our parents had no hobbies, and from mother I got very little encouragement in mine, though father always took an interest in them. However, they labored over my soul's interest." By reason of this, perhaps, he applied himself the more diligently to reading history and science, collecting insects on his grandmother's farm, or in canal-boat excursions to Oriskany Swamp after Habenarias, Dalibarda, and Cypripedia.

He was not in any sense the insupportable " good boy " of the story book. If his pranks and scrapes were few, it was doubtless owing to his abundant occupations. Here is a memory of a boyish accident, told thirty years after it occurred : " How well I recollect sending a ball through the parlor window of Sam. Stocking's house when he lived next to my father on Broad Street, and my errand to the house with money to pay damages, and a promise a yard long never to do so any more! He very civilly took both silver and salutation, and I hardly ever spoke to him afterwards until my return to Utica in 1846." His success at throwing was often more than he could bear. " I could hit that old hen from here," he once exclaimed to his brother, as they strolled one Sunday over his grandmother's farm and spied a vagrant from the poultry yard. The brother naturally dared him to try the shot ; and Wells, to the amazement of both, laid the poor fowl low at a distance of two hundred feet. The good old lady's indignation knew no bounds at this double desecration of her hennery and of the Sabbath-day, and in consequence thereof Wells went supperless to bed.

There is not much which need detain us upon the first decade of his life, either of eventful experiences or of picturesque environment. Blessed, as we have seen, with parents whose treasures were mostly those laid up where neither moth nor rust doth corrupt, he matured under conditions not at all tending to a contemplative life—rather those helping toward supporting the many needs of a busy household, where the domestic concern was entirely conducted by its constituent members. This is a glimpse at his mother's *ménage*, which occurs somewhere in his letters:

" Saturday night ! How busy is memory about the walls of the brain collecting a tableful of old, half-forgotten incidents ! Wood must be piled up in the stoop, high enough to put the passer-by in imminent danger from its eminent elevation ; the cow must be milked, shoes greased, coffee ground, horse fed, faces washed, feet cleaned, S.-S. lesson overhauled and furbished, explanations got from mother, questions asked by children ; lastly, prayers and a kiss, and then to bed."

By reason of such a childhood came habits of industry which in the course of his life never tolerated an unoccupied hour, would scarcely condone an idle minute. It was fortunate, moreover, that the boy was built up physically by abundant duties and healthy exercise, and that he acquired thus early the practice of counteracting the results of over-study by active bodily exertion. For at a very early age books and reading had become his passion ; as soon as he could spell out the printed page, no reward so great to him as to be allowed to return to the half-finished volume and study it out to the end. As soon as he could clamber unaided about his father's book-store, whole days and weeks were spent in pouring over the books which came within reach of his little arms—often with no more critical selection than that of beginning at one end of a shelf and reading its whole array of volumes as they stood. His was a mind which would swallow a bushel of chaff rather than lose the few precious grains of truth which might lie concealed within. Such a hungry intellect, indeed, he afterwards thought was rather to be lamented, and urges a favorite brother (Frederic) to follow some of Dr. Todd's ideas : " It was a great mistake my bolting whole so many books, and never digesting any ; a mental dyspepsia has been the consequence, and this is not yet eradicated." But the supports of an attentive memory and a well practised habit of observation presently supplied the regulating medium and rendered him even as a youth notable for his accurate and general information.

To those who appreciate the influence of childish traits and occupations in the moulding of character, the following letter from one of the boy's schoolmates, Mr. Thomas Allen Clarke, now of Albany, will be read with the interest due to its importance.

My Dear Mr. Williams : Other than of my home I have no earlier memories than those of your father. They are all precious. Clad in frocks at our homes and at our first school of my aunt Sarah Clarke, changing to trowsers and roundabouts in the advanced schools, and there until we were nearly prepared for college, we were together almost constantly. He and James Dana were about the same age, a year or more my seniors. They led in all our sports and pursuits, and received color from each other. While they were much with their juniors, they were heartily prized by older companions, among whom some in after life became prominent—Horatio Seymour, Ward Hunt, and others.

The sports in which your father led were those drawn from the actions of men, and while he imitated he sometimes also improved. I will relate an instance briefly : The village was small but enterprising ; a public garden had been opened, the rear of which adjoined your grandfather's store, and all of us who were intimate had free access by this means. I believe the first balloon experiment in our country was made here ; it was of that primitive kind, made of paper with a small opening beneath where a sponge held by a wire ring was saturated with an illuminating fluid. The balloon ascended a short distance, throwing a considerable light until the fluid was consumed, when the whole affair came to grief. Your father thought that this exhibition might be improved, so he and Dana prepared (we small boys proudly helping with scissors and paste) another balloon, under which they hung an old oil bottle of very thin glass and surrounded with a protecting wire net-work. Breaking off the neck of this, they filled it with the fluid and put in a large wick, duly supported. The balloon was sent up from your grandfather's store yard, and was a great success for those times. Its light was brilliant and enduring, and crowds were drawn to the garden over which it floated for a long time, sinking at length with its dimmed flame. I remember well the keeper of the garden saying to me: "If you make any more balloons, bring them here and I 'll help you." He profited by the show.

This is apparently a trivial incident, but it serves to illustrate both the primitive times of our youth and that trait in your father, as in Sir Philip Sidney, of striving to be and become a man though really a child. And indeed I might best sum up his boyish character in those words of Lord Brooke concerning Sidney : "Of his youth I will repeat no other wonder but this, that though I lived with him and knew him from a child, yet I never knew him other than a man ; with such staidness of mind, lively and familiar gravity as carried grace and reverence above greater years. His talk ever of knowledge and his very play tending to enrich his mind, so as even his teachers found something in him to observe and learn above that which they had usually read or taught. Which eminence by nature and industry made his worthy father style Sir Philip in my hearing (though I unseen) *lumen familiæ suæ.*"

Your father was always studious ; he was also kind to his companions, freely sharing with them all he knew and could acquire. His was a noble spirit, of undeviating truthfulness, anxious solicitude for the weak and poor, and a faith unshadowed in the Lord Jesus Christ, the master of all his actions.

You may imagine how pleased I was when I heard of your father's employment by Commodore Perry, with whom I had had many friendly relations during the Mexican War. It was a singular coincidence that two boyhood friends, separated during all their subsequent lives by thousands of miles, should afterwards have been brought into close contact with an historical character of such eminence.

I must say that it has been for no lack of interest in my subject, but the contrary, that I have written *currente calamo.*

Faithfully yours,   T. A. C.

"As to his childhood and youth," observes Mr. T. W. Seward, "I cannot say that they differed remarkably from all the other childhood and youth that grew to manhood in his company. His individuality was not so much that of disposition and of character as of manner, which had in it a certain austerity. He held very positive opinions, and amongst his associates was not slow in expressing them, and sometimes the expression took the form of sharp criticism. Nevertheless by the naturally discerning and discriminative mind of boyhood he was always respected, even if he was not always liked. His school life in the estimation of his instructors, as well as of his fellows, was well-nigh faultless. His earnest, serious nature would permit no trifling with study, nor waste even of fragments of time. He was rarely the subject of school discipline, even in matters of small importance. Not that he was deficient in that fund of animal spirits which is so apt to prompt into transgression even the best of youthful natures. He was wont to regard all manifestations of an unruly spirit not so much with disfavor as disdain. He was never known to be among the foremost in youthful sports, although he by no means abstained from them. He preferred to devote his hours of leisure to things useful, prompted thereto by the counsel and example of a mother whose nature he largely inherited. At home faithful attention to home duties and no small amount of work were required of him ; and it was not uncommon to find him during short vacations helping in the ceaseless and multiform work of his father's printing and publishing establishment."

This stiffness of manner was owing to an unfortunate

shyness, his own appreciation of which we shall soon see in a letter written from school to his father. He perceived and lamented his unlikeness to those of his own age, and occasionally remarked in later life that his keenest regret when a schoolboy arose from the consciousness of his being less popular than some of his companions. Like Dr. Thomas Arnold, his boyhood had the tone of one who had lived chiefly in the company of his elders, and, as in the case of the famous master of Rugby, this peculiar formality was the more observed by those who knew the joyousness and simplicity of his latter years. Though sincere and strong his friendships were not numerous or indiscriminate; excepting with James Dana, his near neighbor, he seems to have made no intimacy by whose congenial sympathy he could nourish his intellectual life. A bond of union existed between these two, however, which was remarkable, enduring through their widely separated lives, until the days came which found them side by side among the professors of Yale College.

Much of the activity of his young mind found scope in the Sunday-school, the organization of which was due to his father. Under the stimulus of this flourishing and influential institution, then just commencing its godly work in the community, Wells' religious feeling acquired at once greater solidity and his piety became more elevated. Sunday-schools, like all other human institutions, have changed with the times. The stupendous project of making every child commit to memory the entire body of the Holy Word was consistent with the nature of these great-hearted and devout men, who assembled their children on the Sabbath-day to search the Scriptures in earnest. Thirty-three years after his departure for China, Mr. Williams contributed to a jubilee celebration in this Sunday-school some reminiscences which describe its early features:

"My first remembrance of it was standing up in a row with many other children to say our catechism and sing one of Watts' children's hymns. That excellent man, Truman Parmele, became superintendent while I was a young scholar, and remained at the post during all my connection with the school as such. His influence over the boys was of the purest and strongest kind, and his memory, I have no doubt, remains in each of their minds as one of its best inheritances. It was his aim to make the scholars love their lessons and regard the Sunday-school as a pleasant place for all who came to it. The morning school opened at half-past eight o'clock, and the afternoon session immediately after church was out; the two sessions comprising about four hours. In the morning the lessons were recited to and explained by the teachers in each class, and in the afternoon the superintendent questioned the school at large. It was a point of emulation to answer each question instantly, and to repeat the verses of the lesson perfectly. Some boys learned much more than they otherwise would in order that they might be able to answer in the afternoon examination, and the exercise made all familiar with the words and meaning of Scripture. Occasionally the school was collected in the church on Sabbath evening for a general examination, and some of the boys spoke suitable pieces, while others received rewards for diligence and good conduct. I remember myself receiving a book on one of these occasions, with some surprise, for having learned the New Testament through. . . .

"I became a teacher in the school after its removal to the basement of the church in Washington Street, and have as pleasant a recollection of this part of my Sunday-school life as when I was a scholar. Though I have not much knowledge of the subsequent history of my scholars, I am sure that if they derived half the benefit from my instructions that I did in trying to teach them, we have all much reason to thank God for the Sabbath-school."

The emulation among the boys presently increased the lessons to gigantic lengths, so that there was hardly time in two hours of active and uninterrupted recitation to complete the round of the class; finally, when on a certain Sunday, every lad in one of the classes had repeated whole chapters from the Gospels, ending with Henry Ivison, who rehearsed *five hundred* verses without an error or interruption, the teachers wisely perceived that in such contests the spirit would speedily be forgotten in conning the letter of the Scriptures, and forthwith limited the lessons to fifteen verses. What a sincere enthusiasm in a community when lads stole the moments from their play to study Bible verses during the week that they might prepare for triumphs in the Sunday-school! Where among the girls as well, the superintendent of the female department reports a total of some forty-four thousand verses recited during ten Sundays by her department of forty scholars! Full of the emotion of a long-remembered ardor, one of these pupils relates how, upon a certain occasion, when the various titles of our Saviour were repeated in rapid sequence by the boys, the imposing succession of these glorious names, shouted forth with the whole vehemence of a hundred eager young voices, arose to a mighty and swelling chorus so tremendously inspiring as to draw tears from the eyes of every listener in the great room.

Such was the stimulus which cultivated and increased the religious fervor of his nature, and here Wells first decided to enter upon a missionary life; in a school which, during fifty years, furnished more than thirty missionaries and ministers, it is not strange that the spiritual child should have developed into the Christian man.

Among his father's apprentices a young man named George S. Wilson was gifted with a heart so peculiarly sympathetic towards lads of his community, that his influence upon Wells cannot be entirely passed over. With his Sunday-school class as a nucleus, he organized a little band entitled the "Juvenile Society for Learning and Doing Good," holding its meetings every Wednesday evening. Its memory is still cherished in Utica. "Mr. Wilson exerted only a supervisory and restraining influence over his society," says Mr. T. W. Seward. "He held no office in it, but after framing for them a suitable code of laws, he wisely left the management to the boys. But no meeting could be held without his presence. What pride they had in it! With what grave decorum was the routine of parliamentary forms gone through; business despatched, what a fine variety of amusement and instruction followed. But much as we loved our society and each other, we all felt that its soul as well as its brain were incorporate in its beloved founder."

The "Juvenile Society" must have cost its generous instigator dearly in blank books, but his promise of a new journal to the boy who would fill the one given him with original matter was always redeemed. One of these, entitled "Samuel W. Williams' Journal No. 2," is dated December, 1823, and contains "something more about Niagara," describing a trip taken to the Falls in that year. It is the work of a thoughtful and intelligent boy of eleven:

"Everybody must think it makes a great noise [he writes, after mentioning some incidents of his visit], so loud that they can't sleep nor read ; but it is quite the contrary. You can read most as well as if there was no noise. The sound is so hollow and of a kind of grumble noise. This is all I think of now about the Falls of Niagara, the greatest and most celebrated Falls in the world. It is said that eels live under the pitch. You can go under the pitch, but it is very dangerous. By every wind you are all wet over, and by every vapor you are all dry again, so that it is a kind of artificial bathing place.

"There was a gentleman, whose name I do not know, about a month before I came there, that lived in Manchester. He was crazy, and while he was there he took off his coat, hung it upon the tree that was close by, and prepared to jump into the water. He did so and got drowned. I do not know whether he had any wife or children to lament his untimely fate. How rash some people, who act when they are crazy. Sometimes they kill themselves by suicide ; God does not call them into his presence, but they must go. Nothing can restrain them ; they will kill themselves by any way they can get hold of. When every thing else is put out of their way, they will not eat any thing and will try to die anyway. But stop, I am wandering to far from my story ; I must go back.

In another portion of this little journal are the minutes of one or two more meetings of the " Juvenile Society," given in dialogue form with circumstantial detail ; also notes on the sermons heard, the general criticism of which among the boys was one of Mr. Wilson's apt methods of quickening their attention to the Sunday preaching.

Wells' schooling commenced at the age of six or seven, with Mrs. Sarah K. Clarke, an amiable lady, whose efforts to win and teach her scholars were peculiarly successful. After her came one McCloskey, an Irishman, whose badge of authority and instrument of discipline was the "taws." One of his pupils recollects him vividly—" a cripple, who could move about from place to place only by aid of two crutches; nevertheless, it was not safe to defy him. Wells and I formed a reading class of two at this school, in the 'Autobiography of Dr. Franklin.'" While still a little boy he was sent to the school of Montgomery R. Bartlett, the terror of whose wrath he long remembered, and would sometimes illustrate by the story of this furious teacher's hurling his ink-stand across the room at a little girl. An instructor of higher calibre than this was H. G. O. Dwight, who left his school not many years later and became a pioneer of the American Board of Missions in Turkey. At the end of a few terms here Wells attained to the dignity of the old academy, then under the management of Capt. Charles Stuart, an eccentric but worthy man, whose peculiar genius it was to flog and love his pupils with equal warmth; though a man of great purity and simplicity of character, this impulsive temperament made his rule rather a trying one to quiet children.

In the fall of 1827 the boy was sent to improve his mind under the Rev. Ely Burchard, a Hamilton College graduate, who at this time opened a classical school in the village of Paris Hill, a few miles from Mrs. Wells' farm. How many cold mornings were spent over Murray's Reader or "Virgil Delphini" in this little wooden school-house, perched upon rude stone abutments, which elevated its four corners like the legs of a wardrobe, admitting a free circulation of wind, snow, and cold beneath! A single stove, which stretched its pipe breast-high along the entire room for economy of heat, slightly raised the temperature within, and if the pupils complained of chilblains or of frozen fingers they were bidden to warm their blood by chopping wood for the fire. The boys boarded with their teacher and his father-in-law, Gen. McNeil, in a farm-house opposite the school, and here and over the neighboring hills they found sufficient material for the exercise, sports, and adventures necessary to school life.

"Wells was always studious, and in his spare hours was almost constantly reading some book—usually one brought from his father's shop at home—in which he was ever deeply absorbed. One habit which I remember was the use of an ivory paper-cutter in a new book, whose leaves he would split only as he read, so intent was he with the matter in hand. Every visit home brought him back with a new volume, which, however, never lasted him long. On one occasion Mr. Burchard had purchased a book written by a clergyman who was recently returned from the Sandwich Islands, giving his account of experiences and observations there, and this narrative Wells read with a very lively interest, and often talked it over with his teacher. It is not impossible that his taste or choice for missionary work may have then been first formed; the interest he took in this book and the labors of Dr. Judd's family were at least deeply graven upon his heart at the time.

"When out of school and at play he had plenty of fun and frolic, and his whole soul was in it, though he was never mischievous. He was a general favorite, not only with his teacher but with all his acquaintances, and was so universally well-informed that Mr. Burchard often referred to him to answer some question that the others could not. The reliance placed upon his perfect truthfulness was shown once when all the boys having been called upon for some scrape, and each having denied his personal guilt, Wells was finally reached, and said quite simply: 'Yes, I and all of us did it." 'There,' said Burchard, 'I knew I should get the truth from Wells!' During all the time we passed together in the same room I never knew him to engage in a quarrel of any sort; occasionally he was a little impatient at the pranks of Oren, one of our mates, a fat boy, who was up to any thing funny, but they always agreed. And again, he used to tell a joke or help on a story at the expense of any chap who deserved it, though never in a malicious way." *

Of these days there occurs a picture in one of Mr. Williams' letters which is not so flattering to the village or himself:

"When I went to Paris Hill Mr. Weeks was pastor. I listened to his preaching without much relish, for the church was cold, the seats hard, the service long, the preacher monotonous, and the subject distasteful. Religion was not pleasing to me when young, but I could not break away from parental restraints and maternal suasion, nor overpass lightly the bounds they set me. God be praised for their training!"

The establishment of an excellent school under Charles Bartlett, whose institution, known as the Utica High School, and afterwards as the Utica Gymnasium, gained considerable celebrity throughout the State, brought Wells back to town in 1829. Here he found most of his old schoolmates again, many amongst whom (besides Professor James D. Dana) attained in later life more than common fame: Horatio Seymour, a Governor of the State and leader of his party; Alexander S. Johnson, Judge of the U. S. Circuit Court; Lewis Cass, Jr., a son of the Secretary of the State, and himself afterwards a Minister to the Court of Rome; General Morris S. Miller; and not least of all these, Isaac Smith, the inventor of condensed milk. Mr. Bartlett's most admirable quality, in Wells' estimation, was his hearty recognition of the importance of the natural sciences in a liberal education, and the attention given at this school to these sub-

* From a letter of Mr. A. O. Osborn, of Waterville, N. Y.

jects was as delightful to his tastes as it was unusual to the time. From these lectures and lessons in chemistry, geology, and botany came his first accurate knowledge of the sciences, the pursuit of which he carried with increasing pleasure throughout a long life as the study of his recreation, the *Nebenfach* to his professional work. Under Fay Edgerton, and after him Professor Asa Gray, as teachers in this department, the older boys imbibed a taste for the rare and curious in nature which turned several of them into naturalists of creditable rank; while during his long vacation trips or shorter holiday rambles the zealous and sympathetic Edgerton gave to his pupils the impress of religious character that was more precious, perhaps, than his knowledge.

A letter to his schoolmate who had now gone from school to Yale College affords an idea of the annual exhibition of Mr. Bartlett's school:

TO JAMES D. DANA.

UTICA, January 27, 1831.

DEAR JAMES :—This is the remainder of the short letter I wrote you a while ago. You must have thought that that was hardly an apology for one, but it exhausted all my stock of ideas, complaints, and every thing else. However, by the enclosed order of exercises you will see that the annual ordeal was passed by the members severally and individually of Bartlett's school. It was in the First Presbyterian Church, for it would seem that this year the trustees are not afraid of dirtying their seats. A stage covering the pulpit was made—covering, as it seemed, an acre, for it extended between the galleries and out from the pulpit ten or eleven slips. The scholars, thirty-three in number, were tricked out in their Sunday-go-to-meeting clothes, all in due order. For a faculty Charley * sat

* Mr. Bartlett.

in the middle before the pulpit all alone. The house was full, not to overflowing, but comfortably full. Cross's and Smith's were Greek pieces, Billings' and C. Miller's Latin, and J. Devereux spoke in French ; the remainder were vulgar English. The judges sat under the gallery in the broad aisle ; I did not see who they were, but Mr. Whittlesey delivered the prizes, the first to Alex. Johnson, second to C. D. Miller, and third to G.* Hunt. Charles Miller's original Latin declamation and song was the composition of Mr. Whiffin, and was a kind of recitation of the sports usually practised by boys and a salaam to the audience. The song had a chorus in which all the boys joined, he singing alone the other part. The singing was very good considering the circumstances—a crowded church and he on the stage. I don't know how he managed to keep his voice up, but he sang it without wavering. The music was Palestine and The Gospel Banner, a new piece written by Hastings and learnt by the boys. . .

Since I wrote you my last letter an infant brother of mine has closed his short and painful life. He died of a fever while nursing at a Mr. Root's in Schuyler. You have probably seen it in the *Elucidator*, a number of which I shall endeavor to send you weekly—and if you find any information in it you are welcome to it. His name was Alfred Pell, named after a friend of father's in N. York.

I remain your firm friend forever,
S. WELLS WILLIAMS.

A month after this letter was written, Wells, in company with his brother Frederic, made a profession of faith and joined the First Church of Utica. It was a year of unusual religious activity in the community, though this action on his part was due rather to a sense of the fitness of his publicly confessing a truth long believed, than to any influence of those about him. The act was attended, however, by the blessing of God, with a

---

* Montgomery.

genuine regeneration of his nature, which, beginning with the more severe control of a naturally impatient temper, became conspicuous to his acquaintances when in the fall of this year the death of his mother seemed to rob his life of every vestige of the joy and beauty of living. From this time forward something of the sweetness of that holy woman seems to have entered into his character: his boyish faults disappear; his disposition becomes broader as well as deeper; the habit and desire of shaping his daily duty and conversation with reference to a personal and ever-present God, whom he considers as Socrates did his Demon, begins now, never again to be diverted or vanish away. Nor from the time of this bereavement could any one who knew him well fail to note that out of its lessons and experience first came to him that profound realization of a higher life, and that habit of bringing it to mind even in his busiest moments, which was for him the real meaning of religion and the moving spring of his whole career.

Colonel Williams' business did not warrant the outlay of sending the boy to college with his friend Dana; the disappointment was severe, though not so great, perhaps, as in after life, when he regretted that he had not insisted upon entering Yale and working his way through. Had he foreseen the course his life was to take there would have been little hesitation in the matter of preparing himself, at least in some degree, in the methods of scholarly thinking and vigorous expression. But the father, though not averse to a thorough education, intended Wells for his own occupation, and with this in view he put him behind the counter during many of those after-school hours which others boys spent in play. It soon became manifest that whatever his abilities might be, they did not lie in this direction. The Greek lessons which he studied for Mr. Bailey, while working the printing-press, occupied his mind more keenly than the completion of the job in hand, and before many months' experience in the shop he could explain the contents of the books much better than he could sell them. As an illustration of his defective business instinct and tender conscience, it is told of him that he was once overheard advising a customer not to buy a certain algebra enquired for, and of which one copy remained in stock, as a new edition was soon to appear. It became evident to his father that he could better afford to send such a salesman to college.

The death of his mother hastened his decision as to the choice of a higher school, and not many days after the sorrowing little band had followed their counsellor and guide to her grave, Wells gathered his few clothes and precious collections of plants and stones and departed by canal for Troy. The school in that town, which had attracted the boy from Utica, was of a kind to foster his independent habits of study and strengthen the self-reliance of his nature. It had been founded in 1824, by Stephen Van Rensselaer, known as the Patroon, under Prof. Eaton as teacher, in order to encourage the application of science to common purposes. With the design of furthering the education of the tenants upon his vast and remote estates, the old Dutchman established in this case a more effectual monument to his own name than he ever knew of; from its humble aim of advancing the science of common things, the Rensselaer Institute of Troy has now become one of the leading schools in the country, while the material development of the United States has found and obtained hundreds of helping and directing hands in its carefully educated civil engineers. When Amos Eaton was chosen by the aged Patroon as the first instructor in his institute, he was little more than a perapatetic lecturer on natural sciences, who had lately extended his instruction to the people by means of the Lyceum of Natural History newly organized in Troy, and was favorably known from a manual of botany published some years before. It is an interesting side-glimpse at the condition of education outside of New England three-quarters of a century ago, to read that in 1818 Gov. DeWitt Clinton invited Prof. Eaton to deliver a course of lectures before the Legislature in Albany, and that the discussion of public affairs was laid aside while the members were delighted and instructed by an account of the recent disclosures of science from the lips of the young professor.

Until the death of its founder in 1839, Amos Eaton comprised the sum and substance of the Rensselaer Institute. Of itinerant proclivities, with no resources save the Patroon's bounty, and no attendants but the poor young seekers after science, the professor was located at this time in a building in the "old bank place," near the east end of the dam in North Troy, and was followed by half a dozen students upon his mineralogical and botanical excursions about the neighboring country. Despite roughness of mien and rudeness of apparatus, however, the professor and his school were by no means poorly adapted to the times. His practice of supplementing field investigation by requiring each scholar to tell what he knew to the public of the school-room was peculiar and successful. Maintaining that understanding came from instructing rather than from hearing, he made every boy in turn teacher and lecturer to his classmates, in this manner adding to a zeal for experiment and investigation the no less important accomplishment of ready and lucid explanation. His idea was not however a pure charity; during the latter years of his life he suffered much with asthma and was inclined to devote the limited energy of his failing health to the preparation of his text-books, leaving the pupils clustered about the botanical press or chemical table pretty much to their own devices. In the winter evenings of his first term Wells was set to the task of writing out all the derivations in the Text-Book of Botany, an occupation more congenial to his tastes than lessons in logic or algebra, and here his name for the first time appears in print.

Presumably the fame of this institution and the name of its head were greater at the distance of Utica than in the little coterie of students gathered at Troy. At all events, the appearance of both upon his arrival was so contrary to his expectations that it was hard to conceal his disappointment in his first letter

TO HIS FATHER.

TROY, November 23, 1831.

DEAR FATHER :—I arrived here Tuesday at 3 o'clock P.M. rather fatigued and with a severe headache, but a good night's rest restored my health and raised my spirits. With this I send a kind of prospectus for the current year, that you may see all the requisitions of the institution. You will perceive by that paper that the 1st, 2d, and 3d sub-terms are confined to mathematics, logic, etc., studies that formerly were pursued in the spring, and chemistry in the winter. Last winter they studied chemistry, but now that is removed to the spring. Before I came here I thought chemistry was studied in the winter; this was the reason of my being so desirous of coming this fall. However, as I am now here, it will be just as you, my dear father, say, whether I stay or not. There are only six students here at present, two more are soon expected. The whole appearance of the school to me at present is like that of the city of Lisbon, fine in the distance, but full of mud and filth. This may be premature; my ideas may be irritated by coming here in a snowstorm, and may wear off when the sun shines. Six scholars I think is rather a poor number for such a place as this. If I stay I have to furnish bed and bedding. For a bed send a kind of case to put straw in, and as many or few clothes as you or Miss Sanford may think best. Send immediately, for I am now using Prof. Eaton's only spare room. I am tolerably pleased with him and his lady, and may be better after a longer acquaintance. Remember me tenderly and kindly to the folks at home. Does Dwight care for his soul any more yet?

Your dutiful and affectionate son,

WELLS.

TO JAMES D. DANA, NEW HAVEN.

RENSSELAER SCHOOL, TROY, Nov. 23, 1831.

DEAR FRIEND JAMES:—You see by the heading, I have got here at last; but alas! such a disappointment: tell it not.

I started from home Monday morning in the packet, and reached here in due time; meanwhile a violent snowstorm came up, and in that I got here. Six students are all they have in the institution: only think, six students, and this is the eighth year of their operations. I expected to find twenty at least: but so it is. "As it is, so it must be," is *our* motto. This winter is studied mathematics, logic, etc. But I can tell no more about the school. To tell you the truth, James, I never, never experienced such a disappointment, such an utter failure of expectations, in my life. But tell it not, I am contented.

You of course know before this time of the death of my dear mother. Such a loss you have never yet experienced, and may the day be far distant. She left this weary pilgrimage in the full hope of a glorious immortality beyond the grave. Oh! I hope you will before long, yes, even now, prepare for such a scene; it will come certainly. She was taken sick Monday afternoon, and Friday evening was a corpse; so sudden was her call. Her death was a commentary on her life: resigned and acquiescent in God's will she waited her summons. I cannot write more of her now; emotion stops my pen; but had you, dear James, been near her dying couch and heard the gracious words from her, you would have thought that death, judgment, and eternity were realities, that religion was not a thing of convenience. I never knew what death was before. Come now, O James, come now to the gospel feast; it is all ready, and Jesus is waiting to be gracious.

I would send you some crystals of carbonate of strontian, but they are at the bottom of my trunk: but stop, I will get them for you, as that is rather a poor excuse. You must not criticise this letter, nor think it is meant for one, being only an apology; for my spirits are much down on account of the looks of the school. It has seen its best days. When Fay was here it was much better, but Eaton is getting old and now he is very childish; he will tell long yarns, etc. But this may all be altered, and I may think quite differently by a week's time; first impressions are often erroneous. But facts are stubborn things: six scholars are a small number for an institution like this. I should have wrote before, but mother's death took away all thoughts of any thing else.

Your constant and sincere friend till death,
S. Wells Williams.

His disgust at the condition of the school did not soon disappear, though by the following April its vehemence is suppressed into "Rensselaer Institute!?! Troy," by way of date to his next letter to James Dana. The homesickness and disappointment, however, soon wore away, and on Christmas eve he confesses to his father:

"The small number of scholars instead of being a dis-is quite an ad-vantage, the professor has more time for each student, and we can also get much nearer the stove in cold weather. We have just finished the subject of navigation (quite a study when the thermometer is ten below zero), and next week shall take up that of algebra. . . . I am more and more satisfied with the internal policy of the institution, and no doubt with a blessing from above shall spend a year very satisfactorily here. The advantages of the library, or of such a one as we have, is not within the reach of every one."

The following letters indicate more in detail the organization of this school, and how his time was spent there; also in some degree the tendency of his mind and the descriptive powers at his command:

TROY, January 21, 1832.

DEAR FATHER.—I received your esteemed favor of the seventh instant on my return from a walk to Albany, where I went to obtain the map of the stars published by the Society of U. Knowledge. I was in the city but a few moments, but intend to go often during the vacation, and endeavor to do as you wish. I do not know as it is wrong to say it, but I always have had, and for aught I know always will have, a sort of timidity in going into the company of those with whom I am unacquainted, even at public houses. I had much rather stay out-doors or in the hall than go into the room where the fire is, although it should be very cold. This I do not attribute at all to a fear of offending or interrupting, but it seems to be a part of my nature, and however much pleasure I may derive from the proposed intercourse, yet the first introduction I often look back upon with a degree of pain. Yet it *must* be overcome, and I shall go and see Mr. Jermain upon the first opportunity.

This school is one of the most oddly organised that I ever attended; a student can learn the most, if he is so disposed, and also can get along with the least amount of study, if he is disinclined to application. I have been perusing the course on Astronomy used in Cambridge, and of all the books on that subject it excels in elevating the mind of the reader and raising his thoughts to that Being who overrules and governs all these immense bodies, and sustains them in their places. One idea is worthy of penning : Dr. Herschel supposes that all the large stars which we see in different parts of the heavens belong to the nebula to which the sun does, and that this nebula, vast as it is, is only of the third magnitude, or of the same size as the smallest of those we see in the milky way. To take, if possible, the full extent of this supposition (whether it is true or not has not yet been determined strictly), we must consider that when we look at the nearest of these stars, at a time when the earth is in one part of her orbit, and then, six months after this, look at it again at a spot 200 millions of miles from the first one, yet the star appears to be in the same place, such an amazing distance is it. This, at least, gives a feeble idea of the extent of God's material universe, and also of the vast size of those stars or suns which we see in the milky way. Yet the goodness and infinite wisdom of the Creator is as much shown in the formation and habits of the water-spider as in these suns, the size of which we cannot conceive. Dick supposes, and not improbably, that the occupation of those who, thro' much tribulation, shall inherit the promise, will be to study the material works of their bountiful Creator, to all eternity.

Last Saturday I went over to see the Cohoes Falls in the Mohawk ; I was well paid for the walk, tho' that was rather tedious, on account of the snow giving away at every step. The falls were nearly covered over with ice, and the water appeared really beautiful, making its way thro' the ice, and seen only at intervals. That famous bridge, which crosses the Mohawk just below the falls, we had a last look at, for yesterday as the Hudson and Mohawk ice broke up, the collision of the ice proved too powerful, and it came sailing down past the school in fine style. In four hours, I believe it was, the river rose 17 feet, and the large cakes of ice going over the dam near the school were quite grand. . . . This bridge is not the Waterford bridge across the Hudson, but that across the Mohawk. The cost of it, Prof. Eaton says, was $12,000. He also says that the river was never known to rise so high before ; the force with which the ice came was so great as to force large pieces twenty feet on shore.

. . . The bills of wood, oil, and washing have reduced my funds to a minus, and a new supply will be needed. I am unable to say how much it will cost to go through the chemical course ; we have to furnish all the apparatus and substances needed, and then take them away when we leave. I should like Fred or Dwight to send me the remaining nos. of the Soc. of Useful Knowledge, which I left, Dick's books, Darwin's Botanic Garden, mineral hammer and wedge, and press with papers for botany. They may be in the ware-house ; perhaps the wedge is in the kitchen on one of the shelves ; I wish they might be found. Also send a shell of each kind that we have, for the purpose of naming ; let them be done up in tow or cotton safely. The above need not be sent all at once, but at intervals, as also the clothes, etc., for summer. I think I shall pass the vacation pleasantly enough ; four of the students are also to remain. I am quite well.

Your dutiful son,

WELLS.

These are the trifles of a boy's letter, but if they are properly given and read it will not be needful to cast up methodically the average deduced to obtain his character at home and in school. On all sides nature teaches us to

> Think naught a trifle, though it small appear ;
> Small sands the mountain, moments make the year,
> And trifles life,—

and the love or hate of life enters into them, smoothing or roughening the path, developing the tastes and feelings of youth into the character of manhood.

The winter passed away pleasantly enough in school work, and with the ending of his first half-year Wells had about fixed his mind upon the career of a botanist, when a note from his father, proposing to him the plan of taking charge of a missionary printing press in China aroused him from the natural drift of his lessons and at once altered the purport of his cogitations. A printing-press and types had been sent out by the Bleecker Street Presbyterian Church, of New York, to the recently established mission of the American Board in Canton, in recognition of the need of printed books as aids in evangelizing the heathen. When it was requested of William Williams to find a young man qualified to superintend a mission printing office under conditions such as those existing in China, he promptly suggested his eldest son; mission work was not new to him; the love of Christ and of his cause on earth was the most important of all things; giving the gospel to the heathen was the most direct way of serving his Master. His faith in his son was not ill founded; the call was indeed a sudden one, but after a single night of meditation and prayer Wells returned the following answer to his father:

TROY, April 23, 1832.

DEAR FATHER :—Perhaps, from the short length of time that has elapsed since I received your last, you may think that I have not sufficiently considered the question, Will you go? It is, I must say, a very important question when its bearings are considered. But did you, my dear father, know the tendency of my thoughts on this subject, and what they had been since a year had passed away, this question would be different. To come to the point. If *one* objection can be done away to my satisfaction, I will go. This is: is it possible, after the course is finished here in October, to learn the printer's trade sufficiently well to take charge of such an undertaking? I should not be willing to leave here till the course and tours were all finished. For chemistry and botany have a great bearing, and a very useful one, upon the common occurrences of life. Now if, after these were thro', I could sufficiently learn that part of the trade which I do not know, I am willing, and indeed would esteem it a privilege, thus to serve the cause of Jesus. I do not in the least know any thing about a pressman's duty, and I much fear could not bear the work of learning. How this is you would best know. If fifteen months is the time allowed, it would leave but nine months to learn that part. Will that be enough? If staying here till the term is finished is an objection, I would rather it would remain than obviate it by leaving.

Such is the result of what I have thought on the subject. Yet I would say (not by any means that I wish to be excused), why would not Shepard be a better one to go? So deeply has the love of the works of God, and thro' them, Him, got imbued into me—and is almost now a second nature,—that I fear, if I went, any object of natural history would interest me more than any thing else.

If this takes place, it will alter my course of life, which was to be a naturalist. I should have informed you before this, when I received a letter from you some time since inquiring my choice. But as I had not then thought much about it, was hardly prepared to answer. There are places enough to have a choice, and good ones too.

Perhaps there was an ingredient of adventure in the career of pioneer missionary work which unconsciously actuated his prompt decision. Much more of the romance than the reality of life in the extreme East had come to the ears of civilized peoples; their peculiar customs, the result of centuries of seclusion, their unexplored territory, their unknown literature, the wonders of their works of industry and art,—these made the Chinese a principal object of the world's curiosity, and China the golden land of bold and hazardous enterprise. But that it was not the determination of a visionary thus quickly made, the following letters, as well as the language and conduct of his later life, clearly manifest. " The resolution to enter upon this work once taken," he said many years afterwards, " I thank God that no shade of doubt as to the triumphant result, or regret at having engaged in it, has ever arisen in my mind." A spirit of sturdy tenaciousness and entire devotion like his was the fit material for the thankless work of introducing Christian truth and civilization to an intolerant and unwilling empire.

RENSSELAER INSTITUTE, June 18, 1832.

DEAR FATHER :—Your welcome communication from Syracuse *via* Utica was received here on Friday ; it was what I had been looking for some time, and the value of it was enhanced in proportion to the subject on which it was written. It is a continual matter of cogitation, but I do not know that I have any thing new to offer. One thing, however,—that is the extent to which it has attained. By this I mean the multitudinous number of those who are aware of the fact of my determination. I have done as you advised me ; not a single person far or near has had even an intimation of such an event, and last Saturday I received a letter from James Dana, asking for more particulars of a report he had heard from Mr. Lawrence on board the steamboat from New York relative to this matter. How Mr. Lawrence was informed of it is more than I can divine ; and even Fred has written me a letter asking Are you going anywhere, and when, and how, and all about it ?

The object principally of this is to inform you of the near approach of the cholera to this city. No well authenticated cases have occurred nearer than Whitehall, but boats laden with Irish that have just come from Montreal and Ireland are continually arriving here. Every boat containing passengers, no matter of what kind, is stopped immediately close by the school, or rather a little above the lock in the town of Lansingburgh, and there they are detained until they can be examined by the corporation of Troy. About a dozen boat-loads are now landed on the opposite side of the river and a large pest-house erected for their especial accommodation. No case of sickness of any kind (except beastly intoxication) has yet occurred, but if they are detained long, they of themselves will soon produce some disease or other, for I never saw the same amount of filthiness, dirt, vice, laziness, and every other attendant of the lower class of Irish, collected in the same small compass. Yesterday, which seemed to be more than ever a day of excess, because it was Sunday, more than half of the men were drunk, and the women were washing and swimming their children in the river. Last evening the city guards were ordered here, and patrolled the banks all night to prevent their landing. To-day they have all been carried over the river, and are there at present to the amount of several hundred. The corporation of Albany this morning sent up three parcels of men to ascertain the state of affairs, and to assist the Trojans, for the report had obtained there that the Irish had effected a landing in spite of the city guards. On Saturday night a report was in Troy that the Rensselaer students had lodged several sick with the cholera, and that during the night six had died with it! More boats are now constantly arriving and the number is increasing pretty rapidly. Nearly all acknowledged that they have come direct from infected places and from among those that have died with it. It is on that account very uncertain as to what will be the result of their detention, but if it comes, and probably it will before this week is out, it will make terrible havoc among them. The vicinity will then be converted into a quarantine ground, and this school included. The passing to and fro of the inhabitants of the city, from the locks and back again, is great, and added to this are about fifty more Irishmen at work on the canal close by, who also will go over to their brother Irish in the boats; these causes operating would spread the disease greatly when once it made its appearance. If the corporation of Troy conclude to make their quarantine grounds or pest-houses near the school, Prof. E. is then off, and his scholars may go as they list. *What shall I do?* May we be conformed to God's will.

Yours affectionately in life or death,
S. WELLS WILLIAMS.

RENSSELAER SCHOOL, TROY, July 12, 1832.

DEAR FATHER.—Your kind letter of the 5th inst. reached me, and I am very thankful for permission to go on the tours, if all events transpire to favor my going. I imagine that the route pursued will be a very interesting one, and one which will present many of the wondrous works of the Author of nature. I am much pleased with the study of chemistry, although some of my experiments fail. One very peculiar trait in this science is that nothing can be learned until you have performed the manipulation.

On Tuesday of this week I received a communication from R. Anderson, of Boston, concerning the station of printer. He informs me that I must be ready by spring at farthest, and probably to go this coming fall. But to go as soon as fall or spring is what I cannot do; for I do not wish to go and not know what I am to do or how to do it. On receiving his letter I thought it best to write you before answering him. He says that in the fall five or six other missionaries are also to go to the East, but to what particular station he does not say. They, however, go to Batavia. Or I am to go in the spring in a vessel of a Mr. Olyphant, of New York. Nine or ten months is the least time in which I could be prepared to go, and I should not care about going and not know my business. . . .

The enclosure to Dr. Anderson submitted to his father ran as follows:

TROY, July 20, 1832.

DEAR SIR.—As soon as I received your favor of the 7th inst. I wrote to my father: the object of which was to enquire of him why the time which was to elapse between my leaving this school and being ready to go on this important mission was so much curtailed. He had informed me that twelve or eighteen months would be allowed to finish my course of studies here and to get ready. I would not wish to have a longer time than reasonable, but if it is necessary absolutely to go by next fall or spring, I must say that I cannot possibly be ready. I cannot obtain a sufficient knowledge of the business to be able to do any one justice, and you would not wish to send one who was incompetent. In that short space of time I would have to learn all the pressman's and foreman's department, and also other small matters, though these would be the principal. All the knowledge I have of the printing trade has been learnt by stealth, while engaged in other employments. The whole would therefore have to be reviewed or learned. I have also an idea that the pressman's department will be somewhat difficult to learn, though my father assures me to the contrary. It would be very unfortunate, when I should arrive at the field of action, to have half a preparation—as a bayonet without a gun, or a handle without a tool. I could not offer myself without I was satisfied that I was in a measure prepared, and the Board would not want to find that they had an apprentice where they expected a workman. I could not under present circumstances consent to leave the school, and the session will not be finished until November.

I believe that I have, by the light which God has given us in the Bible, examined this question, and as far as I am acquainted with my own heart, I am willing to go. Many doubts and difficulties arise, and also many first impressions of times and places which are dear are to be considered. But I also look at the other side and see three fourths of the world in a state of heathenism or half-idolatry—then that side of the scale weighs heaviest. The way of duty is the plainest and in the end the easiest. "Go ye into all the world" still remains as a last command, and one which should be considered attentively. I should think but little of that Christian's ardor or sincerity who cannot do any thing for his Saviour. The reasons, however, why I could not be ready as soon as you wish, you have above. I also think that if I could wait even a still longer time than specified it would be better, as nineteen is a young period of life to be sent on such an expedition.

This, I should think, would be a consideration, though its weight could be judged of by others better than myself. These are all the views I have to give on this momentous subject. If a printer is absolutely indispensable by fall or spring, I should think that one might be found in some quarter or other. There are enough, I should imagine, who would wish to be sent, and esteem it a high privilege.

Perhaps I have not taken this subject into such prayerful consideration as I ought, but it has been the constant theme of my thoughts, and I believe that by the help of the Holy Spirit, I can see my way clearly. If I should go I should expect to collect specimens in Natural History, as that is my favorite pursuit; the study of nature is a pleasant one and carries its own reward along with it. The Asiatic cholera is, I think, on the increase in this city, tho' it has been much favored when compared with Albany and New York. The public institutions in this vicinity, as Union College, Troy Female Seminary, are about closing, tho' it is probable that this will not do so.

                       Yours truly,
                                   S. WELLS WILLIAMS.
To R. ANDERSON, Boston.

The cholera alarm soon passed away from the immediate vicinity of the school, and the term was allowed to draw quietly to its conclusion. In Utica, however, it had forced his father to give up business, family, and friends in his unflagging efforts to help the sick and arrest the panic created by the spreading epidemic. The tribute to his character, in an address of Mr. Wm. Tracy, reflects a certain lustre upon the whole generation of which such a man was a member:

"They who survive of the inhabitants of Utica, during the first visitation of the cholera in 1832, will never forget his services to the sick and dying, as well as to those who, from poverty, were unable to fly from the pestilence, and whose daily earnings were cut off by the suspension of business. It was not only from morn to night, but from early morn to early morn was he seen driving from house to house prescribing for, comforting, and encouraging the sick, smoothing the pillow of the dying, and distributing to the needy, until he was himself stricken down with the disease, slowly to recover."

Meantime, Wells, with his father's approval, joined his schoolmates and Professor Eaton in a scientific excursion across the State of Massachusetts and into New Hampshire. It was a month of precisely the kind of pleasure into which he threw himself with the liveliest joy:

"How well I remember—yes, indeed I do!—every town I visited on this tramp. Almost every tavern I can bring to mind; only the rainy days are forgotten. I never read again the journal I and all of us kept, but the exercise of writing it appears to have been like a nail fastening it in a sure place. Then we took with us, too, the elation of having all graduated near the top of our class; it was not difficult, since there were only three of us."

Upon returning to Utica in the fall, the influence on his disposition, of his long absence from home, and of the close companionship of his fellows at Troy, was gladly noted by those who knew and loved him best. An exceptional and highly retentive intelligence had sometimes led him to exact from others more than might reasonably be expected from them, and this seeming asperity of manner had made him the dread of some whose abilities were moderate. Faults of this kind, when the heart beneath is good, are sure to wear away in the healthful friction of contact with strangers and equals. Instead of his former censoriousness, bred of a too keen and critical mind, appeared now a kindly and sympathetic demeanor which won the friendship of all. The change is worth noting, since those who remembered him in after life for the benignity and charity which seemed inborn, could never have mistrusted that these qualities were the outcome of many inward struggles against a temper naturally rebellious, and that only by the exercise of vehement self-control did the ungracious youth become a man " lovely and of good report."

No time was lost in commencing the drudgery of the printing-office for the great end in view. For him there was no golden period of indecision, which, in the case of many, follows a college course and determines the complexion of a life. The Secretary of the American Board having allowed him until the opening of summer to prepare himself for his work, his one object was to learn as much as possible of the arts of printing and binding before that date.

In March of this year (1833) his father married Catherine Huntington, of Rome, a noble and devoted wife, a gifted woman, an unselfish mother, who gathered under her care the sadly scattered and untended group of children, and gave them, through a long and eventful life, her entire devotion and love. Wells, owing to his departure for China, came into the close intimacy of home life with her less than any of his brothers; but the difficult task of welcoming a second mother was honestly and warmly performed by him, whose loyalty to his family would have warranted a much severer trial than this proved to be. The springs of his attachment to his father and his admiration of his qualities were deep in his nature, and in his letters occur many expressions of this strong sense of filial duty and love which characterized his whole subsequent career. The following letter to both father and mother intimates this feeling, and records at the same time a few of his doubts and expectations while preparing for the voyage. Some of the accounts which came to him from those who had visited the far East were at once encouraging and tantalizing.

UTICA, April 2, 1833.

DEAR PARENTS.—Having received a letter from each of you, I thought that (if it would be no disrespect) I would answer them together. For them accept my sincere thanks. I have just returned from a visit to Rome, whither I went with Dwight on business ; we stayed there very pleasantly between three and four hours, and returned the same day.

The intelligence that I received concerning the ship in which I am to sail, afforded me a good deal of satisfaction. I think I can become more prepared to go by tarrying to the first of June : more prepared with respect to baggage, books, plants, etc., etc. Mr. Frazier, with whom I have had some conversation respecting China (he having lived at Canton a year), has been *very* obliging in telling me several particulars concerning a residence there, laying before me its dangers, temptations, pleasures, privations, and difficulties. They are to one solely intent on the accomplishment of his ends, and who entirely relys on the assisting grace of God, easily overcome. They result principally from the tendency that a continual habit of smuggling has on the moral principles, to vitiate them radically ; also from looseness of social ties, resulting from an entire want of female society. This latter, he says, is, after a time, most deeply felt ; it begins to be missed as soon as you realize that all whom you *can* associate with are men of loose habits, morals, and principles. But shall I not be obliged to associate more with the natives than he did ? I have been imagining that would be the case, and if so these temptations will be in some considerable measure removed. To be prepared, however, to withstand all the dangers will require a large supply of grace from above, a daily, yea, hourly modicum of that help which is spiritual, not mortal. I hardly realize the fact that I *am* going as yet, though, as the time draws near, it comes up before me in pretty glowing colors, the vividness of which sometimes almost startles me. But turn the page and consider the object, to evangelize the world ; consider the immediate portion of labor, the mighty population of China now at this time shaking to its very centre, and these are enough to recall to mind the fact that he who has hold of the plough has but one way to look. . . .

The end of April found him ready for the long journey. Continuous industry and a mind quickened by the exceptional interest and importance of his task had enabled him within six months to serve a hasty apprenticeship in every department of book-making. From the compositor's room he followed the types to the press, thence with the printed sheets to the proof-reader, then to the folder, the sewing frame, and process of binding ; it was possible in his father's establishment to finish his training in these departments very thoroughly. It was not in the least a six months suited to his fancy. " Full of business, we have been," he writes James Dana at this time, "but such business as I hate." To this eager lad, who had always a student's love for, but never a dealer's interest in, books, 't was a dry and irksome drudgery, mitigated only by the sense of duty present and future.

When in Boston, receiving his final instructions at the office of the Board, he learned that the ship *Morrison*, in which that large-hearted merchant, Mr. Olyphant, had offered a free passage to him.and his fellow missionary, Rev. Ira Tracy, had postponed her sailing until the middle of June. The delay gave them both more time than they cared for in New York, during which some gentle Christians there cherished the young men with social attentions that rather embarrassed them.

NEW YORK, June 10, 1833.

DEAR MOTHER.—The few lines you dropped me in one of your letters were very pleasant. In return I can say but few words, as he will tell you of all that is interesting. I am not sorry that we came as we did ; it has given me an opportunity to go to Philadelphia and see the wonders of that city.

I shall probably go this week, Thursday or Friday, and pray that the God of Jacob may go with me. I am very much troubled with the kind and well meant attentions of more friends than I can number. It is a source of great disquietude to me, but it will soon be over, and I shall be on the great deep. But all the friends? here do not begin to erase from my mind the real friends that are in Utica. I am calling them up ever and anon, and their mental presence gladdens my heart. Remember me to all and believe me
Sincerely yours in love and Christian affection,
S. WELLS WILLIAMS.

It was not easy work saying farewell to old friends and new acquaintances at once. Referring to this in a letter to his father a year later he intimates the kind of strain put upon a sober, self-contained nature.

"You remarked in one of your letters that many had asked if I went willingly. On this observation I have thought somewhat, since I left home, as I would not be certain but that (when I thought of and saw all I was leaving) I had dropped some expressions of regret. But if these were said, they were all left behind in America on the 15th of June, 1833. My return to Utica for so short a time when I came from Boston may have generated the opinion that it was hard for me to leave. And so I confess it *was ;* but I did not come back on this account. And, as you have said, I did not say much to anybody concerning it during the whole winter."

SHIP MORRISON, June 15, 1833.

DEAR FATHER AND MOTHER :—I have kept the last letter for you, and the blue broad sea is in view while I write it. Now I begin to see my way clear, and humbly trust I can look forward to my field of labor, putting my confidence in that Saviour who has sent me. I know he will not forsake me, and he can give me strength to bear all the trials of my long voyage. We have an excellent captain, Briggs by name, and our ship is well manned ; the crew are well chosen, and look like intelligent, active sailors. A very good field of labor ; may we be blessed in all endeavors to do them good. They have opportunities for praising God in the perils of the mighty deep, that if improved will result to their own good. The captain is a pious man : what a favor of God to us notwithstanding wickedness ; and may we be thankful to him for it. We had a last and good prayer-meeting at Mr. Olyphant's last evening, and as I knelt before the throne of grace my thoughts would go home and hold converse with those who are left there, hoping again to see them in heaven, if not before. And now, as my last look is taken of the shores of my native country, my heart is, I know, filled with the sweet unction from on high, which is better than any other blessing. Let me put my trust in Him, and go on doing my duty, and what more do I want ? Pray for me, and pray with an object. . . . Goodbye, and a long farewell, but in hope to see each other again, in heaven if not on earth.

Yours affectionately,
S. WELLS WILLIAMS.

TO HIS FATHER.

SHIP MORRISON, INDIAN OCEAN, Sept. 24, 1833.

I have had good health all the passage, and (except a few days while sea-sick) have not omitted a meal, which I consider a good criterion. For exercise I have climbed the rigging, and as far as that is concerned have become quite a sailor. The accommodations are very good (for *now* I speak in the present tense) ; we have not wanted for any thing necessary, except now and then would we send a desire home, and a desire would be all we got. All the hands have also enjoyed as good health as usual, for calomel and jalap is liberally used on board a ship, and there are many who want it. We lost our steward when two weeks out, from a fit, as we suppose. He lay down at 11 A.M., and at 3 P.M. was a corpse. He had complained of a pain in his head and went to sleep, but awoke in eternity, and to all that was known of him, an eternally miserable one. He was deposited in the deep, Brother Tracy reading the English Church service, which is inimitable in such a situation. He (Tracy) has preached every Sunday that it was practicable, and prayers also are held in the round-house every evening that it is convenient. These services are well attended, many of the men staying to them when they have been on deck eight hours of the night and consequently require sleep. When they were first collected I thought I had never seen so motley a crowd, but now they look like other collections, and, for all I can see, as well as any finely dressed congregation.

My watch has been tried with the chronometers on board and runs like a lame hare, sometimes walking, sometimes trotting, then galloping, and afterwards standing still. What is the ailment I am not watch doctor enough to say, but this ought not so to have been or now be. I have while I felt disposed learnt something of navigation, tho' as it is an easy study it has not taken much of my time; but the book has been earned by its use.

This day, after 103 long, tedious, cold and warm, stormy and pleasant days, we hailed the is-*land* of Christmas, and it was a pleasant sight to all. It is an uninhabited land, but produces cocoa-nuts, etc. One thing is worthy of telling you of—the accuracy of our chronometers. After a hundred odd days of sailing, having gone by the log more than fifteen thousand miles, and exposed to variations of from $50°$ to $112°$ Fahr., we are only two miles out of the way. If this does not show their accuracy, I don't know what would; we saw not a sign of land between Sandy Hook and Christmas.

(Sunday.) We are now at Anger, having come up the Straits in the light of the full moon. But few live here, and these few are so poor and sickly that they hardly live. We only stop to get water, provisions, etc., which we stand greatly in need of.

The wine was duly drunk, one week ago to-day, and many a desire was sent up that it may commemorate the beginning of a new life.

This refers to a bottle which at the last moment of his leaving home a thoughtful mother had stowed away in the bottom of his leather trunk.

"On the 22d of September, 1833 [writes his cousin, Mr. Thomas Seward*], somewhere in eastern seas, our missionary printer contributed from his private stores to the captain's table a single bottle of current wine, which, we take for granted, was found to be of full flavor, served to emphasize one day in the weary monotony of days in an ocean voyage, and did no harm to the company. The wine had been set apart by a happy father from his own vintage of 1812, to be solemnly drank on the twenty-first anniversary of the birth of his eldest son. No horoscope of the child's future revealed Indian seas, the ship *Morrison*, nor the restricted life in Canton."

* Memorial of S. W. Williams.—Oneida Hist. Soc. Transactions, 1885-6.

CHAPTER II.

ON the afternoon of the twenty-fifth of October, 1833, the ship Morrison anchored at Whampoa, twelve miles below Canton. Here lay the great fleet of East India merchantmen,—many of them the finest vessels afloat and manned often with more than fourscore sailors—lining the wide river for three miles with their hundred hulls, and awaiting their annual cargoes of silks and tea. The missionaries Tracy and Williams were rowed up to the city in the ship's gig and landed at the "factories," being consigned to the care of Kingqua, a hong merchant who, on the principle of securing due obedience from all strangers, became sponsor to the Chinese government during their residence in his factory. They never saw the merchant while living under his tutelage, or did him the annoyance of breaking the "regulations" of this singular residence.

The position of foreigners and conditions of their life in China had at this time scarcely altered since the commencement of a tentative and limited trade by the East India Company in 1664. They constituted a community by themselves, housed in a tiny space without the walls of Canton, subject in their mutual dealings chiefly to their own sense of honor, while their relations with the Chinese were about what lawyers call a state of nature. In the crowded group of buildings known as the factories, occupying a plot of some fifteen acres along the river, about three hundred foreigners of all nationalities lived and trafficked with the Chinese, and the confinement, the contumely, the insecurity, the restrictions, the forced separation from families, the monopoly and surveillance of the "co-hong," the obstacles in the way of learning the language or spreading Christianity—in short, the degradation by the Chinese authorities of every "barbarian" who ventured to their territory, existed as a political system in 1833, just as it had been maintained during two centuries; and doubtless it would have continued forever except for the resort to force, which in striving to resist this contemptuous policy culminated in the war of 1841. Until that event China remained in sentiment and civilization a survival of the middle ages.

As to the *Shap-sam hong*, or "Thirteen Factories," enough has been heard of them in Chinese history to merit a description. "They were," says Mr. Williams in some "Recollections of China,"* given in the later years of his residence there, "placed close side by side of each other, forming as it were a row or 'terrace' fronting the river, but each hong consisted of a series of buildings placed one behind the other from the river backwards, for a depth of from 550 to 600 feet, to the first street running parallel with the river. They were, in fact, modeled on the Chinese ground-plan for the building of extensive houses, viz., court within court in as long a series as may be possible or desirable. The approach to those in the rear was through the basement of those in front. The interval between the houses was from thirty to sixty feet,

* Journal of the China Branch Asiatic Soc., No. VIII., Shanghai, 1874.

or more. The upper stories of these buildings were divided off by partitions, some of them having only two stories, others three. The old factories had been entirely destroyed by fire in 1822, but were rebuilt at the expense of the hong merchants, who owned most of them."

The word factory, it must be noted, was the term employed throughout the East, to designate the establishments of the *factors* of the East India Co., and had no sense at all synonymous with "manufactory." From the river this row of brick and granite houses presented rather a substantial front, the various national flags upon masts in the gardens before them adding dots of color to the group and emphasizing the contrast to the fantastic emblems and squalid buildings of the Celestial Empire. Within, however, these establishments afforded at best but poor accommodations, being neither sufficiently spacious nor airy. The main building occupied by the East India Company, with its great banquet-room, offices and chapel, was indeed sumptuously equipped, and those fronting on the river afforded a few good habitations; but the majority were forced to take up with quarters as unhealthy as they were inconvenient and disagreeable. The damp, stenching atmosphere of a ground-floor room in a back factory was quite unendurable at certain seasons of the year, and all who could do so avoided the pestilences of summer in one by a flight to Macao.

These buildings—distinguished in Chinese by euphonious titles, such as "Assembled Righteousness," the "Factory that Insures Tranquillity," the "Wide Fountains," etc.—were for the most part owned by the "co-hong," a body of thirteen Chinese merchants who alone were officially recognized by the government as shippers and foreign traders, and were made responsible for the conduct of the "barbarians" to whom their dwellings were rented. Owing to this monopoly, and as manufacturers of most of the goods exported, they had individually and collectively amassed great wealth, while a number of them, by means of their relations with the foreigners had become intelligent and large-minded men. Their chief in wealth and influence was Howqua, who was in many respects a very remarkable man. "These merchants [to quote Mr. Williams' 'Recollections'] were the intermediaries between the Chinese authorities and foreigners. When the foreigners wished any thing from the Chinese, the plan was to draw up a petition and take it to a certain gate of the city known as the Oil Gate, where it was received by a policeman or some low official who was generally at hand. But sometimes the hong merchants refused to receive or transmit said petitions. On one occasion a Scotchman named Innes, a man of great energy, brought a petition to the Oil Gate, but the hong merchants having got a hint of its purport, refused to receive it. He waited at the gate all day, but they persisted in their refusal. As night approached he gave orders to his boy to go and fetch his bed, as an indication that he intended to stop there all night, and when the merchants came to know that, they received his petition. On another occasion before my arrival, Mr. Jardine, the head of Jardine, Matheson & Co., having taken a petition to the gate in question, received rather hard usage, some one having struck him a rap on the head. He, however, never stirred or gave any indication that the blow had hurt him, from which circumstance he came to be known and spoken of by the Chinese, during all his subsequent stay in China, as *teet tow lo shu*, 'the iron-headed old rat.' This gate—a very small one in the southern wall of Canton City—I have myself very frequently visited, but never with a petition."

Another quotation from the same source illustrates excellently well the kind of wardenship exercised by the mandarins over these pent-up foreigners:

"The East India Company had so arranged the large factory occupied by them that they had managed at great expense to lay out a garden on its river front, extending to about half an acre, which was nicely kept and afforded a very pleasant promenade in summer time, as being walled in it was free from the intrusion of beggars and hucksters. This garden they had enlarged by extending their wall so as to include some land that had silted up from the river and was dry at low water. Soon after this acquisition had been made, the Fuyuen of Canton suddenly appeared one morning in front of the factories, having with him a large band of attendants, several of whom were armed with shovels with which they forthwith began to shovel this new piece of garden into the river, reducing the company's pleasure ground to its original size. The mud thrown into the river was carried down a short distance and there collected, and being increased by subsequent siltings, formed a nucleus of a bank. The Governor having, as he flattered himself, effectually put an end to such foreign encroachments, returned to the city, but the hong merchants rather laughed at what he, no doubt, thought a very valorous exploit. . . . .

"In those days the greatest difficulty was experienced in getting properly qualified persons to teach us Chinese. I secured a teacher of considerable literary attainments, and he took the special precaution, lest he should be informed against by some one, of always bringing with him and laying on the table a foreign lady's shoe, so that if any one he was afraid of, or did not know, should come in, he could pretend that he was a Chinese manufacturer of foreign shoes. This he continued to do for months, till he became convinced that his fears were groundless. One of Dr. Morrison's teachers always carried some poison about him, so that if he found he had been informed against to the Chinese authorities, he might take his own life and so avoid their tortures,—for such a charge was then regarded as one of the most offensive and dangerous that could be brought against a native. This I afterwards learned from one of his fellow teachers. .

"One remarkable feature of that time was the small number of foreigners who were students of Chinese. I can in fact remember only five, during the time that Lin was commissioner—leaving out of view the Portuguese of Macao, few of whom, however, knew any thing of the character. One of the five referred to was Mr. Robt. Thom, who afterwards became H. M. Consul at Ningpo, another was Mr. John Robert Morrison (son of the great missionary), and a third was Dr. Gutzlaff; these three were the only men available to the British Government as interpreters, after 1834. It was a very distinct fact that the authorities of Canton during a long course of years, by their intimidation of natives who aided us, did much to prevent foreigners from acquiring a knowledge of the language. The fear these poor men had of being in any way identified with us was indeed intense. So afraid were they of being accused of having assisted us to learn Chinese, that I remember frequently there were Chinamen to whom I spoke Chinese and who knew perfectly well what I said, but who always persisted in replying to me in English. Thom's practice of talking freely with the Chinese who came to Messrs. Jardine's office did something, however, to overcome this apprehension. . . .

"Residence in the factories (so far as regarded our social relations) was exceedingly pleasant. We all lived together on the most friendly terms, probably because we were so close together, and the interchange of social courtesies was most agreeable. And then when the tea season had passed, and the summer heats assailed us, we started for Macao, where we could enjoy the sea and the cool breeze, and could get a little more room to stretch our legs. At Canton our range for pedestrian exercise was rather limited. We could sail on the river in boats, but on shore we could only walk round the city at very considerable risk of being robbed. . . . When one looks back on the then state of things, it is difficult to understand how we could have been there so long and yet have known so little about the people, and been known so little by them. When Canton was thrown open to foreigners as late as 1858, some missionaries went into the city and found Chinese who had never seen a foreigner; who had never heard that places for preaching had been opened; who did not think it possible that any foreigners could speak Chinese."

In a letter written to Dr. Anderson not many years before the death of the famous Board Secretary, Mr. Williams thus describes his environment and the nature of his impressions on first reaching Canton.

"At the date of my arrival, missions to China were regarded as directed more to the foreigners living in it than to the natives—which latter were to be influenced by the way, as chances offered. I was reported to the hong merchants as a trader who had come to live in the Hong of Broad Fountains, and the hong merchant who owned the hong was security for my good conduct, though we never saw each other. I was introduced to Dr. Morrison and his good son John, and with Dr. Bridgman and Stevens, six of us partook of the communion. Some days after this I saw the only convert, Leang Afa. Yet the work never looked otherwise than hopeful to me, and this small beginning produced no discouragement upon my mind; it seems now, sometimes, as if it ought to have done so. . . . The books to aid in learning the language were as few as the opportunities to use it, consequently my progress was slow. In addition to the work which I was sent to superintend, we made an attempt to have Chinese tracts and the Gospels printed from blocks, but this resulted so disastrously to the natives employed, that thirteen years passed before another attempt of this sort was made.

"When I look back upon those times, I see how nicely

political events were ordered for the good of this nation, gradually preparing it for a better understanding of its own rights and position, and loosening by degrees the restrictions of ages. I cannot doubt but that God has yet great things for so large a part of the earth to do."

Elijah Coleman Bridgman, who welcomed his countrymen to Canton, was the first missionary sent from the United States to the Chinese.* Reaching Canton in 1840, commended by the pious and generous merchant, Mr. D. W. C. Olyphant, he joined Dr. Morrison in his lonely labors, and at once earnestly entered upon the study of the language and the task of fitting himself as an active agent for the evangelization of China. Not unlike the great English missionary in character, Mr. Bridgman was endowed with exceptional intellectual qualities and a retentive memory, which in his case was quickened and refined by the culture of a college and professional education. With the assistance of Morrison and his great dictionary, his zeal and application had brought him in three years to a good knowledge of the language, in which he had already commenced to hold regular religious services, to translate and write acceptable tracts, and to assist in other ways the propagation of the Gospel. His influence upon Mr. Williams was most fortunate; they found in each other especial sympathy of temperament as well as of interest, and between them there arose a friendship which lasted with unabated warmth during many years

*Dr. D. Abeel, his coadjutor was obliged by impaired health to return to the United States in May, 1833. He came back to China in 1839, but, after struggling five years with his illness, returned home a second time, to die. Mr. Williams' esteem for his character amounted almost to veneration. At considerable personal expense he had a steel engraving of him inserted in the first edition of the " Middle Kingdom."

of close companionship in China. The circumstance of their duties lying very near together in editing and printing the *Chinese Repository*, brought the two men immediately into intimate relations, and to this professional connection were added the cementing ties of their family life in the cramped quarters of a back factory, as well as a sense of the isolation of the little missionary band in the midst of a selfish and gain-greedy community. Bridgman's age, as well as his superior education, placed him at first somewhat in the position of a mentor to the young printer; his advice was clearly of the best, and always followed with advantage. The language must not be his only thought (he said), because his first duties were to the printing-press; the necessity of constant and accurate observation of the peculiar people among which they lived; avoiding the temptation to consider merely the odd and picturesque elements of Chinese civilization; training his daily life to bear the minute and suspicious scrutiny of a hostile society,—such were the rudimental lessons whereby the new arrival was shown that missionary work consisted in doing not what he came expecting to do, but to do rather what was set before him. "What a difference it would have made with me," wrote Mr. Williams, " if I had been joined in the first years of my residence here with a freaky, impulsive man! I should probably have gone away from the country. Blessed be God for Bridgman's example and influence!"

The *Chinese Repository* had been commenced by Mr. Bridgman in May, 1832, as a medium of information in matters relating to the extreme East. His way was made clear towards the prosecuting of such an enterprise by the font of type recently presented to the mission, while as encouragment to its success he had the very valuable aid of both the Morrisons, and the use of the Chinese types belonging to the East India Company. Upon Mr. Williams' arrival the management of the printing office was at once given over to him, and before many months were passed he began his contributions to the pages of the *Repository*, which continued until its termination. His first articles on "Chinese Weights and Measures," and "Imports and Exports of Canton," appeared in the February number for 1834. These were followed during the next few years by papers on the natural history of the country, which subject was uppermost in his mind until familiarity with the language brought with the ability to read Chinese an interest in its literature and construction. Not much can be said for the style of these early essays, except that by means of them he succeeded in making his researches known. A consciousness of his literary unskilfulness once impelled him to try and improve his diction, and for this purpose he sought a model and example in his favorite author, Charles Lamb. But the attempt to treat a scene in Canton life after the fashion of the "Essay on Roast Pig," resulted in a parody so naïvely bad that Mr. Bridgman begged him, with tears of laughter, to put his fine writing in the fire and return to dull and plodding prose. It is a notable circumstance, and one worth emphasizing as an encouragement to others, that a man so ill-equipped in the use of his own language should, by dint of perseverance, have succeeded in moulding it into sentences of singular vigor and expressiveness in one of the most difficult of modern sciences. Though never free from a certain clumsiness of diction in his longer works, the terse and direct quality of his dictionary definitions has received the commendations of multitudes of students, and contributed distinctly to the advancement of philology.

The following letter to his father, sent by the earliest return ship, records some of the emotions aroused by a first glance at his new home:

CANTON, November 6, 1833.

I have been here a week, and in that short time have seen enough of idolatry to call forth all the energies I have. A city which at a reasonable calculation must contain as many inhabitants as all the State of New York, which has its enormous influence in the Empire—a city like this demands a deal of Christian labor. The tide of beings which flows through any one of the city gates here is like the deep current of a powerful river. To pass across it you must "sail down a-ways" before you can reach the other side of a street six or eight feet wide. This flood is continual, and once in it, all scepticism vanishes concerning the population of China. To take a circuit thro' one of these streets about eventide, and see the abominations practised against the honor of Him who has commanded, "Thou shalt have no other gods before me," and not be affected with a deep sense of the depth to which this intellectual people has sunk, is impossible to a warm Christian man. The number of incense sticks burning in every shop, at every corner, on every door-post, and indeed in every place where room can be found, is so great as to raise a cloud of smoke over the city, and almost to blind the eyes when walking abroad at such times. And is not such a mass of fellow immortals entitled to deep commiseration, to large and combined effort? They are an easy people to work upon where their prejudices and government do not interfere. By this I mean where government does not in a manner make the prejudices.

Along with this letter I have sent two tracts in Chinese, the smaller one containing Scripture extracts, the other a school-book for girls. And what I want to direct attention to is the cheapness with which these books can be manufactured. The small one can be furnished in any quantities after the blocks are paid for, at *one cent* per copy. This includes paper, silk, and ink, and many thousands of them have been distributed among the natives. The other can be furnished at a cent and a half, and is of the same size as the Bible, which is in twenty-one volumes, sold at one dollar and five cents. These books the Chinese receive willingly, and appear to read. To make them, natives are employed; the first convert (Leang Afa) was made by reading the blocks he was cutting. He is now engaged in making books as fast as he can, and has distributed many thousands. A short time since there was an examination of literary candidates in Canton, and more than twenty-five thousand came. Leang Afa got some coolies to take his boxes into the hall, and there he dealt out the word of life as fast as he could handle them to intelligent young men. This he did three days together, but when he repeated the attempt some eighteen months later, he got bambooed. Thus is the word being put before their eyes, and they are already somewhat acquainted with it in this vicinity. Leang Afa is a venerable-looking man about fifty years old; his countenance expresses benevolence, and at first view you are prepossessed.

The young missionary's duties were as queer as his surroundings; many of the hands in his office were Portuguese from the Colony of Macao, and rather to his own surprise, he found himself first studying that language, instead of Chinese, in order to direct his printers. It was in some respects fortunate for him that the publication of the *Repository* was the only work which could at that time be safely done in the printing room, and that he was able to devote his first year in China almost wholly to teacher and dictionary.

The general indifference to the Gospel saddens him

most. Writing in December, 1834, he complains that, "The congregations on the Sabbath are small indeed. One or two weeks ago, when Gutzlaff preached, we had forty-three, the largest number since I have been here. The service is held in the same room that we eat in every day; we arrange some chairs and put a desk on the table—that is all. Would you not say that it is a day of small things?"

Concerning the practical bent of his character at this period and the manner in which he viewed his work, we have his own testimony in a reminiscence written many years later, as to what was the underlying stimulus to continued effort:

"I did not think much about the matter of my own incompetence until I reached China and was fairly a missionary in the field, when it came upon me very strongly and troublesomely. I learned, however that it grew by nursing, till I was likely to have nothing else to think or muse upon, nor could I even perform my immediate duty; so it came to pass that I cried out, 'I am as inefficient as a wisp of smoking flax, as weak as water, useless, and sinful; but I have something to do *now*, and can do it if I try, whatever else more remote and difficult I cannot do.' So I got myself to feel that I had not the whole Chinese language to learn, but rather a few characters then before me; not the whole nation to convert, but rather a few servants in the house to bless as I could by my presence, and show that I wished to do them good. . . . Afterwards I had very little anxiety as to the haps which might befall me, and strove to become of that tranquil state of mind so enviable and satisfactory, yet not so much as to lose all interest in the enjoyment of society and others.

And again, the following throws a side-light upon his disposition:

"Whenever I see a friend for whom I have more than a complimentary respect, I shake hands with a thoroughly good grasp. With regard to this, indeed, I 've acquired rather an unenviable reputation for squeezing people's hands to the great jeopardy of their fingers and joints. Again and again I resolve to be less rough, but all these good intentions vanish when I see one from whom I 've been long absent and in whom I really delight. . . . Yet I have never been an adept in the expression of feeling and do not possess much tact in making others believe them. When I first came here [to Macao], I had the greatest desire to please those around me, but having signally failed on several occasions of getting credit for good intentions, I thought I should do better for myself by retiring into my own thoughts—very much as snails do when they think their self-love is touched,—letting the people around me take care of themselves. This plan had the effect of rendering me as unhappy and cross as a man with a toothache in a smoky house on a cold and rainy day, insomuch that one lady was heard to observe that she did n't believe I loved four persons in the world. So my plan would n't do; I did love four—nay, fourscore, at least, but the retroactive effect of my own conduct had made me so gloomy that I determined at once to throw it off as a matter of duty and put on as cheerful a face as I could assume, loving all mankind and trying to get those to love me who could."

TO HIS FATHER.

CANTON, February 23, 1834.

Our family is now about to settle, and each one of the four, Bros. Bridgman, Stevens, Tracy, and myself, is fully occupied. Indeed we have so much to attend to that it is difficult sometimes to give each its proper attention. But my old maxim of one thing at a time I find accomplishes much. The *Repository* is the most arduous work, but whether the most profitable or not remains to be seen. If its effect on the Christian world is adequate to the importance of the subject, our labor is not for trifles. The enlightening of those who are the patrons of this great work is not a vain object; therefore circulate those that are sent to Utica, and make the three copies you have do the work of thirty.

We have eight children now under tuition, but none are pious or serious, though they make good progress. I have two Portuguese and three Chinese in the office, and but two of the five speak English. When I first went in I had to talk mostly by signs, but soon got a smattering of both languages, and was fain to use sentences made up in part of Portuguese, Chinese and Canton-English—this last being a mixture of all three. Truly I have often smiled after I've been talking largely, to think of the *Babel-lingo* I was uttering. Now, however, I have made some progress in both the genuine languages, and can separate the two into something intelligible. My office is rather a cold place, as it has a stone floor, is partly out-doors and has no fireplace. Fires you must know are used here from December to April on account of the cold and damp. . . . If you think there are two many *I's* in this letter, I knew I was writing to a father who liked to hear about *I*. I am very well and to keep so take daily rides in a boat on the river which we row ourselves; by this means we have an opportunity to distribute some books, though cautiously. We have explored all the banks of the river for two or three miles, but when either walking or rowing outside of the factory confines we do so at our peril and may sometimes fall into violent hands.*

To his mother writing on the same date:

"I had the rare pleasure, if it can be so called, of attending a Chinese dinner last week; it should be more properly termed a gratification of curiosity than any pleasure. It was a curious affair. The room was about thirty feet long and fifteen wide,

* This happened once to a party of four of them who were walking around the walled city, when a gang of fifty or more sons of Belial pounced upon them, threw snuff in their eyes, robbed and beat them. It was indeed a narrow escape for their lives, but the only redress or satisfaction they received from the authorities was a warning to keep within their fifteen acres. All alien races being known to the natives merely as foreign devils who smuggling opium into the country, they were regarded as fair game.

having three recesses on the side. In one of these recesses or rooms was a stove, in the second the ancestral tablet which they worship in their private houses with an altar before it laden with first-fruits and other offerings, and in the third were the dishes. The sides of the recesses were ornamented with lattice-work, as was also the front of the large room, made with little eye-holes of glass to look out into the river. This lattice-work is very pretty when handsomely constructed, and is often worked with green and yellow ornaments. Perhaps Sisera's mother looked through some such affair. The view from the room was interesting, looking down on the river with its thousands of inhabitants moving in all directions. At 7 P. M. the dinner began with a soup of birds' nests which we ate with chop-sticks; these we used somewhat clownishly at first, as it required a little practice to eat a soup with two ivory sticks. Then followed dishes whose names and contents were unknown, but which tasted pretty much all alike. They were all in cups about the size of tea-cups, and when given to each guest always eaten with these same chop-sticks. In eating liquid dishes, as soups, the mouth is put down to the edge of the dish and the contents shovelled in. They will eat rice as fast again in this way as I could ever manage with a spoon. Some of the dishes we had were birds' nests, lily roots, pigs' tongues, fishes' stomachs, sharks' fins, biche-de-mer, fishes' heads—and others to the number of fourteen. After this a European dinner was served, but rather inferior to the other. Instead of bread they eat watermelon seeds and baked almonds, which are placed by the side of the plate. Wine is drank in cups that I do not believe would hold more than a large spoonful, not a swallow by any means. The custom is to show the bottom of the cups, a thing that can easily be done. Their wine is made of rice. This dinner, which we finished by about ten o'clock, was given by Quanshing-qua, a brother of Shunshing-qua; *qua* meaning Mr."

On the evening of August 1, 1834, occurred the death of Dr. Robert Morrison, the pioneer of Protestant mission work in China, and the greatest name in the evangelical history of that country. His work was almost done when Mr. Williams reached China, a lifetime which may properly be compared to the foundation of a great edifice, not less important though hidden from view. The spirit of seclusion, then in the fulness of its might among Chinese officials, joined to equally restrictive rules of the East India Company against attempts at converting the natives, made the open propagandism of Christianity impossible during his whole life at Canton; but patience and assiduous study enabled him to compass important preparatory labors in the cause. Despite obstacles put by Chinese officials in the way of his learning the language, by the Company in the way of his translating the Bible, by the Roman Catholics at Macao in the way of his preaching there, Dr. Morrison succeeded in accomplishing the two great two objects placed before him by the London Missionary Society, rendering the Scriptures into Chinese and preparing the first Anglo-Chinese dictionary. His noble character and godly life enabled him to win many friends among the foreigners in Canton and to remain in the factories amid, and almost in defiance of, harassing uncertainties and orders from the Company at home for his dismissal. He was naturally looked upon with esteem and affection by the younger missionaries, who considered him the great representative of their common cause and chief adviser in their undertakings. "It should be stated, however," Mr. Williams adds judiciously in another place, "that he was not by nature calculated to win and interest the skeptical or the fastidious, for he had no sprightliness or pleasantry, no versatility or wide acquaintance with letters, and was respected rather than loved by those who cared little for the things nearest his heart." But to the sympathizing band which followed his body to the cemetery at Macao his death was a cause of sore loss and mourning.

TO HIS FATHER.

MACAO, August 8, 1834.

The occasion of my being at this place is one which we are, as Christians and fellow-workers in the cause of Christ, both called to deplore. To any one who had seen the face and heard the recital of the pains of Dr. Morrison for the last twelve months, the impression would have been strong that his race of usefulness was nearly done. And he was himself of the same opinion. But his death has come suddenly, especially to his near friends, who having become somewhat habituated to the complaints which attend the gradual dissolution of nature, did not lay peculiar stress upon his last illness. The disease was invidious and sure, yet not apparent to any alarming extent till its work was finished. And we have cause for much thankfulness that this indefatigable servant of Christ's was permitted to work to the last week of his life. His mind was of such a cast that if he had been confined on a bed for many weeks its restless activity would have aggravated the disease.

The tenor of his conversation for many months past had been towards heaven, and he was in a frame of mind that was looking towards his rest and wishing (if it was the Lord's pleasure) to be at peace in His kingdom.

The anxiety caused by the uncertainty of the new arrangements in the English government, by which he was kept in suspense for three months, undoubtedly aggravated the disease. He described himself as in a constant uneasiness, unable to eat or sleep, stand or sit with any comfort. Pain was his allotment for months before his decease, and the patience with which he bore his afflictions, both mental and bodily, gave testimony to the stability of his trust in his Master. Much of his labor latterly was done under prostrations of energy to which most men would give way. This want of bodily strength was severely felt by him, and he endeavored, as far as he was able, to resist it; but the efforts of his mind were too much for the disordered state of his body. A great deal of the weakness to which Dr. Morrison was subject for several years before his death was owing to the want of exercise, which as certainly will be productive of disease to the body as that combustion will produce decomposition. He was on his arrival in China very thin and poor, but gradually became corpulent and indisposed to bodily exertion. If his constitution had not been of wonderful durability from his early occupation of coal-heaver and farmer till twenty years of age, he would not in all probability have lived half the years that he has in China. On dissection, his heart and liver were found in a great measure covered with fat, while the lungs were adipose, and adhered to the sides of the body.

The anxiety which he has had concerning the future support of his family since the decease of the E. I. Company also aggravated his maladies; and the sudden entering upon his duties as translator to Lord Napier after a period of quiet, together with a cold caught in a squall coming up to Canton, were the more immediate causes under God of releasing him from this world. His prayers were unceasing for those of his coadjutors who remain, and for his eldest son, who is in China, that we might have a courage and zeal to go on with his work. He has fought a good fight, and held out to the end. For twenty-seven years, almost, he has contested the kingdom of darkness in China, twenty-three of them alone as to any one assisting him in China. His dictionary would never yet have been printed in all probability, if it had not been for the E. I. Company, and they were the means of his being enabled to maintain his ground against Chinese and Portuguese authorities. He has been neglected by Christians (nominal ones) here, and forgotten by them at home, but by the grace of God he has been enabled to publish a Chinese dictionary, to translate the Bible into Chinese, and to found a college for Chinese youths. Let no man say that Dr. Morrison has lived in vain.

That famous trading corporation and monstrous monopoly, the East India Company, came to the end of its control in China upon the expiration of its charter a few months before Morrison's death. The policy of this concern, which in India and China assumed all the prerogatives of a government, had been to maintain accord with the native authorities by systematically opposing any efforts on the part of British subjects towards diffusing a higher education or Christian doctrines in the far East. Intercourse of this kind could not impress the Chinese with any lofty or true idea of the character of the English people, though its duration through nearly two centuries without any open rupture had convinced the Directors of its expediency. The termination of these exclusive privileges and the resolve of the British government to insist upon the recognition of a consul in Canton was therefore the cause of considerable satisfaction among foreigners outside of the company in China. Its work was accomplished, as Mr. Williams wrote, "when western nations no longer looked upon these regions as objects of desire, nor went to Rome to get a privilege to seize or claim such pagan lands as they might discover, and when, too, Christians began to learn and act upon their duty to evangelize these ignorant races." * But for its assistance in printing Dr. Morrison's dictionary it did little else as a body during its long life to help the cause of civilization in China, and latterly had put every obstacle in the path of missionary enterprises there. Morrison's continuance in Canton was largely due to the personal friendship of an English merchant whose daughter he married, and to his useful-

* "Middle Kingdom," II., 463.

ness to the company as interpreter and translator; but after occupying this position under them for twenty-five years they never awarded him even the empty compliment of enrolling his name in the list of their "servants." However uncertain the prospects of commercial intercourse with the Chinese when the medium of the company was taken away, its dissolution was not regretted among foreigners in China; the next step toward the extension of trade, the abolition of the corresponding Chinese monopoly of the co-hong, would, it was hoped, soon follow, but this did not come until the government learned the real meaning of foreign commerce by the lesson of war.

TO HIS MOTHER.

CANTON, July 22, 1835.

To give you some idea of the place we live in, I send you a description of what I saw from the terrace on top of our factory one evening last week. How they look you can learn from the view of them I sent you by Mr. Cooper.

Towards the east was the river stretching away among the paddy fields, and defended on each side by hills, some covered with grass and others sterile, but all cut up and roughened by a vast number of graves. The two forts, called Follies, in the middle of the river were conspicuous from the dense foliage which entirely hid their warlike defences. The masts of the junks, all covered with gay streamers, were very numerous and apparently filled up the whole river. On the south side lies the island of Honan, and a small village of that name is immediately opposite the factories. Hills are seen far away on the horizon, and between them and the river-side, patches of paddy (or growing rice), with here and there a tree or a clump of bamboos, open a green vista which appears quite inviting.

Near by, the suburbs in which are situated the factories present a very dull aspect. Indeed, you can hardly imagine how dull a collection of Chinese houses look, when the spectator is placed above them. Behind the city, that is on the north, is a very high hill and many smaller ones, all constituting a range called the "White Cloud Hills," a designation apparently given from their dark and sombre aspect. Forts appear on two or three hills just behind the walls, which command the city entirely, and the turrets of the wall can be seen overtopping the houses. This wall, however, is mostly parade, for I observed that it had fallen down in a good many places, and the road we took in going around the city led over the top of the ruins. It is covered with plants, and I have seen trees of six inches in diameter growing on it. It is about 20 feet thick at the base. A pagoda is situated in about the middle of the city, and two or three temples are also visible, besides which there is nothing to interrupt the dull appearance made by its smoky-looking houses. The poles of the mandarins were to be seen in all directions; a dismantled gallows will give a fair idea of their form and size; they have a frame work about two-thirds of their height, and some of them are 40 feet high. The ground within the walls of the city is entirely covered with buildings and the roofs are occupied with wood-piles, or with clothes swinging in the air. No mansions of size and taste are visible; even the governor's house is undistinguishable, and the streets are so narrow that no ground could be seen from where I stood. On the top of the houses near me I saw a miscellaneous assemblage of piles of wood and clothes, mixed up with people cooking and parties eating and smoking. Immediately before me, as I was descending, there were a few foreigners walking up and down the square, which has now, since I've been surveying fields and hills around, diminished by contrast to a space not much larger than the premises I left in Broad Street, about two years ago.

TO REV. R. ANDERSON.

CANTON, August 20, 1835.

The revision* is proceeding quite rapidly, Bros. Medhurst and Gutzlaff being almost constantly engaged on it. At this

* Of Morrison's version of the Bible, commenced before his death.

present moment in Canton, however, we are much hampered on account of a recent search which was instituted by the provincial authorities at command of the emperor, in order to find any natives who had been engaged in the manufacture of two Christian books which had been sent to Peking by the governor of Fukkeen. This edict caused some alarm and our teachers instantly left us. Search has also been made at Macao for traitorous natives, but we do not hear of any who have thus far been apprehended. The four Gospels were put into the hands of the printer to cut the blocks, but the work was secreted immediately on intimation of danger. Leang Afa is still at Malacca, and his son Atih is at Macao, while his wife and daughter are at Whampoa, or near Canton. The government would probably seize any of them, should they make their appearance in Canton.

Thus are we hindered more at present than ever before. We cannot get a book printed, and those now printed can neither be sent away nor distributed prudently in Canton; and we cannot procure a teacher with whom to study the language. These things may soon change, but the liability to be so hindered at any moment in our work of studying the language and of procuring teachers induces us to think of prosecuting our operations out of reach of the officers of this government. Whether such an establishment cannot be organized nearer China than Singapore, is a point not yet settled. We greatly need a vessel to be stationed somewhere beyond the reach of the Chinese authorities, or a house at Macao. But these matters need much discussion and prayer before a decision can be attained.

Owing to the increasing hostility of the native authorities, the mission at Canton was now, more than ever, cramped and confined in its operations, and perplexed beyond measure. The arrival of Dr. Peter Parker from New York in 1834 had added to the force an enthusiastic missionary of exceptional vigor and ability, who by his medical training was able to introduce a new factor that has performed a service of the highest importance between foreigners and Chinese by removing their mutual misunderstandings. This was the establishment at Canton of a dispensary and hospital for the free treatment of natives. No branch of mission work in the East is now better known or more universally successful than this of medicine; its direct use in spreading the Gospel among all classes of the people has been inestimable; but at this time the experiment was considered hazardous by the foreign community in China, and was looked upon with suspicion by local authorities. At the end of its first year, however, when thousands of impatient Chinese were clamoring for admission to the crowded dispensary, the residents of the factories cordially agreed to pay back the sum advanced to Dr. Parker by the mission, and formed the "Medical Missionary Society" by subscribing sufficient funds to carry on the benevolent work. The hong-merchant Howqua, as soon as he understood the object, gave the free use of a large house during twenty years for hospital purposes.

In this manner a great burden was taken off the shoulders of the little band of missionaries and a new opening made in the direction of an acquaintance with the Chinese. If discouragments occurred in their mission work it is noticeable that these were followed by unexpected blessings and generous donations, without which, indeed, the early days of this mission might have been its last. Eminent amongst American merchants there was Mr. Olyphant, who had returned to Canton in 1834 to conduct the house in person for three years, and whose munificence and encouragement were greatly needed.

"He is always our near friend," writes Mr. Williams, "and aids us as much with his counsels as with his riches. When we go to Macao we live at his table, and in Canton we often dine with him; he does all our exchange business better than we could for ourselves, and in many ways is continually aiding us. May the blessing of the Lord rest upon his family, himself, his basket, and his store."

Many years afterward, when leaving China for the last time, he refers to the great debt which missions there owe to this munificent and large-hearted man:

"American missions to China owed their origin in 1829 to the suggestion of Mr. Olyphant. He supported and encouraged them when their expenses were startling and the prospect of success faint. He and his partners furnished the mission a house rent free in Canton for about thirteen years. The church with which he was connected in New York, at his suggestion, in 1832, sent out a complete printing-office, called after its late pastor, the Bruen Press; and when the *Chinese Repository* was commenced he offered to bear the loss of its publication if it proved to be a failure, rather than that the funds of the American Board should suffer. He built an office for it in Canton, where it remained twenty-four years. The ships of the firm gave fifty-one free passages to missionaries and their families going to or from China, and these and other benefactions were always cheerfully bestowed if thereby the good cause was advanced. The memory of such men is blessed, and their works follow them."

TO HIS FATHER.

CANTON, November 23, 1835.

Instead of dating this at Canton it ought to be Whampoa, where I am now on board the American ship *Albion*, and can perhaps profitably fill some of this sheet with an account of the exercises and meeting held on board to-day. When Sunday morning came the Bethel flag was seen flying from the main of the *Albion*. At half-past ten eight of us got into a small

Chinese boat, and were soon alongside the Bethel ship. Here we found several captains collected, and some men. One of them, a pious Scotch kirkman, who takes a lively interest in sustaining public worship at Whampoa, came up to me and said, "I always carry my Bible with me," showing me a splendidly bound 8vo Bible, with a morocco case. On opening the cover I was much gratified to read : "To the Rev. Edwin Stevens. Presented by the following English Masters Trading at Canton," followed by the names of six English captains and their vessels. The present was a handsome acknowledgment of their regard for him and his services in their ships. At eleven o'clock the congregation assembled on the quarter deck, in number about fifty. Nearly two thirds of the whole were sailors, the remainder being principally officers. The deck was closed in from wind and sun by awnings, and seats arranged for the audience. Mr. Stevens used his new Bible during the service, and seldom do you find persons who pay better attention to public worship than sailors ; and this congregation was better even than usual. I was chief singer,—not that I made the most noise, but I held the book and started the tune. However, the Scotch captain who sat next to me sung so vigorously that it was with much ado that I could keep pitch or tune, or hear my own voice. But I love to hear good, loud, hearty singing, and at this time the north wind blew so strong that it behooved us to make some noise to overpower the flapping of the awnings. After service the meeting gradually dispersed, and we were soon afterwards called to dinner. In the afternoon Mr. Stevens went around to three or four ships to distribute tracts and converse with the crews ; for my part I remained until evening conversing with a pious captain who narrated to me some of his troubles. This day "can pass for a muster" of Brother Stevens' weekly labors. Out of about one hundred vessels in Whampoa now, with perhaps three thousand sailors, there are but five or six pious masters, and, as I have said, not more than fifty men at church. A very small excuse will keep them away ; but on the whole the encouragement is great to persevere, and if we do so till the end much good will result, as in all things upon which we can honestly ask for a blessing.

In contrast to this phase of missionary work the following describes a visit among Chinese sailors:

"To-day I went aboard some of the junks in the harbor, in company with Mr. Lay, the agent of the Brit. and For. Bible Soc , and we were well received, so far as civility goes. As soon as one gets aboard he asks : 'Have you eaten rice?' which is the same as How do you do? The polite celestial then asks the same question and invites you to a pipe, a segurillo, or a cup of tea. After this what comes ? One talks to them of the things in the tracts and Scriptures, but there are deaf ears which hear; they listen in silence, and, when you pause for a reply, ask how old you are or what country you come from. If the reading in the book is explained they seemingly consent to all you say, but it is chiefly politeness. The subject is strange, the speaker is strange, and the language used is generally in a different style or tone from what they are used to. Ask them however about profitable voyages, tell the price of the cloth your coat is made of, inquire after their families, their fathers, you then touch a string that responds, you find real listeners. Yet these poor men on board the junks are rather above the lowest classes, and are perhaps as promising as any portion of the people.

"The torpor of mind in heathen countries is inconceivable to one who has all his life lived in a Christian land ; almost nothing encourages me more than to hear a question asked that shows inquiry, that evinces a thought or a reflection. It is an evidence of life, a sign of resuscitation. I could willingly dispute all day long with them, but there is none who thinks enough to carry on a dispute, none who defends his religion or his customs. This remark may of course be subject to some limitation, but the fact remains, they generally and chiefly act because their ancestors did so."

As it was not safe to attempt the printing of Chinese books in Canton, the mission decided, in December, 1835, to remove Mr. Williams and his office to Macao, where, under Portuguese authority, he could carry on his work unmolested. Here he made use of the Chinese types of the East India Company, and recommenced the printing of Medhurst's "Chinese Dictionary of the Hokkëén Dialect," which had been left unfinished at their dissolution in 1834. Of its compiler, who had lately come to China from Batavia, the printer writes:

"One would find it well worth while to stop and look at Walter Medhurst if ever he came within hailing distance. He came out to Malacca in 1818, as a missionary printer, studied for the ministry and was ordained there, and then went to Batavia, where he has resided about fifteen years. He has greatly endeared himself to us all; a plain-spoken man, often bringing people up 'with a round turn,' as the sailors say; but his uniform cheerfulness and lively mode of expression, combined with readiness in the native dialects and a knowledge of the springs of human action as exemplified in Asiatics (both Chinese and Malay) render him a most valuable missionary and his company instructive and amusing. . . . I shall be a year, perhaps, fagging away at his dictionary, and it is no trifling job to print one in any language—including Chinese,—but when men and matters are not in the best style or efficiency the work cannot be said to be lessened. . . . During its progress I shall learn much of the language, but with so many other employments it is almost impossible to master any thing as hard as Chinese; one must think, talk, write, and dream nothing else, till he is 'licked into a Chinaman,' as the Jesuits express it."

It was not easy, with the interruptions necessary to his employment, for him to satisfy his own high ideal of attainment in this difficult language. In a letter reviewing this period of his life he says:

"My printers were always required to attend service on Sunday, but I was not able to talk to them before two years had been passed in China; I got along slowly in the language for want both of books and time. The first congregation I had consisted of some lepers who had squatted on the hillside behind the lazaretto in Macao, and used to wait for me on Sunday mornings from six to seven o'clock before going begging. They were gratified at the attention shown them, and I had a good opportunity to practice simplifying and mumbling the truth for minds filled with sin and darkness. The mission had no converts in its records until about the year 1850. A poor and empty record indeed!"

"It was rather discouraging," he writes in another brief reminiscence of these early struggles with a task which to most was quite insuperable, " to sit down with a man utterly ignorant of any tongue but his own, and have no aid except Morrison's quarto dictionary in another dialect, and an imperfect Anglo-Chinese vocabulary; for these comprised all there was. And then if one attempted to use his acquisitions, his dialogist would express much surprise, and wish to know the name of the man who taught him; or he would ridicule his rude pronunciation and try to exhibit his own better knowledge of English in every reply."

This was the common difficulty which every new comer to the threshold of the Chinese language had to meet, and before which many a mere enthusiast would have retired. But Mr. Williams' faculties were of a piece with his moral disposition, and seem to have been steadied and quickened to their highest performance by obstacles which daunted others. Through the smoke of this dull drudgery he saw the bright flame that would leap forth when his intelligence was fairly kindled.

Here are a few extracts describing his new life and surroundings:

"MACAO, Aug. 26, 1836.—The weather has been oppressively hot for the past few days, and to-day I have felt the lassitude, so hardly resisted in these climes, more strongly than ever before. This sensation is one of languor and laziness combined; you wish to do but the flesh rebels. When writing, one hand holds a fan to cool the other, while the perspiration appears to be carrying off all the powers, animal or otherwise, ever possessed. As for thinking—the thought of thinking is enough to draw forth an indefinite increase of perspiration. However, by twelve or one o'clock a breeze comes in from the sea, and something can be done with rallying nature. Moreover this sultry weather is but temporary, seldom lasting over a week at once, although the average of the past month ranges 88°.

"Now that I am well upon my favorite subject of *self*, you may let me go on to describe my house in Macao. People in the East occupy a good deal of terra firma, and I must live in such houses as are to be had. My domicile therefore is a two-story affair with twelve rooms, each twenty feet square, and two lower rooms besides; being built on the slope of a hill it has three stories on one side. Two trees (one a fig and the other an elder) constitute my garden, while beyond this and quite separate from my building is the cook-house. For household I have a porter, a comprador, a coolie, a cook, a printer and four little boys; in all, nine who live in the basement. The printing-office is under the parlor, and is a light room—when the sun shines. ·Besides all the rest there is a verandah on one side of the house, extending about sixty feet, which is a great convenience, indeed an absolute necessity in this weather."

At Macao were living a party of Japanese with whom he was soon to become closely associated; his first acquaintance with them is described in a letter written home:—

"June 25, 1836.—There are three Japanese now staying at Mr. Gutzlaff's house who were brought from Columbia River via London, and are now supported at the expense of the

English commission. One of them named Keokitch was sent on an errand to me to-day, and finding that he could talk broken English, I asked him as many questions as I could think up. He says that he comes from a small town about fifty miles (Chinese *li*, probably, a third of a mile each) from Jeddo. The town is called Sriwasi, most likely a small seaport producing rice and exporting it to the capital. This man and his companions, forty in all, sailed from Sriwasi in a junk, expecting to reach the capital within five days, but they were blown out to sea and unable to return. The junk was not a large one and had a cargo of rice on board; according to his account they were tossed about the ocean for forty* moons (!), and during that time all died but the three now here. They suffered much for want of water, moreover the scurvy prevailed so badly that, as he says, 'their limbs swelled like barrels.' It is almost incredible that with a compass they should have wandered about so long, but according to his account no sail was made nor was any attention paid to the steering. From the arrival of these men here, their secluded and unknown land receives increased attention, which is not lessened from the disappointment caused by the sailing of the *Peacock* direct for the Sandwich Islands yesterday; before the death of our envoy here there was some hope that she might carry these mariners home to Japan."

"MACAO, Sept. 10, 1836.—To-day I returned from Canton, whither I went eight days since on business, in company with Dr. Parker, our missionary physician, and J. R. Morrison. We left the provincial city on the 8th at 10 P. M. in a native boat, called, from the circumstance of having a passport, a chop boat. When the same sort of boat is employed—as is often done—without the pass, it is called a fast boat. How to describe it that you may form a just idea, I am puzzled. About forty feet long, sharp bow, cabin forward, kitchen aft, deck at widest perhaps eighteen feet; the cabin is commodious, providing pretty well for three, allowing one to cook, set a table, place a bed, promenade fifteen feet or so, and write or study comfortably.

* Doubtless a misunderstanding for fourteen, the actual period.

"Owing to adverse tides and gentle zephyrs we made very little progress during the first night. About six o'clock on the following morning we reached a post-house, or place where the chop (passport) was examined, called Tsze-ne. Here Morrison and I went ashore and walked for a half an hour or more, climbing a hill, from whence we had a pretty view over the hamlet; the doctor meantime amusing himself with some children on the shore. The prospect from the hill was a fine one and thoroughly Chinese: rice-fields, clumps of bamboos, groves of lichee and orange, with villages here and there—perhaps five in all. Leaving this station with a fair wind behind us, we got down the stream at a rate rapid enough to make the scenery appear to pass us like a diorama, and in some places it was indeed very beautiful. Towards ten o'clock we came to a large town of perhaps 15,000 people, situated on both sides—in fact, all over the river, for the boats covered the stream so thickly as to almost stop our way from their numbers. We were a gazing-stock to the villagers, as they were to us; the children following us for some distance along the banks, and most of the people coming down to the water's edge to have a look at us. So all day long, floating down the river, whose banks seemed like gardens, so richly did the rice clothe the lowlands and the trees adorn the slopes. Two crops are raised annually here, and the land appears to sustain the draft on its fertility admirably. At Heängshan two coolies from the magistrate's office boarded us to examine our chop and procured the credentials to show that three 'foreign devils' had passed. Three names (fictitious or real seems to be immaterial) are upon the chop; the present of a dozen bottles of foreign wine is added by the boatmen as a peace-offering. After sitting long enough in the boat to show their ill-breeding, the men finally went away and we continued on our journey; the delay was not altogether distasteful to our servants, most of whom come from Heängshan, and who in this way caught a glimpse of their friends. The country below this place rises into hills, the scenery being especially romantic where three or four heights are in view, capped by high pagodas. But darkness and rain came on about the same time, shutting us into our cabin for the night ; we went on, however, with shortened sail, the boatmen having measured wind and distance, so that we reached Macao comfortably by daylight."

"Sept. 27, 1836.—To-day I was honored by a visit from the envoy on board of the Cochinese man of war now lying in the Inner Harbor. I had been aboard of his vessel thrice already, and he had promised when I was there to call upon me ; but from his long delay I had concluded that he demurred fulfilling his promise. He is a member of the Board of Public Works, and perhaps 38 years old, of an open, affable countenance, thin beard, and teeth blackened by betel nut. He was accompanied by two other men, one a civilian, the other a kind of military attaché, all dressed in long, black garments and black turbans. Mr. Gutzlaff came with them to the house, they having called to get him on their way to see me. Seven attendants, including a pipe-bearer, came as retinue, all dressed in a uniform of red long-ells, black turbans, and with bare feet. After they entered and were invited to sit, tea was brought in and they quaffed the *cha* most heartily, carrying on a conversation meantime with Gutzlaff in writing. They had plenty of questions to ask about America, its government and its commerce. They could not understand how the emperor of America abdicated his throne every four years, nor why he removed his ministers so often. The business of election puzzled them exceedingly, as did also the want of an heir-apparent. Altogether, I gathered from their countenances that they thought the Americans not much more than half civilized ; yet the ships of war from the United States that have visited their coasts, the large house they were then in, were evidence of at least some advance in a knowledge of the arts. The head man of the party asked for some newspapers and I gave him a few ; upon seeing this success the civilian also requested some, when the former burst into an immoderate fit of laughter, but what was the particular cause of his merriment I did not perceive.

"On one of my visits to the ship I carried the envoy a specimen book of one of the Philadelphia [type] founders, half full or more of cuts, which pleased him mightily. To-day he was enquiring for more books of pictures, when I amused and delighted him again by showing him a volume on zoölogy containing a plenty of illustrations of animals, etc. He did not understand the uses of all he saw represented, as I could see by the expression of his countenance, but I was almost helpless to explain. After sitting awhile the pipe-bearer, sidling around behind the party, stuck the pipe into his master's mouth without the smallest intimation of his approach ; a few whiffs were taken and the pipe withdrawn. They had a look at my office, but 't was pretty much Greek to them, none appearing to comprehend the press or the types, while none of us knew enough of Cochinchinese to explain. When they withdrew they carefully took up the piece of paper used in writing down the conversation, and put it between the newspapers, lest evidence should be brought against them at some time or other, or perhaps as a note of what we had talked about. They left apparently highly pleased. I noticed that they were divested of that superciliousness always seen in a Chinese, and were mild, pleasant, and courteous. The difference between the friendly and polite envoy and the two haughty, contemptible Chinese was painfully seen on board their ship once when I was there visiting at the same time as they."

TO REV. RUFUS ANDERSON.

MACAO, November 29, 1836.

Mr. Lay, the agent of the Br. and F. Bible Soc., has been living with me for the last two months. We have, during that time, taken two or three interesting excursions in the vicinity of Macao, and he has gone alone a few times. One day, taking with us a bag of books, we crossed the water to an island opposite Macao, intending to spend the whole day in visiting the Chinese scattered about there, and distribute among them the books we carried. We were rowed across by women, who here, as elsewhere in China, perform this laborious business, and landing among a group of huts belonging to the fishermen frequenting the waters hereabouts, we started for a village seen in the distance. The day was most pleasant, and our way through the paddy-fields and among the farm-houses was enlivened by the singing of birds and the playful children who ran out of the houses to see us pass. The supposed village, however, proved to be only a cluster of half a dozen substantial brick houses, in which we found a few females, who treated us quite civilly, and one man engaged in sweeping rice on the threshing-floor. He accepted the proffered book very readily, and invited us into his domicile to rest awhile. The house within did not comport, in our estimation, with its exterior effect; the walls were barren of every thing, saving a few inscriptions, the floor was the cold and naked earth, and the room in which we sat was half filled with agricultural implements, rice, potatoes, and tables. A partition divided this from the kitchen and bed-chamber, and on it was placed the household tablet for ancestors with incense sticks burning before it. We endeavored to direct the farmer's attention to the worship and the God spoken of in the book just given him, and then left him, greatly to the mortification of his wife, who had been busying herself to make us some tea ever since we came in, but whose dispatch did not equal our haste.

We were now at a loss where next to go. No village was in sight except at a great distance, and the bag of books was too heavy to carry back again. While still in this half-settled frame of mind we saw a bevy of females sitting by the wayside resting from their burdens. We made towards them, and found their loads to consist of dried grass procured from the mountains for use in the kitchen during winter. This unsubstantial fuel was bound up in faggots proportioned to the strength of the carrier and hung at either end of a pole laid on the shoulder, in which manner these industrious women had already brought it several miles, and their homes were yet a good distance. They were rather reserved at our first salutation, but soon became sociable, so opening our bag of books we asked an active lad who had joined the group to read aloud one of the gospels. He read a few lines, when the volume was taken from him by a man standing behind and looking over his shoulder. By this time the number of people had considerably increased from those passing by with faggots stopping to see the foreigners, and we were soon quite hedged about with bundles of grass. Applications for books were now general, and the same boy who had before read to us was now engaged in preferring requests in behalf of the women; but they seeing our stock rapidly diminishing, cast aside further bashfulness and themselves came up to get tracts, affirming that they had husbands and sons at home who could read if they could not. Their petitions were not to be resisted, and our bag was soon empty, which called forth loud expressions of disappointment from some of them. "So few books for so many people," said they; "why did you not bring more!" After a little more pleasant conversation they began to take up their burdens to go, and we parted mutually satisfied—on our part for having found a success so much in advance of our hopes, on theirs for the acquisition of a book.

In this interview we had a fair opportunity of seeing the Chinese peasantry manifest their natural feelings towards us as foreigners, and nothing in their conduct could be taken as offensive or rude. Before we separated there had probably fifty people collected, and every one behaved as kindly to us as the same number of like persons would in any part of the world. The influence of the females was apparent in restraining all rudeness. One young fellow of about twenty, who was unable to read, came to me for a book, but was laughed at so heartily by them for applying, that he straightway took up his burden and walked off hastily. I was making a comparison between those of them whose feet were as nature made them, and those with whom they had been cramped in fashion's vice, giving my judgment of course in favor of the former. The comparison seems to have been made at rather an unfortunate instant, for what I said was heard by one just hobbling by, and she, to show that I was no judge of such matters, set out to run with her load, which experiment nearly overthrew the poor girl and excited the merriment of those sitting near us. We sincerely hope that these books were requested with some reference to the fact that they were religious works, for it was not until after they had been examined that the demand became general. One intelligent-looking man, after glancing over a volume of Scripture given to him, began in a loud voice to inform those around of the tenor of their contents. He declared that they taught the practice of virtue, that men should be good, and once made a reference to the name of Jesus, when I reminded him of it, in a manner that one does when a thing is momentarily forgotten. This movement on his part was so voluntary that we were much pleased with the attention and the thought it betokened. We did not count the books, but I should judge that there were fifty volumes in the bag at first, most of which were given to this company. On leaving we could not restrain a prayer to God that he would condescend to bless his own word so cheerfully received.

On another visit to the same island we encountered a party of eighteen or twenty men engaged in burying a man, apparently under the direction of a landlord, who, in his form, manners, and tone of voice, was an excellent type of that class of people. Every one of this party was supplied with a book which they requested before we gave them out; the headman, seeing the bag empty, with the greatest good-will and pleasantry, took up a basin filled with ground nuts and oranges and forced its contents into the bag, rather against my will. "What," said he, "you give away all your books, and I give you nothing in return!" This reception was gratifying, for near this place Mr. Lay, a few days before, had his books returned to him.

In another short walk together we met a Chinese who had made two or three voyages as a ship carpenter, having been as far as London, Bombay, and also up the coast in opium vessels. Several books had been given him by one person or another, most of which he declared he had given as presents to his friends living in different parts of the empire, and that as far as he knew they were read. It is an ancient custom of the Chinese to give and receive gifts at New Year, and it was as such presents that this man had distributed the Bibles given him. Knowing the regard paid to tokens of kindly remembrance among this people, may we not hope that these volumes would be read with attention if only from respect to the donor. The carpenter took several of our tracts, which he said he would give to the village schoolmaster on his return home from Macao.

The hamlet near which we then were was poverty and wretchedness exemplified. The men were mostly in the fields, and the women and children were indeed dirty and ragged enough. Filth and misery appear everywhere to be concomitants of heathenism; a Christian peasant strives to make his poverty clean and wholesome, while a heathen is content to live in such wretchedness and mire as put the more cleanly beasts of the forests to blush. The cabins here were mostly built of mud plastered, and at a distance they appeared very pretty, embosomed as they were in a grove of bamboos. The buffaloes were alarmed at our approach and were inclined to make closer observation of us than was altogether agreeable; they are a larger animal than the cow, but much coarser in appearance and dirtier in habits, delighting to wallow in the mire like swine. Near this village we found the tallow tree growing, a most beautiful tree in its foliage and shape. The tallow envelopes the seed and is separated by boiling in hot water, whence it is taken floating from the top and run into candles. These are covered with a coat of vermilion and have the property of never becoming hard.

In all these excursions there have probably been one hundred and fifty volumes distributed; a small number, I know, but the politeness and interest with which they were received is indicative of the success more extensive distribution might meet with.

Soon after the opening of another year Mr. Williams chronicles his first great bereavement in China, the loss of Edwin Stevens, "the friend and companion of us all":

"He died at Singapore (on the 5th of January), whither he had gone in the *Himmaleh*, upon the expedition which Messrs. Olyphant & Co. have sent to spread the gospel in Southern Borneo. I had not heard that he was sick until the news came that he was dead; only last December I saw him embark from Macao in good spirits and health, deeply sensible of the hazards of the trip, yet willing to do whatever God had marked out for him. Truly I was afflicted; for many days my mind could not be brought to believe that one whom I had so lately looked upon was before the throne on high, tuning his harp to the praises of his Saviour. Ah! how beloved was he by us all! He was a friend in the highest sense of the term; we shall seek far and wide in this world for one dearer. Living as we four did, and as I have more than once described to you, in one house, meeting at the same table, uniting at the same social altar (without any tender and fair one to cheer and enliven us), we became wondrously knit together and enjoyed much sweet communion. But Stevens was the joy of the quaternion; his humor pleased, his good sense instructed, his judgment counselled, his piety threw a grace over all he said and did. His voyages up the coast afforded him topics of conversation and added to his speech the savor of an experience that made his advice weighty. Often have I gone to Whampoa with him and been comforted by his earnest appeals to sinners and incited by his zeal in visiting his flock. Miles has he thus gone about preaching to seamen, and I can assure you that it is no small trial to be here and there among a fleet on the river in a bit of a tanka boat, on a July day, when the sun beats upon the glassy stream like fire; but he would only lament the small good he seemed to do. Four years in this land—or rather on these waters—has he labored, 'if by any means I can save souls,' to use his oft-quoted expression; and the account he has already given of his labors cannot be vain."

The close companionship of these early missionaries and their joy in a holy calling inspired them with generous and large-hearted views of their common Christianity, to which the narrower vision of mission boards at home does not often attain. To Mr. Williams, throughout his life, it was sufficient, if a man had the cause of Christ in his heart, to give him the welcome and assistance of his house—where was "neither Greek nor Jew, circumcision nor uncircumcision, barbarian, Scythian, bond nor free: but Christ, all, and in all." In one of his letters, written about this time, he tells of the pleasure occasioned by the arrival of the famous ship *Morrison*, with two Americans: " Episcopal, or, more properly, Christian brothers. I am getting to have a great disrelish of those sectarian terms of denominations which are used in western lands. Here it is enough and far better to be as Christ, and not as Paul or Luther—for neither of the latter died for us. Herein is love. Dr. Morrison never called himself any other than a Christian missionary, and I 'm sure I don't know to-day what denomination of dissenters he did favor."

TO HIS FATHER.

MACAO, July 2, 1837.

The dictionary which I have been printing was finished about a month since and appears to give as much satisfaction as I expected. There are but few, however, who will personally use the books, but many take pleasure in patronizing such undertakings, and give their money to advance a cause they wish will succeed. It cost Olyphant & Co. more than $2,000 to pay the printer, and now they must wait for the slow returns of selling every copy. I hope you have seen Mr. Olyphant ere this and conversed about the things concerning the Kingdom of Heaven.

To-morrow I expect to leave Macao on a short trip to Japan, in the old ship *Morrison*, in company with Mr. and Mrs. King, and Dr. Parker. Gutzlaff has preceded us to Lewchew Islands, where he has gone in H. B. M.'s ship *Raleigh*. The occasion is to return a parcel of shipwrecked Japanese sailors, who have been Providentially cast upon our charity at Macao. Gutzlaff has acquired enough of their language from them to hold a conversation on most topics, and with them and him we hope to make and tell a pretty good story: "That these men were shipwrecked on the American coast, were afterwards brought to Macao, where we have learned their language from them; that we have come to Jeddo to return them to their homes, and cultivate a friendly intercourse with the Japanese, heal their diseases if they are willing to be operated upon, and trade a little." We carry no books this first time, lest a good beginning be marred by exciting their fears, but will endeavor to show them the practice of the Christianity they hate by trying to do good. I go to do ———. I'll tell you what I have done or seen, should God allow us to return. What the result will be I have few apprehensions. I think God is willing, as he is able, to take care of us, and whether life and success or death and disappointment comes, we can all say, Thy will be done. Peace be with you all.

Affectionately, your son,
WELLS.

TO REV. R. ANDERSON.

CANTON, September 10, 1837.

DEAR BROTHER :—I write you a line in order to inform you of the return of the ship *Morrison* from her cruise to Japan. You were, I believe, informed by Dr. Parker of the object of the expedition, which was to return to their homes seven shipwrecked Japanese, and by so doing endeavor to open some communication with that people.

The voyage was planned by Mr. King, and had for its ultimate object the extension of civilization and Christianity. He was accompanied by his lady and a female servant. Dr. Parker, provided with a large stock of medicines and instruments, and myself were also attached to the party. We set sail from Macao on the 4th of July, and on the 12th anchored in the harbor of Napakiang, a port on the southwest side of the island of Lewchew, the same that was visited by Captains Hall and Beechey. We remained in the harbor three days, during which time we had much pleasant intercourse with the inhabitants, going on shore daily, and receiving visits from the officers on board ship. The intercourse was somewhat restrained on account of the slowness of communicating with each other, which was chiefly by means of the Chinese character. This when written was legible by both parties. Many of the educated persons whom we saw could converse in the Mandarin dialect, which made the exchange of ideas easier; and in our visits on shore, we usually met with quite a number of persons who could talk short sentences in this dialect.

This group of islands is supposed to contain about twenty thousand inhabitants, and numbers nearly fifty islands, some of which are nothing but mere barren rocks. The largest is sixty miles long by fifteen broad; and a few of the others are capable of supporting a sparse population. They are under the control of the Japanese, who monopolize many of the offices, and exercise a vigilant supervision over the whole. The language of the people is Japanese, with perhaps a dialectical variation. Our Japanese could make themselves perfectly understood; and there were seven junks of that nation in port. We saw no Chinese, nor were there any Chinese junks. When we asked the officers what they would say to a foreigner coming to live among them and learn their language, they said that they could not permit the least trade with foreigners; how much more, then, could they not allow one to reside among them. So decided were they not to trade, that we could not force them to take money in payment for the provisions they had given us. The country is probably under Japanese influence, more entirely at the present time than ever before, and consequently it would be a very doubtful experiment for one to attempt to settle among them.

After having taken Mr. Gutzlaff from H. B. M. ship *Raleigh*, which met us here by appointment, we set sail for Yedo, the capital of the Japanese empire. We came in sight of the bay at the top of which Yedo is situated, on the 28th of July, and were obliged to beat up against a northeasterly wind for sixty miles. The number of fishing smacks and junks in sight was very great, and they gave notice of our approach to the officers of the several villages lying on the sides of the bay; and probably also information was carried to the capital. During the night of the 29th we had penetrated about forty miles up the bay of Yedo, with much difficulty making the course, on account of the darkness and fog. The morning was misty, but we could hear the firing of cannon far ahead of us, although the weather was too thick for the men on shore to see the ship. About noon it broke, and we could see the shot falling about three fourths of a mile ahead of us, being fired from a fort situated on a hill near the anchorage of Ouragawa, which we wished to gain. On seeing the shot, we came to about four miles below the fort, casting anchor a mile and a fourth from the shore.

As soon as we had anchored, several fishing boats laden with natives came on board, curious to see so unusual a sight. Mr. Gutzlaff conversed with them freely, requesting them when they returned on shore to tell the mandarins that we wished to see them. Nothing was brought off to sell, every one coming from mere curiosity; yet they were friendly and talkative, inviting us to come on shore and ramble about. This we promised to do as soon as was practicable.

During the night we observed no intimation of any hostility; but as soon as the morning broke we were surprised by shot falling about us, fired from four guns that had been brought down from the fort at Ouragawa and placed on the bank directly opposite the ship. Upon these manifest indications of hostility we weighed anchor and left the bay, judging that after such a commitment on the part of the government they would not enter into any communication. The firing was continued long after we had weighed anchor; and one shot struck the vessel, but did no damage. Several gun-boats were sent out which fired at us with small guns. We endeavored, but unsuccessfully, to induce some fishermen in the small boats that were in the bay to come on board in order to give them a paper to hand to the mandarins on shore stating our nationality, character, and object.

Still desirous of executing the object of our voyage we bore away for some port on the southern shore of Japan, and arrived on the 10th of August at the bay of Kagosima, in the principality of Satzuma. As soon as we reached the entrance of the bay two of our Japanese were put on shore in order to find an officer with whom we could communicate, and bring him on board. After an hour's absence they returned, bringing a petty officer, who declared the inhabitants of his village were so terrified at our approach that they should have fired on us if the Japanese we sent had not come to explain. This officer soon left us with two others of our men in order to gain their deposition before a higher magistrate farther up the bay, at Miabara. After an absence of three or four hours they returned highly delighted with their reception and at the "sweet words" which they had heard. Their deposition was very minute, and was delivered in the presence of several hundreds of natives, all of whom joined in praising the "benevolent foreigners." After it had been taken down in writing it was sealed and sent to Kagosima, the capital; and they were directed to tell us to come to anchor where the pilot sent should direct us, and wait three days for an answer. Every one who heard the deposition (as we were told) was of the opinion that our message would be received, and that a high officer from court would be dispatched to take our papers and the shipwrecked men.

We accordingly came to anchor, though the situation was not a very desirable one, and waited from the evening of Thursday until Saturday morning for a messenger from Kagosima. Excepting a single cask of water, nothing was brought off for us, although we repeatedly requested water, fruit, and provisions; nor were the common people permitted to come on board after we anchored, while a guard was stationed to watch our movements and prevent our landing. The Japanese on board were also strictly confined to the ship.

About 7 o'clock on Saturday morning, we observed the people on shore much excited, running in all directions and mustering in little parties on the eminences near the beach. Soon after we saw several strips of cloth, blue and white in bars, stretched across from trees, among the stones of a graveyard. Beyond the cloth were many persons having flags and guns assembled, and officers on horseback were seen hastening to and fro, all betokening some hostile operations. As soon as our Japanese saw the canvas bearing the arms of the Prince of Satzuma, they said that a messenger had probably come from the capital, and that his orders were to drive us away. Our suspicions of attack were strong, and we accordingly began to weigh anchor, though in such a manner as not to excite the notice of those on shore. Before we showed any sails on the ships the party behind the canvas battery began to fire at us with musketry, that falling about half-way to the vessel. Although there was no wind, we concluded it best to make sail, and get beyond their reach before any cannon should be brought to bear on us. In doing so we narrowly escaped getting foul of a rock towards which the tide was drifting us, and we were carried five or six miles farther up the bay than we had yet been before the wind arose. As we came out, which was very slowly, cannon were fired from the opposite side of the bay; but we were cautious in approaching the coast, and none of the shot hit us. The firing was continued from both sides of the bay, until dark. No attempt was made to come on board by any one after the firing was commenced, although we had repeatedly told the officers that we would depart at the first intimation of their unwillingness to receive the men. Perhaps, however, the execution of our rejection was committed to other hands than the guard who had been stationed over us.

After leaving this bay we concluded that there was little prospect of being received at any other port; moreover our men declared that their lives would be in jeopardy if they should now be received anywhere, or if they should attempt to steal ashore under cover of night. The risk of detection in the latter case was greatly increased by the minuteness of the deposition they had given at Miabara. Their disappointment was great, for their expectations had been raised to the highest pitch; and three of them shaved their heads like Buddhist priests, in order that the hair might grow equally, thereby showing their determination to live among foreigners. All of them agreed to go quietly back and become perpetual exiles.

After a pleasant passage down the coast of China, we reached Macao on the 29th ult., thankful that we had been preserved from all dangers. Mrs. King was somewhat indisposed during the voyage, from the heat and reflection from the water, but otherwise all enjoyed excellent health.

In an article published in the *Chinese Missionary Re-*

corder, in 1876, Dr. Williams sums up the result of these fifty-six days on the *Morrison:*

"Commercially speaking, the voyage cost about two thousand dollars, without any return; and the immediate effects, in a missionary or scientific way, were nil. But not finally. The seven men brought back were employed in one way and another, and most of them usefully. Two remained with Mr. Gutzlaff for many years; and two worked in my printing-office at Macao; these four aided us in getting some knowledge of their language, so that between us the books of Genesis and Matthew, and the Gospel and Epistles of John, were done into Japanese for their instruction. Rikimats, the youngest man, went to Nagasaki with Admiral Stirling in 1855 as his interpreter. He and Otosan, who lived at Shanghai, both showed in their correct lives that the faith which they had professed was a living principle. They were the first-fruits of the church of Christ in Japan, whose numbers are now flocking in like doves to their windows. For nearly two years five of them maintained daily prayer in my house at Macao; and their harsh repulse was one of the arguments they used to implore the Governor of Nations to send the Gospel to their countrymen. Whatever Prof. Tyndall may believe, or not believe, upon such a matter, I think that those prayers were heard and are now being answered."

So ended the episode of the *Morrison's* trip to Japan, a novel enterprise, from which, though undertaken with no high hopes of success on the part of the little band of Christians, they returned saddened, but not downcast. The path of missions and civilization in that country seemed still closed, but something could yet be done toward preparing means for the enlightenment of its people; to this end Mr. Williams began a serious study of the language from one of the most intelligent of the Japanese brought back to Macao. During the ensuing winter, with the assistance of his sailor-teacher, he prepared a translation of the Gospel of Matthew into Japanese, for the instruction of the seven who had all been given employment by foreigners. This was followed by a small vocabulary of Japanese words, and this two years later by a translation of Genesis into that language. Only two or three copies of these little books were made in manuscript by the two sailors who could write, and none have been preserved, Mr. Williams' copy perishing with his books at the destruction of the factories in 1856. By these efforts he achieved the conversion of at least two of the sailors and gained a knowledge of the language of the common people sufficient for conversational purposes; what he himself thought of the nature of this acquirement we shall see presently. As workmen in the printing-office these Japanese left much to be desired. "They are uneasy people," he writes, "for they love their fatherland as much as any nation, and do not at all relish their unwitted exile. However, they are fain to make the best of it at present, and—seeing that there is no chance of returning to Japan—are willing to be useful in their way."

CHAPTER III.

WITHOUT attempting to follow in detail the course of events in Southern China during the period of her gradual embroilment with foreign powers, their influence cannot be entirely overlooked in a narrative of the missionary life before us. The withdrawal of the East India Company having essentially altered the position of British subjects in China, a Superintendent of Trade, Lord Napier, was sent from England to oversee the traffic which was now open to all. He made an attempt to communicate with the Governor-General at Canton upon a footing of equality, but was contemptuously refused, thus raising a direct issue between the Chinese and British governments. Lord Napier unfortunately died soon after his rebuff. The outline of some incidents which followed is related in Mr. Williams' "Recollections":

"The Superintendent of British Trade in the person of Lord Napier having been so badly treated at Canton, the office of the Superintendency was removed to Macao to await the advent of better days. It remained there for some years, a clerk only being kept at Canton to receive ship's papers and such other official business as might be necessary. During the years 1837 and 1838, commenced the remarkable proceedings of the Chinese government with a view to putting down the opium trade. . . . Lin, who was appointed anti-opium Imperial Commissioner, had previously been Fuyuen (Governor) of Kiangsu province, and his memorials in the *Peking*

Gazette had already drawn attention to him as a man of superior ability. Dr. Morrison told me that Lin's memorial on the effects of a severe inundation in Kiangsu was one of the ablest state papers he had ever read. . . .

"When Lin arrived he soon gave proofs that he was thoroughly in earnest in his resolution to faithfully discharge the trust committed to him, but how to get about it he was as ignorant as one can well imagine. The trade in opium was very dull at the time, the fact being that people were afraid to deal in it, and so it happened that the stock on hand was large. Lin adopted the plan of keeping himself incognito for a fortnight or so after his arrival, during which he used all diligence in endeavoring to collect information about the opium trade; but the information procured was as incorrect as might have been expected when obtained from such a people by this method. He never communicated with Captain Elliot [Lord Napier's successor], nor sought to learn from the foreigners the information which they were willing and able to furnish. But, proceeding in the underhand manner just described, he all at once came to a resolution as to his course of action, and one day foreigners at Canton suddenly found themselves shut up as they had been immediately after Lord Napier left Canton. About 4 P.M. one day a man went up and down thro' the factories, calling out in Chinese, and warning every Chinese servant to leave; and in two hours there was not a single native servant in all the thirteen factories. A line of boats was also placed in the river abreast of the factories, so that escape from that side would be impossible. All their three hundred residents had for the time to depend on the assistance of the Parsees' servants, who knowing a little of the Cantonese dialect were able to go into the adjoining markets and purchase some things. But the supplies they bought were inadequate, and we had to make a careful inspection of our store-rooms and larders to see what resources were left us; and what between laying tables, washing dishes and trying to cook, we considered that we had rather a hard time of it. It was no small privation to be forced to go down ourselves and carry unfiltered water from the river. By and by the Governor took pity on us and sent us some bullocks, pigs and poultry. These, however, the foreigners refused to touch, and indeed some of them were allowed to starve at our doors. I suppose the hong-merchants gave the Governor a hint that this was hardly the way to get on with us. At all events, greater freedom was soon allowed, and facilities were afforded us to procure wood and water, which—especially the latter—had been almost unprocurable. We were put to many a strange shift during this blockade of three months.

"Captain Elliot was at Macao when these occurrences took place, but as soon as he heard the news he came up to Canton, Lin being no doubt glad to have some responsible head of affairs to deal with. It is not necessary that I should follow in detail the history of the measures and negotiations which led Elliot to surrender under protest 20,283 chests of opium, being all the drug at that time in the hands of British merchants in Chinese waters. This immense quantity was brought together at a place a little below the Bogue Forts and destroyed, in the summer of 1838. While these negotiations were going on, foreigners were kept within their own bounds very strictly; but within these limits there was no further restraint on their personal liberty. Business was of course entirely suspended, but no one suffered any loss or damage, no one fell sick, and those in the ships at Whampoa were supplied with food during the entire blockade.

"Few foreign officials who have come to China have been superior in talent to Capt. Elliot, or better fitted than he to fulfil the important duties devolving upon him. He had also the advantage of having as interpreter and adviser John R. Morrison, Dr. Morrison's son, a man whom it was impossible to know without loving, and who, born in the country and familiar with Chinese from childhood, was in some respects better qualified than his father to act in these capacities. He was a man whom I remember with a respect and love that I feel it hard to describe. He received me when I came to China with that kindness which never failed to leave an impression. Both he and Captain Elliot recognized very clearly the ideas which the Chinese have on the subject of their unchallengeable supremacy over all other nations—ideas that appear to have grown up in the earliest period of their history and are to be found in all their writings. Indeed, it is hardly to be wondered at if they felt themselves vastly superior to the handful of foreigners who dwelt in the Canton factories, intent only on trade, which as you know is the lowest of the four categories into which the Chinese divide human professions and pursuits. It was by no means pleasant to live among people cherishing such self-conceited and supercilious notions regarding us."

The way for direct mission work among the Chinese was still closed, relations between natives and foreigners having become a curious mélange of traffic and hostility; an attempt to print portions of the Scripture in Chinese style had resulted in the imprisonment of two of the block-cutters and further constraints placed upon missionary efforts; during the year 1838 Dr. Parker was forced to leave Canton and his hospital; while throughout the neighboring districts the distribution of Christian tracts had almost entirely ceased.

In view of such a threatening future, when the mission was half determined to move in a body to Singapore, it was hard to turn in any direction; "to the eye of man the prospect indeed seemed gloomy enough that China would ever be rendered accessible to the efforts of Christians." It was rather owing to these untoward circumstances than to any especial reluctance toward changing the line of his work that caused Mr. Williams to reject the suggestion of preparing himself as an ordained missionary; another recommendation, that of studying medicine and opening a hospital elsewhere, appealed more strongly to his scientific tastes, and had he divined the near opening of China, it is probable that he would have turned his attention to this field. But to him and his coadjutors it seemed the better way to continue preparing and printing books designed to aid others in learning the language, since for this labor he was especially well adapted. Mr. Bridgman, in addition to his translation of the Bible and contributions to the *Repository*, had so far completed his "Chinese Chrestomathy in the Canton Dialect" that the first part was ready for the printing-press shortly after the return of the *Morrison* expedition from Japan, in 1837. Mr. Williams gave himself entirely to the enlargement as well as printing of this work, collecting idiomatic phrases and translating or selecting extracts from Chinese authors, and by the time of its issue from his press (in 1841) he had furnished about one half of the subject-matter to the volume; in consideration, however, of the just rights of Dr. Bridgman to its inception and plan, he would not allow his name to appear on the title-page either as part author or compiler. The chief interest of the Chrestomathy lies in the fact that it was the first practical manual of the Cantonese dialect prepared in China. It proved during its lifetime and in the absence of all rival lesson-books a very welcome assistance in the study of the language, but its size—a quarto of 734 pages—made it a costly as well as cumbrous affair, while its plan was too extensive to be logically carried out even in this generous space. Like all the books which bear the imprint of the Mission press, it has long since become excessively rare, and is now remembered chiefly by the small body of Anglo-Chinese bibliophiles.

During his residence at Macao, most of the time with the English missionary Mr. Lay, Mr. Williams regained both health and spirits. The confinement of his quarters in Canton had begun in two years to make serious inroads upon his constitution, in spite of abstemious living and the utmost attention to diet and exercise. Probably at no time in early life was he in robust health, though his active habits and natural inclination to out-of-door recreation had stimulated his muscular development and given him a prodigious amount of endurance. In later years he often referred, for example, to his being able to lift and shoulder a box which two Chinamen could hardly carry, and in his wherry on the river he used to enjoy "pulling round" his side of the boat, in great glee at his companion's unsuccessful efforts at holding his own against him. It was his invariable custom, when in control of his own movements, to devote at least an hour of the day to some such exercise as walking, rowing, or, while in North China, riding; and from this practice, maintained through his lifetime, more than from any other cause was due probably his long life and freedom from illness. Good health he esteemed the most important of earthly blessings; the warning of Stevens and Abeel and Tracy, all of whom succumbed to the climate, as well as Dr. Morrison's comparatively early death, doubtless impressed him with the necessity of caring for it, and taught him the fruitlessness of overwork in a tropical country. How important such care was in his case may be apprehended from Dr. Parker's statement that at one time he was convinced that they would lose him, for all his salutary habits and wholesome regimen. His daily round of duties at this period appears from the following letter, which describes his life at Macao for several successive years.

TO HIS FATHER.

MACAO, January 21, 1838.

You have but a faint conception of the vividness with which I paint you all at home sometimes, when a morbid sensitiveness, as it were, comes across me, and my thoughts rove like the fool's eyes, apparently without my volition. These reveries are a sort of intellectual intoxication, and productive of no good ; yet they are ofttimes so delicious as to drown all sense of their vagrant tendency. I now and then offer to excuse myself to myself by suggesting whether or not you may be at the same time musing with me. I have no doubt that I am not seldom brought to mind ; at least I gather much comfort therefrom, whatever may be the truth of the supposition. This tendency to think of those far away is strengthened by the circumstances of friends at home being a constant topic of conversation among the residents here. No one considers this country other than an exile place, to which they distrain themselves to come for a limited season in order to occupy and get gain and then joyfully return to their homes and kith. How then should I become so stolid as not to catch a little now and then and also take the chariot of Aminadab to pay you a visit ! Do not give these vagaries a thought and suppose I am getting homesick. I was merely making an episode on reveries. You expressed a wish some time ago to know somewhat of our manner of life ; and I have been on the point of giving you a *coup d'œil* several times, but have hitherto been puzzled to know how to put the matter rightly before you. Yet I 'll try.

I get up about half an hour before sunrise, at this season half or a quarter past six, and throwing on a few clothes, sally out to take a stroll and a breath of morning air. In these walks I usually talk a little with such Chinese as I happen to meet, but for the most part they are too busy for any thing else than to sell their vegetables. When I come back, I dress ; and then enjoy communion with Our Father, alone and at family prayers, until nearly breakfast time at eight. The breakfast is usually boiled rice, and a relish of curry, eggs, or fish, as the case may be, and as the comprador chooses. Tea is the only drink. Cakes made of boiled rice, and toast are often brought on the table, but no meat. The breakfast being ended, I settle the comprador's, or head servant's account of daily expenses, and tell him what to provide for the day. We literally, here, have daily our daily bread; you can hardly imagine it possible to have so little overplus of food in the larder, as is the habitual custom here; the servants eat every thing up you do not prohibit, leaving the cupboard all bare.

After these things are straightened I hear the scholars recite their lesson; set them a new one, and read it with them. Then write letters, or study or what not, until ten o'clock, by which time the Chinese have done their breakfast, and the teacher comes up. He goes into Mr. Lay's room, and I hear the boys recite their lessons. This is a set term and does not convey the idea, for the truth is they learn but little except while they are with me; the Chinese think but little, and study consequently is dull as well as hard work. When their recitation is over, the Japanese man comes, and we sit down again; I doing what little I can to learn his language, his ideas, and his modes of expression. The helps we have in this study are few; an imperfect vocabulary of terms ill arranged, and a few pictures are all, so that I can derive my knowledge of his idioms, his formation of sentences and rules of pronunciation only from continued practice. Neither grammars nor easy lessons are to be had; but we get along. This study is pursued until dinner time at half past three; by which time I am hungry and tired. After dinner I take a walk until dark. In the walk we go among the Chinese and talk and chat with them in their shops or houses, or by the way as opportunity offers. Sometimes we get civility, and then again receive abuse. Sometimes we are called foreign devils, and then others salute us as teachers, or gentlemen. Thus we get acquainted with the Celestials and find but little among their customs or characters which deserves the name.

In the evening I write or translate after hearing a third recitation from the boys—attend to business, if any is required, or evening meeting for prayer or whatever else is on hand. The day closes about 10 P.M. with social prayer.

Thus the days wax and wane—I shall probably resume printing operations shortly, when my routine will be a little modified, but still this round of duties will not be entirely laid aside. On Sabbath days the boys learn a portion of Scripture which is explained as lucidly as a stammering tongue can do it. They are uneducated in their own language, and consequently do not easily catch the new terms I use, nor understand the still newer subjects they hear me speak of. God must aid me in sowing the seed, and watering it, how then can I expect an increase except by Him! The mind of a heathen is dark enough, too dark to describe to you; a long work of patience and persevering labor is necessary before the fallow ground, with the luxuriant growth of vicious weeds now flourishing on it, can be upturned or made soft, even with usual success. Our sufficiency is of God. And if the hearts of sinners at home, in Christian America, are so obdurate, will it be surprising if the consciences of the heathen are scarred with a hot iron?

Therefore do not be disappointed if the answer to your prayer of faith is delayed, and we trust a long time before the early and latter rain is sent—" Lord increase our faith," should be the supplication of all.

TO HIS FATHER.

MACAO, January 26, 1839.

Now I am once again quite alone, Mr. Lay having gone home to his family and friends in England. He has lived with me all the time of his stay in China, and we have got on very well and usefully together. But it is dull work describing a stranger to a third person, and that, too, in a letter halfway round the globe. Since I wrote you last we have had strange times, and, as foreigners, we have had a new chapter in Chinese intercourse. The mob of Dec. 12 was caused by an altogether unprecedented command of the Chinese government to execute a man before the foreign factories, and the mob itself was described to me as being a fearful index of what a Chinese mob c^d do when aroused and heedless of consequences. Things are now moving on quietly, however, and after a cessation of trade of nearly two months business appears to be very brisk.

I am very busily engaged in Macao in studying the Japanese and Chinese languages, and in printing an elementary treatise for learning the latter tongue, which will be completed, perhaps, in a twelvemonth hence; there are few reasons for saying this; indeed, the chiefest one is that it *ought* to be completed by that time. I have one of the oddest printing-offices you can possibly imagine; 't is quite unique, I am sure, in its way. In the first place there are the Chinese types, which are arranged on frames on the sides of the room, so as to expose their faces, for they must all be seen to be found. There are sixty cases of the large type—which is about the size of four-line pica—and there are upwards of 25,000 types, hardly any two of which are alike. The small type stands on frames, one case above another, and justifies with the Gt. Primer, being contained in twenty cases, all so arranged that the type stands on the base, exposing all the faces. So much for the Chinese type, which fills up half the room. There is one clumsy, English press of iron, and three composing stands. But my workmen are really the most singular part of the office furniture. There is a Portuguese compositor, who knows not a word of English and hardly a Chinese character, yet sets up a book containing both; I speak to him in Portuguese, after a fashion, tho' imperfectly. A Chinese lad, who knows neither Portuguese nor English, sets Chinese types, and does his part pretty well. Lastly a Japanese, who knows nothing of English, Portuguese, or Chinese (hardly), picks out the various characters, and makes plenty of errors. When all hands are employed I must talk to each in his own tongue, and direct them all to print a book, the contents of which not a single person engaged on it knows any thing of; yet I think it will be printed tolerably accurately notwithstanding. I am sometimes much amused at the mutual endeavors of my motley group to hold intercourse; but conversation is so tedious, and withal so imperfect, that my office is much stiller than No. 60, 3d story, used to be whilom.

Mr. Lay had not been gone many weeks before his

place in Mr. Williams' house—the so-called prophet's chamber—was occupied by a new arrival from America, Rev. S. R. Brown, sent out as a teacher under the Morrison Educational Society. Of this institution, well-known in the annals of China mission work, it may be necessary to say that it had been organized by subscriptions from benevolent foreigners of all nationalities in Canton and Macao, as a memorial to Dr. Robert Morrison and for the purpose of educating Chinese boys in English and Chinese. About six thousand dollars, and many books, were subscribed soon after the great missionary's death, to the lasting credit of a few noble-minded men from the trading and shipping community of foreigners; and with this in hand as a basis, plans were devised for developing and carrying out the objects of the society. There was, however, some delay in finding a competent teacher or principal, none being willing to come from England; Mr. Brown was at length recommended by the faculty of Yale College upon request of Mr. Olyphant, and immediately sent to China with his wife, arriving in Macao in February, 1839. "At the anchorage," he says, "we were met by Mr. S. W. Williams, who came off in a covered boat to convey us to his house. At that time no lady was allowed to go to the city of Canton, and foreign ladies were forbidden by the Chinese authorities to land even at Macao; but as the government of that place was half Portuguese, the latter winked at the violation of this prohibition, and by landing at the Portuguese Custom House the ladies from our ship were safely and easily housed on shore."

After reporting to the officers of the society in Canton, Mr. Brown spent seven months with Mr. Williams, preparing himself for his position by study of the language, and during this interval commenced an attachment which became for both a most intimate and valued friendship, lasting through life. Mr. Brown's success in founding and conducting his school was notable, while his influence upon the future of China through a number of his pupils, who became distinguished in various professions has been second, probably, to that of no other foreign missionary.

The mob referred to in the last letter quoted is described as being "the most serious of many provocations inflicted by foreigners upon the authorities." An opium dealer had been brought to the square in front of the factories to be strangled there, in order that the "barbarians" might be impressed by a visible instance of the punishment inflicted upon such miscreants as were caught in this trade. The foreigners, observing the unusual sign of a small cross planted near the American flag-pole, of a wretch bound legs and arms, of a petty official smoking and superintending from a tent erected hard by, ran out to the number of seventy, or more, and insisted that no execution should desecrate their restricted pleasure-ground. The mandarin, hardly comprehending such sentimental objections as repugnance at the horrible sight, declared, properly enough, that the square was simply a portion of His Celestial Majesty's empire, and that his orders were explicit. An English ship's crew, however, appearing at this moment, in high glee at prospects of a scrimmage, knocked over tent and cross, drove out mandarin and officers, and would have jeopardized the lives of all the foreigners in China, had not the residents checked their frolic. But a native mob almost instantly collected after the ejectment of the executioners had become known, and the factories were subjected to a siege during the afternoon by a furious mass of the lowest and vilest Cantonese. The foreigners held their ground behind the gates and bars of the buildings, and were fortunately restrained from firing at the rabble; otherwise the factories and every one therein would have perished beyond peradventure before the ten thousand ruthless miscreants, who had assembled as much for plunder as for revenge. An end to the danger was at length brought about after two American gentlemen had stolen over the roofs of some adjacent buildings to Howqua's hong, and through that energetic merchant obtained the despatch of some hundred troops by the city magistrate. These, with whips and gongs, in characteristic Chinese fashion, drove the mob, helter-skelter, into the river and down the narrow lanes, and by the end of twilight the foreigners breathed freely again. The poor opium-smuggler had, meantime, been strangled quietly in the execution ground. The military who came to their aid had not a word to say to the foreigners relative to their flagrant and cavalier action, treating them with the forbearance due to children, and seeming to consider that their fright was a sufficient punishment for their indiscretion.

Trade had now almost entirely ceased, and its vital importance to Canton was confirmed by the irritability and distress which followed upon its suspension there. At Peking, however, the government was determined to utterly destroy all intercourse with foreigners, the profit from which was secured by a comparatively small community, while the demoralization of opium and the enormous drain of silver which paid for it was a strain and a burden to the whole country. For the furtherance of his end, therefore, the Emperor appointed Governor-General Lin, one of the ablest statesmen in the Middle Kingdom, as a special commissioner, to proceed to Canton and force a speedy conclusion of the business. He arrived there in March, 1839: his actions were the first step to an inevitable conflict between East and West, the discredit and glory of which alike belong to England, as the instigator and victor of the Opium War with China.

The anomalous position and condition of foreigners before the outbreak of hostilities is illustrated in the letters and extracts which follow:

TO HIS FATHER.

MACAO, April 3, 1839.

Since I last wrote you affairs have thickened a good deal, and now all the foreigners in Canton are close prisoners, and what is still worse, deprived of all their provisions and servants. If we were permitted to go out and buy in the market at any time, the deprivation of servants could be better borne, but in Canton we live through the native servants. The emperor has sent down a commissioner from Peking, vested with extraordinary and irresponsible powers, to put an everlasting stop to the opium trade, and he has demanded from the foreigners all the opium in China, valued at two millions of sterling money, which they have agreed to give up. So complete is the imprisonment that no provisions enter the factories, and 300 people are threatened with starvation unless they give up one of their number to the Chinese, at the demand of the commissioner, with a very slender chance of his life in case of so doing. Guards of soldiers are placed in front of the factories to prevent all communication, and letters are with the greatest difficulty sent out of the city, either to Whampoa, or Macao. The ships are all detained at Whampoa, and no provisions carried to them, but they are better able to endure a siege.

One incident of these troubled times is thus narrated in the "Recollections" already quoted:

"While Lin was superintending the destruction of the opium he sent a messenger to Macao to request Dr. Bridgman to go up and see him. The Chinese portion of the Mission press had been taken to Macao, and the rest went there as soon as foreigners were allowed to leave Canton. Only a few American and other merchants remained in the city, by whose means trade was still carried on; vessels arriving to British merchants stopped at Macao, and were re-consigned to some of those of other nationalities remaining at Canton. Dr. Bridgman was sent for at the suggestion of a former pupil of his who spoke English very well, and who was employed by Lin in translating into Chinese such portions of foreign newspapers as were of interest for him. And here I may observe that of all the Chinamen I have ever seen, Lin was decidedly the finest-looking and the most intelligent. He was indeed a very superior man, and if he had only been better informed he might have brought the difficult business intrusted to him to a much more creditable issue than he did; but this his ignorance and the conceit that accompanies ignorance prevented. I saw him only once. He was naturally much elated at his rank, and the absolute power entrusted to him led him to commit acts of rashness which recoiled upon himself.

"Dr. Bridgman remained at the Bogue for a day or two, Lin wanted him to carry a letter to Captain Elliot. This the Doctor agreed to do, provided Lin would make him aware of its contents; but Lin declined to do this and Bridgman declared that he would not carry letters like a common postman. The Governor then agreed to write the letter, but when Dr. Bridgman called to take leave it was not ready, and it was never sent. Lin did, however, write a letter to the Queen of

England, and a singular document it was. It showed how fully he appreciated the perplexities of the situation he was in, and how helpless he felt to extricate himself from them. He implored the Queen to put a stop to the opium trade."

TO HIS FATHER.

MACAO, August 28, 1839.

If my leisure for writing was in proportion to my inclination, I could fill half a dozen sheets with an account of what has taken place since last March. But I must trust for assistance in keeping you informed to various other channels, and I suspect they will add much to your stock of news, if the interest excited in America concerning recent events here bears any proportion to their true value. I wrote you last by the *Morrison*, since which we have been permitted quietly to remain at home; but all our English friends have been compelled by the proceedings of the Chinese authorities to leave Macao, and go on board the shipping in the anchorages, and at this time there is hardly a single Englishman in the place. The proximate causes of this harshness flow from the law of the Chinese, which under all circumstances requires blood for blood,—a law that at any moment may come down upon myself or any one living here. About a month ago some sailors were ashore near the anchorage, and getting drunk, made an attack upon this village near by, and most inhumanly killed a man passing by. Captain Elliot held a court on board of the shipping, but was, after the most diligent search, unable to convict the murderer, though he sentenced several to imprisonment. The Chinese were, however, not so easily satisfied. After a while a demand is made by them for the murderer, and a threat that in case he is not given up they will proceed to extremities in order to force the surrender. Soon after this another edict was received, saying that in three days the servants should all be removed unless he was given up their provisions stopped, and no communication allowed them. Upon this, Captain Elliot called a meeting of the British, and told them he never should give up a man who had not been proved guilty, and even if a man was convicted he was not to be executed by the Chinese. He therefore recommended them to deliberate, and some prepared to leave. After three days not a Chinese was allowed to come near their houses, and they were supplied with provisions through the Portuguese for about a week. The commissioner, finding that the English were sustained in this manner, sent an edict to the governor of Macao telling him that if he did not send the English away the town should be invested with troops. Upon this, those still remaining prepared to depart, and by Monday night, the 26th inst., not one was left; men, women, and children all having to go, or be held as guilty, and in imminent danger of being seized by the Chinese as a hostage for the murderer. Hundreds of people have thus been obliged to leave their business, forsake their homes, and go on board confined ships, their dwellings containing thousands of dollars in furniture, books, pictures, etc., all remaining at the mercy of those behind. These are some of the consequences resulting from a glass of grog, a thing that many would not deprive the sailor of, lest his comforts be reduced and his burdens increased. O when will people call things by their right names, and trace effects to their proper causes! What else will ensue we cannot tell; but all these things—bad as they are—shall work together for good.

The Americans have in the troubles consequent upon the murder been undisturbed, except so far as so great a change in the circumstances of all our neighbors makes it imperious upon us to aid them as we can. Our servants were not taken away; and this is equivalent in China to living; for no foreigner is permitted to go into the market, and purchase provisions. It was, however, almost impossible to do any thing, for the servants were sometimes terrified, sometimes quiet, one day they would work, and the next they would refuse. But amidst all these trials there is enough to be thankful for, and I am sure that the hand of the Lord is in all that has taken place, and that he is using the chief actors in doing His plans, and before they are completed His people will be made to give up their non-intercourse system, and receive foreigners as fellow-men.

Commissioner Lin after these proofs of his determination to rid the country of the British, allowed them to remain unmolested until aroused to further action by the outbreak of hostilities. Trade though prohibited to the English at the end of the year went on from Macao in American and other bottoms, and opium smuggling flourished exceedingly as soon as the destruction of the twenty thousand chests surrendered to Lin became generally known. The inevitable crisis, which led finally to the beginning of an honorable intercourse between the nations, arrived with the appearance of an English fleet and army off Macao in June, 1840, and their capture of the island Chusan, opposite Hangchow Bay, a fortnight later. The Chinese authorities made what defence they could, here and wherever they were attached on the mainland, but the contest was very unequal, though needlessly protracted through the deceitful promises of yielding on the part of the Chinese and an unwillingness to carry the war up to Peking on the part of the English. Lin was degraded and recalled after the first reverses and succeeded by Kishen, an astute negotiator, who was in a fair way towards adjusting the difficulties and arranging a truce, when the Emperor issued an order to "destroy and wipe clean away, to exterminate and root out the rebellious barbarians." Thus from various causes the desultory conflict was continued for two years in various places on the coast, while the small circle of missionaries remained in Macao, spared from the horrors of war and indiscriminate hostilities, pursuing so far as they could their ordinary duties and looking forward with hope to the speedy opening of the country.

An incident of the war, which occurred just before Lin's removal is described in the following:

TO HIS FATHER.

August 20, 1840.

About three weeks since, Mr. Stanton, one of our number, was seized by the Chinese while going alone very early to bathe beyond the walls of the town. He was carried to Canton in a rough manner, but after undergoing an examination there before the Governor and other high officers, has been treated with kindness, supplied with a change of clothes, a servant and other conveniences, the officers considering him as a prisoner of war, not to be severely handled. Capt. Smith, the senior officer on this station made a demand upon the Portuguese governor of Macao for Mr. Stanton, inasmuch as Macao, being considered a neutral place for all parties, no English troops had been landed for the protection of the English residing here. The Governor demanded him of the Chinese, and the taoutai, or Intendant of the place, started for Canton to get Mr. S. from the Governor. However, instead of procuring his release, it is said the Governor was highly indignant with him for having allowed the English to remain in Macao, (as it appeared on Mr. Stanton's examination that they were there), took away his button and sent him back to Macao post haste to order the Portuguese Governor to drive the English away from the settlement, telling him that he (Gov. Lin) was coming with thousands of troops to help him. Capt. Smith on hearing such an answer, waited a day or two, but nothing being done by the Chinese that indicated an intention of delivering Mr. Stanton up, yesterday anchored two sloops and an armed steamer near the barrier which separates Macao from the Chinese territory and opened a fire upon the troops stationed there. This barrier is a solid stone wall built across an isthmus, having a few houses on the Chinese side of it, but clear of every thing on the Port side, except a large temple where several hundred Chinese soldiers were quartered. Nine war junks were anchored in the mud on the opposite side of the barrier. As soon as the ships opened their fire, the barrier fort and the junks returned it, the latter keeping up a scattering fire with them for an hour. The ships were so far off that their shot did little execution, and the troops were landed beyond the barrier in Chinese territory about two hours after the firing had commenced. The Chinese made little or no resistance, nothing like a line being formed, or a volley of musketry fired from their hundreds. As soon as the English troops landed they took possession of the barrier, as every one had fled from it, and began to fire upon the troops in the temple. Many shot had been fired at the temple from the ships, but a projection in the hill and the building itself protected them, the balls passing overhead. As soon as the sepoys opened a fire of musketry upon the temple the scattering shot warned the soldiers there to get out of the way, while a discharge from their field piece silenced the junks. The Chinese soon left the place, and the English after setting fire to the buildings at the barrier went aboard ship again. The number killed among the Chinese is said to be five, but it is probable there are more, as many shot hit the junks, and the muskets of the sepoys were directed towards a number of Chinese.

This morning Mr. Bridgman and I went to look at the temple. There were great numbers of natives thereabouts, looking at the damage—what little there was,—and talking over such an unexpected event. Thousands of them covered the hills, witnessing the action, and many of them were not displeased to see their braggadocio troops routed. They walked over the ruins of the Barrier, where were now no more insulting soldiers ; for to understand this feeling it should be mentioned that a body of soldiers is one of the greatest annoyances to a Chinese village that can infest it. Many of the soldiers fled into town, only to leave it again this morning for the country, and to-day there is not a soldier in the place. During the action no excitement or irritation was seen among the populace ; they quietly looked on, and when the action was over, returned home to tell what they had seen. One spectator, unluckily wounded in the leg, came to-day to the hospital to be cured ; the ball was cut out, and he will probably soon go home quite well.

It is well that one cannot pry into futurity ; if we could, it appears to me, that the vista which would open through this land would so fill us with horror, doubt, and grief, that all our energies would be unnerved, our hope go out in gloom, and our faith wellnigh be lost. The passions of 360,000,000 of unsanctified spirits cannot be let loose at once, they cannot all be shaken by the same causes, but the prospect now is that they will be in detail. The bonds of social intercourse among the Chinese are strong for a healthy nation, and God's hand should be seen in thus forming their social polity ; but it is not based on the knowledge of His truth, His designs to a world through His son, nor on His overruling Providence. It is better to leave all these cases in His hands ; we are quite willing to do so when they look favorably, but we think we must help Him a little in caring, when we think the prospect is gloomy and results troublesome to ourselves.

TO HIS FATHER.

MACAO, April 26, 1841.

By the ships which are now so rapidly departing, you will infer that trade is going on very thrivingly, yet the merchants, if we are to believe what they say, are very discouraged, and do not like the change or the prospects. Perhaps if they had their own wishes they would be quite as little pleased. The Chinese rulers at Canton have been very quiet lately. Indeed, I suspect they are beginning to find out that an edict is not so dreadful in its effects as they wish it to be, and conclude to make the best of present troubles, and let the English alone in these parts. What the English will do next is not known ; perhaps Captain Elliot's acts will be modified a good deal by what the Chinese themselves do. This instruction of the Chinese Government by degrees into a knowledge of the power, forbearance, and resoluteness of foreign nations will, I think, be, in the end, much more salutary and beneficial than an overwhelming attack and great slaughter, and this means may be used by the Allwise Disposer to make China peacable towards far-travelled strangers. It is to be feared, however, that the English plenipotentiary will not do so much, after all, to extend the intercourse as we wish. His ideas are rather to put the present plan for trade, which the Chinese Government itself has sanctioned, upon a permanent footing. He can force a residence in other parts if he chooses, but that would be what the Chinese will resist to the best of their ability, which, indeed, is not very great. The whole expedition is an unjust one in my mind on account of the intimate connection its sending here had with the opium trade, but we shall find very few expeditions that have not had a good deal to find fault with in them. There is a way some have of saying that "it will all work well, and that good will come out of evil," which is only a sheer excuse for leaving themselves in indolence. For my part, I am far from being sure that this turn up is going to advance the cause of the Gospel half so much as we think it is. England has taken the opium trade upon herself nationally, and can that be a cause to bless? for the success of her arms here would extend that wicked traffic ten thousand times more than the Church is ready to extend her stakes here. The 50,000 chests now annually brought to China would rise to hundreds of thousands shortly, and only think of the destruction of it. . . .

I am in usual health and as busy as ever with the *Repository* and other duties, while some of our number have days of illness allotted to them, and can hardly work at all. Dr. Parker went home last July, and his hospital has been long since closed, though not forgotten by the natives who have been benefitted by it. No foreigner is so extensively known among the Chinese as its conductor; his gratuitous treatment of their diseases has done much to place foreign character on a better footing in this region, and show the Chinese that we are not exactly the devils they take us to be. Three Japanese have lately reached Macao; I have seven now living with me.

The Chinese at length, thoroughly beaten, and amazed at the prowess of the British, came to terms after the capture of Chinkiang, and acceded to all the demands of their enemy. A mere skirmishing party of English and

Indian troops had in two years conquered and subdued the whole available force of the Empire of China. "The world has seldom seen," as Mr. Williams says elsewhere, "a more conspicuous instance of the superiority of a small body possessing science, skill, and discipline, over immense multitudes of undisciplined, ignorant, and distrustful soldiers, than was exhibited in this war." By the treaty of Nanking, signed in August, 1842, the Chinese agreed to surrender the island of Hongkong; to acknowledge and receive foreign representatives; to permit trade at five open ports; and to establish a fair and regular tariff. The barriers of Chinese ignorance and pride, which had so long been effectual in obstructing the spread of a higher civilization, were thus partially overthrown, and an entirely new era of civil and political intercourse opened. The history of modern China may be said to commence with the downfall of the co-hong at Canton and the admission of foreigners to trade and residence in other coast towns. Various missionary societies, recognizing the importance of the vast field thus opened, sent out as many as could be found to establish new stations there, permission now being also given to foreign women to live in China, while those missionaries who had been employed among Chinese colonists in the Archipelago were with a few exceptions transferred to China. "The ways of God's dealings with this people began at length to open, and he entered into judgment with them, that he might show them his mercy."

Before the necessary and creditable task of the "Chrestomathy" had been completed, Mr. Williams was busy planning a cheaper and more suitable introduction to the study of Chinese. The habit of attending more or less simultaneously to several pursuits, which most hard workers are apt sooner or later to acquire, had been forced upon him early in life; and like all minds trained to continuous industry, his recreation consisted chiefly in turning from one form of mental activity to another. His delight in a multitude of engagements seems to have increased with his capacity for fulfilling them, and appears again and again in his letters. "I rather like to be driven with occupation and duties," he exclaims in one, "and have no doubt but that we enjoy life and ourselves much better when thus pressed, than when we are more at leisure. Therefore give me always enough to do!"

The little volume of some three hundred octavo pages which he commenced printing in the spring of 1841, under the title of "Easy Lessons in Chinese," * was designed to supply to those who undertook the formidable task of learning that language, an aid somewhat analogous to the grammars of European tongues. It is a matter for wonder that an attempt of this sort was not made earlier by those who had struggled unaided with this monstrous speech; but the fact that trade under the old conditions had been carried on by means of the ridiculous jargon known as "Pigeon English," a medium invented and learned by Chinese interpreters and adopted by foreigners, left few who cared to undertake the serious study of Chinese. The "Easy Lessons" issued in 1842, with its simple and practical exercises and interlinear translations, after the

* "It surely demanded," says a writer in the *North American Review*, "a more cheerful faith and elastic confidence than those of the mere linguist, to coin the title of '*Easy* Lessons in Chinese.' "

manner of Ollendorf, appeared at precisely the fortunate moment, when the opening of China created an eager demand for text-books on the language among foreigners, who were now flocking to the country in great numbers.

A second work from his pen, prepared during the year 1843, was the *Ying Hwa Yun-fu Lih-kiai*, " An English and Chinese Vocabulary in the Court Dialect," a convenient manual of five hundred and twenty-eight octavo pages, published in January, 1844. This was undertaken with the design to further the object of the " Easy Lessons," in facilitating intercourse between natives and foreigners at the newly-opened ports, at all of which, of course, the court, or " Mandarin," was the language of officials and educated men. " Much of the ill-will and difficulties which exist between these parties has been owing to a mutual misconception of their words and wishes," was a frequently expressed opinion of the author; and the task of overcoming the mischief resulting from such ignorance was one to which he applied himself with redoubled ardor, now that the gates of the country were opening.

A smaller publication, called " A Chinese Commercial Guide " (octavo, pp. 370), was compiled and issued this year, to furnish foreign merchants with useful information respecting trade and navigation under the recent treaties. Although an original publication, and containing matter which was necessarily new, this little guide appeared as a second edition to one compiled by J. R. Morrison in 1834; for this reason Mr. Williams omitted to put his name on the title-page until a fourth reissue had altered and enlarged it into another work. A practical compendium of geographical information, which he first presented in a series of *Repository* articles, also came from his press in 1844 as a book of some hundred pages, entitled " Chinese Topography : an Alphabetical List of the Provinces, Departments, and Districts of the Chinese Empire, with their Latitudes and Longitudes." If to these publications are added the Japanese translations already mentioned, and his regular contributions and editorial labors in connection with the Chinese *Repository*, the record of these years will be found to be one of pretty continuous application to his various duties. It frequently fell to his share, also, during 1843 and 1844, to conduct Sunday services in the British chapel at Macao, in lieu of a regular clergyman.

The United States Government was among the first to take advantage of the new treaty and arrange terms of intercourse with China. For this end President Tyler sent the statesman and scholar Caleb Cushing,* with a letter addressed to the Emperor and full powers as commissioner to negotiate a treaty between the two countries. He arrived in Macao in February, 1844, where he remained six months, making no attempt to present his credentials at the capital, but establishing his miniature court in the house of a former Portuguese govenor and creating in the colony a profound sensation by the novelty and magnitude of his mission as well as by his attractive personal qualities. He was met by the Chinese Commissioner Kiying, who had signed the Peace of Nanking, and who afterwards, owing to his connection with foreign affairs

---

* The honor of making the first treaty with China was given to Mr. Cushing at this time as a partial compensation for the Senate's refusal to confirm his appointment to Tyler's Cabinet.

in China and frequent personal interviews, became the best known Chinese statesman abroad. A treaty which Mr. Cushing had drafted was discussed by the two commissioners at their meetings in Wanghia—a village suburb of Macao—and presently signed in July of this year. This document, from the clearness of its terms and its able definition of the rights of foreigners in China, remained the leading authority in all disputed cases until the second great war and admission to Peking. In his negotiations the American Minister appointed the missionaries Bridgman and Parker as official interpreters to the legation, and availed himself of Mr. Williams' press and translations as long as the embassy remained at Macao. His letter of acknowledgment to the latter concludes:

"I beg you to accept my best wishes for your future happiness and prosperity; and I am very respectfully and truly,
"Yours, &c.,
"C. CUSHING.
"To which I add the expression of the great satisfaction that I have enjoyed in your society during our short association, and my high estimation of the service you have rendered the Government directly, and indirectly the general cause of religion and civilization in China."

Mr. Williams' letters to America at this period contain frequent allusions to a project which he entertained of interesting his old church at Utica in raising funds for a font of Chinese metallic type for the Canton mission. His own enthusiasm in this branch of his profession was so full and eager, his readiness for personal sacrifice so constant, that the suspicion of any possible indifference in the matter on the part of other Christians does not seem to have occurred to him. His interest had of late been excited by accounts from Singapore of the labors of the English missionary Dyer, who had for many years been engaged in making steel punches for a font of Chinese types, many of which were now completed; these it was desirable to add to the antiquated and imperfect font at Macao before satisfactory and acceptable books could be printed for distribution among native scholars. The history of his endeavors in this direction has been kindly furnished by his early friend, Mrs. E. Throop Martin, whose personal efforts and assistance contributed largely to the final accomplishment of his purpose.

"I recall with deep interest a visit which I paid many years ago in Utica to Mrs. Thomas Clark, the sister of Mrs. William Williams, in whose affectionate heart the love for her nephew Wells was as strong as for any of her own children. The good woman was then on her death-bed and confided to me the response which she felt it our duty as a Christian church to make to the appeals of her nephew in China regarding funds for a font of Chinese movable types. She put in my hands several letters from him extending over a period of two years and containing urgent pleas for this help in spreading the gospel among the Chinese. The American Board was then struggling with a debt which drew the attention of its supporters from all new enterprises and left the earnest appeal of the young missionary printer unheeded. Disappointed in not receiving that sympathy and coöperation from the church of which he was a member and which he was so ably representing abroad, he wrote as follows:

"'There seems to be a dreadful apathy in the churches at home about their missionaries abroad. It is vastly more disheartening, more weakening to us than short allowance or spare wardrobes, and I am exceedingly grieved to see how far gone in this spirit of covetousness are the good people of Utica. If I had that font of type now it would be a great help to me, and I entertain some hope that it will yet come, for I cannot believe that all spirit has departed.' And again: 'If some of the good people with you felt that I was their agent in China for the cause to which they had dedicated themselves, it seems as if they would be more anxious to know how their interest prospered. I love this cause more than ever I did, and wish that every one could see, as I do *sometimes*, how cheering it is to know that God is on our side.' Under date, March, 1842, he wrote : ' I await very anxiously your reply to the request I made last year, when you told me to send for such things as I needed ; but better far than the types would be the assurance that the church was aroused to a sense of the eminent danger the heathen are in.' "

It was stated that at least $1,000 would be required before any punches could be ordered, a large sum in those days when the widespread charities of societies and individuals so common at present were unknown. The prospect of raising the whole amount was doubtful, but an effort was made, and a reply to this effect sent to Mr. Williams in December, 1843. Before this date, however, Dyer had succumbed to a tropical fever while on a visit to Macao, leaving his work unfinished and the prospect of a complete font of Chinese type more uncertain than ever.

Eleven years had now passed since the missionary printer turned his back upon the old home, and every year increased his desire to see his birthplace and its people once more. His letters plainly indicate the strength of this wish, generally strongly repressed, but breaking out from time to time into a yearning which every message from his family, urging him to apply for his fully earned rest, made it hard to resist. A special motive, appealing to his deepest affections, had lately arisen in the sad intelligence of his father's failing health. Owing to the collapse of his publishing business, William Williams had left Utica in 1836 and settled with his family in Tonawanda, in western New York, where he undertook the management of some farm lands. When in a fair way to regain his prosperity an injury received in a stage-coach accident brought on a slow disease of the brain, which soon prevented his working and reduced him at length to complete imbecility. Before his illness had reached its most serious phase, the family removed to Rome, near Utica, from whence Mrs. Williams entreats her son, with a woman's warmth of appeal, to return ere it be past his father's power to greet him. But the straitened circumstances of the Mission Board were unable to provide means for his passage home, while the secretaries were reluctant to lose his services in the printing office.

TO HIS MOTHER.

MACAO, September 21, 1844.

It was a melancholy recital of the work of ruin which disease and injury have made on the mind of father, that was contained in your letter of April 15th. Diseases of the mind have their peculiar features of sorrow, and to those who see the daily and mournful decay of all those powers which before entertained and instructed and comforted them, the sight is different, but perhaps not less painful than to see the body dissolving while its tenant is able to cheer the hearts of friends. But *I* had no definite idea before of the extent of his malady, and the weakness to which it had reduced him ; it is a comfort to me, who have never seen him otherwise than in vigor of mind and body, and who must make imaginings from your descriptions, to remember that behind all this feebleness the spirit itself is unimpaired, as is the sun when hid behind a cloud. We too have this consolation, that if his mind grows daily darker, its final emancipation will be in realms of light so joyous and so pure, that even the light of sun or moon can add nothing to their glories. This is indeed a source of much consolation, and to you who see the constant decline, it must prove a never-failing support. As for me, I cannot but adore the Hand which takes away and which gives most when it takes. The comforts of this life are felt to be most transitory after they are gone, most unsatisfying after we have tried to suck the greatest comfort out of them; but the hidden joy of the everlasting Comforter makes large amends to us for these earthly deprivations. We are all under unrequitable obligations to you for the care you take of our father, also to Sophia, who supplies the place of all her brothers; between you two he can want for nothing that assiduous care prompted by affection can supply. It is a principal motive of my desire to visit the United States to see you at Rome once more; if it is only a matter of a brief call, it will be well worth the time. I shall consider it my duty to go, but I must not be anxious to know when that time shall come.

A way was unexpectedly opened for his return to the United States by the generous offer of the American merchant, Mr. Gideon Nye—a friend to whose impulsive and magnanimous heart he was already indebted for a multitude of kindnesses,—who proposed that he should accompany him upon a journey homewards by way of Egypt and Europe. Their plans were soon matured and passage taken in the November packet from Hongkong, but business matters detained Mr. Nye at the last moment. Rather than cause a double disappointment by the delay, he induced Mr. Williams to go on alone to India and await him there, but, as will be seen, the trip proved a solitary one to its end; Mr. Nye did not leave Canton until his friend had reached New York, though he assumed the entire expenses of the trip, as originally contemplated.

Leaving Hongkong Mr. Williams arrived nine days later at Singapore, where he found that after Dyer's death all the apparatus for cutting type had been sent to Siam, and the workmen dispersed; the disappointment of this hope to the editors of the *Repository* was the greater since they had already advanced $500 for a partial set of the types, in anticipation of securing enough to work with. Very little was returned to them for their outlay. From Singapore a steamer brought him to Bombay, via Ceylon, by the middle of January, 1845. A joyous note is sounded at Colombo that testifies to the gratification with which he ever recognized any sympathy with missions from the imperturbable and sordid merchant or official classes in the East:

"The few days I spent there were passed in Sir Anthony Oliphant's house, who takes great interest in the progress of missions in Ceylon, and highly esteems our brethren at Jaffna. He is Chief Justice of Ceylon. It was no small pleasure to me to hear one holding the liberal views of Sir Anthony speak in such terms of commendation of the operations of missions and of the harmony and Christian love exhibited by the missionaries in their intercourse with one another. After all, it is living Christianity which is the way to teach it."

In Bombay, where he remained two weeks in the congenial society of Rev. D. O. Allen and other American missionaries, the opportunity of acquaintance with other fellow-workers was as interesting as was the comparison between the two mission fields of India and China. Especially were the printing operations of his host related with his own work.

"Mr. Allen is engaged in the office all the time, superintending the men and reading proofs. He does ten times more

English work than we, and five times as much as I thought this mission did. The office, indeed, almost supports them, so that they have hardly drawn upon the Board for eighteen months. I have been looking a little at what I 've had time to see among the people around me. The aspect of the land hereabouts is indicative of less advance in agriculture, and the squalidness of the natives and the shattered, half-built condition of their hovels betoken less comfort and health than among the Chinese of the same class."

It was a great regret in later life that he could not fulfil his desire for a second trip to India, to renew the friendships of this visit, and witness the elevating influences of Christianity upon its people. As a parting memento of his sojourn among the missionaries in Bombay, he presented to a museum of natural history in charge of one of them a collection of plants and minerals from Central New York, which he had taken with him to China, and to which he had added many specimens gathered in the neighborhood of Canton. These much-travelled herbs and stones probably remain for the edification of the Bombay youth to this day. The monthly mail steamer took him on the 1st of February by way of Aden to Suez, where he arrived on the 17th, and was carried by the post route at once to Cairo. The companionship of Dr. Pickering (the American naturalist and author of the " Races of Man "), returning from India, greatly increased the pleasure of the voyage. After a few weeks in Egypt, this is his first reflection :

" The large bazar is always covered over in towns, but the dust and flies envelop every thing. What a plague was that when the *dust* of Egypt was turned into lice, for in most of the villages it is ankle deep in the thoroughfare. You walk along in piles of dust, which in times of high wind is whirled about the country and fills the air like fog. You can hardly realize the universal diffusion of the soil upon and in every thing; and then imagine it *all* turned to lice. Not a step could be taken without stepping upon and in them; the bed would teem with lice; the clothes would instantly crawl with them; the plants, the trees would swarm with these loathsome insects. A camel would be a moving mountain of lice; a buffalo would bellow with the torment of myriads suddenly enveloping him; sheep and goats would almost die with the weight in their fleeces. Every thing is covered with dust; every thing would be covered with lice. The first step I took in the dusty lanes of a village, after reading the account in Exodus, showed the extent of the infliction upon the people of Pharaoh more that I had ever before thought of it. No wonder the magicians said, ' It is the finger of God ! ' "

While awaiting the coming of Mr. Nye in Cairo, he made the acquaintance of an agreeable and intelligent French gentleman, with whom he hired a dahabéeh for the Nile trip. Their plans resulted in an expedition of fifty days spent upon the river, a wholly delightful and profitable tour. Returning to the capital to hear of fresh reasons for delay from his friend in China, Mr. Williams prolonged his journey with his companion, and crossed the desert into Palestine. The country at that time was suffering from the ambitious wars of Mehemet Ali and his son Ibrahim, so that travelling was not altogether uneventful or entirely safe.

TO REV. E. C. BRIDGMAN.

JERUSALEM, May 12, 1845.

Since my last to you from Cairo, I have come to this city by way of the desert, having been fourteen days on camels and horses; a tiresome journey, for out of this time we only travelled one hundred and twenty-one hours. I was accompanied by the same gentleman with whom I went up the Nile, and together we had five camels and three Arabs to take care of us and of our servant Ibrahim. On the first three days our route took us along the edge of the desert, stopping from time to time in villages, but after that were no marks of habitation until we reached El Arisch, at the S. E. extremity of the Mediterranean, the last town in Egypt, and *so* sandy, barren, and desolate. During our five days of the desert, there were shrubs and a little grass on every hill, but near El Arisch every vestage of vegetation disappears; the sand covers all with one uniform coat of yellow. The town is partly composed of stone hovels with matted mud roofs, clustered around a large fort, and partly of black Arab tents, which looked more like cloth hung out to dry on four sticks, and kept from blowing off with strings pinned to the ground, than human habitations. When we entered the town the women belonging to the tents were wailing for a dead person, slowly moving in a circle and holding one another's hands as they uttered their notes in slow tones, sounding lugubriously as they came over the plains. These Arabs are dressed in long robes, with a striped yellow and brown cloth on the head tied with cords, the peculiar head-dress of the genuine wild Ishmaelite, who wears no turban, and scorns many of the customs of his more stationary countrymen. These fellows are the most villainous looking ruffians you can imagine and I think they are devising plans against my life or my pocket whenever I see them or they me. They stopped us near El Arisch in the desert and demanded money for the right of going through their barren wastes, which is indeed no other than robbery, but conceded because they are feared, and their demand is only fourteen cents for each *kafr* or infidel. They sometimes meet parties of travellers whom they let pass free, because of their numbers and weapons; but most of those who go along this route are obliged to accede to the charge. In one case, the claimants being unauthorized to levy, our men hooted the scamps, whereupon they seized a poor donkey travelling in our party, and incontinently straddled and rode her off, while our servants scurried off in pursuit, and liberated the brute only with piastres. On this route we saw half a dozen women on their knees reaping oats by pulling it up by the roots, while their lords stood and looked on, holding weapons in their hands, prepared to defend their crops. I thought, as we passed by, how Christianity has changed all this, and restored woman to her proper level in society, but God alone can ever make the Bedouin regard her aright.

Goats and sheep were in plenty, almost always in one flock, and attended by children; when a shepherd here " divides his sheep from the goats," it is simply to shear the former. Some herds of camels were seen, and of all lubberly, ill-contrived beasts, a camel's colt will bear away the palm; it looks like a badly stuffed bag of wool on stilts, with an ostrich's head and neck attached to show the way. Riding camels is not at all unpleasant; it is almost impossible to get them out of a walk, but a trotting dromedary shakes all consistency out of one, speedily reducing your mind and body to a uniform pulpy mass. I sometimes tried to speed my camel at a trot, but a little of this was quite enough; fortunately he would not go far at such a pace.

Gaza, a beautiful city of gardens surrounded by olive groves, was doubly pleasant to us after the renagates of the desert. A day in quarantine there gave us time to look at what is shown, the hill up which Sampson carried the gates being about all that is worth seeing. He carried them 100 rods, at least, up a hill about 250 feet high, the ascent being gradual. The pillars he pulled down, the gates, and his tomb are all shown, and can all be disbelieved, for he was not buried here, and the pillars are much too short for a building whose roof held 3,000 people. However the tradition is vouched for by all the Moslem inhabitants of the place. . . .

Later from Jerusalem:

It was with such feelings as you have in no other city that I went around and about the hills, across the valleys, stopping at all that was so new to the eye, so familiar to the mind. The nearer view of the plain of Jericho I afterwards enjoyed only added to the impression of its beauty and desolation. The Jordan is a small, muddy, turbulent stream, just like my school-boy river, the Mohawk, of little other use than to drain the country—yet who can see this rapid stream running as it now does through a desert filled with Ishmaelites, wilder than any savage beasts, and not recall the times when it was thrice divided that man might go across it dry shod, or the time when its Former descended into its waters to fulfil the righteousness he came to perform? I could not, and I think no one can see or wash in the Jordan as he would look at or bathe in any other river.

Reaching Jerusalem early in May, he and his companion remained about a month in its vicinity, delighted and at the same time incensed at the manifold sights of the region; for while his tastes led him to examine with eagerness the physical features, natural and political history, ethnology, and peculiarly interesting associations of Palestine, the spoiler had long been in the land, and Mr. Williams was not one who easily forgave or overlooked idolatry in any form. "I have been twice," he writes, "to the church of the Holy Sepulchre, but my incredulity spoils all the sights there. The monks have contrived to place many remarkable spots together under its roof, as the spot where Christ appeared to Mary, the place where his mother stood at the crucifixion, the grave, the spot of the cross, the stone which covered the grave, the stone on which Christ was embalmed, the grave of Nicodemus, the grotto where the crosses were found, etc., etc., for most of which there is no proof at all." But perverse and foolish practices were carried on elsewhere. In detailing a visit to Mount Carmel, he says:

"In the convent you are shown a grotto where Elijah lived, and there is a ridiculous image of him over an altar, representing him as a crooked old man. I dislike to see such things, for they cling to one's ideas of the persons they represent, and when I read of the wonderful event which once took place on this range of hills, I am afraid that the little humpbacked, red-faced, gray-beard in the den on Mount Carmel will be the impersonation of the wonderful prophet. I cannot see how men, with the Bible in their hands, can make such things, or when made worship before them. When one who does not agree with the ritual observed visits these places, the friar shows you all over without an attempt to make you do as he does; he is down on his knees straightway, and while you are looking at whatever is before you, he is tacitly reproving you by his silent praying. . . .

"From the convent we went down to Haifa, a small village on the coast across the bay from Acre, and upon inquiry there found that it would be easy to make the excursion to Nazareth and the Sea of Tiberius. There were others, too, intent upon the same expedition, and the next morning our company mustered nearly forty horsemen in all, of whom fourteen travellers, the rest servants and troopers to serve as guards—though it was confessed by all that they were the greatest cowards on earth, and that in case of a brush we should no doubt be obliged to defend them and not they us. Such miscellaneous companies always move slowly; I found the slow walk of our day's journey much more fatiguing than the camel ride across the desert to Jerusalem. . . . We reached Nazareth by about sunset, though in time to see what the friars had to show us before it was dark, and also to give the cooks an hour to prepare dinner for our company."

He continues with an account of the grotto where the Virgin lived, of Joseph's workshop, the Virgin's fountain—"the only one of the whole at all likely to be anywise authentic, for it is the only watering-place in the village," —and other places, but enough has been given to illustrate the nature of his impressions in this country. From Nazareth the party returned to Acre, from whence

Mr. Williams travelled alone to Beirut, and after ten days with the American missionaries stationed there, "went down half sick, half well to Alexandria."

From Malta, July 7th, again to Dr. Bridgman:

"I was liberated to-day from quarantine and have removed into town to the house of Mr. Hunter, the father of the printer to the Mission at Beirut, to whom I had a note of introduction, and who to my surprise invited me to his house in town until a steamer left for Marseilles. This does not occur for a week to come, and I am by this unlucky quarantine detained here for half a month, which to my very great disappointment will probably prevent my reaching home in time for the annual meeting [of the Am. Board] in September. I have chosen this route so that I may go to Paris, where I want to make inquiries about getting a font of Manchu type, its price, sizes and form; I believe there is also a font of Japanese type in that city. I wish to get some of the books published concerning the Manchu language, which ought I think to be in our* library. Nye's letter of March reached me in Alexandria, and I am sorry indeed to learn that he cannot come on; his note of that date is like all of them very kind, and he expresses his regret that his business is in such a position that he still must stay to attend to it. I had calculated so strongly upon his being at Alexandria that when I arrived there I almost sent a note ashore addressed to him, and did inquire by messenger where he was. But instead of him I got his signature and directions to send his letters on to Bombay, there to await his arrival. The quarantine detention at Smyrna has prevented my going to Constantinople to see your old class-mate Dwight, who whilom was my schoolmaster, and has hindered me too from going directly to London. . . .

"I find it difficult while seeing so many scenes in this world to keep heavenly scenes in such nearness as I wish. 'T is easier to the natural man to grow in every other way than to grow

---

* The Canton Mission, for which he picked up many works about China on this trip.

holier. I discover that seeing holy places has no effect in getting a better apprehension of heavenly places; there is no royal road to heaven except through our King. But I'm grateful for the privilege I've had of seeing Mt. Zion on earth and other places in Palestine, for it has made me understand much better many of the events mentioned in the Scriptures."

Leaving Malta by a line of Neapolitan steamers which allowed him to stop at two or three places on the route, he directed his course along the Italian coast to Marseilles, making hasty visits at Syracuse, Messina, Naples, Rome, and Genoa. Upon reaching the French port he went by steamboat up the Rhone valley and thence to Paris by diligence—a trip which he often referred to as being about the hardest travelling in his life. His time in Paris was largely engaged in the business of looking up types already referred to. What impressed him most vividly, he tells his friend Bridgman, was the fact that—

"Sabbaths are almost unknown here, so far as the different aspect of the city on that day goes; shops are open, hucksters are crying, cabs and omnibuses are rattling along, and people hurrying to and fro in multitudes, as on other days. . . . The sights to be visited in Paris are much more instructive than those in Rome, where art and architecture are the principal things worthy of notice. Here there is more science, more pleasure to those who are not critics in painting and statuary, but who like to examine works of nature; collections made to illustrate the Handy Works found in this city are unsurpassed in the world. That in the Jardin des Plants, for example, is alone worth a visit to Paris, even if one saw nothing else here."

The penchant of the naturalist asserts itself; it may readily be guessed where one, who found more delight in a single flower than in the most glorious painting from the hand of man, employed his spare moments in this capital city of collections.

At the conclusion of his fortnight's stay here, August 25, he writes:

"I have occupied the last week in looking at what is most interesting in this great city, and in procuring specimens of the fonts of type, in which I have been successful, so far as the permission from the Minister of Public Instruction could take me. With the Manchu types I shall be able to get matrices made by means of electrotype, and thus we can print all we wish to in Manchu with the same elegance as the Imprimerie Royale. The font of Japanese does not please me at all, and I think that, if I can compass it, I shall get punches cut for the Katakana, for which only 100, or 80, are necessary. The Imprimerie Royale employs 800 workmen and can print in 36 languages, among which is ancient Egyptian, a new and beautiful font of hieroglyphics having just been cut. . . .

"I wish you would send one of the vocabularies to Stanislas Julien, and when the translation of 'Prémare' is finished, send one to him and to Mr. Bazin; both of these gentlemen will be glad of copies and will, on their part, send us what they publish. I have received so many attentions from M. Bazin that I am really ashamed of being the object of so much trouble and kindness; he has made my visit to Paris all it could be. We leave Paris together for London (D. V.), he having no other object than to see and talk with Milne's teacher, for whom the French govt. have furnished him 900 francs. The collection of books in the Royal Library here is immense, and the Chinese department is exceeding full, there being many works in that language which it would be difficult to procure in China. The great topographical descriptions of each province are all here, as well as many beautifully printed works in both Chinese and Manchu, encyclopedias, large editions of the classics and laws, a huge array of small books, novels, etc., etc., the most of them being bound in morocco, making altogether the finest and handsomest Chinese library in existence —for altho' there may be larger collections in China, there cannot be any so handsome as this. Julien is the conservateur of the Chinese books, and receives nearly as much for taking care of them as for teaching their contents. Bazin is merely a professor, receiving $1,000 salary. He tells me he has about twenty in his class at the commencement of his lectures, and five or six at the end of them. It is singular to me to see these French savans digging with such zeal after the treasures in all languages found in the library, spending their lives in rummaging the records of human learning, while so far as I can see, hardly one of them troubles himself about a religion for his own soul. Of course I know none of them myself besides Bazin and a few of his friends, but the fact of any of the learned men here being a decidedly godly man w^d certainly have been noised abroad and come to my ears. The Imprimerie Royale may almost be said to be at the service of these professors and wise men here; they easily get their translations and works printed there at no expense to themselves, while all the profits from their sale comes to their own pockets. If they had half the trouble to get a book through the press that we have, I am disposed to think that Paris would hardly send forth so many oriental translations. The government here is every thing; the people look too much to its help, its directions, to gain the best results from their own resources."

In London, where he remained twenty days, his concern was almost wholly in missionary affairs; very little appears in his letters about the sights of the place, except in the incidental explanation that the distances were too great and the time too short to enable him to see much of the city. A long and frank interview with Mr. Browne, a secretary of the British and Foreign Bible Society, seems, however, to have given him great satisfaction. It is not easy to realize in these times of rapid communication, how numerous and exasperating must have been the doubts and misunderstandings in missionary matters, resulting from the tardy mail service with the East. Certain puzzling questions in the choice between the many Scripture translations which had already appeared in China, and the terms for God employed in them, threatened somewhat the peaceful relations of several of the societies and their missionaries abroad; and Mr. Williams' statements were instrumental in enlightening the home secretaries on numerous points, as well as in furthering their solution. His friendly reception in England was gratifying in the extreme; long catechizing and many inquiries about what is doing in China is the account he gives of many of his evenings in London, where "they all seemed to have the utmost liberality toward American missionary efforts, and considered themselves as fellow-workers with us."

But the most joyful news which he has to tell his friends relates to that branch of mission work nearest his own heart. "Through Mr. Nye's liberality [he writes], I have been able to procure a font of Manchu type and the matrices, all complete. The matrices are to be cut by Mr. Watts, one of the first type-founders in England, under the superintendence of Mr. Stallybrass, formerly a missionary among the Buriats, in Siberia; this gentleman has an intimate knowledge of Mongolian, the letters of which are much the same as the Manchu. Mr. Borrow, whom you have heard of from his Bible in Spain, is also to have a look at these same type, so that I hope the whole will be arranged completely and we shall be able to add something to our knowledge of Manchu." Correspondence with Herr Beyerhaus, of Berlin, did not prove quite so satisfactory. The famous Chinese font, for which Mr. Williams had so earnestly and often entreated his friends at home to subscribe, had been lately attempted on another scale by this benevolent German printer, but his operations proved to be as yet hardly begun, its maker being unable either to get assistance for the work or, owing to his poverty, to carry it on himself. Even here, however, came a grateful surprise from an unexpected quarter. "From Beyerhaus I received a note recently [Mr. Williams writes from London] stating that the minister of the Prussian Government, in whose department the matter lies, hearing that I wished to get a font of Chinese type, has of his own accord offered the use of the matrices cut by Le Grand in Paris, and belonging now to the gov. Of course I have no reason to avail myself now of this kind offer, as Cole's* workshop is already in China, and I do not like the system of divisible types."

At the close of this month he left Liverpool in a liner for America, arriving in New York October 15th.

TO REV. E. C. BRIDGMAN.

NEW YORK, October 18, 1845.

Within five weeks of a year from the time I left you all in the *Balcarras* I arrived here, where I was glad to learn from your kind note of last May that you and the many friends around you were in good health. I am truly glad to hear that you had about concluded to go back to Canton,† and hope soon to learn that you have been able to procure a house in the city or suburbs large enough to hold the printing-office and school. In

---

* The American missionary Cole had undertaken the completion of Dyer's work, and by 1851 produced small but beautiful fonts in two sizes, which are still used.

† The head-quarters of the China Mission of the American Board had been moved to Hongkong upon the cession of that island to the English; the printing-press was taken from Macao to the newly built Mission house there after Mr. Williams' departure; but the influence of the colony proved detrimental, and the station was abandoned for Canton in 1845.

going up to Canton one of the most important points regarding the choice of a house (for I suppose you are not going back to No. 2 [the Factories]) is to get one as secure from the chance of fire as possible ; for should we be so unfortunate as to lose the small font of Chinese types, it would indeed be disastrous in the extreme. Perhaps I think more of fire now from having lately heard that the Delano's at Macao were burned out last summer, and lost nearly or quite every thing. Mr. Olyphant is also much pleased to learn that the American Missionaries are going away from Hongkong, and here the general opinion is against making that settlement a leading station.

CHAPTER IV.

SOON after reaching New York Mr. Williams succeeded in enlisting the effective aid and sympathy of Hon. Walter Lowrie, the Secretary of the Presbyterian Board of Missions, in his project of obtaining a font of movable Chinese type from Berlin. His own Society was too poor to commence such an undertaking, and some of its officers were inclined to diminish rather than enlarge its printing operations abroad. With their consent and advice, however, Mr. Williams resolved to devote his furlough to the task of raising a sum at least sufficient to encourage and continue Beyerhaus in making the steel punches. His presence and inspiration naturally greatly facilitated the movement inaugurated for this end in the First Church of Utica, among whose members Mrs. Martin's energetic endeavors had already raised some six hundred dollars before his arrival. Finding after a brief visit to Rome, that he could be of no service to his parents there, while the spectacle of his father's infirmity only saddened his stay, he determined to commence at once the preparation of a series of lectures on the social life, history, and institutions of China, which he delivered in Utica and its neighboring towns. Their success was considerable, owing both to his extended and accurate knowledge of the subject and to the general interest which the recent war and opening of the country had excited in the minds of all intelligent persons. Invitations came from many cities to repeat his lectures in churches and public halls The vastly increased facilities for travelling admitted of his carrying on the same course in two or three towns simultaneously, allowing intervals of a few days to elapse between the lectures. Thus he visited in turn most of the important places in New York and Ohio, losing no opportunity of doing what he could to increase the acquaintance of their inhabitants with China. One letter out of many written at this time will serve to show the sensations with which he entered upon this new work.

TO HIS MOTHER.

CLEVELAND, March 3, 1846.

Yours of the 24th found me in usual health and as pleasantly situated among many who take an interest in me and my work as I could wish. I have been many times paid for coming, and hope that the information the people have received, regarding China and the wants of the natives there, will not end in mere curiosity but produce more sympathy in behalf of the moral life of that nation. I do not yet know how much I shall get, nor do I greatly care, for I trust that the money—though an evidence of the real interest felt—is the least of the good obtained. I spoke an hour and a half on Sabbath evening last and described what I could of the operations now going on in evangelizing the Chinese by Romanists and Protestants; 't was a largish audience, say two hundred or more. Last evening I lectured in the big church and to my surprise kept the audience two and a half hours ; all the lectures here have been two hours long and well attended.

I have written to Pittsburgh to see about the prospect of delivering lectures there, and the probability is that I shall go to that city by Monday next, the 9th. I shall not be at Utica for a long time yet, since Dr. Armstrong rather dissuades me from going on to New York, and thinks that the actual net receipts there are not likely to be much if any more than they would be in such places as Cleveland, Utica, etc.; moreover the relative influence in the latter places is far greater than in New York, where one new wave of interest washes with a single sweep upon and over the preceding old one. In such a matter as this I am persuaded that Dr. Armstrong's opinion is worth more than a handful of others who never having been in such a position as his can get no idea of the influence of lectures. It is not well for missionaries to lecture in New York for pay, for there this object of mine will not be distinguishable from that of others who keep the money for themselves, so long as the hearers pay and I receive it. I had rather lecture a dozen times in places and communities like this, than once in a huge city like that.

The profits from these lectures were not great, but the sums added to the "type fund" slowly accumulated until the success of his enterprise was finally assured. Instead of a thousand, it became necessary to raise six or seven thousand dollars* in order to provide the new printing office with the equipment desirable for its Chinese press. More than a hundred of these lectures were delivered from first to last during the years 1845 and '46, and the strain and weariness of this frequent repetition, the physical fatigue of constant travelling, the mental stress which comes from successive efforts to attract the attention and gain the sympathy of untried audiences, can hardly be appreciated except by those who have passed through a like experience. The lectures were seldom written out in full, but spoken from notes, which could be expanded to meet the apparent receptiveness of the listeners. From the limitations of the lecturer's style it

* Of which the Presbyterian Board agreed to furnish half.

may be surmised that they were more instructive than exciting, given with the sober purpose of informing the serious-minded rather than attracting the listless auditor, full to overflowing of carefully gathered facts supported and illustrated by personal observations, always bearing upon the great end of China's advancement by means of the gospel. The material gathered in this way naturally and easily suggested its arrangement into a compendious work on China, which Mr. Williams in 1846 determined to prepare by writing out his lectures. For this purpose he went to New York to the house of his brother, H. Dwight Williams, where with occasional breaks for delivering other lectures he remained until its completion.

TO HIS MOTHER.

NEW YORK, September 15, 1846.

The meeting of the Board at New Haven last week was an unusually pleasant one, if the opinion of those who have attended more of them than I have can be taken as evidence; I for one was very much gratified. I went up on Tuesday and returned on Saturday, and not only saw and heard much which was encouraging, but also had a pleasant visit at Professor Silliman's house, where I stayed by invitation. There were nearly 500 members present and upward of a thousand visitors, which, with the persons belonging to the city itself who attended, made the meetings quite full, though not crowded. There was a discussion on the last day, Friday, upon the subject of polygamy, which brought out a little unpleasant feeling on the part of some who had heard strange reports and mused over them until they had got the idea that mission schools contained people who possessed half a dozen wives and that their pastors upheld them in their harems. I was amused, surprised, and grieved to observe the strange construction and inferences drawn from a single case, and to see how little confidence was reposed in the men who are sent abroad to gather churches—

as if they required explicit directions sent after them as to their guidance of converts who should be admitted into communion. Some people seem to be constitutionally careful about the footsteps of others, lest they slip, and wondrously solicitous for the purity of churches, lest there be some one in them from among the heathen who is not quite up to their mark. I wish that all converts from heathenism were angels as soon as they passed from ignorance to knowledge, from death to life ; but since this is not the case, and will not be the case in this world, we must do the best we can with the materials we have. . . .

You must be somewhat lonely in comparison, now that my good sister is gone and the care of two invalids [his father and her father] falls chiefly upon you. I sometimes wish that I could do my writing where I might see more of you, but this city is much the most convenient for my purpose, since all my books are here.

Oct. 24th.—I keep as busily at my writing as I can; but I am much hindered. I have now a course of lectures at New Haven, and application has been made for one at Bridgeport ; I would, however, that the latter had not been sent me, for I neither want to go nor do I wish to refuse ; I have not time to attend, since every course keeps me the longer away from my field of labor—yet one would willingly impart information where it is asked for, when, too, the doing so will aid the work of missions.

My health is as good as usual, and my occupation affords it constant employment. I am most of the time busy in the house, but I have running enough to keep the circulation up, and hope to get through this winter as well as the last. I have no expectation of going to Oneida Co. until the time of my departure approaches, for my engagements here will keep me, in all probability, until the spring ; after they are done I shall get off in the first ship that presents a good opportuntity. The longer I stay the less people like it, and constantly ask me what I am doing *here ;* I shall feel happier out of their way.

Industrious as he was, and eager as he seemed for the completion of his task, Mr. Williams was still essentially social in tastes and habits. It was not long before his ready information and his ability as a conversationalist, always a distinguishing trait, became known, and he was on terms of intimacy or of friendship with nearly every person in New York City whose acquaintance offered the slightest prospect of an interest in China or the work of foreign missions. By these he was invited to appear before churches, Sunday-schools, scientific boards,* and educational institutions, or in private gatherings, where he showed the art of improving and continuing a friendship once begun without seeming to claim the attention due to long-standing intimacy. This was owing in a great degree, doubtless, to the directness and simplicity of his nature, which was the farthest possible removed from the inclination or capacity of posing before men. To him a friendship was a holy as well as a joyous relation—an impact of heart and mind, the influences of which were for all time; and one whose amusements all tended to self-culture could not fail to inspire in others a certain degree of attachment, though the occasion of meeting may have been merely an evening's diversion.

One of these friendships, begun during an entertainment at his brother's house, ripened on his part into an

---

* Among these he was elected to the American Oriental Society and the American Ethnological Society, both recently formed. Before the latter, which held its weekly meetings at that time in the house of Albert Gallatin, its first President, he read a paper on the "Present Position of the Chinese Empire in Relation to Intercourse and Trade with Other Nations." The famous old statesman and savant was then preparing his last work on the Indians of Northwest America, and acknowledges in his long Introduction thereto his use of Mr. Williams' researches in China. Another officer of this society, Mr. John Russell Bartlett, Secretary, in his "Progress of Ethnology," mentions a similar obligation.

admiration and interest altogether different from any which he had ever before felt. One whose heart and affections were as warm as his required a deeper and closer sympathy than even the most genial amity could supply. After a comparatively brief acquaintance with Miss Sarah Walworth, a niece of the distinguished chancellor of New York, who with her family spent the winters in the city, he found her at home in Plattsburgh, while lecturing there in the spring, and became engaged to her by letter soon after returning.

TO MISS WALWORTH, PLATTSBURGH.

ST. JOHNSBURY, May 29, 1847.

MISS WALWORTH :—It was my purpose when I saw you last Thursday to have requested the favor of corresponding with you, but the presence of company and the hurried leave I was obliged to take to be in time for the boat prevented me, so that in doing so now I do not know but that I am taking an unwelcome liberty. The object of my making such a request would perhaps not be difficult to conjecture, though I cannot say that I have the least reason for supposing that you would receive it with any particular favor. Brought together in the most casual manner, we can have none but the slightest acquaintance, though that has been quite enough to give me a very favorable estimate of your character, and to wish to make a further acquaintance.

In a word, my chief object in proposing a correspondence is to learn whether you are disposed to engage in the good work of missions and are willing to consider any proposal to accompany me. I hope I shall not be deemed abrupt in thus briefly stating the subject to you without further preliminary, for I do not wish to intrude a correspondence on you, and the mere statement is sufficient to lay the whole matter before you. I am quite sure from what I have learned of your general tastes and pursuits that the subject of missions is not a new one to you ; but am at the same time willing to leave the consideration of personally engaging in it at your own decision. I have no new arguments to bring forward in its favor, no objections to state not already well known. I have gathered from others that you are used to engage in works of benevolence, and the work of doing good is the same in kind in China as elsewhere, though varying of course in character.

The climate and salubrity of Canton and its vicinity is equal to most places in Asia, though there are some drawbacks to a pleasant residence there, as well as some peculiar advantages to compensate. For myself I enjoyed uninterrupted health, and so have the majority of foreigners of both sexes who have sojourned there. We are immortal nowhere in this world; we are immortal everywhere till our work is done.

It is not climate, however, which I fear will form the principal point of consideration in your mind. We should be more acquainted, each with the other's disposition and habits, and better know those less apparent traits which require a longer intercourse to be manifest. Here I am willing to leave the case in your hands; a correspondence conducted with Christian frankness will enable us to do something in this important particular.

I trust you will not be so much surprised at this no doubt unexpected note as not to consider it, and have hopes too that you will not say me nay. I should have been glad to have remained longer in Plattsburgh, but having written to gentlemen here that I was coming I could not well delay further. In receiving this you will be the sole recipient of its contents, as in truth you ought to be. I lay my suit entirely in your hands. I would, I think, be willing to return to Plattsburgh from here next week, had I not promised to be in New York the coming week. You perhaps already know that I am carrying a work on China through the press, which will probably be published in September next. I have been engaged the year past in writing it, and am now obliged to return to the city on account of the illustrations which are being engraved.

There are many other points on which I might enlarge, but until I hear from you it does not seem necessary or proper to do so. The missionary work in China has so many branches that you can choose any one : literary labors, education, visiting, or training a few youth in your own house ; all these can be done, and each affords abundant scope for the talents which you can bring to bear upon them. Each of us can assist, encouraged by the assurance that no sincere efforts in such a cause will be in vain, nor any labor be so humble as to be useless. I could fill up a sheet with such views, but I prefer to leave the proposal rather to your own good sense, though hoping, indeed that the conclusion will be favorable, even if you wished first to make such previous inquiries as that same good sense would suggest.

For my part, I can assure you of a sincere desire to do every thing to make you happy, and am sure that the effort will not be unsuccessful.

Her reply has not been preserved, but from the tenor of the correspondence which followed, this brave demand could not have met with entire disfavor. It is hard to imagine how out of a world of women he could have chosen one better fitted to round out and complete his nature, or one possessed of a disposition so harmoniously supplementing his own. She supplied that important and peculiar influence which somehow it seems to be the indispensable part of women to bring into the lives of all superior men. The rich and tender inspiration of her thoroughly womanly qualities strengthened and sweetened his moral life, while her strong sense, active head, and determination to surround his home with the external conditions most agreeable and favorable to his tastes, contributed more than any other human cause to the success of his undertakings.

A few extracts from his letters written to her during this period will illustrate his mode of thinking and living, without unveiling what was revealed for her eye alone. The lectures on China, written out under the title of "The Middle Kingdom," after being refused by nearly every publisher in New York, were at length being printed by the firm of Wiley & Putnam.

TO MISS WALWORTH.

NEW YORK, August 23, 1847.

Time passes quickly with me and I may truly say pleasantly, for I feel that I am not wholly misspending it. I do not think that we are required to deny ourselves the gratification of an approving conscience, and we surely can tell amid all our deviations from rectitude when we do not so wander, but do act up to the light we have. I am not mistaken as to some of the motives which induce me to undertake the publication of a book upon China, and one of them was to increase an interest among Christians in the welfare of that people, and show how well worthy they are of all the evangelizing efforts that could be put forth to save them from disorganization as a government, degradation as a people through the effects of opium, and eternal ruin to their souls. Ignorance is a cause, an explanation, and a motive for indifference to a subject, and to remove this ignorance removes some of the reasons for inaction. Perhaps other motives have mixed with this in a large proportion, but this is formed as a leading reason for commencing it. I am not insensible to the gratification of having afforded instruction to persons of refinement and education, or of adding a work of some value to the literature of the country, and shall do my best to make it worthy of acceptance and repay perusal. However, this, like every other means, is in the hands of God, and he can use it to the advancement of his designs more or less as seemeth him good. It *is* a joy to me to assist in great and good objects, and spend my life to carry out such ends as serve to make the world and me better. The reward comes with the consciousness of doing it for love's sake. . . .

You see, I am the chief subject of my letters, the main argument of my writing; in a degree purposely so. Prevented from enjoying each other's society, we have need to become acquainted most honestly and intimately to the degree we can; and I lay open all my heart to you. Wherefore I make up my letters of myself rather than of news, and only wish I was as good at darkening the description as I am at brightening it; for if I make myself out to be so good the excess of light and excellence will lead to the inference that what requires so much care in delineation and nicety in description, is therefore the less likely to bear examination from behind. I have pride enough to supply a nation, and conceit mixed with it; while pride, to my sorrow, mixes itself with even my religious duties, literary labors, social enjoyment, and daily conduct. I have no measure to gauge its amount or density with that existing in the hearts of others, but am sure I have enough to destroy my soul forever if the blood of Jesus Christ do not wash it all away. If one feature more than another appears desirable in the happiness of heaven, it is that I shall be totally free from pride, both knowing my own qualities and attainments, and as willing to give every one else his due for knowledge, holiness, and humility. About humility there is an inexpressible charm; it is a true, genuine knowledge of one's own proper position in the scale of creation, in the sight of God, angels and men, and an unaffected willingness to take and keep that place; feeling that in the sight of the Most Holy all is originally vile, but not so now if he has implanted any good thing; that in the sight of angels our mental faculties have been debased by sin far below their original strength; that in the sight of men a close regard to the commands of our Heavenly Father will always obtain their better judgment, and that our endeavors to keep his law will teach us greater dependence on him. Humility is like a transparent mantle, through which every other virtue appears, while unseen itself it protects them and adds increased charms to their beauty.

NEW YORK, Sept. 6, 1847.—Your mother arrived late last Saturday night, and although I fully intended to go and see her a moment yesterday, I could not compass it. Firstly, I went to a Sunday School on 6th Avenue, and talked to the children there about an hour; they wanted me on account of the absence of the teachers, it being the first Sabbath after the recess. Then I went to the dedication of the new church in 13th Street, just finished by Mr. Burchard's people; the crowded house made the heat of the day seem hotter still, and most of the audience still more uncomfortable. From thence I returned home and stayed a half hour or more, when I was obliged to start without my dinner for the Tabernacle—spite of the rain—lest I should be late, since I had engaged to talk to a Sunday School there. By the time I had finished doing so I was rather tired, and was glad to rest during the afternoon service, after which I went home with the superintendent, and took tea with him. From his house near Duane Street I walked to Mr. Olyphant's on 20th, and with him had to hasten to the monthly concert, where I spoke another hour. I was not excessively tired when I returned home, but rather more so than I wish to be on the Sabbath, for I think that bodily rest is no small part of the intention of that day; I shall try and avoid the wandering, weary walks of yesterday on another Sunday.

Sept. 13th.—I was busily engaged all last week in preparing a Chinese map, and have made a very fair job of it. The Chinese teacher whom Dr. Cumming brought with him came very opportunely, and is not only willing to assist me, but does his writing better than legibly, even handsomely, in spite of having to write all the characters backward on the stone. This map is made from the one I have now in the engraver's hands, by taking the plate before any lettering was added to it, transferring the drawing to the stone, and there filling up with the Chinese characters. In this way I shall have a neat and accurate map of China in Chinese to give or dispose of to the natives, thereby showing them more of the topography of their own empire than most of them know. These maps will moreover be of use in the mission schools.

Sept. 27th.—I work away at my book pleasantly enough, and hasten its accomplishment with all my power, despite the hinderances of calls and disappointments, which, however, are not very serious. Every page brings me nearer its end and you, and both in the distance seem alike pleasant, while the work itself is agreeable and useful. I am querulous sometimes about the form of a sentence, and hesitate concerning this and that sentiment or expression, but these delay me only a little, and I am satisfied with perspicuity and cohesion. My literary labors have ever been pleasant in their progress, and thus far useful in their result. The "Easy Lessons in Chinese," which I published five years ago, is now nearly out of print, and I should not wonder if on my return I found it expedient to print a new edition. It has proved of value to many a beginner in the long journey of acquiring the Chinese language. I am not careful about the success of the one I am now issuing, rather preferring to let it fare as its merits and demerits shall allow, while all the good it does I shall give to the praise of the Author who allowed me health and ability and friends to bring me where I am.

NEW YORK, Nov. 11, 1847.—I wrote you Monday concerning Dr. Anderson's ideas respecting our sailing during the coming winter, and that he wishes me to come to Boston to have a consultation upon certain points before leaving. In reference to this I proposed two plans: one for me to go as soon as liberated here and spend Thanksgiving with you, see what arrangements were needed, then to Boston, and so return to Plattsburgh to be married, and leave there "for good"; the other, which may suit you better, is to make our preparations now, leave Plattsburgh for a parting visit to Utica, and then returning, leave you at your home, while I go to Boston and back, a chilly journey which you belike would greatly mislike. There is time yet for discussion of this, for my eagerness has far outstripped the case, and more time is absolutely necessary than I had allotted. To-day leaves only four days to complete the whole work yet remaining, which indeed could not be done if the entire book was to fall through in consequence. Some of the MS. is still in my hands, and the index cannot of course be written—not to speak of printing—until the chapters are all in type. I find my manuscript stretches on like a long-standing account of lawyers' fees in a chancery case, and I wish 't were clipped up or else transformed into letters such as I 'd like to send you. I 'd cheerfully forego the laudations of posterity and propinquity both—whatever they together give me for my performance—for the sake of your entertainment. The proofs which came to me last evening were full seventy feet in length, if they should be stretched out, and these I have to read over thrice.

The conclusion is that I must stay here next week. If you are agreed to be married erelong, set any day you please after the 22d, which will allow me time to accept the invitation. The manner of the wedding I prefer to leave with you, to have it by morning, noon, or night, in the house or in the church, before many or before few; I am not over partial to a great wedding, yet as I like to see it made a pleasant occasion in others, so I am willing to reciprocate the compliment. Your relatives will, I imagine, include a good share of the village, while of mine I can expect none, or almost none.

The wedding took place in Plattsburgh on Thanksgiving Day, November 25th. After the ceremony and feast the bride and groom went down Lake Champlain to Whitehall and Saratoga, and thence to carry out pretty accurately the second programme outlined in the last letter.

TO HIS WIFE.

CHARLESTOWN, December 13, 1847.

How many times I've regretted that you did not come with me to Boston, for by not bringing you we have missed making the acquaintance of several excellent friends whom you would have been glad to know. I am now writing from the Navy Yard, Charlestown, where I have been staying since Saturday morning. Yesterday I did as much in the way of talking—preaching as most people would call it—as on previous Sabbaths, and quite to the gratification of one clergyman at Cambridgeport, whose health was so weak as to appreciate the relief very sensibly. I am glad to be employed indeed if of any use in this way.

Dr. and Mrs. Anderson would have been much pleased to see you here, for he particularly wishes to make the acquaintance of every one who goes out in the employ of the Board, besides a more special desire in this case on account of Uncle Ruben. There are many warm friends of missions here, and such people are usually estimable on other accounts too, so that you would have seen the élite of this society.

I am to manage my own departure pretty much as I like and get ready to sail at my own convenience; still I think that we had better go as soon as we can. There is nothing to be gained by delay for the separation must come, and the sooner we are off the easier will be the struggle, inasmuch as it will not be protracted. Now the decision is like a grumbling toothache, which seems likely to be more painful the longer it is let alone. We will therefore get ready soon to go on to Utica, where there is not much to be done except bidding friends farewell—a tedious routine of foretastes of our lot until we bid our native land good-night. Yet we have each other, and will delectate ourselves in this refreshment. Let us keep nothing from each other.

The reception accorded to "The Middle Kingdom" was an indication of the degree of interest in its subject and expectation of usefulness to a community hitherto without any authentic source of information on China. Except Davis' "Chinese" there had not appeared a comprehensive work on that country that deserved to be quoted, while the few books on special topics printed in China were both scarce and unsatisfactory. The author's object, stated in the preface, to attain the "golden mean" betwixt an encyclopedia and a primer, fixes the keynote of his production; a work for reference rather than for recreation was his ideal, and Mr. Williams, who realized his own limits while he kept well within them, was sometimes annoyed by the carelessness or sneers of those who from time to time criticised his solid and sober volumes, as though seriousness on a subject like the Chinese were preposterous. He did his best indeed by this book to put an end to "that peculiar and almost undefinable impression of ridicule," which, he complains, was universally bestowed upon them; "as if they were the apes of Europeans, and their social state, arts, and government the burlesques of the same things in Christendom." The real purpose of the work was "to set them in a fair position by a plain account," giving a rational and satisfactory answer to the question so often asked as to the reason of Chinese singularity in thought and action, and the perpetuity of these modes through many ages. Above and beyond all this, moreover, was the desire—the ruling motive of his entire life—to advance the interest in the cause of evangelizing China, and to increase the sympathy in foreign missionary labor by increasing a knowledge of its field of action. "If that knowledge shall further tend to induce in any one the desire to diffuse among them an acquaintance with the chief source of our own civil and religious liberties, and encourage those now engaged to greater efforts, then will the pains taken in its preparation be increasingly rewarded."

Some reference to his map of China has been made in one of the letters already quoted. This map of the empire, which appeared on a folded sheet with the first volume, had been compiled from the survey of the eighteen provinces made by Jesuit priests under the Emperor Kanghi, from the British Admiralty charts, and from whatever published authorities were accessible. It was a matter of considerable solicitude to the author to present with his book a map which should so far as possible be reliable, a difficult ambition where the greater portion of the territory had never been visited by civilized man; but before long the reward of his care appeared in that most honest of literary compliments, a pirated English edition, and until recently his map of China has been issued in all standard atlases. The Chinese edition was sold only in China.

Like Dr. Johnson he realized that "the place of books in the public estimation is fixed, not by what is written about them but what is written in them," yet it cannot be denied that he felt an honest and natural delight in the commendations which followed the appearance of "The Middle Kingdom." Union College, upon Dr. Nott's suggestion, conferred on him, in the summer of 1848, the honorary degree of LL.D.—a dignity less universal at that day than now, and one which rather chagrined and overwhelmed the recipient, whose modesty would have been better content with less notice. The title was taken more in earnest in China than at home, and came to be generally applied by friends and acquaintances on ordinary as well as on formal occasions during his subsequent career in the East. The personal taste of a victim to a sobriquet being rarely consulted, he accepted the designation as such and judiciously held his peace; but a mild protest was heard when a letter for his wife was addressed to "Mrs. Dr. Williams."

TO MRS. THROOP MARTIN.

NEW YORK, March 14, 1848.

The sale of my book has been such as to afford me much gratification as to its general acceptance. The price is so low, however, that twice as many must be sold to repay the cost of manufacture, let alone any returns for authorship or interest on the outlay. The book does not appear to me to be a dear one, if you consider merely the number of pages, map, and engravings; but perchance many of the purchasers would already rather have their money returned than wade through so many pages. The second edition is now printing, the first having been distributed rather than all sold.

A recital of the incidents connected with the first appearance of "The Middle Kingdom" ought not to close without reference to two gentlemen, both recently deceased, whose kindliness and generosity were instrumental in its publication. To Mr. J. Russell Bartlett's good offices with Wiley & Putnam was due their acceptance of the manuscript after several others had refused to receive it, and from Mr. Gideon Nye came the prompt offer to make good any losses sustained by the publishers, without which substantial guaranty they were unwilling to hazard the experiment. These circumstances regarding a book which commanded a steady if moderate sale for over thirty years, are noteworthy as an indication of the public interest in China at that time.

Mr. and Mrs. Williams left New York in a sailing vessel for Canton, via the Cape of Good Hope, June 1, 1848.

TO HIS BROTHER, REV. W. F. WILLIAMS.

CANTON, February 24, 1849.

Our passage to China of 90 days, over 17,000 miles, was more than usually favorable, and a delay of three or four days in the China seas, by the good hand of God upon us, prevented our experiencing a tyfoon of unusual severity, which might have proved our destruction had we got into its midst. One vessel of 650 tons was sunk at her anchors, and most of the crew in her.

On arriving here (Sept. 1) we found all our friends well. We remained at Hongkong for almost a fortnight before coming up in the ship, and then reached this place after an absence of 46 months, during which I experienced more mercies, privileges, and pleasures than fall to the lot of most people. We found the mission-house in rather an unwashed condition, and moved in towards the end of the month, having remained at Dr. Parker's house for the time being. On the 18th of October a new source of happiness was opened to us both in the birth of a son, whom we have called Walworth, and who is now upwards of four months old, and thus far has enjoyed good health to eat, good lungs to cry, and good spirits to play. It is a new sensation to hear the wailing of one's own child and feel that an immortal spirit has been intrusted to our care to bring up in the fear of God and consecrate to his service. I feel as if this dear boy was more in my keeping than all the Chinese, and that his salvation more depended upon me than upon any other person.

Since January we have got into a new house, which, unlike the old one, does not require a lamp to be lighted night and day in the entrance to guide people up-stairs, but where light and heat and air can enter and ascend. I shall not attempt to describe our hong, but refer you to former descriptions, inasmuch as every one who has been here declares that no idea of a hong containing a dozen houses could be formed. They never would be built anywhere but in China ; our best houses are far inferior to the pleasant dwellings of Beirut and Abeih, with the clear sky and green fields near by.

We have just received our notice of the allowance of our mission for 1849. Three families and two bachelors and three assistants—thirteen in all—are put on $6,000. I have just rented a house at $750, and my allowance is $1,300, or so, whereby I have $550 to subsist on, hire a teacher, support a wife, and such other needs as may come along in the path of life. I am sure I do my part to reduce the debt of $60,000, by being scrimped up so that I can't increase it ; but I trust to the goodness of God to get along, since I have a promise of bread and water being sure. This constant harping on funds and allowances, reductions and contractions, in missionary life and practice, has not the best effect in the world upon a devotion to the great business of evangelizing the nations—yet it has a good effect in raising one's views to the Source of men, means, and mercies, and to feel that there is still a great hope of the world through Him.

The *Repository* engages my time somewhat, and every thing has come upon me since I returned, for no help do I get, or can I get from my fellows. However, I keep on and hope to fag through. Canton is likely to be my residence for many a day, and as we have begun now to preach to regular congregations, in which I take a part, I hope, if I have the health, to do more than I did. Since my arrival the Morrison Education Society has fallen through, the community having suffered the school to run behind in funds to such an extent that we must disband the boys and fall back on our permanent fund till its interest pays up the debt and enables us to resume operations. Mr. Brown has decided to remain in the U. S., and by last accounts hoped to get the charge of a school near Rome, N. Y.

A rescript of the Emperor Taokwang, in reply to Kiying's memorial, had granted a general toleration to the practice of Christianity in China soon after Mr. Williams' departure for America.* On his return to Canton he found regular and open services conducted in Chinese, in which he at once took part, while hopes were high for the speedy evangelization of all the coast towns, and many new missionaries coming to the country. The work of revising Morrison's translation of the Bible had been jointly undertaken by a delegation of the Protestant missionaries in China, Dr. Bridgman being now in Shanghai in order to carry on the version with his coadjutors, and establish a mission station at that port.

* It is not likely, however, that Taokwang's edicts respecting Christianity were ever much regarded by provincial governors in China. The notions of emperor and officials alike were extremely hazy on the subject, and neither was inclined to persecute except in case of political organizations.

This revision of the Scriptures in Chinese brought to the surface a mooted question of suitable words to represent *God* and *Spirit*, which had early been raised among missionaries in China, and has since become memorable as the "Term controversy." A brief notice of this discussion, which enters more or less into the biography of every missionary to China, is necessary in tracing Mr. Williams' career, both from the heartfelt interest which he took in its development and the contribution he made to its literature. His "Controversy on the Chinese Translation of the Words God and Spirit," printed in the *Bibliotheca Sacra*, 1878, furnishes the only succinct account of this matter which has been published in this country, and may be condensed into something like the following statement. The fact that such a controversy has arisen in China alone of all heathen countries, indicates some peculiarity of its people or language, and in the latter lies a partial explanation of the trouble; its origin is also indebted to Chinese pantheistic cosmogony, which being in itself very vague has never led native philosophers to any adequate conception of Deity, as Creator and Source of the universe, nor to the association of definite terms in connection with such fundamental ideas as those in dispute. The difficulty of fitting these conceptions with appropriate words in China early disturbed the Roman Catholic missionaries, who contested the point hotly and vigorously among themselves for almost a century, when the matter was settled for them *ex cathedra* by a Bull from Clement XI., who did not, however, discuss the merits of the case, which had become for Catholics personal rather than religious. Among Protestants the debate has turned chiefly upon the use of *Shangti* or *Shin* for God (Elohim, the Almighty), and *shin* or *ling* for spirit, though many other words have been suggested by way of compromise. The first term is the chief deity of Chinese state worship, as definitely acknowledged as the Greek Zeus or the Scandinavian Odin ; the second, translated both as God and spirit, melts away into meaning every thing and nothing, as soon as we bring it to our more accurate tests. In general, it may be said that those on the first side have endeavored to find the name for deity which will come nearest in the Chinese conception to the true God, and through that name lead them up to Him as the only object of worship, while their opponents have sought for the word for gods (θεόι) in Chinese which includes them all, and can be made most effectual in teaching Chinese idolaters that there is only one God demanding their worship and obedience, and thus overthrowing their polytheism.

Mr. Williams, with most of the American missionaries, was in favor of adopting *Shin* (or *Shên*) for God, translating *ling* as spirit, their argument being that Shangti will never be understood in any other sense than he now is—the active exhibition of the soul of the universe, which no one but the emperor is permitted to worship. " Jupiter and Zeus (he says) were never regarded by the Jews, or Apostles, or Christians, as having been at any time used by anybody as names applied to or designating the true God. When Paul was at Lystra he had the opportunity to preach the being and attributes of God through Jupiter, whose temple and priest were before him, but he called him a *vanity*. And so is Shangti."

Dr. Bridgman's absence in Shanghai threw upon Mr. Williams the sole charge of the *Chinese Repository*, which he now edited alone up to the time of its conclusion. The removal of many of its supporters to other ports or to Europe had so far diminished its circulation that it was now issued at a loss to its publisher; few articles were contributed by its former supporters, and upon the editor came chiefly the burden of filling the monthly numbers —one of which was actually composed from cover to cover by his unaided pen. Beginning with the year 1849 he compiled and printed an "Anglo-Chinese Calendar," a small octavo of 100 to 130 pages, which contained besides much useful official and statistical information, a brief summary of events in China during the previous year, and a list of foreign residents at the open ports. This, like the "Commercial Guide," was an idea taken from John Robert Morrison, whose little "Calendar" was first published at Canton in 1832, but was not continued. From the year 1841 the succession is uninterrupted until the destruction of the factories in 1856, the first eight being compiled by Dr. Bridgman, the last by Mr. Williams, who printed editions of about 300, and sold them at some profit to his press.

TO REV. W. F. WILLIAMS.

CANTON, March 26, 1849.

The principal topic of conversation and importance here at present is the probable result of the reference to Peking about fulfilling the stipulations of the treaty made two years ago as to entering the city gates; the citizens of Canton being determined not to let the barbarians come into their privacy within the walls, if they can help it—which they cannot. The steamers now lie off the factories, ready in case of need, and the people have begun to amuse themselves, and parade the streets by night in uniform and armed with spears, matchlocks, and muskets. Perhaps ten thousand have been enlisted during the past month by the headman of the various neighborhoods of this huge city, ostensibly for the purpose of defending themselves against the myriads of ragged, poverty-struck desperadoes now swarming in the streets and suburbs, yet equally efficacious if the government should direct them against us. I have no idea that the latter will be attempted, for rulers and ruled stand in awe of the steamers and ships lying off the factories, one of which is the *Dolphin*, U. S. brig, just arrived from Singapore. Consequently we are all in a state like that at election times, or worse,—if that be possible—quite unfitted for attending to any thing, and going about among the people at some risk. When I went down to service last Sabbath, about two miles through the streets, I think every tenth shopman uttered a malediction against me, as one of the hated foreigners; *Shat*, "kill him!" or *fankwai*, "foreign devil!" came from every side. But these words are harmless weapons, and I felt little apprehension of any harm. If these men had the personal courage of the Druzes or Kurds, we should stand a chance of getting our blood let much more frequently than we do; as it is we do not feel much afraid of their attacking us, except when they assemble in an overwhelming crowd around two or three whom they are sure they can overpower. Two English officers were killed at Hongkong this month for insulting a female, the incensed villagers rising upon them and spearing them to death. Most readers of the evidence think that a Chinese would have received less mercy at the hands of an English village crowd, had he conducted himself in the same manner, and that his murdered body would not have been deemed worthy of all the notice these men received. We are not very fond of having the just chalice returned to our lips in such matters, but sometimes it is done and the indignation is corresponding.

The discovery of gold in California to such an unlimited extent has thrown our community into the same ferment as elsewhere. The rapid settlement of that region will cause a steady trade between Oregon and China, and tend to induce the Chinese to resort to California in large numbers. The stories we hear are wonderful; the El Dorado seems at last to have been found. I have seen one piece of $375, and many thousands of $ worth have already come here to purchase goods with. It must erelong tend to alter the comparative value of gold with silver and food . . .

June 22d.—If you could see the packed-up way in which we have to live here—crammed as close to each other as jars of sweetmeats in a box of bran, no yard, no out-houses, no trees, no back door even—you would feel as keenly as I do the pleasure of sometimes seeing growing green things. Our residence being a back factory gets no breeze, and is shut off from many other things—lights as well as shades. This summer is not much hotter than usual, that I'm aware of, but it has heated our house to a degree that almost prevents our doing anything, and is especially severe upon poor Sarah who is not accustomed to any thing like this weather. We become quite used to 95° by day and 89° by night. One of my good friends has invited us to Macao for the remainder of the summer, and she and the boy will soon be rejoicing in its fresher air and pleasant walks.

MRS. WELLS WILLIAMS TO MRS. WM. WILLIAMS.

MACAO, July 21, 1849.

I have been now three weeks, staying at the house of Mrs. Wetmore, one of the most charming of my friends here, who treats me in all respects as kindly as a sister. Wells came with me and 'twould have gladdened your heart to see how he enjoyed his holiday; he was like a school-boy on a vacation and not satisfied until he had taken me to see every one of his old haunts and familiar places—living over with me all his past in present enjoyment. So I went with him to the house in which he lived with Mr. and Mrs. Brown, where afterwards was commenced the Morrison School; then to Camoen's cave and Island, climbing all the hills and getting all the views that were to be seen far and wide. It was a genuine delight to have him give himself up so completely to the enjoyment of an entire relaxation from labor and study. His duties have been so absorbing since his return—always hurried, ever with a dozen matters needing immediate attention, and at night often so tired that he could hardly sleep. I am sure that this little jaunt has been of the greatest benefit to him and hope he will be able to repeat it by coming for me when I go back to Canton. As for me I am delighted with Macao, the beautiful scenery, the company, the freedom of going out unmolested upon the shore and hills around; I am sure no one need complain of being condemned to a life here.

TO REV. W. F. WILLIAMS.

MACAO, September 12, 1849.

A most tragical event has thrown a feeling of gloom over the people in this place. Their (Portuguese) Governor, Amaral, was assassinated in open day by six Chinese, who fell upon him as he was riding, pulled him down from his horse, cut off his head and his hand, and escaped. The assassins have not been discovered yet, and I fear are not likely to be just now, for the people in this vicinity are greatly incensed against him for his efforts to revive the declining fortunes of the settlement and infuse more energy into the government and people. One probable cause of the murder is the ill-will excited by his having opened several roads through the island, in doing which he removed a large number of graves, and according to the Chinese belief seriously impaired the good luck of the families whose dead lay there; they treasured up this imagined insult, and their feelings were wound up higher by inflammatory meetings and placards, caused by the forcible removal of the custom house here, and the departure of many large Chinese trading establishments to Canton; this involved great sacrifice and loss to a large crowd of dependants, who most unwillingly left with them. It is supposed that full five thousand persons left Macao within two months of the removal of the custom house, and the villagers round about were wrought to a wonderful pitch of ill-will by their clamor. I am of the opinion that the governor lost his life by the hands of some of these villains, who had previously been hired and bribed by their countrymen. Gov. Seu is generally held guilty of connivance, or at least of sheltering the assassins, but I have no evidence of the truth of such a charge and am doubtful of its probability. The murder had a great effect on Sarah, who passed the unfortunate man not five minutes before his death, she being on her return home as he was riding out. His death has left the colony as headless as is his own trunk, and I think if it were not for three or four ships of war we should see some further fighting steps taken by the Chinese. At present all is quiet, and the Portuguese are putting their forts in a state of defence; they can expect no help from home beyond a governor to take Amaral's place.

I have been seriously deliberating about stopping the *Repository* and turning my attention to a Chinese magazine, trusting that if such a periodical as the *Repository* is really needed another will soon be started. The class of merchants here now take very much less interest in the condition of China than they used to do, and the publication is carried on at a loss—which, as in the case of slaveholding, is another strong argument for its abolition. I like editing a paper of this sort well enough, but I am doubtful of my fitness, and still more of the propriety of spending life in such an indirect means of benefiting the Chinese.

A month later, speaking of the nature of his duties, he says:

"I am busy as editor of the *Repository*. I am getting up and out a Vocabulary, Chinese and English, a Tonic Dictionary, —as Sarah says, to be taken in small doses. I make almanacs, and print the first sheet to-day. I tend babies at intervals; I preach at Dr. Parker's hospital every Sunday morning; I am writing the annual mission letter, while others of the mission are declining it; and lastly, I write more letters than I wish to be obliged to on every subject and for everybody, sell all the bills of the Fuhchau mission, look after all the bundles, letters, boxes, barrels, bales, and business of this and other missions. I tell you I have almost no time to eat, and often get up from dinner to see if a job is printing correctly, for the office is next door to the parlor. Yet I am where God has placed me, and where I try and do his work.

"It is bad for our missionary operations living as we do in such an unsettled political time, and surrounded by people who rail and sneer at us; our progress is slow indeed, discouraging at times, but we feel that this feature is as much a part of the whole face of things as any other, and quite as much under the controlling power of God as the idolatry, the priesthood, or any other obstacle. Our preaching is listened to by few, laughed at by many, and disregarded by the most. Our names are mixed up with the general community of foreigners, nor have they but hardly begun to know us as a body of men desirous of doing good to the people. After all we can do, it is the motive which is more to be looked to than the amount of labor. The succession of political troubles, disasters by sea, the news of death and change at home, the experience of troubles here, combine to produce a sense of instability in living in China which is much like sojourning in an omnibus or canal-packet. One gradually acquires a feeling of I can't tell what unfixedness, the result of abiding in a community so changeable. It should lead us to set all our affections on high, to live loosely to every thing but heaven, and aim to read our title there; but I fear me much it does not have that effect."

TO PROFESSOR JAMES D. DANA.

CANTON, June 22, 1850.

It is so pleasant to get a line from you that I do not mean to have the reason fall on me for not getting another as soon as I can. We both have enough to do, I doubt not, and find little enough time to do it in—for the more we are qualified to do, the faster comes the work to us; indeed I find myself to have exceeded my strength latterly, and that my head is crying out from overstraining. I am cautioned thereby to relieve myself as much as possible, yet I see little prospect, short of the grave, of being relieved. Nor in fact do I desire to be laid on the shelf of *otium*, but rather prefer to have something pressing on hand as long as life lasts.

I am writing in such a furnace—I had almost termed it—that I can hardly put any ideas straight upon paper. The thermometer at 88° is not the true index of this heat, for I am sweltering as if in a steam bath, and the feelings induced by such a constant perspiration are not the most favorable to collectedness of ideas. Then, instead of having a quiet, pleasant room for writing, where only those who have business might come, I am scribbling within ten feet of my printing press which is going all the time, and close to the printers—all of them Chinese and loquacious as ducks—every few minutes asking for proof, copy, or instruction ; then, in runs the nurse with the baby crying at her bent for something to eat or to be attended to, and I have hardly minded them when a visitor is announced, or a note must be answered. Thus my days are spent, now with more, now with less interruption, and (I hope) some useful duties. I am well satisfied with my position, but earnestly desire more purity of motive and singleness of heart in God's service, more love to the Chinese, and more humility. It is much easier loving the souls of the heathen in the abstract in America than it is here in the concrete, encompassed as they are with such dirty bodies, speaking forth their foul language and vile natures, and exhibiting every evidence of their depravity. My printers call for much patience, and I have not so large a supply of this as I thought I had ; they steal my type, my books, my tools, selling them for a mere song, of course, but spoiling a whole font or set of books for the sake of a few pennies. I am soon to be released from my editorial position, for the *Repository* is to cease in a few months, the demand for it by no means recompensing the strain upon its manufactors. The other work in the office has supplied the deficiency for three or four years past ; at present we find that the openings for other work are so great that we cannot spend so much time as the *Repository* demands to make it worthy of its position.

TO REV. W. F WILLIAMS.

CANTON, July 20, 1850.

In missions we are on the whole finding encouraging success. At Amoy six are propounded for admission and six were baptized at Shanghai not long since. The New Testament is finished, and the delegates have been chosen for proceeding with the Old Test.; the term for God has not been determined upon, and in fact a *usus loquendi* must grow up before it will be decided. Out of 60 missionaries in China only 16 are in favor of Shangti, but unluckily in our mission here, two are for each term. The controversy has caused considerable coolness and taken away much labor from proper work. The Englishmen who advocate Shangti, by some singular process of segregation all belong to the Lond. Miss. Soc., and all the Americans on their side to the A.B.C.F.M. At Ningpo and Fuhchau all are in favor of *Shin*, and at Amoy all preach Shangti as God, but here and at Shanghai there is a sad result in the minds of inquiring natives at the discrepancy between the two terms. I think if we had a singular and plural in Chinese the use of *shin* would become general, but the plural idea connected with the word is a great obstacle to teaching monotheism, while Shangti is confounded with a god of that name in heathen mythology ; thus we teach idolatry while we think we are teaching truth. However, I think the God of Truth will enable all inquiring minds to come to the knowledge of it, and the blessed Spirit will himself lead them to the fountain of truth.

Dr. Parker has succeeded to full powers as chargé d' affaires, now that Mr. Davis* has returned home. The continuation of intercourse between the Chinese and English is fast bringing up a cloud of difficulties between them, not so much from overbearing acts on the part of the latter as from the ignorant and irritated pride of the natives leading them to presume greatly on their power, foolishly making and raising difficulties. The poverty induced by the opium trade is pressing harder and harder upon them, and the lower classes are devoting themselves to robbing, piracy, and emigration in order to procure food and work. Altogether the new Emperor has

---

* John W. Davis sent as U. S. Commissioner to China in 1847 to succeed Alex. H. Everett. The notable feature of his term was an interview—the only one by any foreign representative—with Seu, Governor-General and Imperial Commissioner at Canton.

the prospect of a thorny seat, and in his inexperience seems inclined to act Rehoboam's part, discarding the counsel of the old men who stood by his father and taking very stringent measures. In this port there is a very strong effort now being made to reimburse the empty treasury by imposing an extra duty upon tea by means of a system of warehousing, charging a sum to the men who bring it to town of some two cents a pound before they can remove it to the shipper's warehouse. The English authorities at Hongkong have a force quite large enough to bring our silly governor to his senses and make him observe the treaty, but I hardly think they will do that at present.

William Williams died in Utica, June 10, 1850.

TO HIS MOTHER.

MACAO, September 25, 1850.

The tidings of your last note called forth both sorrow and joy, regret and satisfaction; for how c^d one be wholly sorry that such a dear friend had passed from death to life, that affliction, pain, and darkness had given way to ease, joy, and light? But it is impossible to refrain from sadness at losing so near a relative and friend, one whom I can never lose again. To you the vacancy thus made must at first appear very great, and always be more or less recalled by the scenes with which he was so closely connected. My remembrances of him are mixed with his appearance when I first left home and when I last saw him, a sort of blending of manly vigor and animal decrepitude which I have not tried to analyze. He has long been an object of the past to me, and when I heard of his death it was with a more vivid recollection of what he was seventeen years ago than I had had for months. To you I have no need of bringing up any sources of consolation, for few can have them nearer or be more practised in applying to them. God portions his afflictions to us with as much wisdom as love, and we do well to trace both object and manner in all his dealings with us. The little insight we can have here of the purpose of this or that particular providence will by and by be exchanged for fuller knowledge of the whole business of training immortal souls for endless happiness. What a delightful study it will be for us to review the way by which God led us to himself, and how many new sources of humble wonder and adoration will it open. We may therefore well trust for the whole what seems so well done for the little embraced in our knowledge, waiting until we have light granted us by which to read the obscure lessons of His providence. It is gratifying to hear that though father had retired so entirely from society these many years his memory was respected by all, and that so great a number of friends was found about his grave at the last.

TO W. F. WILLIAMS.

CANTON, December 25, 1851.

Our attention is turning just now to supplying the emigrants, leaving here for California in great numbers, with tracts and SS. The total emigration of Chinese in this direction is estimated at already about 10,000, of whom most are from this region ; fully 2,000 have gone to Peru. A plan is now started to supply laborers to complete the railroad across the Isthmus, as it is found that Irishmen cannot stand the climate. Ships are loading with Chinese laborers for Panama and Callao, while emigrants flock to San Francisco at the rate of $60 each for passage money, which they pay themselves. No women have gone, and there is difficulty in overcoming the dislike of the sex to going abroad, and even of their husbands and brothers to taking them. Hundreds of unhappy victims of lust could be bought, and one such cargo was shipped from Hongkong the other day, but such unfortunates do not make emigrant settlers—to say nothing of the horror of such business. It is a singular direction for Chinese settlers to take, but they go wherever money or work is to be had, and are content with a little. It surprises us to hear what a good character they bear in general among the settlers, being more peaceable, quiet, industrious and manageable than almost any others who have gone there. They seldom fight, and gamble in a small quiet way compared with the blacklegs who have resorted there. I hope some good to China may react from the thousands now gone and going off to the universal Yankee Nation.

I have lately brought the *Repository* to a close; as soon as I get the index published, I have some idea of commencing a newspaper in Chinese, or of making something for them of a less serious and religious nature, which will make known facts of a different character. It is not so easy to get the people here to read our books as it is to make the books; I find my confidence in distributing tracts lessening, especially when unaccompanied with oral teaching.

The conclusion of the *Chinese Repository* at the end of its twentieth year is so important an event in the life of Mr. Williams as to deserve a few words. We have seen how the editing and printing of this periodical claimed his attention as soon as he reached Canton, and during every month of his subsequent residence in China its management formed a background of care, a never-ceasing responsibility. "The work was done," says Mr. Williams in his 'Recollections of China,' already quoted, "at the Printing office of which I had charge, without any outside help in the way of funds. The office supported itself by the works it printed, of which the *Repository* was one. The result so far as the *Repository* was concerned, was not encouraging from a pecuniary point of view. During the last seven years of its existence there was an annual deficit of from 300 to 400 dollars; in the last year it had only 300 subscribers at three dollars each, which hardly paid the workmen's wages." A complete set of this periodical, the value of which as a compendium of information and a record of contemporary events is almost inestimable to the student of Chinese affairs, brings to-day from $150 to $200, the price having greatly increased owing to the destruction of the 6,500 volumes remaining in the factories in 1856. In all there were about 21,000 entire volumes struck off, the editions averaging about a thousand copies, all printed on native bamboo paper. An exhaustive Index of Subjects contained in the twenty volumes, with a classified list of the articles, giving also their authors, was the work of Mr. Williams, and covers 168 pages. From this list it appears that he was the author of more than a hundred distinct papers, besides his share in the editorial department of the magazine.

TO PROFESSOR JAMES D. DANA.

CANTON, April 22, 1852.

DEAR JAMES:—Your letter of August 11 came to hand after a passage of 160 days, none the worse, that I could see, for the considerable navigation it had had, and still deserving a reward in kind. It is rather odd, indeed, to compare our letters to and fro now with those which the mail once carried between Troy and New Haven. Then 't was about trilliums, violas and lysimachias, zeolites, spodumeni, and terebratulas, iodides, oxides, and chlorurets,—and as many more hard words as you like to remember; mere playthings and foils for the mind to give itself an idea that it knew something because it could use such. Now we talk of books and babies, work and writing, having passed from the playday of life to the reality, and seeing one after another of those whom we used to look up to pass away to their graves; and now some are beginning to look up to us in the same way. "How changed!" every one readily says of such a place, since such a time, etc., and well it is so. I am not sorry to live in a world of change, and hope that I can find assistance in changing to better and better, until I am where I need have no fear of losing in the race set before me.

I am still at work at my vocabulary of the Canton dialect, and expect to get enough to do out of it for the next twelve months. Dictionary-making is not one of the most enlivening studies a man can pursue, and I am conscious of having a great deal of boggy ground under my feet which I have not properly sounded, and cannot fully measure, in our present limited knowledge of this language. It is somewhat like pounding out specimens in mineralogy to puzzle out the meaning of Chinese characters from native dictionaries; the fraction of error which enters into the definition of a vast number of the characters, arising from the difference in habits, ideas, and knowledge between the Chinese and ourselves, renders Chinese lexicography tedious and unsatisfactory. When one has the whole language packed away in a small compass, as Genesius had Hebrew; or when there is no literature at all, as among the Indians and Africans, I sometimes think 't would be easier work than with this ancient speech chipped off the Tower of Babel and its enormous bibliography. However, toil must accompany every labor in this world, and I am sure you know what toil is. Since I have done with editing the *Repository* I have not that driving whip behind me I had last year,—that exhausting care as to what Maga should eat and drink and clothe herself withal. I have an Index in hand to add to your set erelong.

TO REV. W. F. WILLIAMS.

CANTON, June 21, 1852.

The worthy secretaries in Boston have nearly concluded to bring my printing-office to a conclusion and get all our printing done by other offices at such rates as we can arrange by the job. Dr. Anderson seems disposed to subordinate and surcease all printing-offices, schools, and hospitals, and turn all the energies of the missions hereabouts into preaching. We are now engaged in a long correspondence (which is likely to be longer before it is ended), and as a preliminary I am urged again, as I was in the United States, to be ordained. Nothing has yet been decided, and probably will not be for months. Amid such a valley of dry bones as China, subsidiary means, like schools and hospitals, in which to teach and practice the principles of Christianity, are worthy of not a little care. Dr. Parker's hospital still goes on, supported by the charity of foreigners, and the Gospel is constantly made known there;

so also at other hospitals. I will not deny that too much stress and time may be given to these departments, but it is difficult to tell beforehand what will prove the most promising path. Blessed is the work of doing good in any line; all finally run into the same Sea of Glass where its earthly agents will one day be so happy in casting their crowns of glory before Jesus, that they will quite forget the discussions as to whose rill was straightest, and deepest, and had the purest water. My vocation seems to be rather hereditary, and I think I should be dissatisfied if I had no printing-office to look after, though belike I am not now well able to judge. We get along pretty well in our mission, and are learning more about the rafters in each others' upper stories, so that we do not knock our heads so often against them.

A large fleet of United States ships of war is here at present, and Com. Perry is soon to arrive with three more, making, in all, three steamers and four sloops, to visit Japan and tell the Siogoun that he must treat our whalers more civilly. If he will not "reverently hear and tremblingly obey" (as runs the jargon of oriental courts), I suppose some long nines are to drop their ferro-cyanic pills into his ears, just as he once sent some hundreds of the same at us in the ship *Morrison.* Doubtless Japan must yield up her seclusion and receive her fellow-men; and I hope this visit of her cis-Pacific neighbor will be instrumental in quietly furthering this end. I am not aware what particular points are to be insisted upon by Perry, and so am not able to state what views I ought to take of such an expedition. . . .

The children are in excellent health just now; we have about a dozen of little folk in the foreign community, so that they are not without playmates. My knowledge of Chinese serves as no small check on the servants, who, perhaps, do not venture to act lies to them as much as they otherwise would, knowing that these infants will tell every thing they learn. The Chinese in the houses of foreigners have great desire to learn English; ours talk half of each language to the children, all English to their mistress, and all Chinese to me. Walworth's aptness in translating from one tongue to the other is a gift I often wish I had. The other night the adobie gate fell down, leaving a wide opening in the garden wall which could not be securely fastened until the next day ; and he was telling his mother that the gate had "fallen open and the steal-man would get in night-time," these being the Chinese terms and idiom almost exactly.

Mr. Williams' second child, Katherine, was born May 19, 1850, and a week after the date of this letter his family was further increased by another son, Olyphant, named in grateful recognition of his friend.

CHAPTER V.

THE command of the expedition from the United States to Japan, sent out in 1851, was first intrusted to Commodore Aulick, who arrived in China in the summer of that year, but was recalled soon afterwards, and the position given to Commodore Perry. The change was in every way a fortunate one; it is improbable that the service contained any one better fitted by experience or natural qualities to carry such a delicate and peculiar business as this to a successful termination. Perry was vigorous, acute, tolerant, straightforward; and long and varied experience in command on land and on sea had taught him all the essential lessons of conduct and control in combat or negotiation. His apparently intuitive perception of the measure of patience and dignity needed in combination with severity and show of force when dealing with Oriental magnates has probably, thus far, never been equalled by foreign diplomatists in Asia— though approached in some degree by the Scotchman, Lord Elgin. It is a gratification and an honor to all Americans that the name and career of Matthew Calbraith Perry, his victories in peace and war, his success in diplomacy, his initiative and reforms in the navy, should at length have received the due reward of an appreciative biographer,* whose recently published account

---

* Rev. Wm. Elliot Griffis, D.D., Boston, 1887.

of his eventful life renders any detailed notice unnecessary in this place.

The motives which prompted a peaceful expedition, with a force sufficient to command respect, to a country under so fanciful a condition of isolation as Japan forty years ago, are not far to seek. With the exception of a few Dutch merchants, who persevered in an unprofitable trade at Nagasaki, under conditions more humiliating than those of the Canton factories, no foreigner had been allowed to land in that country for more than two centuries. There was a belief generally entertained among American naval officers and others, whose attention had been aroused, that a few well-armed vessels might, by a spirited policy and some display of strength, secure an audience with the Shogun, or temporal ruler of Japan, and persuade or frighten the government into admitting foreigners, before the friction and ignominy of his exclusive pretensions should force a war, as had happened in the similar case of China. Other inducements offered. The increase of whalers from New England in Japanese waters brought numbers of shipwrecks upon her coasts, and many Japanese sailors had been picked up and returned since the attempt of the *Morrison* in 1837. Upon the United States government, therefore, fell the natural duty of protesting against the imprisonment and abuse of mariners cast upon the coasts of Japan, and demanding some guarantees for the future.

With Perry's appointment the East India squadron was strengthened by the addition of some of the most powerful vessels in the navy, twelve ships and steamers being promised him for the expedition, though this number was never got together in one place. He reached Hongkong on the 6th of April, 1853, and immediately after his arrival made inquiries for Mr. Williams, whose knowledge of Japanese had suggested his name as interpreter before the Commodore sailed from America. How the missionary left his press for this unusual service is related in his journal, from which his entire connection with the expedition is briefly traced in the following pages. He seems to have yielded to the solicitations of Com. Perry, backed by many foreign residents in China, with extreme reluctance and a profound distrust of his ability to perform the duties involved in such an office. A letter from Mrs. Williams, written soon after his departure, is significant, and declares that—

"Wells went with Com. Perry rather against his own (and much against *my*) will, in consequence of leaving his office of Chinese printers in unexperienced hands, and feeling his own want of preparation for such a position. His reputation as a Japanese scholar is based upon the slight ground of his having studied that language ten years ago, under a sailor teacher!— nor has he since that time had the opportunity to practice a word of it. You may imagine his chances for success with such a meagre capital to begin with, and in the event of failure no allowance, of course, will be made for any want of knowledge on his part. However, the Commodore seems to have based his plans upon his accompanying him, and my husband is not disposed to do any thing which may thwart or disarrange them upon the very threshold of the enterprise; so he goes disposed to do what he can for the furtherance of an endeavor that *may* open a country of many millions of heathen to Christian influences."

It was, however, a decision which he had afterwards no cause to regret. The journal begins as follows:

"On the 9th of April, 1853, I received a request from Commodore Perry to accompany him to Japan as interpreter, adding that he wished to have me ready by the 21st, his day of sailing. Upon his reaching Canton I had an interview with him, and learned that he had made no application to the Secretaries of the Board at Boston respecting assistance of this sort, nor had he informed them of his intention; this he said had indeed never occurred to him, for he had repeatedly heard in the U. S. that I wished to join the expedition and would be ready to leave on his arrival in China. Dr. Bridgman was with me at this interview, and we spoke of various topics connected with the enterprise taken in hand to improve the intercourse with Japan, from which we inferred that the visit proposed for this year was intended chiefly to ascertain the temper of the Japanese in respect to the propositions which would be submitted to them; at any rate, no hostilities were determined on, except indeed to repel an attack or actual aggression. The Commodore added that he had refused to employ von Siebold as interpreter, because he wished the place for me,—doubtless a compliment to me, but not wise in him, so far as obtaining efficient intercourse with the Japanese goes.

"In conclusion, I told him that unless I could get some person to take charge of my printing-office I could not possibly leave Canton. At the next meeting of the mission it was concluded that Mr. Bonney should leave his station at New Town and come up to manage the press. The next day (21st) I told Commodore Perry that I would go with him, but could not be ready to leave until the 5th or 10th of May; I stipulated, too, that I should not be called upon to work on the Sabbath, and that I should have comfortable accommodations on board ship. Moreover I told the Commodore that I had never learned much more Japanese than was necessary to speak with ignorant sailors who were unable to read even their own books, and that practice in even this imperfect medium had been suspended for nearly nine years; he must not therefore expect great proficiency in me, but I would do the best I could. I am not yet sure that I have been rightly persuaded to enter thus ill prepared upon the duties of this position. It is very strange how attention seems to have been directed to me as the interlocutor and interpreter for this expedition, not only from the people hereabouts, but from the United States."

He left Macao in the *Saratoga*, which had been detailed to wait for him there, by the 12th May, on the run to Lewchew. The weather was stormy and his old enemy sea-sickness rendered the passage a trying one.

"Such motion disorders one; old Sieh, my Chinese writer, and I have been lying abed, weak and heady most of the last fortnight; he feels, besides, a great weakness from the disuse of his opium. I suppose I shall be comforted for all the discomfort of this tossing, queasy, and confined life on board ship by being told 't'will do you good,'—I shall be pleased to find that it does me no hurt."

The *Saratoga* found the squadron in the harbor of Napha-kiang (or Napa), the chief town of Great Lewchew, and Mr. Williams was soon transferred to the flagship *Susquehannah*, where he found permanent quarters. Cards from the chief man, or regent, were soon sent on board and a visit received from the islanders.

"It was told them that the Americans entertained most amicable feelings towards Lewchew, and that the present visit was to open further intercourse. Refreshments were handed round and the Regent's servants brought pipes, one of which the Commodore took from his hands. He seemed half stupefied at times (but occasionally spoke excitedly to his attendant and the interpreter) being probably amazed at his novel position. Upon a motion of the guests to rise, Perry observed that he should be ready to return this visit on the 6th prox. at Shui, the capital, and thank the king in person for his civilities. With some consternation they at once began to offer excuses, that it was far, that the king was sick, that he was a mere child, that this call was only a form and the presents contemptible and beneath notice. It was stated, however, that propriety required him (Perry) to return the visit, and he should not fail in his duty. The decorum of these islanders on board and their subdued way of looking about, was almost comically earnest, but it did them credit. Conversation with them on general topics was very slow and almost impracticable, as much from their apparent anxiety as from the tedious method of written communication by means of the Chinese character which we both could understand but pronounced in an utterly different manner. The party seemed in a measure to enjoy their visit, but such a melancholy set of faces, fixed, grave, and sad, as though going to execution, the *Susquehannah* probably never saw before.

" Lewchew is apparently a dependency of the Japanese prince of Satzuma, rather than subject to Japan ; that prince probably monopolizes the trade and manages the foreign relations and policy of the islands, allowing a voyage of homage each year to Fuhchau in order to keep up a profitable trade and a shadow of independence among the natives. The power is wielded by the gentry, whom long usage has formed into a caste, and these sway the timid, defenceless people by a system of espionage which spreads distrust and mutual fear over and through the entire community. The gentry maintain the spies and are the depositories of all learning, education, and office, doing nothing to elevate or improve their serfs. Apparently their sway is a mild one for no swords are seen in the hands of soldiers or whips among the guards ; resistance has probably long since ceased and a motion of a fan or a wink is as effectual as a blow.

" June 6th.—Our visit of ceremony was performed to-day at the capital, in spite of the continued protestations and objections of the authorities. Nothing could have been prettier than the long procession,—band, marines, light artillery, officers on horse and in sedans,—winding up the narrow valley road to the citadel. I will not describe the feast and ceremony of presentation, which the official reports will, in time, give fully ; we were properly, though not cordially, received, and the Commodore is satisfied at having carried his point.

Two other disputed demands have also been yielded us, a house on shore to serve as a hospital, depôt, and general headquarters, and acceptance of pay for supplies, about which they have been very stubborn. The poor officials are unquestionably afraid of some unseen power, to which the swarms of spies report all their actions, and this blocks their more natural impulse towards making friends with us and taking advantage of the great profit arising from the presence of so many strangers. I cannot forget or accustom myself to the curious impression produced by the crowds which always encircle us upon our walks through the town, or about the neighboring country. Men, women, and children run before in hundreds and follow in thousands, yielding the way wherever we turn, yet seldom touching us, and never speaking above a whisper, or making a footfall that can be heard. 'T is like going with Dante through the flitting throngs of hell,—purgatory, rather, for there is not much misery seen. Peaceable, noiseless, agile, preternaturally serious, but not unfriendly, they are, nevertheless, most animated and curious, as though taking in with every sense the opportunity, which may never occur to them again, of seeing the foreigners. As we push away to the ships in boats, they line the coral beach, noiseless and now motionless, wondering to the last, and presenting to our view a base line of bare and dusky shins, a middle stratum of blue rags, and a crust of bare heads, each adorned with two copper pins glancing in the sun, every man riveted to the spot so long as a boat remains to be seen.

"June 11th, at sea.—We are on our way, with the *Saratoga* in tow, to the Bonin Islands, there being now not much of an official nature to do with the Lewchewans, but every thing in showing them the equitable and firmly just conduct proper in our dealings with them, letting them see that it is their own interest to treat us with courtesy. The other vessels remain to do this, having, among other things, landed some fine cattle and sheep to present to the natives after they learn how to care for them. All our officers and men are ordered to be scrupulously careful in treatment of the natives or their property, and thus far the results of this policy are as favorable as I expected them to be; the authorities will, I hope, refrain from their subterfuges when we show that we mean what we say.

"To-day the poor old teacher, Sieh, was committed to the sea. He did not recruit at all after reaching Napa, and though every care has been taken of him he has never recovered his spirits or appetite. He had brought along all his opium apparatus, though he constantly asserted that he had none of the drug with him; I would not let him smoke, but he took it in some pellets, which he called 'nourishing-life pills,' and swallowed in large doses. He presented a sad spectacle of ghastly emaciation, mumbling, talking, or moaning, now about home and now about money. I told him a week ago that he probably would not recover, and tried to direct his attention to the Saviour, of whose salvation he was not ignorant; but he paid little heed to it all, and died with no sense of his sinfulness. He was bound up in his mat as he lay, and with all his pills, pot of opium, and a lot of cakes, and beloved pipe, was sewed in canvas and put overboard. I never saw the death of an opium-smoker before, and had no idea that the use of this drug so enfeebled the nervous system and rendered the powers of mind so weak, or the whole man so foolish. He was a shocking sight, a melancholy ruin."

Arrived at Port Lloyd, the only settlement on the largest of the Bonin group, parties were sent from both vessels to explore the islands. The occasion found in Mr. Williams so eager an amateur in arranging and classifying the minerals and flora brought on board, that the Commodore exclaimed delightedly: "Why, our interpreter is as good an interpreter of nature as he is of the people of these regions!" The lack of a professional botanist and geologist connected with the expedition lessened its contributions to science in these branches, but Mr. Williams' unabated love of nature supplied every moment which he could spare from his duties with delightful and congenial occupation, and in the end the flagship returned with very creditable collections. His journal of the five days' visit to the Bonins is almost entirely taken up with notes and observations upon its natural history, many of which appear in the official report of the expedition. A single extract will serve for sample:

"Near Mr. Savory's house the water is shallow, and the bottom covered with fine sand, washed down from several small rills hereabouts, and allowed to spread itself over this secluded bight without being carried off by the tide; the drift in some of these rills shows that at times violent torrents roll along their beds. The net in this bay brought up large quantities of mullet and a species of silver perch, which finds its food in this silt. Bits of dead coral are scattered about here, doubtless mixed too with remains of fish, land crabs, tropical and temperate vegetables, and trap rock, all washed into the basin. Now, if this patch should be raised up as sandstone by some volcanic force, what a miscellaneous assortment of relics would be found imbedded in it as petrifactions—surely enough to puzzle the most acute. Yet we can see how natural is the process by which such heterogeneous constituents have been brought together in this spot, while in other spots of the harbor there appears nothing but coral covering the bottom in all but the deepest holes. After such an illustration it is not hard to understand the manner in which the older rocks have been formed.

"The various things found in the trap rock of this island seem to have been deposited in the most irregular fashion, for in one place we have views of ironstone, in another of quartz in different forms of chalcedony, obsidian, greenstone, etc., in a third, a bed of iron pyrites, then sulphur without the iron, and discoloring and decomposing the rock, and again a fine-grained isomorphic, half-crystallized basalt, approaching the columnar form. Most of the rivulets are sulphurous, some of them unpleasantly so. Is the tropical type of the flora here (lat. 27°) due to the heat of these rocks being increased by their proximity to the internal fires which crop out at Volcano Island north of them? It seems difficult to account for tropical vegetation in the latitude of Chehkiang province."

Upon his return to Lewchew, Commodore Perry learned that the regent who had entertained him in the palace at Shui had been deposed and disappeared, not improbably, as was afterwards discovered, in consequence of this forced act of hospitality. His successor, a man of hardly less taciturn demeanor, was appropriately fêted on board the flagship, and in a subsequent interview with him it was agreed that a vessel should remain at Napa, and that the building given up to the Americans might continue in their hands while the squadron was absent.

Anchor was weighed and they left for Japan on July 2d. An extract from Mr. Williams' journal upon the passage is given, both as characteristic of his feelings at this moment, and as having an interest of its own in bearing upon certain objects of the expedition. His estimate of the Commodore was greatly raised before the end of their connection.

"July 4th.—To-day has been a holiday, and a salute was fired at noon from all the ships. The outburst of patriotism does well enough to announce to these remote waters the coming of the universal Yankee nation to disturb their apathy and long ignorance, and I hope that nothing worse will come of our visit hitherwards than firing salutes and making a noise. I pray the Governor of Nations to so prepare the hearts and allay the fears of the people we are visiting, that this mission to them shall be as peaceable as is the tenor of President Fillmore's letter to the Emperor, and that their sovereign and his advisers may be led to entertain these proposals favorably. I am sure that the Japanese policy of seclusion is not in accordance with God's plan of bringing the nations of the earth to a knowledge of His truth, and, until it is broken up, His purposes of mercy will be impeded—for His plan is made known to us, and we have no knowledge of any other. To immortal glory at His right hand the Japanese can have no entrance so long as they are idolaters ; if they have known Christianity only through the medium of Romanism, and have never been given the means of studying the law of God for themselves, regarding this new-fangled doctrine as only a cover for political schemes, it is to be lamented, but seems to me to present no good reason why the nation should be still left in ignorance and seclusion. As to the real views of the United States Government or the plans of Commodore Perry, I have less confidence since I have seen more of his character ; the previous experience of victory in Mexico may strengthen his determination to drive by force matters which can be attained only by long and patient treating. Let us hope, however, for the best till we see the worst, trusting much to the over-rule of God to make the wrath, the ambition, the pride of man to praise Him and advance His glory. It is a matter of rejoicing to know that He *does* rule the affairs of all nations, and this rule will as surely be exhibited here as it has been elsewhere."

In the sense of these constantly expressed convictions he writes to his brother describing the first visit of the expedition to Japan.

TO REV. W. F. WILLIAMS.

U. S. Str. *Susquehanna*, YEDO BAY, July 16. 1853.

We reached this bay a week ago last evening, having hitherto had only official intercouse, and this not very frequently. As soon as we had anchored the authorities of Uraga came off to us with a dozen boats full of people the beginning of the usual guard, I suppose, to surround the ships, but after considerable parleying we allowed only two or three officials to board us. This sort of usage, and the utter refusal to let them board the other ships was new to them ; and when we declined to tell the dignitary who came up, our size, or armament, or purpose, or any of the particulars he usually learned from vessels, and further ordered him to keep all boats away from guarding any ship lest trouble should arise, he was in a query as to what manner of people we were. We would have nothing to do with him on important matters, and on our asking him to go ashore to get a superior officer to receive a letter to be forwarded to Yedo, he departed in a huff and some fear too. There were several well-manned boats pulling around the four ships, the boatmen in which were large brawny fellows, within a hairsbreadth of being stark naked, and all making a huge clamor. The other vessels were instructed not to receive anybody on board, and none but these few dignitaries had the privilege of coming on the flagship. Our orders were obeyed, rather to our surprise, from what we had heard of the treatment of former vessels here, and by sunset not a native boat was near our fleet. I can hardly imagine any cause so likely to have produced this great change in their conduct as the sight of our big steamers with their 68-lb guns, coupled with our express command to keep away from us, if they intended to guard us as prisoners. I suspect the authorities at Uraga were amazed at the apparition ; and four rockets sent up soon after we anchored doubtless apprised the Emperor at Yedo of our arrival, which would be futher illustrated by the despatches of these officers, and intimated audibly, perhaps by our evening gun.

Next morning the highest officer at Uraga came off to inquire further respecting our mission, advising us that we were breaking their laws by coming here instead of going to Nagasaki, and exalting the strictness of Japanese laws ; whereunto we told him that his high and puissant mightiness the Cæzar of America had sent a high officer with a letter to the emperor of Japan, and that the laws of the American realm were stricter than those of any other, and must be obeyed to the letter, adding that this mission was peaceful and neighborly and hoping it would be so received. The letters were shown him, and he was requested to take a package to forward to Yedo, in which were copies and translations of these letters from our august sovereign. We were fully up to him in all these adjuncts of glorification, and when he saw the beautiful boxes (containing the President's letter) he realized, I suppose, that it was no child's play now; he asked why so many ships came to bring so small a cargo as these two boxes, and when he was told, "Out of respect to the Emperor," his countenance indicated doubt in no doubtful manner. He was not allowed to see the Commodore, but every minute or two Perry would send for one or another present to give some new order, or to learn how the interview went on. We managed to make an impression. The meeting ended by their promising to make full representation at Yedo, and our agreeing not to go ashore. The coast line in full view looked so pleasant and inviting from its verdure and cultivated slopes, its alternating towns, trees, fields, and woodsides, that we considered our side of the engagement as involving as much denial and sacrifice as theirs. Much surprise must have been felt at our refusal to receive supplies until our letter was taken, and the threat to molest every boat which was set to guard the ships, or which interfered with our boats when out on the bay, showed them that we were in earnest and not to be trifled with. The communications were carried on in Dutch, one of the Japanese from Nagasaki having probably been stationed at Uraga to await the arrival of the expedition, and his Dutch was far better than my Japanese. Indeed I found that I had forgotten most of the easy habit of forming sentences, and a disuse of eight years had made me very misty in a language of which I had never more than a smattering, and that obtained altogether with common sailors. It was a relief to me, under the circumstances, to learn that full communication could be carried on in Dutch, but I had more than expected we should find some Japanese who could speak it well.

At last firmly maintaining the single point with which we had set out, that we had a letter from the U. S. President, to be delivered through a high envoy to an equally high envoy of the Emperor of Japan, our object was accomplished, and on the 14th of July, the meeting was held near our anchorage at a fishing village called Gorihama. Here Commodore Perry met the Prince of Idzu and the Prince of Iwami, dressed in their full robes of ceremony, and delivered the letter of President Fillmore and his own credentials in two beautiful boxes, for which they gave a receipt. There were about 400 foreigners landed from the ships, all of them armed with loaded guns or pistols, or swords; of these about 50 were officers, as many musicians, 112 marines, and the rest sailors. In the Japanese side there may have been 1500 troops, 50 officials, and perhaps 3500 spectators, all of whom maintained the utmost propriety, and kept the most entire order. It was the meeting of the East and West, the circling of the world's intercourse, the beginning of American interference in Asia, the putting the key in the door of Japanese seclusion, the violation of the sanctity of Japanese soil, and, to me alone, a full revenge for the unprovoked firing on the defenseless *Morrison*, which took place not over half a mile fom this spot, sixteen years before. The day was not very hot, and every movement went off admirably under the direction of Captain Buchanan, who was the first American to land in Japan with the consent of the authorities.

At the meeting nothing was done except giving over the boxes, no refreshments even being offered us; we had previously agreed not to discuss the points in the letters, therefore it was a brief interview, and apparently not a pleasant one to the high Japanese officials, who sat perched on a couple of camp-stools as demurely as though doing penance. Their dresses were gay and rather grotesque, not showing much taste, and very far from making as good an impression on the beholder as the long robes of the Chinese. The bare legs and woollen socks with a thumb-toe division contrasted oddly with the brocade mantilla on the shoulders and the two swords. To my notion the Chinese and Egyptian official robes are the most elegant and showy of any nation. The Japanese always squat, and their dress is arranged to produce its best effect when the wearer hides his feet under his legs. The two long swords are mightily in the way when sitting in a chair, but arrange themselves if their owner squats. It is curious to see a group of Japanese take to their haunches so naturally, and remain for hours in a position which would make me giddy.

Compared with the Chinese the Japanese impress one as a people of more mind and energy, but I doubt if they have more comforts, and am pretty certain they have not so much freedom of action, and are not so industrious. Perhaps they have better and more elevating elements of character, and may by and by take a higher rank than the Chinese when both come to understand their relations with other countries.

Before and after the meeting at Gorihama boats were sent out to survey the fine Bay of Yedo, and we moved about in the ships wherever we pleased, on one occasion going within twelve miles of Yedo, which is about fifty or sixty miles from the outer capes. We could not see the city, for it lies in a plain at the N. W. corner, but we saw the long row of masts of the junks anchored at Shinagawa, its port. Our vessels were all too big, and it was perhaps unsafe to send surveying boats alone so near as to plainly examine the city. The two war steamers, the *Susquehanna* and *Mississippi* are each of them nearly 2500 tons, drawing 18 or 20 ft. of water, and it was best to run no risks. The probability is that large vessels can run nearly or quite up to Yedo, at least near enough to be seen by the people, and it will not be difficult to ascertain this at some future time. Perry told the officials he would come next year with a larger force to get their answer to the points mentioned, which are good treatment for all Americans visiting or wrecked on the shores of Japan, a port at which to get coal for our steamers and provisions for the vessels coming after coal. These are our ostensible reasons for going to this great outlay and sending this powerful squadron to the Japanese waters; the real reasons are glorification of the Yankee nation, and food for praising ourselves. Behind them and through them lie God's purposes of making known the Gospel to all nations, and bringing its messages and responsibility to this people, which has had only a sad travesty of the truth as it is in Christ Jesus. I have a full conviction that the seclusion policy of the nations of Eastern Asia is not according to God's plan of mercy to these peoples, and their government must change them through fear or force, that the people may be free. Corea and China, Lewchew and Japan, must acknowledge the only living and true God, and their walls of seclusion must be removed by us, perhaps, whose towns on the Western Pacific now begin to send their ships out to the opposite shores.

The Bay of Yedo is one of the finest imaginable, extending nearly a hundred miles on the eastern shore from N. to S., and perhaps seventy on the western side (that on which we remained), everywhere furnishing good anchorage. The shores are bold, rising nearly behind the water in most places, in others affording a little level land for the accommodation of villages and patches of fields, but nowhere that we saw sloping enough for easy tillage. The peak of Mt. Fusi rose in the distance about twenty miles off, upwards of 13,000 ft. high; and there were others of a respectable (6000 or 8000 ft.) altitude; generally, however, the country seemed to be level, and all parts looked green and inviting to us who were walking the planks. If the squadron visits these waters next year these banks and fields may perhaps be explored—I hope not by hostile hands.

In returning from this brief preliminary visit to Japan, the squadron touched again at Napa, and, during a few days' stay there, the Commodore, through Mr. Williams as negotiator, succeeded in persuading the authorities to allow the free sale of their wares to the Americans. This was brought about by establishing a bazaar stocked with all manner of native goods; the promise to abandon, in future, the odious system of shadowing the foreigners with spies was another tardy but unmistakable sign of a free and profitable intercourse which the policy of this expedition had succeeded in inaugurating among the suspicious islanders.

Mr. Williams reached his family in Macao by the 7th of August, and, a week later, had resumed the management of the printing-office and his labors upon the "Tonic Dictionary."

Once more at work in Canton, the tide of his busy life flowed again in its usual channels, immersing his thoughts and attention so completely that he declares in a note: "I'm as humdrum and commonplace now as though there were no Japan expedition or incompetent interpreter to recall his part in it." It was the good fortune of a practical temperament, as well as his habit of self-command, that enabled him to throw off the work just accomplished and enter upon a new undertaking with less of the friction of pre-occupation or self-interest than frets the nature of most men. No daydreams of a more brilliant career, where his experience and knowledge of the East gave him reasonable promise of worldly eminence, tempted him from mission work; his spirits, on the contrary, were brighter and his life happier when the arrival of the fleet in Hongkong brought his contract with the Commodore to an end, and he was able to resume his place by the press and in the chapel; nor did he look with much favor upon the suggestion of his renewing the connection with the expedition in the spring.

Commodore Perry had no sooner reached winter quarters in Macao than he was besought by the American merchants and other residents to dispose his vessels in the open ports for the better protection of their lives and property from the Tai-ping rebels. This movement had grown from a rising of peasants and mountaineers in the province of Kwangsi, in 1850, to an enormous insurrection of ungovernable fury and indiscriminate slaughter, which threatened the existence of the empire. Of the leader of this remarkable civil war enough has probably been written to make any account of his life here unnecessary. His conversion to Christianity, or to a few of its doctrines, was due to his chance reading of some of Leang Afah's tracts, and the religious and puritanical aspects of his revolt against the government were pronounced enough to attract attention and raise the fondest hopes of Protestant missionaries for the immediate subversion of paganism and the conversion of all China. It was during the absence of Perry's expedition that the insurgents had advanced across the country from the south to the Yangtsz' River and taken Nanking, the second city in the empire, thus coming for the first time within reach of foreigners. No time was lost, as may be imagined, in visiting Nanking, where they had established their capital, and investigating the causes and features of their extraordinary success. The Tai-pings, it was found, had accepted and proclaimed Gutzlaff's version of the Bible and set up their leader Hung Siu-tsuen, as Emperor, clothed in yellow, thus attacking at once the religious as well as political assumption of Hienfung. Viewing the despatch of a great army directly upon Peking in the light of their almost uninterrupted successes thus far, it was generally thought that the downfall of the existing government could be a matter of only a few months. Subsequent events have shown that the defeat of this expedition and the eventual overthrow of the rebellion was a result of unmixed benefit to the welfare and happiness of the Chinese people. Two letters from Mr. Williams to his brother in Turkey afford some idea of the position and sentiments of foreigners at this time towards the insurrectionists.

CANTON, August 20, 1853.

The progress of the insurgents in China has been such as to lead most of us to regard the downfall of the Manchu dynasty, and a re-establishment of the native Chinese princes as very likely. We are in daily expectation of hearing of the capture of Peking and expulsion of the Manchus from the capital, and have some fears of the safety of ourselves and property in this city, when it is fully known that the dynasty is overthrown. I suppose that both English and American ships of war will soon be brought up the river, as near to the city as they can be, and perhaps a guard of marines landed to defend the Factories,—which can be done without much trouble or interfering with the native authorities, and rather to their relief than otherwise. The leaders of the insurgents have shown considerable skill, and their plans indicate far greater foresight than we had given them credit for, while our only means of information was the travesties of the Imperialists, whose officers were apparently unable to speak truth of their enemies. They have some knowledge of the Pentateuch and Gospels, destroy idols, keep a Sabbath, and mix up with this much that savors of Mohammedanism and paganism; their cause finds favor among a few, perhaps, on account of their tenets, but more from their general fair dealing with those of the people who do not resist them and furnish supplies—which are paid for. Their Christian tenets, imperfect as they are, would not find much acceptance among the mass of people whose regard for idols and the worship of ancestors is not so easily turned; however, this last is not much meddled with, and probably is not discarded by the insurgents. We are surprised at the amount of Christian knowledge displayed by them in their books, mixed up, doubtless, with many errors and fanatical notions, especially respecting direct revelations from God and constant personal guidance, which the leaders receive from heaven. I have hopes of the movement resulting in good, at last, and even to this generation, but there must come a vast deal of suffering to all parts of China from the dislocation of the old order of things. Blessed is the assurance that God, even our Saviour, overrules all these changes, and can make them advance His cause.

CANTON, September 24, 1853.

Since my trip to Japan I have been quietly at home, going on as usual, printing, proof-reading, and studying as if I had not been away. We have quiet times in respect to missionary work here now, preaching in more places than ever before, and finding no opposition. Perhaps the remarkable religious turn taken by the insurgents, and the prominence given to the names of Jesus, Moses, and other Biblical characters (all of which are put on a level by the people in their ignorance) may have attracted a degree of attention to what we have to say, in order to learn something reliable. The people hereabouts are greatly excited as to the result of the struggle at the north, and are regarding the change of dynasty as an event likely soon to take place, and one pregnant with unknown consequences, on which they like to speculate. There is very little loyalty in these Asiatics, for their governments are not founded on any principle in which the people participate heartily, but there is some love of country and any amount of pride among this long-tailed race. The emigration to California has given great impulse to the desire to know somewhat more of foreign countries, particularly along the maritime districts. The settlement of foreigners at Shanghai has also brought thousands into intercourse with them who before had only a mythological idea of other peoples, and their better knowledge is spreading. Consequently there seems a fair prospect of free communication ere long with all parts of the country, and steams tugging their loads up the Yangtsz-kiang and Yellow river and their tributaries, where people are now agog to see and learn more of us. Opium has gone in, unobstructed, and it is high time to let some other influences, some other exponents of western arts and religion than the bane of China be seen in her remote cities and rivers. In this vicinity we find that, in villages where opium smokers most abound, there is the worst feeling against foreigners, and more unthriftiness than elsewhere. I suppose the same can be predicted of remote parts of the land.

At present the insurgents are gradually advancing northwards to Peking; large bodies of them have left Nanking and gone towards the Yellow River, taking town after town—without either people or patrol rising against them in any serious degree. I know not where they are just now, but probably not yet in the vicinity of the capital. The people everywhere allow them to advance, neither strongly joining nor resisting them, selling them provisions as they pay for them, and leaving them when they have passed by; at which time the old rulers assume possession of their offices, and things go on as before. There is too little known of the religious element in the rising, and still less of the actual power of the faith in Christ necessary to salvation, upon the leaders or their men, to predicate any thing as to the progress true religion has made among them. Extravagant notions are entertained by foreigners that the new dynasty will, when well established, set up Christianity as the national faith, and make its reception a test of allegiance. These European reformers have little idea of the slow progress of truth among a pagan nation, for most of them have no notion of a radical change in their own hearts, and no higher standard of opinion than society. Yet there are reasonable grounds for hoping, when these rebels become rulers, for much better days in China than the Manchu government allows us at present. But I fear a long day of misrule ere this comes about.

TO REV. W. F. WILLIAMS.

CANTON, December 6, 1853.

Since I wrote you last, I have had the first illness since I came to China, but by the goodness of God I have now quite recovered, and feel as well as before I was taken. The twentieth year since reaching this country was just completed when I exposed myself unknowingly to a north and piercing wind, by going down to Macao in the overloaded steamer, and caught cold, which was further aggravated, I suppose, by going out in the sun unduly protected; the end was a nervous fever which required Dr. Parker's kindest, careful attention to manage, but it gave way to his medicaments, and I was off his list in twelve or fourteen days, thankful to the Giver of health for its restoration. It is the first illness I remember much about, and during it I was led to review all the goodness of God in this respect. . . .

I am ere long again to go with Com. Perry to Japan, and may be kept busy in those regions longer than I was last summer, for probably he will not come away until something has been done to bring about a better understanding with the suspicious people and rulers of that land. One thing that leads me to think that his mission will be successful is that movements in this region of the world seem to indicate that the time of God's working has come, and that the utmost East can no longer be secluded and seclude herself as she has done. Two centuries have passed away since these lands were as completely boxed and sealed as the Egyptian monarch in his pyramid; now the signs indicate a breaking up of the indurated customs and seclusion of these suspicious races, and the infusion of higher aims, knowledge, and hopes—with perhaps dreadful revolutions and bloodshed in their train. The conflict will not be as severe or terrible as were the wars of Europe between light and darkness, Pope and Protestant, for the energy of those half-enlightened nations is not at all equal to that of G. Vasa, or Louis XIV., or Frederic; moreover they are all of them as afraid of European power and guns as the beasts were of Noah when they left the ark.

It was thought by many that a book would be the result of his visit to this unknown country; but apart from the promise which all members of the expedition were under, of giving their notes and journals to the Commodore upon its conclusion, the busy missionary considered himself no book-maker, as an extract from Mrs. Williams' letter (of May, 1854) indicates:

"My husband has *no* thought of writing on the subject of Japan, so you will have to get your information from other sources—or wait until he goes home and shows you the private diary of his trip, which he keeps very carefully. I have no ambition, nor has he, for his producing another book; one is enough in a lifetime, if it be a good one. Yet Commodore Perry is anxious that he should 'get up' a book on Japan; but Mr. Williams is not the kind of man to write a popular account which is meant to take for a time and then die. He would only write after reading and studying well, and lying off within gun-shot of land does not give one any profound idea of a people and their customs and country."

The following extract from one of Perry's notes to Mr. Williams, written at this time, throws some light on the Commodore's sentiments regarding the new administration of Franklin Pierce:

"U. S. S. F. *Susquehanna*, HONGKONG, Jan. 5, 1854.—The only additional book I have is entitled 'Memorials of the Empire of Japan,' published by the Hakluyt Society; it is mere compilation, you can make a much better one during the cruise, therefore bring all your materials, or rather references.

"My letters from government and from all sources prove to me that the present administration are disposed to sustain me. Though they give me no new instructions, the tenor of their communications indicate much interest in my doings. News of our Japan visit had not reached the U. S. at last dates.

"This intelligence could have caused no diminution of their favourable intentions; the truth is if they do not hamper me with new instructions I shall get along the better. As a proof of what I conjecture as to their feelings towards the Japan expedition, I subjoin an extract of the only public letter received by the last mail, referring to the *Saratoga*, out now a year over her time.

"'On receipt of this order, *unless the further detention of that ship is deemed by you essential to the important objects of your mission to Japan,* send her home,' etc., and promising to send another vessel out to relieve her.

"My best respects to Mrs. Williams. Yours very truly,
"M. C. PERRY."

The expedition left Hongkong for its second visit to Lewchew and Japan, January 14, 1854.

CHAPTER VI.

MR. WILLIAMS' Journal is resumed January 17, 1854:

"I depart from my home in full confidence of my being where duty calls me, and leave my family under the care and governance of our Heavenly Father, who has hitherto watched over us all. Mr. Bonney has unwillingly taken care of the office again until I return. I have secured the assistance of Lo, a teacher of good attainments and no opium smoker, so that I hope to do more study than I did before.

"I came on board the *Susquehanna* on Friday evening, and, all being ready, the ship weighed anchor about nine o'clock on Saturday morning, and steamed out of Hongkong harbor. To-day we have passed the southern end of Formosa, progressing rapidly on our course; the sea is smooth, and a fair view has been obtained of the shore (distant about two and a half miles) which offers few signs of inhabitants, some cultivated and stubble patches, a house or two, and roads leading inland. Most of the shore was covered with low woods, and large areas appeared as if untouched by man. The soil was generally good enough to produce grass or trees, and no bleak, barren patches speckled the hillsides as about Hongkong. This portion of Formosa has been lately made infamous by the capture of the *Larpent's* shipwrecked crew, most of whom were driven ashore hereabouts and murdered by savage natives; a few having obtained safety among Chinese villages finally escaped to the *Antelope*, as she passed through the strait in sight. Such miscreants as dwell at this end of Formosa should be severely dealt with; perhaps the desolate aspect of the apparently fertile coast may be owing to their driving away peaceable settlers, while the savages are still afraid of themselves living within reach of others who might punish them. Some blackfish and two black terns were seen as we passed the straits."

TO HIS WIFE.

NAPA, January 31, 1854.

We have been here now wellnigh a fortnight, and will, in three or four days more, be off to Yedo, whither all the sailing ships started this morning. We left Hongkong on the 14th, and got here the following week, Saturday evening, without any sea-sickness on my part, nor much unpleasant weather The Lewchewans sent off a deputation to salute the Commodore upon his arrival, and, excepting three days of windy weather, when it was impossible to go ashore, I have been to see the authorities almost every day, scolding, advising, exhorting, and coaxing, as seemed most to further our objects. The common people here have become far more social, and gather about us when we stop, while the children exhibit no fear as formerly. We have compelled the rulers to receive pay for the coal-shed built last August, and made them give receipts for the money—a great achievement, you will say, yet it has been attended with some difficulty and the exercise of patience. The dozen old weather-worn sailors, who are to be left here in a sort of half-pay half-sick way to look out for the coal-shed, will serve still further to familiarize the people with our ways. Some of them have already picked up a good deal of English, and as we go along the streets now we hear from time to time : "How do you do?" "Good-morning," "American," and other phrases chirruped out by little boys, who then hop quickly back into the dirt and oblivion they emerged from. Some of the harridans in the market-places seem disposed to sell an article occasionally, but they are mostly afraid of such public contact with foreigners, and rather avoid it.

Feb. 1st.—To-day four of us were despatched to Shui to hand in a letter to the Regent, and, in order to make it impressive to both people and rulers at the capital, about a hundred marines and musicians were sent with us. The hour was early and the visit entirely unexpected on the part of the Lewchewans ; it was therefore a magnificent surprise and treat to the natives to see so fine a show and hear the music; but to the authorities nothing could have been more startling than our appearance. They supposed, I presume, that our intentions were nothing less than to take them all as prisoners to the ships; they therefore hurried out in the greatest fear and trepidation, while the evolutions of the marines seemed so to surprise and threaten them that I had some trouble in quieting their fears. The regular interpreters were not on hand, so that our communication with them was slower than usual. The Regent acted as if quite out of his wits, got up, sat down erratically, took us by the hand, and did what he could to prevent the Commodore's visit, which is promised for Friday. After having shown through all these months our friendly desires towards them, it is strange that these islanders have still such a horror of us.

I am, ere long, to transfer my traps and followers into the *Powhatan*, where the Commodore will move when the squadron reaches Yedo. The vessel we came in is to be put at the service of Mr. McLean; I suppose he will like to take a few excursions in so desirable a yacht. This compels Perry to get into another ship, greatly to his own inconvenience and the discomfort of others, but I am likely to be quite as well off.

TO HIS WIFE.

BAY OF YEDO, OFF KANAGAWA,
Powhatan, March 11, 1854.

Commodore Perry had his first interview with the Commissioner (whose name is Lin in Chinese, and Hayashi in Japanese) on Wednesday last, the 8th, at a place called Yokohama, where four or five houses have been erected for this purpose and for displaying the presents. The interview had been delayed nearly a fortnight by the endeavor of the Japanese to get Perry to return to Uraga, where preparations had at first been made to receive him, and where they doubtless expected to bring him. Instead of going down, however, the fleet pushed up the bay, within fifteen miles of Yedo, where we now are, much safer than below, and not liable to delays from high winds preventing our landing. The Japanese at length agreed to hold the meeting here, and brought their houses or pavilions all the way from Uraga, thirty miles, reconstructing them on the beach opposite our fleet. Their extreme desire to get us down rather than up the bay seems to indicate that they will do all they can to prevent our reaching Yedo, knowing perhaps that they cannot make us as " respectfully submissive " as their Dutch visitors, and fear that in consequence they will lose caste among the people. As for the common natives, they have neither fear nor dislike of us, and already an intercourse has commenced among them from our surveying boats, which is plainly a voluntary exhibition of their good-will and laudable curiosity toward "far-travelled strangers." This gradual entrance into so peculiar a land—one thing gained or developed after another—is not the least of the charms of our experiences on this expedition.

Captain Buchanan gave a dinner to Yezaimon and his friends on the 1st March, ten Japanese sitting down to table with six Americans for the first time in the experience of any of the party. The dinner was well served, and the Japanese seemed to enjoy themselves like genuine bon vivants, drinking healths and joining in the toasts, as though perfectly used to the custom. Yezaimon proposed the health of the President in return for that of the Emperor, and in all respects acted with a propriety that certainly spoke for a very high breeding and superior tact, which reflect great credit upon the culture and social life of his country. Every one of our guests behaved well, excepting one Saboroske ; his restless curiosity—not to add impudence—led him up and down the cabin, prying into every conceivable thing—putting on the captain's cap, and looking at himself in the glass, hopping behind Yezaimon to take notes, bawling across the table, asking the English for this and that, and making himself as obstreperous as any common braggart He is a clever fellow, however, despite all his quirks, even if he did pour out a glass of oil and drink it down for wine. All the visitors took away parts of the dinner in their nose-papers, wrapping up morsels of turkey, asparagus, pie, ginger, sweatmeats, and the like, and stuffing them away in their capacious bosoms ; to his root of ginger Namura added two spoonfuls of syrup, and thrust the tissue-paper parcel into the folds of his gown—which must have been a pretty accurate sample of the inside of his stomach by the time he arose from his meal, so that he could illustrate as well as describe his feast to the wife and gossips at home.

But to return to the interview. In the morning we observed that they had erected long lines of curtains on the beach, as well as rows of posts hung with mats extending from the house to the shore, and quite excluding all the view from the space thus enclosed. This rather annoyed the Commodore, since it looked like the same sort of fencing which had been done with boards last year at Uraga; accordingly, he sent Capt. Adams and me to have them taken down. As a matter of fact these screens are designed entirely for show, and to do us honor, but Perry wants honor in his own fashion, or not at all. A half-dozen officials came down to meet us in some concern, evidently, lest the Commodore was sick, or something had happened to prevent the meeting. I told them that every thing was well, and that he expected to be ashore at noon, but that we had come to see the arrangements, etc., beforehand, adding casually that as there would be more than thirty boats it might be better to remove the screens on both sides so as to allow more room for landing. Instantly, and almost as I spoke, the curtains were folded up, the stakes and ropes removed, and a clear beach presented for our escort. So the Commodore had his way, and I am sure that it is good that all obstacles to a view or a ramble on shore should be removed, but it pleased me more that I obtained this as the result of a suggestion rather than a demand. The rapidity with which the "fortifications" disappeared greatly amused the people on board ship. . . .

The ceremonies upon our landing constituted something less perhaps than a pageant, but they were effective, the escort on either side being more guards of honor and less guards of fear than last year. . . . But I need not detail. Com. Perry and his immediate suite were invited into a side room, where, after a few compliments, Commissioner Lin brought out the Emperor's answer to President Fillmore's letter, written on a few pages of coarse paper. It acceded to the demands for good usage of shipwrecked sailors and supplies of provisions for ships, offering also a port for trade, to be chosen by us, and supplies of coal to be there delivered as soon as needed. A Dutch translation was handed in, but the original of this paper was not given us, as they had no signed copy with them.

Our draft of a treaty and explanatory letter were now handed to the Commissioners, and we proceeded to dilate fully and freely upon the desirableness of their forming a treaty with us which would fix our international relations with Japan upon a substantial basis. To these observations and papers they are, of course, to reply presently in writing. It was very singular, and to us repulsive, to see the way in which our friend Tatsnoske, the interpreter, crouched down on hands and knees before these high dignitaries, never rising, but shuffling from one to another and always addressing them in the lowest of whispers ; what respect can a man have for himself in such a position ? . . .

Since this meeting I 've been busy translating Perry's answer to the Emperor's reply. The President's letter asked for one port, now Perry wants five ; that desired simply an assurance of good treatment, now the Commodore demands a treaty, and suggests, in no obscure terms, "a larger force and more stringent terms and instructions," if they don't comply.

The presents for the Japanese Government are all on shore, and the railroad and telegraph lines are now being put up at the house where the interview was held ; the lot of agricultural implements which we've brought may, perhaps, suggest something new and useful to the natives here, but of their adaptation I have some doubts, since most of them are labor-saving, and labor is abundant. The railway engine and car are on a miniature scale ; the car has some fifteen pairs of seats, all covered with damask, its floor is carpeted, its tiny windows made to slide up and down, and nothing wanting to complete the illusion of a real lilliputian railway, except the pigmies to ride thereon. The wheel-trucks are no more than nine inches apart, so you may guess that the whole affair is tiny and cunning ; on the whole it pleases our men quite as much as the Japanese, and when a dozen of them straddle the car and steam is got up we see a good deal of fun. The telegraph is too mysterious to attract their attention at first, and we have found the corn-cracker and rice-huller more popular, but Colt's revolvers carry all before them, everybody wanting one. I should think that we had already given away more than a dozen of these.

My Chinese clerk, Lo, inquires for news, and I wish he had a line from his family. I tell him all the news from your note which would interest him, and he seems to think in hearing it that a wife may, after all, be made of some use. He is an excellent man and is making friends among the Japanese by writing poetry on their fans for them; they often communicate with him on paper, there being many who can read and write Chinese readily, though no one talks it. Both of us have plenty to do, so time passes quickly and pleasantly.

In a reply from Yedo the Japanese Government signified its willingness to negotiate a treaty of friendship with the Americans, submitting at the same time a draft in return for that which the Commodore had presented to the Commissioners. During two or three weeks their views were exchanged and topics discussed in an amicable and tolerant spirit, the business interviews being varied by banquets on either side, and the return of presents from the Shogun, in the name of the Emperor, in acknowledgment of those brought to him from the United States. By yielding some minor points the Americans succeeded at length in obtaining the first treaty ever concluded with the Japanese on terms approaching equality. The most important stipulations of the contract were those opening to American trade the ports of Simoda and Hakodadi, permitting consuls to reside at these places, and granting free access to the country surrounding them; good treatment and safe-conduct to either of these two ports was also guaranteed to Americans shipwrecked upon any coast of Japan. These concessions, which established the preliminaries of possible commercial relations rather than a treaty of commerce, were the least which Commodore Perry would accept and the uttermost which the suspicious Japanese would relax from their laws of voluntary and determined isolation. It was hardly to be expected that these independent islanders would at once permit a foreign trade upon even the restringent terms which had been wrung from the Chinese after half a century of acquaintance and struggle; but in securing such proofs as these of their willingness to enter into friendly relations, while distinctly refusing to submit to any such humiliating restrictions as those borne by the Dutch in their prison island of Dezima, the Commodore probably gained from the Japanese the most favorable compact which could have been achieved without actual war. It is a striking testimony to the strength of the feudal system in Japan at that time, that the Shogun* refused to treat for the opening of ports in Lewchew and Matsmai as being under the control of their respective princes and only nominally within the jurisdiction of the empire.

His Journal describes the signing of the first treaty to which Mr. Williams was witness.

* Or Generalissimo. "The Mikado kept his seat, the prestige of antiquity and divinity, and the fountain of authority at Kioto, while the Shogun, or usurping general, held the purse and the sword."—Griffiis' "Life of Com. Perry." p 327. The Mikado never received the presents brought by this expedition, the Shogun, or self-styled Tykoon, being probably afraid to turn them over to his master.

"March 31st.—Last evening Kenzhiro came on board with the Chinese version of the treaty done from the Japanese, and after the correction of one important error respecting the distance allowed for rambling at Simoda, the copy was agreed upon. This morning a fair transcript was made, and a little past noon the Commodore left the ship. On meeting the Japanese Commissioners they exhibited three copies of the Japanese version, and one each in Dutch and Chinese, while we had, besides the two latter, three copies in English. First opening theirs at the end, they showed the rubrics attached to the name of each Commissioner instead of a seal; then the Commodore signed his copies in their presence. The two Dutch versions being thereupon compared and found alike were exchanged, and one signed by Mr. Portman and one by Yenoske. After this the Chinese copies were compared and one character erased in one of them, but upon my desiring them to sign and date their copy, a difficulty arose, for they would only affix the date in Kayei's name and year, while I required both their term and ours, as in the Dutch; they declined to write the characters for 'our Lord Jesus Christ,' and the Commodore allowed the omission; so at length they dated the paper and Matsusake Michitarō signed it with his rubric, when I signed the other copy and gave it in exchange. Thus was completed the negotiation and signing of the Treaty of Kanagawa, the first compact of the sort ever made by the Japanese. Long may they rejoice over the blessings it will bring them, and may the Disposer of nations make it the opening whereby His great name may be declared unto them. After this long-continued seclusion He has inclined them to listen to this application to loosen the strictness of their laws; I know not how else to account for the unexpected and peaceful attainment of our objects here—may the same moving Cause grant that they may never have occasion to repent of the privileges ceded on this day."

Mr. Williams' acquaintance with the Treaty of Whampoa between France and China, which contained the "most favored nation" clause, led to his suggesting a similar provision in the compact with the Japanese; the Ninth Article, accordingly, was introduced in his words, as follows:

"It is agreed that if, at any future day, the government of Japan shall grant to any other nation or nations privileges and advantages which are not herein granted to the United States and the citizens thereof, that these same privileges and advantages shall be granted likewise to the United States and to the citizens thereof without any consultation or delay."

An interesting incident relating to this treaty has recently come to light, and is thus recounted by Mr. Griffis in his biography of Perry:

"Unknown to any of the Americans, Nakahama Manjirs, who had received a good common-school education in the United States, sat in an adjoining room, unseen but active, as the American interpreter for the Japanese. All the documents in English and Chinese were submitted to him for correction and approval. He was afterwards made curator of the scientific and mechanical apparatus brought by Perry and presented by the United States government."

"April 10th.—We told the Japanese yesterday that we had made up our minds to go up the bay, since the President had ordered the expedition to do so, and the Commissioners had presented no objections when this proposition was first made to them. Yenoske and Kenzhiro and their train came on board the flag-ship, and were loud in their protestations that we ought not to do this; that Japanese laws were very strict; that the bay was shallow; that an awful commotion among the native shipping would ensue; that the Emperor would be irritated; that serious personal consequences to themselves might occur—intimating almost jeopardy of honor and life if we persisted and they were implicated—and a hundred other reasons *quia non*. But Perry of course insisted, only promising that the ships would not anchor unless they grounded; and then the whole party, as if perfectly willing to get what good they could from this evil, began to beg permission to go with one of the steamers and see the working of the machinery!

"By 8 o'clock this morning the squadron was bound for Yedo. The day was tolerably clear, and the Japanese visitors seemed to have little fear of any dreadful result of the day's excursion. By noon we had gone about ten miles from Yokohama, and seen the suburb of Shinagawa, with its numerous rows or detachments of boats. We then passed within about eight miles of a long row of stakes stretching along in front of the capital city, and—turned about in one hundred feet of water! If a man is a Commodore, I suppose he can do as no one else would under like circumstances; but after all we have said about the moral need of our going to Yedo, to stop four miles short of our surveying-boats and fully twice that of the city, does seem rather an imputation upon our common-sense. I was much disappointed, for saving a line of stakes, a long row of trees, a smoky cloud above and plenty of junks below, I saw nothing even indicating a settlement. As one of the officers observed, this should have been the first instead of the tenth of April to make such a humbug appropriate. I have now been three times bound for Yedo, approaching nearer each time; perhaps the fourth trial will land me there, or at least near enough to see the town."

This inexplicable withdrawal of Commodore Perry from securing his end when fairly within reach did not fail to irritate his officers, and raised a feeling of distrust on the part of the Japanese which appears to have in some measure colored their subsequent negotiations during his stay in Japan. The incident, with one exception, occasions the only serious animadversion upon his policy or conduct found in Mr. Williams' journal of the expedition; the other was the too frequent neglect of the Sabbath day in the squadron. The Missionary and the Commodore doubtless viewed the matter from very different standpoints.

"Although to-day is Sunday, there is little cessation from work or business, and if God adds His blessing and enables us to carry out the design of the expedition, it will not be because or in answer to our prayers or regard to Him, but because we are used, as Nebuchadnezzar the ax-helve was, to carry out that which falls in with his plans. In fact no regard seems to be paid here to whatever scruples a man may have about working on the Sabbath. Mr. Brown goes ashore to see about wood, ballast, boats, and coins, all of them objects of minor importance and deferable to another day ; Dr. Smith is ordered to see about a man lying in the hospital—a service really no more called for than if he had been sent to see the condition of the boats lying on the beach. God's day, and by consequence his law, is made subordinate to the will of one man. The alternative of outraging one's conscience is, of course, the accusation of disobedience or mutiny, and of this every officer is extremely wary. Truly the desecration of the Sabbath in a man-of-war is as great as in a pagan country, where it is not known ; as to keeping the day holy, I fear amid such a melée of men talking, moving, and working, the thing 's impossible."

Upon the conclusion of negotiations in the upper bay, and departure of Captain Adams with the new treaty to America, the squadron repaired to Simoda, where it remained a month endeavoring to encourage by friendly treatment a closer and more spontaneous intercourse with the Japanese. Here a general permission was given to the officers to go on shore, and their reception by peasants, as well as shopkeepers pointed to a prevalent willingness on the part of the people towards a mutual acquaintance, which was checked and limited only by the jealousy of the officials. The duties of his position were now much less confining to Mr. Williams than before, and with Dr. Morrow, surgeon on the flag-ship, he made many botanical and geological excursions about the surrounding country. It was with the zest of an explorer that he gathered his herbarium, not knowing, as he plucked the strange and gorgeous flowers now bursting into bloom, but that in any or every specimen he might be adding an unknown species to the world's known flora.* An amusing testimony to his botanical enthusiasm appears in the account which his Chinese teacher, Lo, published after his return to Canton, and which Mr. Williams translated for the *Hongkong Register:*

"The Azalea is very abundant on the hills about Simoda; nor are other flowers rare. My friend [Dr. Williams] made large collections of them, which he afterwards dried and preserved for future study, showing himself worthy to be a disciple of Confucius, who advised his followers to read the "Book of Odes," that they might become acquainted with the names of birds and animals, plants and trees."

TO HIS WIFE.

HAKODADI, ISLAND OF YESSO, May 21, 1854.

I have so much to tell you, so many musings to entertain you with, that the richness and variety of my material rather embarrass me. Happy am I, in all my ignorance of your condition as I am writing, and of your hap since I heard from you at Chinese New Year, in the confidence I have that God is your keeper and will do for you what is best. To trust and commend you and yours into His protection, love, and power is my joy daily, and I am ready, I think, to hear any tidings from you.

We have come up to this place in compliance with a stipulation made with the Japanese Commissioners to survey and

* Many new varieties were found which were analyzed and described by Prof. Asa Gray in the official report of the expedition. One of these he named the Clematis Williamsii, "for one of the collectors, S. Wells Williams, Esq., of Canton, a cherished friend and correspondent, author of one of the best works that have appeared upon the Chinese Empire, and a good naturalist, as well as a learned Oriental scholar."

examine the port, so that American ships may learn something of it and the way into it before the treaty takes effect. Five ships were never before seen in the bay, and they spread such alarm among the people that most of them, supposing us piratically inclined, have sent their families into the country ; thus far, therefore, we have seen only men. I have tried to allay their fears, which, in the absence of all special instructions from Yedo were not surprising, and I hope they will soon resume their usual occupations, seeing that we are friends and may do them good. The non-arrival of the envoy and Dutch interpreter from the capital has thrown the whole business of interpreting upon me, and I can assure you I 've business enough for twenty tongues to be kept up at trip-hammer rate the livelong day. Thus far we have got on so well in bringing the people into our plans, that the want of other interpreters is not so much felt, many even hoping that they will not come at all to interfere with the details already settled. Heretofore, most of my talking having been in a small way and on unimportant matters, if I bungled 't was not of so much consequence ; but now the affair is serious, so I bring Lo into considerable service to make one language help the other, and thereby avoid many mistakes. He takes a lively interest in all our operations and gets on admirably with the natives ; he is, indeed, the most learned Chinaman they have ever seen, and their delight in showing off to him their attainments in Chinese is increased when he turns a graceful verse or two for them upon a fan ; of these he has written, I should think, more than half a thousand since coming to Japan, and nothing pleases him like being asked to do so.

Fortunately for the visitors the Commissioners from Yedo arrived too late to seriously interrupt by their objections or restrictions the amicable arrangements concluded between Commodore Perry and a delegate from the Prince of Matsmai. A lively and in some cases rather a furious desire to purchase Japanese curios and works of art broke out among officers of the squadron, some of whom had to be disciplined for brutal conduct toward the shopkeepers before the trade could be put upon a conventional basis of cash payment for goods received. It may be noted that the extraordinary rate of 4.7 to 1 was found to exist between gold and silver upon this island. The difficult matter of fixing a limit within which foreigners were to remain was finally adjusted by establishing a boundary circle with a radius of fifteen miles from the town. Mr. Williams' Journal concludes an account of the stay here:

"June 3d.—Thus ended our visit to Hakodadi, forming one of the pleasantest episodes in my life in Asia. I expected a dull visit at a miserable fishing village, and found my time and abilities employed to their highest degree, the whole business of interpreting thrown on me, and the duty of removing from the minds of the officers their apprehensions and disinclination to act in the absence of orders from Yedo. Acquaintance produced mutual trust, and as they found themselves fully supported by the treaty, it was soon seen that no little trouble would be avoided by meeting all our reasonable propositions. It was favorable to them that the lack of particular instructions from court left them more at liberty to follow out what the treaty implied; and it was more favorable to us that we found two such persons as Matsmai [a relative of the Prince] and Yendo to deal with, instead of petty-minded and hesitating men like those at Simoda. I have been repaid during the last fortnight for the years of study of this language, and hope that the impression left at Hakodadi may by and by open a way for a residence there to some one who will tell its people of the love of Jesus for their souls."

"SIMODA, June 16th.—Since we returned here, more than a week ago, the weather has been as warm as we have been busy. The five Commissioners of our treaty discussions, together with two others—forming a respectable row of shaven-pated gentlemen,—have met the Commodore almost daily since we reached them here, to consult upon various regulations pertaining to future trade. You would be wondrously amused to see us all sitting in a little room covered with mats and partitioned off by means of folding screens on three sides, the fourth being curtained off from a garden; above is hung a curtain of purple crape, and behind these various screens and mats are the dumb gods of the Commissioners squatting in solemn darkness, unable to prevent this summary transformation of their temple into a council-house. So we sit in this little room, the seven shaven pates on one side in flowing gowns and huge trousers of various colors, their swords stuck in their girdles like skewers through their midriffs, while on the other are the Commodore and his four aids, clad in tight garments and hardly adorned with their few brass buttons; before us all are cakes, candy, and tea, on long benches, and between the two parties waddles the Japanese interpreter back and forth as he speaks to one and another; at the extreme end of the room sit a dozen native officers, of various grades and functions, as still as mice. We form a remarkable group, doubtless, and the import and results of these discussions may prove of great consequence to the nations of both parties.

"The chance of which I am availing myself in writing at this moment is while waiting for the commissioners to come on board to an entertainment prepared for them on both the *Powhatan* and the *Mississippi*—a great dinner followed by a séance of the Ethiopian Minstrels. The latter steamship is already dressed up with flags and various embellishments, and presents an exceeding pretty appearance as her lights shine through the gayly-colored bunting, and are reflected upon the placid harbor. The Japanese are mightily pleased with our music, and the dancing of the Ethiops is diverting in the highest degree; it is funny enough to be using this kind of a *divertissement* as a means of peace and in the hope of concord. The Commodore, on leaving home, was given a large bundle of comic valentines which had stranded in the Dead-Letter Office at Washington, and, taking them one day to one of our solemn discussions, set the Commissioners laughing over them till they cried. In general, we have found the Japanese to be a good-natured people, rationally and easily moved to merriment, and fond of a rich entertainment."

"June 22d.—All official intercourse being over, Morrow and I took a last walk up the valley, over the hill, and around by the side of the river, some nine or ten miles in all, along which we found many old faces and acquaintances, most of whom seemed really pleased to see us. The country was charming, the rice, now mostly transplanted, giving to the hill-slopes and terraces a beautiful light green, which contrasted finely with the heights above dressed in dark verdure; at wellnigh every step we were called upon to admire the successive beauties of the ever-changing scene. Few flowers, I'm sorry to say, were found, most of those along the path having blossomed, and some berries already made their appearance, among which were those of the paper-tree. This was the first ramble I'd had since our abortive expedition with Bent and Maury to discover the seven-*ri* limit for future American wanderers about this port, and the freedom of this was a decidedly agreeable contrast to the hampering presence of the spies and officials of the other. It was sunset and nearly eight o'clock on this solstitial day before we got back to our boat, tired and gratified with our tramp.

"If any one thing has rendered the expedition to Japan more agreeable to me than another, 't is surely the walks and search for flowers about these enchanting hills, and thereby the greater freedom of intercourse I've obtained with the common people. These rambles have been taken too with a delightful companion in Dr. Morrow, so that we have both been pleased with our excursions, with the objects of our search, and I think with each other; certainly I shall always associate them with him as being among my kindliest remembrances of Yokohama, Hakodadi, and Simoda—though elsewise, indeed, I've nothing to complain of. It is rather melancholy to me to observe how few are the sources of enjoyment, occupation, or instruction which those around me have or find for themselves in such a spot as this, where the ordinary amusements and company found in seaports are wanting. Here they employ their spare hours in scolding the Japanese, the Commodore, the expedition, the ship—every thing save their own evil tempers, which alone are to blame."

While the flag-ship with its larger companions of the squadron remained in the two treaty ports of Japan, the others were despatched at different times to examine various points of interest or importance in the neighboring seas, survey the coasts, and report in advance of the Commodore in China. On the 25th of June the five remaining vessels left Simoda Bay—to the unconcealed satisfaction of the villagers, whose provisions had become excessively scarce—and Perry's expedition, its objects fulfilled beyond the bravest hopes of its best wishers, was at an end. Mr. Williams' reflections, written as they steamed out of the harbor, are the counterpart of the prayerful emotions with which he accepted his charge in the enterprise, and bear an interesting likeness to the exclamation of Lord Elgin in the same harbor and upon a similar errand, four years later—" God grant that in opening their country to the West, we may not be bringing upon them misery and ruin! "

"On a review of the proceedings of this expedition no one can deny the assertion that it has been peculiarly prospered by God, and (so far as we are at liberty to say it) was carried out with His blessing as a step in His plans for the extension of His kingdom in this land. The appointment of a naval man as envoy was wise, inasmuch as it secured unity of purpose in the diplomatic and executive chief; and it is not improbable that, as proved by the general prudence and decision of his proceedings since anchoring last July at Uraga, Perry is the only man in our navy fully capable of holding both of these positions. It has indeed been favorable to his unbiassed action that he has had no captain under him whose judgment or knowledge were entitled to the least respect, and so far as

I've observed, all in the fleet, excepting Buchanan, have devoted their intellects to criticising what he did, and wishing that they were going home. The Commodore, in regarding all under him as only means and agents for his purpose, has perhaps too often disregarded the just wishes and opinions of others in comparatively trifling matters; but this extreme is and must be almost unavoidable in minds of strong fibre, trained during long years to command. Further, the remarkable weather experienced since we left Macao last year, fair, pleasant, and healthy, has been such as to draw the attention of all, who have more frequently cried out, 'See Perry's luck!' than been disposed to acknowledge the hand and favor of God therein.

"The Japanese could not easily collect provisions for so large a body of people as were in the squadron, and had stress of sickness or some other need driven us to the extremity of forcibly supplying ourselves with food, even at the alternative of immediate hostilities, I can conceive that the peaceful opening of Japan might thereby have been deferred indefinitely. Now, not a shot has been fired, not a man wounded, not a piece of property destroyed, not a boat sunk or a single Japanese to be found who is the worse off, so far as we know, for the visit of the American expedition. Its ultimate results can only be estimated when time has properly disclosed them, both in respect of trade between the two countries, and intercourse between their peoples; but in the higher benefits likely to flow to the Japanese by their introduction into the family of civilized nations, I see a hundred-fold return for all the expense of this expedition to the American Government. By permission of the Commodore, I drew up a paper of a general character which was sent last night to Commissioner Lin; in it I endeavored to show how Japan could learn much which would be of enduring benefit to her by adopting the improvements of western lands, and allowing her people to visit other countries —adding that it was to set before them the more useful rather than the fanciful specimens of western manufacture and art that the President had sent to them a steam-engine, a telegraph, a daguerreotype, agricultural tools, with books and drawings explaining them. The great and general change in the policy of Western nations from the ideas of two centuries ago was referred to, as removing all grounds of fear of any evil resulting to them from a more liberal intercourse; and I hazarded the statement that no civilized nation now could wish them to do aught which would be injurious. The paper closed by a hint respecting the danger of future trouble if Americans were continually followed about by spies and officials, and that it was only necessary to secure the arrest and punishment of those who actually did wrong.

"In reviewing the proceedings of the last few months, it is fair to give the Japanese officers the credit of showing none of that hauteur and supercilious conduct, which the perusal of books about their country might have led one to expect. Compared with the conduct of the Chinese when Amherst went to Peking, that of Hayashi [Lin] and his colleagues appears far superior in point of courtesy, decorum, and willingness, as well as good sense in discussing the matters brought forward for their acceptance. Perhaps more impracticable men could easily have been found than these seven commissioners—indeed, I suspect that they were chosen rather on account of their progressive views; but the other qualities referred to may fairly be taken as part of the national character, as we have observed them to some extent in all classes. Much more might be said, indeed, without giving way to enthusiasm. In no country could more agreeable and kinder-hearted men be found than old Yendo and Fuzhiwara at Hakodadi, and if one could converse with all, such characters would doubtless appear rather as samples than as exceptions."

On her passage from Japan to Lewchew, the *Mississippi*, to which Mr. Williams had been transferred, touched at the island of Oho-sima, lying nearly a hundred miles north of Lewchew, to ascertain its position, size, and the character of its harbors.

"Mr. Maury went ashore in a boat to reconnoitre, and was met as he neared the beach by a party of armed natives, who wanted to oppose his landing. One among them had a matchlock, and one, who seemed to take the lead, had a single sword; others were furnished with stones, sticks, or spears. Sam Patch soon undeceived them as to the nature of our intentions, and before long most of our men had got ashore, while provisions were brought down to the water's edge. Maury slipped away to the village from whence the natives had issued, and found it a most miserable collection of huts, the abodes of filth, heathenism, and ignorance. The men wore pins in their hair, like the Lewchewans, while the presence of swords indicated their proximity to Japan, with the language of which theirs had also more affinity. They presented a more wretched appearance than any people we have yet seen, and cause one to notice how easily and surely man deteriorates in a small and isolated community where every member is compelled to labor for a bare living, and no surplusage of wealth remains for the support of government, education, or even religion or an elementary civilization."

Sam Patch, it may be noted, was one of the seven shipwrecked Japanese, on whose account the *Morrison* made her voyage to Japan in 1837; he had joined the expedition in China as common seaman, and made himself useful as interpreter among the sailors and upon the survey boats.

During their stay (from the 1st to the 16th July) at Napa, the Commodore was chiefly engaged in obtaining from the authorities proper punishment for the killing of one of the sailors who had been left here by the fleet in February. The fact that the Regent at length bestirred himself to the end of discovering half a dozen culprits from the mob which stoned this sailor, indicated that the influence of the Americans had not been wholly without effect upon these islanders. A compact was drawn up and signed in lieu of a treaty, by which the rulers of Lewchew agreed to maintain amicable relations with America and treat its citizens hospitably whenever any came to their islands. Since the consummation of this agreement, owing to their lying outside of the tracks of commerce, the Lewchew Islands have been visited only two or three times by any foreigners who have left a record of their voyage. Whatever conceptions of regard for their fellow-men may have been instilled into their inhabitants by the sojourn of the American squadron, it is to be feared that their own timid natures and the power of Japan have together pushed them back into precisely the same pitiful and contented ignorance in which they were when first discovered. The imperturbable and passive resistance offered by this peaceful people to all outside influences has, up to this time, proved a successful barrier against missionary efforts among them. So long ago as the year 1846, Dr. Bettleheim, a converted Jew, was sent by a society of naval officers to found a mission at Napa. This enthusiastic and zealous worker, by means of his school and some knowledge of medicine, bid fair, at first, to accomplish the conversion of many intelligent islanders, but difficulties soon arose, he was desired to leave, forbidden to teach, and finally, upon his refusal to obey, was practically boycotted by the natives. In this condition, and in no very agreeable frame of mind, the American squadron found him upon their arrival in 1853, and on their last visit here. As it was apparent that no good could possibly come from his remaining in a state of undisguised hostility to the authorities, he was, at his own request, taken back to China in the *Powhatan*. The satisfaction of the Lewchewans at the departure of this foreign incubus was greatly marred by the appearance of another missionary, with his wife, Mr. Moreton, whom the fleet left to their cheerless exile upon these beautiful islands.

Transferred again to the *Powhatan*, Mr. Williams reached Ningpo, July 20th. His chief occupation on this, as well as on the outward voyage to Japan, was the translation of a Chinese novel, the *Lieh Kwoh Chi*, or "Records of the Feudal Kingdoms," of which nineteen chapters, or some 330 closely written quarto pages, were turned into English.* It is notable, as an instance of his perpetual industry, vanquishing even the plague of sea-sickness, that Mr. Williams found, under these unfavorable conditions, time for the only purely literary effort of his life.

The arrival of the *Powhatan* at Ningpo was opportune for the safety of the American missionary colony there, a bullying Portuguese captain having brought his corvette nearly abreast of their houses in order to fire into some Chinese junks of war lying opposite. The return fire was more keenly felt by the missionaries than by the Portuguese, who continued the scrimmage with great indifference to the lives and property of others, until the unexpected appearance of an American man-of-war brought him to an apology and his senses. The best illustration of the conditions of his life heretofore in China is the sentence in Mr. Williams' description of this visit to Ningpo: "We took a walk through the town with McCartee, and, at last, after 21 years in China, I

---

* He revised and published the first two chapters of his translation in the *New Englander*, January, 1880, as a specimen of Chinese historical fiction.

have this day, for the first time, been inside one of her cities!"

Stopping at Fuhchau and Amoy on her way down the coast, the *Powhatan* joined the squadron at Hongkong, nearly four weeks after leaving Napa.

"CANTON, August 11th.—Seven months from the day I left I am permitted to return to this city in health. The steamer reached Hongkong in thirty-five hours from Amoy, and on Tuesday evening I went up to Macao, to find my dear family all quite well there. How pleasant the meeting was those alone can realize who have been separated thus from the dearest on earth; but God had answered my prayers for their health and safety and loaded us all with benefits! I came up here after two days with them and am already at my old work Thus ends my expedition to Japan, for which praise be to God."

The ensuing letters are so immediately connected with Mr. Williams' part in this expedition as to deserve a place here.

COMMODORE PERRY TO MR. WILLIAMS.

U. S. S. F. *Mississippi*.
HONGKONG, September 6, 1854.

MY DEAR MR. WILLIAMS:—I have had the pleasure of receiving your communication of the 28th ulto., together with your interesting description of Hakodadi, which I shall file with many others of your valuable notes.

I regret much not having had the pleasure of seeing more of you or your family since our return from Japan,—whilst at Macao most onerous and perplexing duties followed me, most of them connected with another squadron, and my health being feeble, I had not time or the spirit to go anywhere if possibly to be avoided.

In taking my departure from China I feel myself called upon by every sense of propriety and justice to bear the most ample testimony to the talents, zeal, and fidelity with which you conducted the important duties entrusted to your management as Chief Interpreter of the Mission to Japan. I say little when I declare that your services were almost indispensable to me in the successful progress of the delicate business which had been entrusted to my charge.

With high abilities, untiring industry, and a conciliating disposition, you are the very man to be employed in such business.

With my best respects to Mrs. Williams, I am, dear sir, very truly yours, M. C. PERRY.

FROM THE SAME.

U. S. LEGATION, HAGUE, December 6, 1854.

MY DEAR MR. WILLIAMS:—I have received your letter of September 9th, and in reply take pleasure in saying that I shall make an effort to secure a liberal appropriation from Congress to enable me to publish in a suitable manner an account of my late cruise; and being aware that the interest and value of the work would be much enhanced by the vocabulary which you propose to prepare, I may in all probability obtain a sufficient amount to authorize the disbursement you will need in carrying out your object, but all is yet uncertain; many of the members of Congress are very odd people, and may throw insurmountable obstacles in my way, and without the aid of Government I shall not undertake the risk of publication; nor shall I be silly enough to venture, like Wilkes and some others of our naval men, to write a book which no one will read, preferring rather to place the editorial department in the hands of some book-maker of reputation, for there is as much experience and skill required in the collation, condensation, and writing of a readable book as in the successful accomplishment of any of the arts. I may claim to be a pretty good sailor, and familiar with naval affairs, but I have no talent for authorship. . . .

FROM THE SAME.

NEW YORK, March 13, 1855.

MY DEAR MR. WILLIAMS:—I wrote you some time since from Washington upon the subject of the report or narrative of my late cruise to Japan, which Congress has called upon me to furnish ; and I naturally look to you, as one conspicuously engaged in the mission, for valuable aid in the way of notes, etc., as also for the vocabulary to which you should affix your name, and of which any number of extra copies can be struck off with no further additional expense than the paper and presswork.

Besides the vocabulary, I know of no one who is so capable of writing an historical sketch of Japan as yourself, with the aid of your valuable library and your own personal observations—some forty or fifty pages or more might be produced which would reflect high credit on yourself and furnish a valuable acquisition to my report. I have no means of remunerating you, but to set aside a certain number of the copies to be assigned to me to be placed at your disposal, and of giving you a share of any ulterior advantage that the copyright would give to me, for though the right would belong to the Government, Congress is generally liberal in giving the officers certain privileges.

I shall be impatient until I hear from you, and hope you will write by return of mail, and write fully. I should be greatly disappointed not to have your assistance. . . . The truth is, every incident connected with the Japanese expedition is looked upon with great interest, and there is one universal demonstration of applause at every event which has occurred, and I feel a nervous desire to make the report alike creditable ; in doing so I depend confidently upon your services in the way I have suggested. You write with so much care and so graphically that it will not give you half the trouble it would many others.

Do not forget to send me some translations of Japanese poetry, as also Chinese done into English, if you have any ; these scraps can be appropriately introduced. The specimens furnished to the *Hongkong Register* by your Chinese clerk are quite interesting. . . ."

Most truly yours,   M. C. PERRY.

The busy and troubled times following Mr. Williams'

return to Canton compelled him to abandon the idea of compiling a Japanese vocabulary and phrase book, which had suggested itself to him during his service on the expedition. Every effort was strained to complete the "Tonic Dictionary," while attending to his usual missionary work and maintaining the press. It is not improbable that upon finishing his Canton Dictionary, he might have enlarged and arranged the little manuscript vocabulary which he had prepared when studying with the Japanese sailors in Macao; but the burning of the factories destroyed this, together with many other possibilities, turning his thoughts to new channels of usefulness, and retaining for China energies that, but for an accident, might at this moment have been diverted and transferred to newly opened Japan.

Mr. Williams regarded his original work and the pecuniary profit of it, from his writings, press, or other employments, as something due already to the Mission Board which supported him. His salary as interpreter in the expedition, amounting to $2,100, was handed over at once to the mission treasury.

The letter which follows contains perhaps the last echo of the fame of his part in the expedition:

OFFICE OF THE BOARD OF TRADE,
BOSTON, June 17, 1856.

S. Wells Williams, Esq. :

SIR :—The Boston Board of Trade honoring the motives which dictated the Expedition to Japan in the year 1853-54, and appreciating the eminent service rendered by Commodore Perry, and by the officers who so ably coöperated with him on that occasion and added efficiency and dignity to the mission, have caused a gold medal to be struck commemorative of the event. And the undersigned, having been commissioned for the purpose by the Government of the Board, have now the honor to present a copy of the same to you, in silver, in the name of the Merchants of Boston, and to ask your acceptance of it as an enduring token of their high estimation of your services in that expedition.

Very respectfully, your Obedient Servants,

    JAMES M. BEEBE, *President.*
    THOMAS B. CURTIS, *Chairman of Committee.*
    ISAAC C. BATES, *Secretary.*

CHAPTER VII.

THE prominent association, in printed reports, of Mr. Williams' part in the successful achievement of Commodore Perry's expedition, suggested his name to the State Department as possessing the necessary qualifications for the performance of similar duties in China. Mr. McLean having resigned his place as Commissioner to China in the summer of 1855, Dr. Parker was appointed to succeed him while on a visit to America, leaving the office of Secretary and Interpreter to the Legation vacant. At the same time Mr. Williams was nominated to this position, and his commission sent to China without waiting to learn his consent or desires. His reluctance to undertake a charge which would remove him from missionary labors was extreme, but the intention of the American Board was to be consulted first. "Whether I shall accept it or not will depend," he writes to his brother Frederic, "altogether on the proceeding of the committee as to their printing-office, for they wrote last year that they would rather like to give it up, and proposed that I should be disconnected from the Board and get a living by making books and doing Bible and tract printing. If they carry out this proposition I shall have to look around for something else to do, for the printing-office won't maintain me. I do not wish to go to U. S., where I can do nothing and have nothing to do it with, but prefer to stay here, where, at least, I can assist in preaching and where I am at home. I am on the whole, however, rather unwilling to take this government position, and look for no enjoyment in its duties, judging from the luck Dr. Parker seems to have had for his ten years of it."

The first intimation of his appointment reached Mr. Williams in the following urgent appeal for its acceptance from Commodore Perry:

WASHINGTON, June 28, 1855.

MY DEAR MR. WILLIAMS:—I have had the pleasure of receiving your letter of April last, and regret to hear of the illness of Dr. Parker, though the circumstance has thrown into your hands an honorable appointment, as I happen to know.

I was yesterday at the room of Mr. Marcy, who made some inquiries about you, saying that it was contemplated to appoint you in the place of Dr. Parker. Of course I was not sparing in my praise of your character, standing, abilities, etc., etc., and whilst reading to him your letter the President entered, and Mr. Marcy remarked that "Commodore Perry had fully endorsed Mr. Williams," and he thought it better to make out the commission at once; I suppose you will receive it by the mail which takes this. . . .

I hope you will not think of declining the appointment, as it can in no way interfere with your missionary duties, but, on the contrary, will give you position and additional influence in the prosecution of your pious labors,—and besides, a larger income will accrue for the benefit of your family if you do not regard money yourself.

You will, I trust, pardon the freedom I take in thus speaking of your concerns. To confess the truth, I feel somewhat selfish in this matter, as I should like my son * to be under so good a chief.

There is nothing new here; politics, as usual, are the en-

* O. H. Perry, appointed U. S. Consul to Canton.

grossing topics of the day,—knownothingism, democracy, soft-shells, hard-shells, silver-grays, etc., etc., of which you know about as much as I do. My book, or narrative, as it should be more properly called, makes but slow progress, as I have been kept constantly engaged in other duties,—at present I am serving as a member of the "Board of Naval Reform." I send you a copy of the account of the presentation of plate to me at New Port, Rhode Island. Captain Adams has reached Washington, delivered the ratified treaty, and leaves for Philadelphia to-morrow. Most truly yours,

M. C. PERRY.

The Commodore's unusual interest in the matter also inspired the following from a mutual friend in Hongkong:

September 27th.

MY DEAR MR. WILLIAMS:—Commodore Perry writes me that the government at Washington requests you to accept the office vacated by Dr. Parker, but he tells me he has no means of knowing if you will do so. In these days it is an unheard-of case that the Commodore advises; such offices, under our government, being so seldom given except on application, then too frequently with little or no respect to the qualifications of the applicant. I look upon this appointment as indicating a sort of *moral* reform at Washington and should, of all things, be sorry to hear there could be any objection on your part to assisting any such movement by accepting their appointment. . . .

I sincerely trust (and I know that every American in Canton will agree with me) that you will accept the secretaryship. Believe me, yours respectfully,

ROBT. S. STURGIS.

Pending the decision of the American Board, Mr. Williams returned a provisional acceptance to the Secretary of State, entering upon the duties both of Secretary and Commissioner-in-charge until the arrival of Dr. Parker, December 31, 1855. Few salaried offices under the United States Government have been so little sought or as lightly esteemed as this, in accepting which Mr. Williams reached the turning-point of his career in China, the dividing line between his service under God as missionary-printer and missionary-diplomatist.

TO REV. W. F. WILLIAMS.

CANTON, December 13, 1855.

This region is fast resuming its usual quiet, and the detail of horrid executions is dwindling to a small number, say 20 or 50 a day, a trifling sacrifice, which the Cantonese regard as a mere bagatelle. The experiment at upsetting the government has not at all succeeded, and I think the people will not renew the attempt soon. There was no prospect of improvement in their success, for although the leaders might have desired a relief of oppression, their followers were as unscrupulous as brigands.

During the whole the mass of people remained loyal and preferred to suffer the outrages of the government troops, which were as bad as the others, to taking part with the insurgents and destroying the imperialists. We suffered nothing in person or estate, but, of course, the foreigners were greatly interested in the progress of the struggle. Our services were well attended in the main, and are still, though we have in our fifty weekly services and meetings not ten regular hearers. There are perhaps 2,500 or more hearers at all these meetings, but I fear they get very imperfect ideas of the truths we would tell them. This language is most meagre and troublesome in explaining and enforcing new and spiritual doctrines, even if spoken accurately; and in the mouth of an imperfectly educated foreigner, it is frequently the merest nonsense and gibberish, at which the people must often laugh derisively. It is not unlikely that the doctrines themselves suffer when delivered so; but it is here truly by the foolishness of preaching that God will deliver his elect from Satan. . . .

But I have not told you of the important event in our family this summer while summering at Macao. I went down from Canton to see them there, when Wally met me at the door of the house as I entered (having stayed at home for this purpose while the other children went on their afternoon walk) and said, with the cunning, playful way of his when hugely pleased : "We've got a *little* sister now." So the proceedings of the Chinese branch of the Williams family are now published in quarto,—two boys and two girls.

A few months before the date of this letter his eldest son, Walworth, was sent to America in charge of the officers of the steam frigate *Powhatan*, in the hope that the voyage and a colder climate might restore the boy's health. Meantime the effect of continual work and the addition of new duties to those connected with the printing-office and dictionary began to tell upon his own vigorous constitution.

TO REV. W. F. WILLIAMS.

SHANGHAI, October 7, 1856.

I have come to this place, chiefly to do the duties of Chinese Interpreter to the Legation, but also for health's sake. The change has done me good thus far, for I have received the tonic of a cooler climate as early as October, while at Canton it is still warm.

At last, through the goodness of God, I have completed my "Dictionary of the Canton Dialect," at which I was engaged for six years. The book has not yet been enough used to enable me to see how serviceable it will prove in other dialects. It is a surprise to myself when I look back upon these years to remark how little I have been hindered in progressing with it. The sheets were printed as fast as they were written, which prevented the corrections I would often have been glad to make ; but this was my only course,—to fix my pages as soon as I formed them, or I could never hope to print it at all.

I am still undecided as to accepting the position of Secretary of Legation, but matters now look much more to acceptance than otherwise. I think the Board wish to reduce their printing establishments, and mine is a small affair, as most of our Chinese tracts, etc., are printed in blocks. Perhaps I shall buy out the office myself. I have heard nothing as yet from the Committee on this subject, nor from the Secretary of State, but as the latter has consented to one of the stipulations I made respecting the post, I am, in a measure, constrained to take it. For the year during which I 've drawn my salary I find that the duties do not take nearly all my time, but this may be different in the future. I wait for God to direct me, and cannot doubt his wisdom.

The completion of the " Tonic Dictionary in the Canton Dialect " was the important event of the year, not alone to its author, but to all foreign students of the language in Southern China, who had looked with longing for a smaller and more accurate hand-book than the bulky and untrustworthy volumes of earlier Chinese scholars. The design of producing a little vocabulary for beginners, which Mr. Williams commenced in 1849, had been altered in the course of the work to the extent of re-writing some fifty pages, when he became convinced of the evident desirableness of a more complete lexicon. At that time the foreigners living in or about Canton so far outnumbered those in other parts of China as to render the adoption of the Cantonese dialect sounds almost a necessity in a work designed for practical and colloquial use. The day for an exhaustive rearrangement of De Guignes and Dr. Morrison had not yet come, but the improvement and advance in Oriental linguistic studies since those great dictionaries appeared could still be embodied in a useful volume ; whatever had been written on Chinese lexicography and was within reach was gathered into this book, and to this was added all that a wide range of general knowledge and a score of years' experience could contribute to the author's purpose. "Thus" (writes Rev. Wm. A. Macy in a review of the work) "in addition to the combined treasures of his predecessors, we have new stores of definition and illustration, and in particular an unrivalled accuracy in the case of terms of geography, history, and natural science. Where previous writers had to content themselves with saying, a river, a tree, a fish, or an insect, Dr. Williams has labored to fix upon the exact place, locality, and individual, or on the true technical name in every case. The size of his work will probably not prepare those who have been used to the dignified portliness of De Guignes and Morrison, for the statement that no other dictionary is so full in its definitions; and this is not only in the abundance of synonymous expressions, but also in the shades and changes of meaning." The dictionary contained about seven thousand eight hundred characters, with introduction, appendix, and index, in nine hundred octavo pages.

A fourth edition of the "Chinese Commercial Guide" was completed and printed in the fall of this year, proving to be the last work ever issued from this press. In the eight years which had elapsed since the appearance of the third edition, important changes—the development of Shanghai, Foochow, and Hongkong as centres of a large and increasing trade, the treaties with the neighboring countries of Siam and Japan—had rendered necessary the alteration and enlargement of this little compendium into a good-sized volume of three hundred and eighty-four pages. Its main *raison d'être*, like that of the "Calendars," was to help support the press which produced it, the profits of all Mr. Williams' books being devoted to the same end. The thoroughness and accuracy of these minor labors are, however, no less characteristic of the man who thought it necessary to use his best abilities in whatever he found to do.

During Mr. Williams' absence in Shanghai, the gradually increasing tension between Governor-General Yeh, of Canton, and the foreign representatives had terminated in a serious rupture when the Chinese officials seized a number of suspected pirates upon a boat carrying the British flag. This—subsequently famous as the "Lorcha Arrow" case—was immediately resented as a significant insult by the impulsive Sir John Bowring, Governor of Hongkong, and there followed a more or less furious warfare of words between China and England. This resulted eventually in the second war with China.

In consequence of acts of reprisal by Yeh, and the total stoppage of trade at Canton, it was deemed advisable to remove the head-quarters of the United States Legation to Macao. While their archives and furniture were being conveyed by way of the Macao Passage, American frigates in the other channel of the river were battering down the Bogue forts in retaliation for their firing upon the United States flag. This sharp punishment on the part of the American Commodore Armstrong carried its lesson as to the respect due his nation, quite as effectively as the English admiral's previous contest at these same forts and his subsequent bombardment of the city. It is notable, moreover, as being the only hostilities ever entered into by Americans in China; and these were considered of such small importance by Yeh that when Dr.

Parker resumed correspondence with him, he coolly replied that "there is no matter of strife between our respective nations,"—an example of assumed indifference which seems to surpass the powers even of a North American Indian.

TO W. F. WILLIAMS.

MACAO, January 27, 1857.

You have heard something of the proceedings of the Chinese and English, I presume, and the destruction of the foreign Factories on December 14th. My printing-office and household gear perished with the rest, and all the books I had on hand, excepting the "Dictionary" and "Commercial Guide." The type and materials are all valued at some $20,000, most of which belongs to the mission; whether we shall ever receive any compensation is a matter of doubt, for the United States is not often in a hurry to collect such claims. I do not blame myself for want of precaution, for I did not believe that the Chinese would set the Factories on fire, and had left them only two days before to see how Sarah was situated in her newly rented house in Macao. The remaining copies of the *Repository* were burned in boxes ready to move, and had I been there most of *them* could have been saved, though not the printing-office. The loss is one I much regret, for 't was in good working order, and I was in hopes of doing something with it.

I have now concluded to be Secretary of Legation, though the duties of interpreter are nearly all I have to perform. The office is not, therefore, one which will take me away from intercourse with the Chinese, nor (I hope) from ever feeling the same desire to do them good. Moreover, I am pretty sure that the Board will not replace the printing establishment, now that it is burned, as I was nearly convinced that the Committee would ere long have sold it or refused to continue it. The fire will doubtless decide them as it has me, though I do not regard the dissolution as final. I have a great respect for the Board and its officers, and believe that it is managed as well and made of as good material as any mission society extant. If I can do as much good to the Chinese now as before, and not use mission money, I shall not regret it. Yet where it will end and where the progress of events will drift me, I cannot say, and have, indeed, some fears.

Our brother John was poisoned by arsenic put into the bread at the general Hongkong bakery, by a Chinese, whereby nearly four hundred persons were poisoned in one morning. It has been computed that thirty-six pounds of arsenic were used, on an average of two grains to an ounce of bread; had a quarter of this quantity been used, probably a hundred would have perished. As it was, the enormous proportion caused vomiting, and not a life was lost thereby. A public thanksgiving was held in the chureh on the following Sunday.

No further doubt now remained as to the course he was to pursue. The destruction of the factories with his printing-office was a burning of his ships, the removal of the last tie which seemed to bind him to his former occupation in China. It was a change, in his estimation, rather of means than of end, his transfer from direct to indirect mission work, where he could "do good to the Chinese and not use mission money." Governor Yeh's act of revenge for the bombardment of Canton would have inflicted an irreparable loss upon Mr. Williams had not the unsold editions of the "Tonic Dictionary" and "Commercial Guide" been taken for distribution to Macao and Hongkong a few weeks previous to the fire.

Mr. Williams' claim for losses in this capacity—mostly in books and furniture—amounted to $1,550, which was allowed in full with interest. His statement concerning the type and mission press, drawn up for the Claim Commission, is of value as comprising a brief history of the first Chinese font ever made.

"This type was made under the orders of the East India Company, and was commenced about 1814. I took charge of it in 1835, at which time it consisted of two fonts, a large-sized one filling sixty cases, and a small-sized filling sixteen cases, besides many hundreds of others in the real and running-hand styles. All of these types had been made by hand on lead or tin blocks, the workmen writing the character on the smooth end, and then cutting it out in relief with chisels.

"The large font originally contained all the characters in the Chinese language, with a few duplicates, about forty-six thousand types nearly an inch square on the face; but of this number many thousands had been lost during the years it had been in use.

"The small and most useful font contained about twenty-two thousand sorts, of which there were many duplicates of the common characters, making the total number amount to about seventy thousand types. During the twenty-one years I have used these fonts I was constantly adding to them, especially to the small-sized one, so that its original number was probably more than kept up. Each type cost from five to six cents, exclusive of the metal, and the lot was probably the most expensive one ever made; the whole was generously given to me in 1842 by the British authorities, through Sir Henry Pottinger."*

---

* The Mission Press at Canton and Macao, during its twenty-five years' existence, printed:

1832–51. The *Chinese Repository*, 20 vols., 8° In all 23,000 copies, including reprints of vols. i. to iv.

1837. Medhurst's "Hok-këen Dictionary." 4°. 300 complete copies.
1841. Bridgman & Williams. "Chinese Chrestomathy." 4°. 800 copies.
1842. Williams. "Easy Lessons in Chinese." 8°. 700 copies.
1844. Williams. "Topography of China." 8°. 200 copies.
1844. Williams. "English and Chinese Vocabulary." 8°. 800 copies.
1844. Williams. "Commercial Guide." 2d edition. 8°. 800 copies.
1845. "Treaties between China, Great Britain, the United States and France." 8°. 100 copies.
1847. Bridgman. "Translation of Premare's Notitia Linguæ Sinicæ." 8°. 600 copies.
1848. Williams. "Commercial Guide." 3d edition. 8°. 800 copies.

Some of the losses of types mentioned were due to thieving native workmen who could not be kept from occasionally pilfering a few handfuls to sell for their worth in metal. In more than one instance it cost hundreds of dollars to replace what was sold for a few cents.

With Mr. Williams' resignation from the American Board the following letter was sent to Dr. Anderson:

MACAO, January 28, 1857.
Rev. R. Anderson, D. D——

DEAR BROTHER :—Your last letter to me has remained unanswered for some months, longer than I intended when I received it at Shanghai, and now it is lost, so that I cannot refer to it, having been burned with others when my house was destroyed December 14th, before all the members of the mission had seen it. I should be glad, therefore, to receive another copy.

From it I gather that you expect that I will leave the mission, and had probably already left it before your letter would be received. I had not, however, seen the way to accept the office of Secretary of Legation at all clearly when it came to hand, but its general tone, combined with the minute of the Prudential Committee of July 3, 1855, showed that the Board had no serious objection to my doing so. At the time the President's appointment was received, October 1, 1855, there

1849–56. Williams. "Anglo-Chinese Calendar." 8°. 8 issues; in all about 2,000 copies.

1849. Meadows. "Translations from the Manchu" (text printed from blocks). 8°.

1854. Bonney. "Vocabulary, with Colloquial Phrases in the Canton Dialect." 8°. 800 copies.

1856. Rutter. "Calculations of Exchanges between England, India, and China." 8°. 300 copies.

1856. Williams. "Tonic Dictionary." 8°. 800 copies.

1856. Williams. "Commercial Guide." 4th edition. 8°. 1000 copies.

The total probably reached some 38,000 volumes, besides a number of pamphlets as jobs. The press earned in all, by its publications and jobs, about $12,000 over and above expenses.

was no member of the Legation in China, and it seemed best to the mission here that I should accept it provisionally—which I did, stating at the same time that I must confer with the Committee, from whom I have heard nothing on the subject. If I had received this minute of July 3d, it is probable that I should have done no otherwise from what I have done.

The subject-matter of your last letter was deferred until I returned from Shanghai, but the extraordinary state of affairs rendered it impossible at that time to hold a mission meeting, my business keeping me in Canton while my family were in Macao. I left Canton on December 11th, to see how my wife was situated, expecting to return in a week, when the destruction of all the Factories by the Chinese on the 14th, placed me in a different position. The question of the disposal of the printing-office was thus settled peremptorily by its entire destruction; the way and means of restoring it to useful operation must be deferred until reference be made to the Committee. All this requires time, and as the Department in Washington had meanwhile acceded to one of my stipulations as to my taking this post, I have accordingly sent in my resignation to the mission, which, I suppose, reached you by the last mail. In it you will observe that I do not regard this dissolution of previous connection as a final one, but rather as a temporary arrangement, made in consequence of the enforced suspension of printing operations. At present I have very much to do in the way of translating official papers, and I hardly know who would have done it just now had I not been here to assist. In fact, during the last eight years I have done nearly all the translating of this sort for the Americans and other consulates,—excepting the English,—and have received no compensation therefor. The burning of the printing-office seems to direct me in the path of conduct, at least until I can get funds with which to procure another press. I shall not be doing wrong in taking the interpretership. I wish you would send me a paper stating the circumstances of the case, for I have not left the direct mission service hastily, but laid the case before the Committee, desiring first to obtain their views. Were not the press destroyed I should have tried to effect some arrangement so that it should not cease altogether.

In all my course in this matter I have kept in view the effect it would have upon the cause of missions. The fact that I am not a minister is well known, while the position I have held has been a secular one and identified with the press. But I wish to have it plainly stated that I leave with the full concurrence of the Committee, so that all who have known me for twenty-four years as one of the mission in China will know why and how I leave it,

I may also say that I wish all success to the work, as much now as ever before, when directly engaged in it. During the last few years of my control of the press here I have had the feeling that you did not altogether like the way in which it was conducted, and wished to discover some good opportunity of getting it off your hands, so that I might be relieved of this work, or you of me. Perhaps I am wrong in this impression, but there seems to be no harm in stating it. You have made arrangements to do away with the presses at Bombay, Madras, and Mampy, and when you said that you saw no necessity for the continuance of the small press here, I presume it would soon have gone too. I have been at times much depressed with this thought, that I did not possess the confidence of those with whom I was working,—but only at times. In going forward with the preparation and printing of the Dictionary (now happily finished after seven years of labor), I felt that I was doing about the best thing I could for the cause, while my efforts were approved of by all the missionaries in the field so far as I know them. But I knew that this was regarded differently at the Rooms if I rightly read the letters we received concerning the printing-press.

This may all now pass, however, for it bears nothing on the feelings I now entertain towards the good cause of missions in China and my desire to do a little towards its advancement. I believe that God has stores of mercy yet to give China, and the way is preparing for her to learn the great things of His law. Ever most truly,

S. W. WILLIAMS.

The year 1857 was one of waiting among Europeans in China and passed quietly, while the governments of Great Britain and France were preparing armaments for a Chinese war. In January, after some useless cannonading, Sir M. Seymour evacuated Canton and awaited reinforcements at Hongkong.

"April.—There have been two or three skirmishes with junks and other government vessels, in which the Chinese have showed more pluck and skill in defending their possessions than heretofore, showing that they are able to learn to fight under proper instruction, and may, in time, become as skilful as other Asiatics. Politically speaking, I think that this is their only chance of preservation, for otherwise they will fall a prey to foreign invaders, and, perhaps, to internal foes and seditions. Moreover, with a better knowledge of war as now carried on they will learn a thousand other things, as well as the trust in foreigners as equals and friends. All this may seem contradictory enough to you, but through war will surely come friendship. If the four greatest western powers could combine, heartily and without suspicion, in forcing the Chinese Government to enter more fully into that intercourse which is its best guaranty of safety, the present gloomy situation with its doubts and fears of convulsion would certainly be cleared away. I would that the Gospel might come among the Chinese without the destruction of their polity and the dismemberment of their dominions, but perhaps that is not to be the way of their regeneration."

As a political forecast, made at a time when the action of the English Parliament regarding China was unknown there, and while the influence of a second combined attack on the imperial policy of seclusion was quite incalculable, this is interesting and remarkable. Meantime the months passed rapidly for Mr. Williams at Macao. "I'm as much at home here as in Canton, though I've not yet got over the feeling that I ought to be reading proofs and printing something. I assist in conducting services on Sunday, of which there are several here carried on by all the missionaries and with good audiences."

The death of his brother John, who had remained in China since his arrival in the Perry expedition, and taken command of one of the steamers plying on the Canton River, occurred at Mr. Williams' house in July. The loss of this warm-hearted younger brother was a keen grief.

In October Dr. Parker returned to America, leaving the Legation in charge of Mr. Williams until the arrival of his successor.

"Nov. 11th.—Mr. Reed has reached Canton, and finds himself in the midst of a whirl of opinion, for every one feels competent to give what costs nothing; he will be perplexed, I suppose, till he learns what it is all worth. I like his bearing much, and think we shall get along pleasantly together. The *Minnesota* is a palace of a ship, and her cabin has been fitted up for Mr. Reed's residence; I suppose he will go up the coast in her, and perhaps I shall go with him. The local matter of Canton must first be settled, so that the people there admit us into the city and give us good locations for our houses; then I presume we shall move towards Peking. I speak of what is generally said, not of any plans fully decided on."

At this date representatives of England, France, Russia, and the United States, all with extraordinary powers, had assembled in China, and were prepared to unite in pressing their demands for renewed treaties and enlarged rights upon the Emperor. The choice of men possessing the qualities and characters of these four plenipotentiaries —Lord Elgin, Baron Gros, Count Poutiatine, and Mr.

Wm. B. Reed—was exceedingly fortunate for the successful achievement of their delicate and important mission; the difficulties of their action in concert were not diminished by the impossibility at first of learning the real complaints and policy of the British, nor by the fact that both Russians and Americans were forbidden by their instructions to lend any active aid to the armed coercion of the French and English allies. The first act of the United States Minister was to request an audience with Yeh, as the representative of a neutral power who volunteered his good offices; the meeting was declined, as a similar offer from the Russians had been a few weeks previously.

TO REV. W. F. WILLIAMS.

MACAO, January 26, 1858.

We are here in the midst of war and peace, trade and plunder, the whole position of society as far as regards foreigners being disjointed, but promising a new and better mortising. Canton was taken with very little opposition by the Allies about a month ago, and Yeh was captured with it, having almost got off, however, when he was recognized by a portrait of him that had been made by one of the writers last summer. He was dressed in common clothes, and one of his followers in official toggery endeavored to personate him, but the enormous size of the Governor-General betrayed the fraud. It has been almost as good as the capture of a province to get this ruthless man in keeping, for, since he was taken prisoner, the next in office, the Governor Pihkwei, has consented to act under the Allies and carry on a local rule so as to secure peace in the city. The apathy of the Cantonese after the fall of their stronghold, and the bitter way in which they talk about their own rulers, gives another instance of the contrariety in their character; they seem now to be inclined to go on peacefully under the oversight of the English, and trade will probably be re-opened erelong. If the foreign residences had not been burned there would be no difficulty in each one's going back to his former quarters and resuming business. The English have restrained their soldiers very well, the French having shown much greater desire to execute vengeance on the citizens and to pillage what they could. On the whole, owing a good deal to the absence of serious opposition, there has not been much damage done. We shall recommence mission work as soon as the blockade is taken off, but I am likely to be a gad-about this year.

"Thus," observes Mr. Reed in his despatch to Washington, " has been consummated that to which so much importance has been attached, the punishment and the humiliation of the Cantonese. The great problem now remains: will this severe blow be felt beyond narrow local bounds, or will this bloodshed be vain? . . . I have no hesitation in saying now that this result has occurred, that it was a disgraceful surrender, without the grace of being voluntary; an indifference to the sacrifice of human life; an obstinate and unreasoning faith in a superiority of race made more absurd by a cowardly dereliction of duty; the insolence of Yeh one day, and his neglect of all means of defence, though with abundance of resources, and running out of back doors the next *; his refusal to

* Mr. Reed's private diary adds some interesting and amusing incidents connected with the capture of the Chinese Governor-General: "Captain Hall says that Yeh is a cowardly blackguard, and that he trembled in every joint as he helped him out of the boat and up the side of the *Inflexible*. He adds that Yeh eats well, drinks well, walks about the steamer, exercises, and examines the engine with interest, and is quite contented. . . . One grotesque scene of his captivity I may describe: The received notion was that, if taken prisoner, the great chief would surely commit suicide or attempt it, and accordingly every precaution was taken to avert this. He was seated in a large chair and two sailors stationed by his side with orders not to permit him to raise his hand to his head or mouth. The consequence was that the moment he tried to pick his teeth or scratch his ear or arrange his cap, Jack seized him by the arm and held it down. It was soon found, however, that he had no such heroic intention, and he was therefore left in peace. On the *Inflexible*, when asked if he cared to send for any books to read, he replied that he had already read every book printed."

receive the visit of a friendly power, such as he admits the United States to be, at a time when some good offices of mediation might have been rendered;—in view of all this I do not hesitate to say that a new policy towards China ought to be initiated, and that the powers of Western civilization must insist on what they know to be their rights, and give up the dream of dealing with China as a power to which any ordinary rules apply."

With such moderate and enlightened views upon the difficult subject of reaching and influencing the Imperial authorities for their own good, Mr. Reed was the first of the plenipotentiaries to welcome and carry out a plan for jointly and simultaneously addressing the prime-minister at Peking upon the subject of their demands. The four letters were forwarded in February through the provincial governor at Suchau, but received no response, excepting a message to Governor Ho for transmission to the foreigners; in this the Emperor's government refer them to a newly appointed Commissioner at Canton, and deny their right to correspond directly with the high authorities at Peking. The reply to such a rebuff, it was generally agreed, must be an advance of the allied powers to the mouth of the Peiho. Many indications pointed towards long and protracted negotiations. Accordingly, before the departure of his legation for the north, Mr. Williams sent his wife and three little children to America on a sailing vessel, which left Hongkong in March, 1858. It was a sad scattering of the family group, for, besides the wide separation of these, his eldest son was now at school in Utica, while the youngest, a baby, being considered too small to travel, was left to the tender care of a missionary lady living in Canton. A natural anxiety for the safety of these continually re-occurs in the Journal kept during his absence, and tinged the interest or enjoyment of every hour; but an unshaken belief that the same Almighty Arm protected 'them now as ever preserves him from giving way to harrowing concern. The exclamation of an aged friend of his boyhood, who saw the letters written at this time, touches the chord to which all his thoughts were attuned. "What a comfort," she said to his wife, "to have him on almost every page commend you all to God!" The comfort, indeed, was his own as well as hers; "Cast thy burden on the Lord" never failed to bring with its injunction the cheering assurance that "He will sustain."

The continuous narrative of his experiences during the next two eventful years is taken from his letters and journals.

CHAPTER VIII.

"April 17, 1858.—The *Mississippi* anchored at about 11 o'clock this morning on account of the thick fog which obscured the horizon, while the zenith was clear, but upon finding our position at noon we took up the anchor and slowly ran up to the mouth of the river Peiho, off which we arrived by three P.M. The anchor was hardly at the bow before a furious gust came down from the north, bringing with it a cloud of impalpable sand which settled over the ship and gradually penetrated through the doors into the cabins, covering every thing with the dust. A slight dash of rain on deck made it smell just as a street does when sprinkled by water-carts—that aluminous earthy odor we all know so well. The sun through this sand-storm appeared as livid and red as I ever saw it in Egypt when the great winds blew. The English men-of-war and the Russian *Amerika* are already here and lying all about us; it is a dull anchorage, quite eight miles from the land, which appears as a dim strip, and that only in clear weather.

"19th.—The morning is calm and bright; the warm sun has turned the whole ship's company into a lively crowd of washermen, some at their clothes but mostly scrubbing the ship from the dust which had settled in and on every part of her. Yesterday, Sunday, Capt. Nicholson had the ship's company assembled to service, which he conducted himself. No sermon was read as you may suppose, but this public recognition of God and the honor due his worship is so much better than it was in most of Perry's squadron that the contrast leads me to speak of it.

"24th.—The French frigate *L'Audacieuse* arrived yesterday. Messengers from the four ministers started this morning, each with a letter for the Gov. Genl. of the province of Chihli, and enclosing another for the prime-minister Yu, granting the

Chinese Government time to send an envoy. Of course there was not much to note in the brief interview with the officer who took the letters, but he expressed a disinclination to receive them on shore and took them from the boat in so tart a manner as to suggest rather an unfavorable prospect toward a peaceful solution of these questions.

"The Russian admiral sent an invitation for us to dine with him this afternoon. He is a plain man, but one who soon attracts you by his excellent sense and extensive information; his suite consists of seven persons, but only three of them were on board to sit down to table. Inasmuch as I.'ve never before dined with Russians you may expect to hear the bill of fare, but under the circumstances it could hardly be taken as a sample of this common style of entertainment on shore. After soup came a pasty-cake in thin slices with tart sweetmeats between them, then further pastry-meat cakes with rice croquets; the sausages and peas which followed were not so palatable, the latter being a bit touched from canning; then beef cutlets—the only hearty dish on the table; for dessert came a preparation of eggs and tart made I suppose like floating-islands, but looking so much like a plate of scoria just out of a volcano, that I could not attempt it until the count assured us that it was light and palatable in spite of its appearance—and so indeed we found it and the cakes which were taken with it. We had about finished our repast when the captain and interpreter returned from their visit to the Chinese officers on shore. These it seems have proposed a meeting between the ministers coming from Peking and the Russians to-morrow. The old interpreter, the missionary Avercoom, who has lived in Peking many years, was chief spokesmen in this report, and like Eleazer of Damascus he would not eat until he had delivered his message: more than that, he would not even drink the glass of gin he had poured out as a whet to his dinner."

TO REV. W. F. WILLIAMS.

U. S. S. *Minnesota*, GULF OF PICHILI, April 30, 1858.

I was interrupted when last writing you by some Chinese officials coming alongside from the newly appointed Imperial

Commissioners, who had recently arrived from Peking to treat with the foreign ministers here. This letter was a copy of one bro't off on the 28th but refused on account of the informality in writing it—the names of their country having been placed about an inch above ours, an indignity much more marked than it would be if we wrote AMERICA followed by china in our despatches to them; the elevation or depression in the written column of a person, title, or country denote the greatest difference in dignity of position and rank in the Chinese language. The Governor General made an apology in returning the paper, laying the blame on his clerk, who had received no practice or sample in such things, and were it not really such a common matter for Chinese officials to show contempt of foreign dignitaries by just such petty indignities we might have accepted his despatch. Mr. Reed's titles take up only a dozen or fifteen characters, whereas the Gov. Gen'l requires something like forty to describe himself, and it may easily have happened that an inexperienced scribe thoughtlessly began the shorter one lower down on the page. The incident gives you an idea of what we have to be prepared for; it is a difficult thing to manage such people, because while one is decided not to take any insult it can hardly be known how much to allow for real ignorance. It needs skilful doctoring not to kill where you only meant to cure.

On the 3d of May the first interview took place between the American Minister and the Chinese Commissioner in the Taku Forts.

"The interview lasted about two hours and was quiet and serious, the attendant Chinese standing with great respect and showing the utmost interest in all that was said. Mr. Martin interpreted while I took notes and suggested such topics as were likely to be forgotten. Without going into a detail of the whole conversation, it ended by Mr. Reed's requiring some satisfactory proof that the letter of the President, which he bore to the Emperor of China, should be properly acknowledged by the latter and not sent back in the mutilated manner of the former letter forwarded by Dr. Parker. A long table covered with eatables and ornamented with an immense table-cloth of red felt was placed before us, but the Chinese ate nothing, hardly sipping the tea, Tan being so taken up with the discussion that he even forgot to offer Mr. Reed a dish—rather unusual in a well-bred Chinese gentleman. Neither Tan, Tsung, nor Wu appear very intellectual in expression, though all that they said was sensible and discreet; only once was there any thing like laughter, and that was somewhat forced. The guard outside were not so easily kept in order, three or four grenadier-looking officers being kept busy walking among them, not seldom ordering the lash to be applied over their shoulders; but curiosity got the better of discipline, which was no wonder. We returned to the *Antelope* half wet through with the spray, but not dissatisfied with the result of our first visit. For my part it seems to me that Mr. Reed in this interview has put himself in a right position before the Chinese in letting them know his sentiments. The poor fellows have no idea of the powers slumbering in these ships. Since I've seen that crowd of conceited and helpless officials, my pity is more excited at their ignorant confidence than my indignation at their refusal of our demands. I am afraid that nothing short of the Society for the Diffusion of Cannon Balls will give them the useful knowledge they now require to realize their own helplessness."

Meantime the English and French Ministers refused to see Tan unless he presented credentials of higher powers.

"May 8th.—Admiral Seymour, Capt. Hall and Lord Elgin all successively came aboard to-day to talk on various points. It seems that on the occasion of the delivery of the letters granting six days for the Commissioners to produce powers like those given to Kiying, the two English interpreters demanded an audience with Tan himself, and after some hard words succeeded in getting into his presence. The Chinese felt this to be a high-handed assumption, and not unnaturally complain of it. I think nothing is ultimately gained by demanding humiliating concessions of this sort which pique their dignity. The English Admiral is not pleased with the occurrence.

"May 10th.—Another visit to the Commissioners on shore to-day. Tan said that he was in receipt of an answer from his Majesty as to accepting and acknowledging the President's letter, but that he could not exhibit the original on account of many other directions therein. This reply was made, I guess, in order that Tan might not run the risk of seeing the barbarians, in presence of all his subordinates, irrevently handle the Emperor's edict. The promise of a copy of the portion which concerned us was accepted, and we are to bring our letter ashore to-morrow if the rescript is satisfactory. It would, I'm afraid, have derogated somewhat from the reverence due this President's Letter (with a large L), if the Commissioner and his company had known that I was writing my notes of the meeting on top of it.

"May 12th.—Mr. Reed left the *Antelope* for his ship yesterday with a bad cold. Mr. Martin and I delivered to the Chinese officials our paper this morning; he went ashore and had the sedan chair brought down, in which at the request of the Lt.-Col. I remained seated while he went to inform Tsin of my coming. The treasurer met me at the door of the tent and we were soon seated at the tables covered perhaps with the identical messes of last Monday. Mr. Martin has now become well acquainted with several of the officers, and they regard him with respect and confidence. The interview lasted two hours. We brought up all the arguments we could think of to induce them to reconsider the questions now at issue, especially those concerning Tan's full powers; they persisting in asserting that he had fuller powers than any official now in the capital. . . . The proposition to go to Peking is excessively obnoxious to them all; they show plainly that they mean to try the issue rather than admit it peaceably. What can you do with such wrong-headed men—men upon whom no impression seems possible except through their fears? 'Do? Why fight them, kill them,' some say, 'until they do as you wish.' I say, try to teach them, patiently, kindly and with hope. Perhaps God has it in his scheme to join these opposites and carry out his own plans of improvement by judgment and mercy joined.

"May 13th.—I made a visit on board the *Furious* this morning in order to make some explanatory statements respecting the results of our interview yesterday. My hap was rather luckless, for Baron Gros came up just as I did, and I saw only Mr. Bruce. The more I talked with him the stronger was my conviction that the conclusion the allies were coming to of making a rupture with Tan in regard to his powers was likely to deprive the issue of much of its moral value. To take the Taku forts because he cannot, or will not, produce a decree like that of Kiying's, authorizing him to settle every point, instead of the higher ground of his refusal of a peaceable visit to Peking, seems likely to divest this more important demand of all its effect. It is to my mind a misstep and a blunder. . . . Baron Gros has just ended a long visit to Mr. Reed, and I had the opportunity of stating fully to him my conviction that Tan has all the powers which he could really get from his government, and that it would greatly weaken the form and moral effect of an issue on the more serious points if it should be made where the Chinese felt that they were right. I think that he rather agreed with me, but he was wary in saying much. The Baron is a pleasant and agreeable man, and one is inclined to trust him, tho'—like a true diplomatist—it is hard to conclude what he means. . . .

"In the *North China Heralds* brought to-day are some ill-natured remarks about 'intrusive neutrals,' and a tone of criticism upon what has been done here that is very annoying on acc^t of its injustice and bad tendency. The objects of these four ministers may diverge to some extent—Russia has a boundary to settle, France has her form of Christianity to strengthen and vindicate, England has her trade to foster, and America has all objects to gain which will enlarge her influence, but all are united in agreeing to the demands which will most effectually open the empire to the access of other nations."

FROM MR. REED'S DIARY.

"May 14th.—Mr. Williams came to my room this morning with the good news that last night about 1 o'clock he was awakened by Baron Ostensacken with a message from the Russian Minister to the effect that the Mandarin Secretary

Pien had come to him yesterday and insisted on an interview to-day, professing a willingness to yield to the demand for an occasional visit to Peking. He thought the news sufficiently important to be sent at once to the Ministers outside. . . . We are all in high spirits, and Mr. Williams and I have been hard at work on a draught of a treaty. I wish my cabin could be photographed for you. In the port cabin, or in his state-room writing for me in the big book, is my son. On the starboard side, in the back cabin, are Dr. Williams, with his pale, intelligent face, and myself, preparing our memoranda for a treaty. And on the other side are his two Chinese writers hard at work with their camels'-hair brushes and Indian-ink saucers, writing Chinese. It would be quite a scene for you. . . . The *Mitraille* a French gun-boat, has arrived, making the 31st man-of-war now at anchor—and this bright morning it is a glorious sight—the numerous lorches, gun-boats, and gigs pulling about from one ship to another, with their flags, red, tricolor, and starry, floating about, and at every moment lines of variegated signals hoisted by the admirals, and answered by the fleets. The *Mississippi* had target practice this morning with her great guns, and the first shot, delivered with the precision of rifle practice, knocked the target all to pieces. (I hope the English and Frenchmen saw it.)"

"May 15th.—Mr. Martin presented an almanac to the prefect of Chau, at an interview the other day. He began to look it over, and coming to the 10th commandment expressed his admiration at such an injunction, and then wondered why the English did not observe this requirement, instead of coveting the lands and towns of China. The next day at my meeting with Tsien the same officer was seated at his right hand, and had the same book spread out before him, evidently prepared with some point. He begged us to circulate many such tracts among the English to lead them to act more in conformity with these doctrines. At a suitable moment he again referred to the little volume, quoting the 6th commandment against the English, alleging that they could not be Christians, for they killed the Chinese with opium merely for gain. How strongly England and opium are connected in the minds of these people can only be appreciated after long acquaintance with them.

"May 19th.—The Emperor has negatived Tan's memorial regarding the admission of foreigners up the river and so to Peking. I am the more sorry, for there now seems to be no alternative but to reject Tan and his colleagues and push on as far as force can go. . . . To Captain Du Pont was intrusted the delivery of the President's letter yesterday. We landed at the boats—some six or eight of us—and proceeded to the marquee, a boy carrying the Letter (!) in his two hands, with four marines flanking him, and walking just ahead of Captain Du Pont. Tan and his colleagues were standing at the door, and as the letter was brought in he requested the Captain to lay it on a small table, before which hung a yellow silken screen. After it was placed there he put his hand upon it in token of acknowledgment, and then asked his guests to be seated, placing them all on his left hand. The interview lasted about an hour, and went off with the usual civilities, tho' there is a degree of restraint in a conversation carried on through interpreters which it is hard to get over.

"Mr. Martin and I went to call upon them again this morning, the Minister wishing us to sound the Chinese mind on the matter of our treaty. Tsien and his assessors, Wang and Pien, were at the door to receive us with a large crowd of inferior officials. After referring to our satisfaction at the reception of the letter yesterday, and the reasons for making Capt. Du Pont the medium of delivering it, it occurred to me to show the Treasurer one of my maps [of China]; he had never seen any thing of the kind before, and was, with those around him, greatly pleased and surprised at it. When I gave it to the old man he took it with many thanks, even rising up to add force to his words. Then to business; some of the articles of our draft were passed without objection, those relating to toleration [of Christianity in China] and the payment of claims were copied off to show the Commissioner, those permitting and regulating visits to Peking were rejected, and others were amended, the colloquy being conducted with considerable animation and constant good humor on his part. We had nearly finished the general examination of our draft when it was interrupted by the arrival of Dr. Bradley with the following letter from the Minister:

"'My Dear Sir:—I have this moment received a communication from Baron Gros, informing me that to-morrow a final communication will be sent to Tan with a summons from the Admirals, and that the forts will be taken *two hours* afterwards. Consider this intelligence as strictly confidential, not to be whispered, for obvious reasons, on shore or even to Mr. Martin. If you receive this note while you are with the Treasurer, or he with you, my positive direction is for you, in the most gracious way, to break off all conversation—simply saying that you have received directions from me to do so. You will, I am sure, see the necessity of the Chinese knowing nothing of the Allied intentions till they learn them directly.

"'Truly yours,
"'W. B. Reed.
"'May 19th.'

"The note came fully an hour too soon for my intentions, as I wished to make one more effort to show the Chinese the folly and danger of resistance. Tsien seemed to attach much importance to the mediation of Mr. Reed with the Allies, and spoke slightingly of the conduct of the Russian envoy—to him they would probably have referred to Mr. Reed in similar terms, such is the usual time-serving conduct of the Chinese. I came away rather dispirited and sad.

"May 20th.—Before noon nearly half the crew of the *Mississippi* had come into the *Antelope* to witness the fray. At eight o'clock Captain Hall took the summons ashore; of course no one expected a compliance. At a few minutes past ten the *Cormorant* began to move up towards the fort on the left bank, the Chinese firing at her from all their guns. The cannonading soon became general as the ship got nearer, and the forts continued to answer for an hour, doing their best to repel and destroy, but with the usual insufficiency of Chinese artillery. The shot came out as far as the *Antelope* in one or two cases, but most of them fell on the opposite bank, proving how high the guns were pointed. The French landed on the left bank first, the Chinese escaping as soon as the enemy entered the forts, and fleeing in all directions. We heard but little musketry firing. The marquee in which I had the interview was pierced by three or four balls, which did it little injury, and on going ashore Mr. Martin found the plates of fruit and comfits still on the table, pretty much as we had left them the evening before. . . . On the whole the Chinese have made a pretty brave defence. Some officers were found in their places who had killed themselves rather than survive defeat—another contrast to our customs presented by these people, for as our efforts in warfare are usually spent in cutting other people's throats, here we see the Chinese cutting their own. Here is a fine variation of the fashion, however : Tah, the Manchu tsiangkiun, when the forts were lost, threw himself into the water, from whence his followers dragged him out alive ; this attempt to clear his fame as a loyal statesman and soldier may suffice well enough instead of the reality of suicide."

During the week following the capture, the plenipotentiaries waited at anchor while the Allied Admirals pushed on up the river to Tientsin. On the 28th, the passage was pronounced by them to be perfectly safe, and the four Ministers proceeded in small steamers to Tientsin ; the American legation, on account of the surly and disreputable conduct of the captain of the chartered steamer *Antelope*, preferring to be guests of Count Poutiatine rather than undergo temporary imprisonment in their uncomfortable tender.

Writing to a friend before starting for Tientsin Mr. Williams says:

"I look upon this quarternion of fleets and plenipotentiaries collected off the capital of China as part of that great course of missionary work. Will the Church send such men to occupy the opening which these great ships and embassadors make? Last week I witnessed the capture of those four forts which guarded the mouth of the river, where about 2,000 foreigners drove away 3,200 Chinese from their guns and blew up their works, and I agreed with Count Poutiatine that even this little encounter will, like Bunker Hill, be probably of more importance to the world than were half of Napoleon's great battles. It is not well to judge beforehand, but if the Emperor does not hear the present demands and prefers the issue of war, he may never again have a chance of bringing peace to his throne."

The fall of the Taku forts had produced an immediate effect in Peking. Upon their arrival at Tientsin the foreign embassadors were given houses sufficiently commodious for the wants of their respective legations. Cards sent to each of them announced that two new commissioners, Kweiliang and Hwashana, had come from the capital with full powers to treat in place of poor Tan, who was now degraded in rank. Negotiations were opened by visits from each Minister separately, Lord Elgin having negatived the suggestion that they should exchange the introductory courtesies with the Chinese together. On Monday, June 7th, came the turn of the American envoy.

" This morning all our party were astir by dawn, so as to be ready for the visit which was appointed for *six o'clock*. Mr. Reed, in a blazing green and vermilion chair with eight bearers, was preceded by Mr. Martin as interpreter, and had before and behind him six marines. Then came my chair, and then those of five others in a long row. The place of meeting was a temple on the banks of the river, about a mile and a half from our house; we were received there with more politeness than Tan had shown us at Taku, Kweiliang and Hwashana receiving Mr. Reed at the door and conducting him to a seat between them, the latter then occupying the chair on his right. Two chairs on Kwei's left were filled by myself and Dr. McClenahan, but their opposites on Hwa's right were empty, no native presuming to sit in their presence. There were seven separate tables altogether, covered with small plates of fruit, sweetmeats, etc., similar in every respect to those spread out in the tent at Taku.

"Kweiliang is a well-preserved man of seventy-four, tall and not too large for his height, placid in speech and countenance, having a stoop of the shoulders and a quavering tone of voice, which more than any thing else indicates his age. It was an interesting sight to look upon this veteran in Chinese politics, an exponent of the policy of his country, vainly striving by appeals to reason, propriety, law, and favor to stem the influences and power now brought to bear. Hwashana is fifty-three, fresh, healthy, animated, talking well ; he has the appearance of being rather a dissipated liver ; he is a Mongolian and Kweiliang a Manchu, but it would puzzle one to point out any difference of type between them and the Chinese standing about.

"The meeting opened by a few ceremonial offices of courtesy, after which Mr. Martin translated *viva voce* a statement of Mr. Reed's views and intentions in coming to Tientsin and the general policy of the United States in respect to China. The paper surveying the proceedings of the past year showed how much China had acted against her best interests in secluding herself and treating friendly nations so coldly, assured the Commission that England did not now desire territory, and declared that the U. S. Minister could hope to accomplish nothing more for China by mediation unless she was ready to yield to reasonable demands. We then handed them the draft of our treaty and Mr. Reed delegated me to meet an officer to-morrow for discussion. Pien, who seems to stand behind the Commissioners as a sort of spokesman and expounder of their views, was suggested, but refused as not being of high enough rank. An officer named Chang, who wore a red button was then named, and he immediately stepped forward like a soldier from the ranks. I was amused at his promptness, but more interested in his intelligent face and manner. He did not mention his office but we were told that he was a hereditary viscount; he was a pattern and model of ugliness.

"Now come up again the old subject of the President's Letter and its reply. They promise one soon. One would think that the answer of Hienfung to Mr. Buchanan required all the Hanlin to draw it up, for two weeks are gone since we handed them the box. The copy of the powers given the Commissioners was then presented to Mr. Reed, and at the same time a paper purporting to be the original was very reverently taken out of a yellow box enclosed and lined with yellow silk. As I looked it over Kweiliang turned around two or three times to see if I handled it reverently, and while I read aloud the main draft of it he watched me very closely as tho' trying to catch the foreign sounds. It was a singularly worded document, restraining the commissioners from doing any thing detrimental to China, but allowing them to grant whatsoever was reasonable, in fact, allowing all or nothing as the results should favor or force the negotiators. My Chinese writer when called upon afterwards to explain some of the terms, commended the style of this edict, assuring me that we spoke altogether too plainly, and that this amphibology was the preferable style. I infer from such credentials that Kwei and Hwa are empowered to give up all if the pressure is sufficiently powerful."

In this wise, by reason of the frankness and comity of the American plenipotentiary, this initial visit of ceremony established the *entente cordiale* with the Chinese, to the great satisfaction of both parties. "Never again," (says the "Middle Kingdom," in an expression which its author more than once made use of), "in the history of nations can functionaries to whom were confided the settlement of questions of so great moment, be brought together in such honest ignorance each of the other's fears, intentions, and wishes." The interviews of the English and French lacked the element of cordiality, some technical defect being found with the credentials, so that in

Lord Elgin's case, as the Blue Book reports, "his Lordship rose immediately, and the Commissioners, after a few vain endeavors, by words and gestures, to retain him, accompanied him to his chair."

During the following week occurred two incidents of interest:

"March 10th.—The Russian Admiral went to-day to the temple where the Commissioners lodged, to see them concerning an article of his treaty, when he found them in a state of high excitement and disgust at the conduct and threats of H. N. Lay, one of the British interpreters. He had forced himself upon the high commissioners, threatening them with a bombardment of the city unless they signed the treaty soon, or unless they allowed the Allies entrance up all the rivers in the country as well as liberty to appoint consuls wherever they pleased. Lay was using extremely harsh language to these high functionaries, who were so alarmed by his threats that the Count [Poutiatine] found it useless to attempt any negotiation, and retired chagrined and surprised at such conduct. Soon after he reached his rooms, the Chinese officers sent to inquire whether it was true that the town was to be bombarded to-night.

"Kiying came on a visit to Mr. Reed this morning as a private gentleman, and was received with respect in every way. He has grown old and infirm and deaf withal, but retains the lineaments as given in the portrait in the " Middle Kingdom." He comes as an advisor and reporter to Kwei and Hwa, and bore a red button to-day. When shown the copy of the treaty of Wanghia, found in Yeh's yamun at Canton, he recognized it, and explained that the three treaties found there were left in Canton by express orders from Taokwang so that they might be readily referred to if it ever should be necessary.

"12th.—Kiying and Mr. Reed had another meeting in the Temple of the Winds near the river bank, Mr. Martin and I accompanying. The old man inquired about Dr. and Mrs. Parker, Morrison, and others. When told I had published a portrait of him in the " Middle Kingdom " from the daguerreotype taken by West, he expressed no little anxiety to see it, and we promised to try and get him a copy; he at first thought that the book was in Chinese, and showed much pleasure in hearing that his name and features were known in America. He made us each take a mouthful from his chop-sticks, and then let us go in peace, evidently gratified with the visit.

"June 13th.—We hear to-day that Kiying left for the capital this morning, having been ordered by the court to return there immediately, but no one tells us the reason; it seems that he and his associates misinformed Mr. Reed the other day when they told him that they had been sent to inquire of the Allies what were their demands. . . . Last night Capt. Du Pont was obliged to enter the city with the marines and demand the return of two of our servants who had been set upon and arrested. A general and bloody scrimmage was narrowly avoided, but the servants were returned. Such *contretemps* rather dampen our hopes of speedily ending our affairs here, tho' the Chinese do not say much about them; in one view of the case, however, they are almost necessary, for we shall get nothing important out of the Chinese unless we stand in a menacing attitude before them. They would grant nothing unless fear stimulated their sense of justice, for they are among the most craven of people, cruel and selfish as heathenism can make men, so we must be backed by force if we wish them to listen to reason. In this respect I sometimes am inclined to think that the Americans would be more respected if they had joined the Allies in warlike operations; yet again, the consciousness of having themselves really no sufficient reason for a resort to arms would show the injustice of such hostilities and nullify their effect."

This entry is the last reference contained in the journal concerning the most dramatic episode of this eventful month. Though rumors of his tragedy reached them before the last of the foreigners had left Peking, it was not until many weeks later that they learned the fate of the poor and aged Kiying, once the chief man in the empire, and on this day a wrecked and decrepit statesman playing his last card in the desperate hope of retrieving fortune and honor. There will always remain a degree of mystery about his sudden appearance and disappearance at this juncture in Tientsin, which time is not likely to remove. He had, probably, in his eagerness to prove his influence with the foreigners, made large promises at court of persuading them to retire down the river, if himself permitted to repair to their councils; and the pressure of fear upon the capital was at the moment so overwhelming that he was allowed to go at his own risk. The theory that he was forced by his enemies to undertake this impossible errand with the certain hope of inculpating himself, though possible, does not seem to be either reasonable or evident, the man being already in disgrace and politically harmless. He appeared before the foreigners in a deplorable condition, mentally and physically, found no credit with them (being without credentials), was jealously regarded by the native commissioners, and in his disappointment and weakness said many silly things. In a panic he fled home without his master's leave, laying himself open to a charge of disobedience, which is treason. The story of his end is brief and perfectly characteristic of an oriental court: Arrived at Peking the silken cord was sent him from the Emperor's hand in "Our extreme desire to be at once just and gracious," and in consideration of past services the old Prime Minister of Taokwang was tenderly allowed to strangle himself in lieu of going out to meet the executioner.

Mr. Williams' chief individual achievement at this

time, that of incorporating an important article in the treaty, allowing the practice and profession of Christianity in China, is told in a letter written many years later:

NEW HAVEN, Sept. 12, 1878.

As the matter of the "Toleration Clauses" in the treaties of 1858 has become one of general interest to the mission body in China, I regret that the statement concerning it in the report of the Shanghai Conference should not have been more accurate. The toleration of Christianity was not brought forward by the Chinese commissioners in any shape, for it was a point upon which they were wholly ignorant as a religious question. The Russian Minister was the first to formulate an article on this subject, and in the discussion which ensued as to his draft of a treaty presented to the Chinese officials, they are said to have expressed their willingness to allow missionaries to travel through the country, inasmuch as these could usually speak the language; they opposed a like permission to merchants, who could not do so, and this ignorance was sure to breed trouble. These officials knew the Russian priests in Peking to be quiet, industrious men, and were doubtless willing enough to admit them to further privileges, but they could give no opinion on the general toleration of Christianity, for they knew practically nothing of its peculiar tenets.

The next day I got the Chinese text of this article and drew up a similar one for the U. S. treaty, leaving out the proviso that "a certain number of missionaries" would be allowed, and inserting the two names for Protestant and Roman Catholic churches, so as to bring the former distinctly before them as not the same as the Roman and Greek churches; it was otherwise different in phraseology but not in spirit. The night before the treaty was signed, a note was sent from the Chinese, rejecting this article altogether, on the ground that Protestant missionaries had their families with them, and must be restricted to the open ports; the inference was therefore pretty plain that the novelty of foreign women travelling about the country had presented itself to their minds as an objection to allowing Americans to preach Christianity. As soon as I could do so I drew up another form of the same article, and started off next morning to lay it before the Imperial Commissioners. It was quite the same article as before, but they accepted it without any further discussion or alteration; however, the word "whoever" in my English version was altered by Mr. Reed to "any person, whether citizen of the U. S. or Chinese convert, who"—because he wished every part of the treaty to refer to U. S. citizens, and cared not very much whether it had a toleration article or not. I did care, and was thankful to God that it was inserted. It is the only treaty in existence which contains the royal law. I have always regarded the present article as better than the discarded one; that in the British treaty was abridged from it, and I understood at the time that it would not have been inserted if ours had not contained such a clause. It must be said, moreover, that if the Chinese had at all comprehended what was involved in these four toleration articles, they would never have signed one of them. In the *Chinese Repository* you will find a partial toleration of our religion by the Emperor Taokwang, but this was only a rescript and did not carry with it the weight of a treaty, and during the fourteen years which had intervened since its promulgation it had pretty much lost its effect.

I could never ascertain who had a hand in causing the rejection of my first form of the article, but think that it was someone connected with the French legation. The harsh and unjust criticisms of some persons on these articles in 1860 was only the beginning of the pulling and hauling they have since received; but it is much easier to find fault and overthrow than to improve and build up. Though Christianity does not depend upon treaties for its progress and power, these articles have proved to be a check upon the native officials, who have been taught therein not to destroy what they did not approve. I thank God that the Imperial Government was thereby bound not to become a persecuting government, as it has more than once since wished to be.

This incident is important enough to warrant some further extracts from his journal:

"About nine o'clock P.M., just as we had indulged in a triumph which I do not think was unpardonable, a note came from the officials addressed to Martin and me, withdrawing the privilege in the most decided terms. The note was accompanied by the draft of an article in which American missionaries were restricted to the open ports where they were to be placed under the semi-surveillance of the consuls and local authorities while they preached religion; the toleration to professors was granted as before. A reply was returned that rather than allow such an article the American Minister preferred that the whole should be omitted—a grievous disappointment to me to see the toleration of the truth likely to be utterly ignored in this treaty.

"June 18th.—I went to sleep last night with the impression that after such a reply from the Minister 't would be vain to urge a new draft, but after a restless sleep I awoke to the idea of trying once more, this time saying nothing about foreign missionaries. The article was sketched as soon as I could write it and sent off by a messenger before breakfast; it was a last chance, and every hope went with it for success.

"At half-past nine an answer came. Permission for Christians' meeting for worship and the distribution of books was erased, while the words open ports were inserted in such a connection that it was rendered illegal for any one, native or otherwise, to profess Christianity anywhere else. The design was merely to restrict missionaries to the ports, but the effect would be detrimental in the highest degree to natives. I decided at once to go to see the Viscount and try to settle the question with him personally.

"Chairs were called, whose bearers seemed to Martin and me an eternity in coming, but at last we reached the house where Capt. Du Pont and his marines so unexpectedly turned up last Saturday. Our amendment was handed to Chang, who began to cavil at it, but he was promptly told that he must take it to the Commissioners for approval as it stood, since this was the form we were decided on. Our labor and anxiety were all repaid and ended by his return in a few moments announcing Kweiliang's assent to the article as it now stands in the treaty. Here it is :

"'The principles of the Christian religion, as professed by the Protestant and Roman Catholic churches, are recognized as teaching men to do good, and to do to others as they would have others do to them. Hereafter those who quietly profess and teach these doctrines shall not be harassed or persecuted on account of their faith. Any person, whether citizen of the United States or Chinese convert, who, according to these tenets shall peaceably teach and practise the principles of Christianity shall in no case be interfered with or molested.'

" After coming so near to losing all of this out of our treaty and being dependent upon the English, French, and Russians for such an important matter, I was joyful indeed at this conclusion. I think the Chinese rather expected to tire us out, and Mr. Reed was determined not to postpone the signing, even if the clause was wholly omitted. On returning to the house, therefore, I felt as though the day not been wholly lost—though the mere insertion of a provision of such a nature in a treaty is not likely to change the feelings of a heathen magistrate or neighbor in favor of a Christian prisoner."

Mr. Reed's despatch accompanying the treaty to Washington further explains the terms used in this clause, and concludes with a deserved compliment to the essential aid rendered by American missionaries in China to their government:

" The recognition of both forms of Christian faith professed by the Roman Catholic and Protestant churches is rendered necessary by the fact that in the Chinese language different terms are used to describe them. The sign interpreted 'the religion of the Lord of Heaven,' is generally understood as applying only to the former, or 'religion of Jesus Christ' is applied to the latter. In the Chinese text of this treaty both characters are used and could only be rendered in English in the form I have adopted, and which I certainly should not otherwise have resorted to, accustomed as I am to regard them as part of a common faith. The recognition of that common faith, and the great principle on which it rests and the immunity of its professors whether native or American are in the broadest terms, and that recognition is hailed here with entire contentment by the devoted men who are teaching the great doctrines of Christianity.

"I cannot allow this occasion to pass without an incidental tribute to the missionary cause, as I observe it promoted by my own countrymen in China. Having no enthusiasm on the subject, I am bound to say that I consider the missionary element in China a great conservative and protecting principle. It is the only barrier between the unhesitating advance of commercial adventure, and the not incongruous element of Chinese imbecile corruption. The missionary, according to my observation, is content to live under the treaty and the law it creates, or if in his zeal he chooses to go beyond it, he is content to take the risk without troubling his government to protect him in his exorbitance. But taking a lower and more practical view of the matter, I am bound to say further that the studies of the missionary and those connected with the missionary cause are essential to the interests of our country. Without them as interpreters the public business could not be transacted. I could not but for their aid have advanced one step in the discharge of my duties here, or read, or written, or understood one word of correspondence or treaty stipulations. With them there has been no diffficulty or embarrassment. It was the case also in 1844, when Mr. Cushing's interpreters and assistants were all from the same class; in 1853, with Mr. Marshall, and 1854, with Mr. McLane. Dr. Bridgman, who was the principal assistant in all these public duties, still lives in an active exercise of his usefulness; and I am glad of the opportunity of expressing to him my thanks for incidental assistance, and constant and most valuable counsel. My principal interpreter for the spoken language of the north has been the Rev. W. A. P. Martin, of Indiana, of the Presbyterian Board. There is not an American merchant in China (and I have heard of but one English) who can write or read a single sentence of Chinese, and the spoken language is the hideous compound that prevails at the open ports, which has no single merit to recommend it, but suffices to convey the imperious mandates one universally bears to inferiors, or the mutual cravings of ordinary traffic. The missionary tries and succeeds in learning to speak Chinese, or in teaching the Chinese to speak English."

Some phases of the religious question in that country are touched upon in an article by Mr. Williams, on "Protestant Missions in China," written after twenty years' experience of these favoring influences:

"The articles in the treaties with China granting toleration to those who preach and those who accept the doctrines of the Bible, and allowing the public exercise of their faith has already proved to be a great protection to the growing Church. It is one of those mile-stones of progress which indicate the advance made, and guide that advance further on to the consummation of the christianization of the whole land. The difficulty of convincing the converts that the degree of toleration granted does not release them from their allegiance to their own rulers, has been increased of late years by a kind of semi-protection claimed by Roman Catholic priests to appear before the rulers in cases of oppression of their neophytes. There is indeed no caste to warn people off from its peculiar inclosure nor state hierarchy or bigoted priesthood to forcibly prevent members from leaving it, but hindrances to the promulgation of the Gospel are to be expected as the renovating, reorganizing nature of its doctrines are better understood, and the rights of conscience are more strongly asserted. It is a cause of great thankfulness that the progress of the faith has been attended with so few drawbacks, persecutions, and causes of just complaint from either party. Three Protestant converts have already yielded up their lives rather than deny their Master; and others have suffered the loss of all things at the hands of their countrymen. The reputation of these converts has generally been good as members of society. I was once talking with Wansiang, the premier, respecting them, and told him that I had never known of a member of the *Yesu kiao* having been condemned before the native courts for any crime, and he said he had not heard of a case."

"JUNE 18th.—Martin and I have been nearly every day in conference with the Viscount, and the treaty is now ready. This evening the Chinese commissioners met Mr. Reed, accompanied by three of his suite at the Hai-kwang monastery, where they signed seven copies of the treaty, four in Chinese and three in English. I went with Mr. Martin an hour beforehand to compare our two copies in Chinese with theirs, and was much mortified to find that by trusting to Ateh to oversee the transcript, one whole article had been omitted in both of mine. I proposed to have the commissioners sign only one copy for each, and send these to them afterwards to be signed and sealed, but they preferred that the missing characters should be inserted on the spot, and all finished up together. Four copies in each language should have been prepared, but the Chinese cared to retain only one in English. It was their idea that a pair of copies should be signed and sealed by each party, and a second pair only signed, their last to be sealed and ratified by the Emperor and President, and the copies exchanged when the latter sends his ratificatton. This seemed proper enough, and was accordingly done. The seal of the Chinese commissioners is a large brass affair in Chinese and Manchu seal characters, rather prettily made; the impression was not clear on the silk, the Viscount, who performed the sealing, making a dirty botch of it, and getting the red ink over the pages. The treaty was thus signed in the side room of the temple, where I had spent the best part of five days discussing their contents and provisions. A thunder squall and darkness came on before we concluded, and old Kweiliang evidently began to weary. A bottle of champagne, which Mr. Reed had brought to celebrate the occasion, was drunk with some gusto by all parties, for the tables laid before us as usual did not furnish much to exhilarate. Hwashana evidently enjoyed the wine, and tasted it probably for the first time in his life.

"The circumstances attending the signature of this treaty and that of Wanghia were as peculiarly different in political aspects as in place. That treaty was based on one obtained by English power after a hard struggle of three years, at the end of which the Chinese were willing to stop at any sacrifice consistent with independence; this was signed before and under a threat of hostilities (which have only been shown at Canton and Taku) as a lion growls a little before he leaps. The Chinese therefore stand here in a defensive attitude, and after learning the demands of the Allies as the price of peace will naturally try to reduce them to the utmost. There Kiying had his ground marked out by the previous treaty which was dictated at Nanking, here Kweiliang treads on miry soil, insecure and hesitating, in need of the greatest prudence and firmness. Their best ally is Count Poutiatine, who has an admirable influence upon them and is leading them in the dark to a better perception of their own true interests. It is evident that Baron Gros is inclined to take up with less than will satisfy Lord Elgin, yet he cannot well break away from him. So betwixt these counter interests and influences it is likely that the Chinese will get off better than if they had John Bull alone to deal with. The Russians are on the watch of the Allies, whose progress in China and all Asia will henceforth be carefully observed, and a consciousness of this now doubtless grievously annoys the English earl.

"The position of the four ministers here is, indeed, something like that of four whist players, each of whom makes an inference as to the others' remaining suits and honors from the cards they throw down. Now of course the Russian and American are partners, but if the Englishman were more *bon homme* and open he might readily have the Yankee to his aid against the others, were there any need of that kind.

"June 22d.—Affairs do not get on so pleasantly with the English to-day as we had been led to suppose. Their overbearing conduct with the commissioners is reported to us by so devious a channel that I hardly know how much of it to believe. An Englishman as a general rule never sees any virtue or excellence in people of another nation until he has been beaten by them, then his measure of respect alters according to the severity of the drubbing. Perhaps this trait in the leading nation of the world is not without its good effects, but in the individual it works great disgust toward him. Lord Elgin's conduct illustrates these national characteristics, and perhaps his agents in carrying on his negotiations develop them to a still greater degree. I am willing to concede, on the whole, that if a good object is in view it is better to frighten Kweiliang and Hwashana than to destroy thousands of human beings in battle or bombardment. . . . However, much as I like the English, their conduct here has been both vacillating and bearish.

"25th.—Mr. Reed and his suite went early this morning to make the commissioners a farewell visit. The discussion of the proposed plan for indemnity for losses by Americans at Canton was carried on in a few decided sentences, and they finally agreed to the same plan, nearly, which they had summarily rejected as an article of the treaty. This is rather easier than that, and may pay up the whole demand in four years, as our rejected clause proposed. Now that this troublesome matter is arranged I feel as if we had wellnigh concluded, but it is discouraging to have such continual pressure upon these officials before any satisfaction is given.

"Later in the day Mr. Reed received a verbal but very polite and urgent request to come and see the commissioners in company with the Russian Minister. The messenger, Major Chang, was quite ignorant of the business in hand, for he only 'ran over the land and wandered over the sea, but did not intermeddle in the affairs of state,' as he expresses himself. On reaching the residence of the commissioners we were taken into their sitting-room, where Kweiliang said that since he and his colleague had left Mr. Reed in the morning they had received an imperial rescript in reference to the demands of the Allies, giving a final decision upon the important ones and suggesting that they should call in the advice and coöperation of the American and Russian Ministers as to communicating it. This ultimatum refused the permanent residence of foreign ministers at Peking on any pretext, deferred the navigation of the Yangtsz'kiang to subsequent negotiation after the pacification of the insurrection on its borders, declined to allow traders to go over the country, and referred the settlement of the tariff and the expenses of both war and indemnity to Canton and Shanghai. This mode of meeting a group of claims and demands of the importance of these proves how careless the central government of this unwieldy empire has become in the most vital matters. However, Kweiliang told us in the most earnest manner that those were his instructions at the moment when both English and French were insisting upon the immediate signing of a treaty including all these things. The dangerous position they were in was rendered the more apparent by the punishment of Kiying, and they desired their friends, if we really were such, to go and see the allied ministers and state to them the impossibility of obtaining the Residence and Yangtsz' Navigation Articles.

"It was recommended to them to adhere to these orders as having come from their master, but we plainly added that they must themselves inform the English, since it would be worse than useless for us to interfere. The two ministers also advised them to sign the French treaty, trusting to the accuracy of the version, for they had been asked to accept the French text as the authorized interpretation, which they not unnaturally demur at, knowing nothing of that language. They assented to this, but evidently thought that our half-promised mediation with the English was not worth much. The meeting was an animated and interesting one, in some respects unlike any previous interview, the proud government of China having at last come down to the point of instructing its cabinet ministers to ask for mediation and advice from other governments to help it out of trouble.

"26th.—Our fears have been relieved to-day by the Count's coming in with gratified face to tell us that each side has yielded something and the British treaty is to be signed this evening. At six o'clock the first signs of preparation appeared in the Allied ships running up long lines of flags and dressing up in parti-colored attire as if by magic, manning the yards as well. Before seven the procession started—marines, sappers, a large party of officers in full dress in chairs or on foot, and the band, in all perhaps some six hundred men. The ships cheered as they started, and an enormous throng of natives lined the streets, quietly beholding the pageant without knowing much of its import. I rejoice at this result of peaceful instead of warlike measures; much of this successful outcome which so gratifies us is justly to be ascribed to the Russian minister who has not ceased to counsel the Chinese where they would otherwise have gone astray. The French envoy signs to-morrow, and after that is done we ought soon to be on our way out of the river."

TO REV. W. F. WILLIAMS.

Minnesota, YELLOW SEA, July 9, 1858.

The visit to Tienstin has brought me into very close contact with the highest officers of this realm, prime-ministers, councillors, generals, governors, and lords of high degree, and I have found them all to be heathen in their ignorance of God's truth, but yet to be quick-witted and measurably regardful of the truth, at least to us. They have been badgered and insulted by the English, forced to yield the privileges of their treaties by threats of war and sackage, and made to feel in every way their weakness and poverty. It has been a melancholy sight, and though their present humiliation may be fraught with the best outcome and promise for the future, I shall not soon lose my disgust for the overbearing conduct of Lord Elgin and his entire set; I may not speak all I feel, now that it is fresh, lest I oversay the matter. I hope God will cause that the new openings made into this citadel of ignorance, heathenism, and pollution, may be immediately improved and occupied by His Church, and the chafing of the Chinese will pass away in the ameliorating blessings of the Gospel. Lord Elgin, who has many good traits, should have been restrained by rather stricter instructions and not backed by thirty men-of-war to add a terrible force to his petulance. However, he has the national and hereditary dislike of his aristocratic clique to Americans, and this will excuse and account for much that he has said and done these past two months. I find I have need of more grace of God to like Englishmen than people of any other name, and must keep the beams of the lamp of love shining pretty bright upon them to render them tolerable. Belike they have harder work to be patient with me.

I don't know whether you have ever been in a man-of-war at sea, but you have never been in a better one than the *Minnesota*. She is a palace of a ship and the largest by far that anchored off the Peiho, but with all her size as manageable as a cockle. The six hundred men on board do not appear to encumber her nor stand in each other's way. Her daily expense to the United States is about $1,000, rather more than the outlay by the Board for all its operations, yet it would be an unfair inference to add that it was wasted or even unnecessary in comparison; still, an estimate of this sort shows us how cheaply men, individually or collectively can do good as compared with the cost of mere worldly plans and adventures.

FROM HIS JOURNAL.

"SHANGHAI, July 17th.—I have already told you of our arrival here on the 12th. Last evening I made known, as well as I could, to all the missionaries who had assembled by special call of Dr. Bridgman, the real extent of the liberty granted by the late treaties to the practice and preaching of Christianity. The article on toleration contained in the treaty with each nation was read, and the purport of their provisions taken as a whole explained as fully as could be from my own recollections of our discussions in Tientsin. The clear evening had brought a great number to hear me, but I fear there was as much disappointment as gratification, for the hopes of every one had been raised to an undue and exaggerated height by the rumors which preceded us. They will find, however, if any of them live in China 25 years longer, that they have not then been able to occupy all the land which these articles give them; they will discover too that laws and treaties do not restrain the wicked heart of man, and that to the end it will be true that 'whosoever will live godly in Christ Jesus must suffer persecution.' It was, however, my duty to tell them just what I thought the Chinese government had intended in granting this degree of toleration, and that we must not suppose that they while quite ignorant of its principles and effects, could grant the same liberty to Christianity which was enjoyed in England or America. I think that the more reasonable among my hearers will be satisfied with the enlarged freedom and do what they can to explain its true bearings, while urging their societies to send hither laborers who shall live as well as preach the Gospel.

"SHANGHAI, July 31st.—An Austrian frigate [the *Novara*] has arrived; a scientific expedition, and well provided, I should think, with appliances to make the most of their opportunities. The commodore told me to-day, what I did not know before, that the 'Middle Kingdom' had been translated into German and was well known in Germany. So I have been talking to many more people about China than I had ever supposed—and, as the genial commodore added, 'telling them no lies.'"

Mr. Reed, with the members of his legation, delayed through the hot and tiresome months of July and August in Shanghai waiting the arrival of the Imperial Commissioners, who were expected to discuss with him there the details of a tariff. The journey from Peking to Shanghai was, however, a precarious matter for officials of the importance of Kweiliang and Hwashana, owing to the movement of the insurrection over many parts of Shantung and Kiangsu; and despite the body-guard of a thousand braves the two high mandarins advanced slowly and in perpetual fear of capture. The Americans being definitely advised that their arrival in Shanghai would be postponed until October, Mr. Reed determined to spend the intervening months in Japan. To Mr. Williams the prospect of a glimpse at the changes which five years of foreign intercourse had brought to the susceptible people of that country, was welcomed with the greatest satisfaction. The pleasant days at Dr. Bridgman's "with their quiet and monotony, relieved with the consciousness of doing a little," came to a close, and by September 20th, the *Minnesota*, with the minister and his suite was anchored in Nagasaki harbor. They arrived soon after the signing of the treaty negotiated at the Japanese capital by the American representative, Mr. Townsend Harris, in which Yokohama was exchanged for Simoda* as an open port, an embassy promised for the United States, and certain minor restrictions removed from the conduct of commerce.

A few brief extracts from Mr. Williams' journal will suffice to commemorate his pleasant visit to a part of Japan which he had not before seen.

"NAGASAKI, Sept. 20, 1858.—A party of officials came on board soon after we were anchored this morning, bearing with them the salutations of the governor to the captain and Mr. Reed upon their arrival in his port. The interpreter spoke English as if he had learned it out of a book, a lump of words at a lesson, for it required no little practice and attention to recognize some of his sentences as belonging to our language.

"In the afternoon I went ashore. The stock of articles in the bazaar is less both in quantity and quality than I had expected, but perhaps the best of the stock is kept in reserve and samples only exhibited. The shops are small and in nearly every way inferior to those in China, all of them being rather stalls than stores. The shopkeepers were courteous and expert, some of them expressing considerable surprise at hearing even a few words of their language spoken. I was asked whether I had visited Yeddo, but there was none of the stupid wonder which the lower classes of Chinese show on such occasions. . . .

"The Island of Desima is not nearly so large as the old factory site at Canton, but the number of people living here has never been so large in proportion. There is a garden, several

---

* The port and town of Simoda were destroyed by earthquake the year after Perry's expedition.

warehouses and guardhouses, besides the residences of the Dutch, whose flagstaff shoots up high over the dwellings, and by its tricolor indicates their position to every ship coming into the harbor.

"Sept. 24th.—I went this morning into a small shop where the position which a woman can reach in this land was well exhibited, and the instance, I judge, was not an unusual one. Bowls and plates and grocery articles were spread in front, while the back of the room was well-stocked with foreign articles of the cheaper sort; one young man'in a corner was reading a Dutch book on mechanics. The woman sat on the floor in the middle nursing her fat baby as unconsciously as if she had been playing with it, while she directed the traffic. Two or three men brought out the various articles as she told them, doing all the running, while the bargaining was left entirely to her, they never disputing or suggesting otherwise. The ease with which all this was done showed that it was her place, and from the large number of women managing the other shops here, I infer that most of the chaffering is done by them."

A fortnight or more was spent by the ship's company in rambling about the city and its environs, gathering in its shops some portion of the rich harvest of Japanese curios and art-works, then so imperfectly appreciated by foreigners, exchanging visits with the governor and courtesies with the Dutch residents of Desima. Some years after this trip Mr. Williams relates:

"I was much impressed with what Mr. Donker Curtius, the Dutch envoy, who had just signed a treaty, then said: that the Japanese officials had told him they were ready to allow foreigners all trading privileges if a way could be found to keep opium and Christianity out of the country. There were also then at Nagasaki [on the *Minnesota*], Rev. Mr. Syle and Chaplain Henry Wood, and we three agreed to write to the directors of the Episcopal, Reformed, and Presbyterian Mission Boards, urging them to appoint missionaries for Japan who could teach the people what true Christianity was. Within the coming year we all had the pleasure of meeting the agents of these three societies in Shanghai."

One of these was Dr. S. R. Brown, the former head of the Morrison Education Society of Canton, whose name will long be held in remembrance as one of the pioneer educators of New Japan.

The *Minnesota*, without visiting the other treaty ports, left Nagasaki for Shanghai, Oct. 7th. Mr. Williams' journal continues:

"Thus ends my fourth visit to Japan, in some respects pleasanter than the others. Hope predominates, and I am sure that God will further assist in carrying on His plans if His people begin missions here in faith and patience.

"Steam and anchor were both up very soon after daylight, and every one was on deck for a last look at this beautiful bay, while we slowly moved out. In my wanderings during the past four or five years I have become somewhat conversant with different sorts of scenery, but none surpasses the harbor and environs of Nagasaki. I shall love to remember the pleasure I've had in looking upon and rambling over its hills and glens.

"We had hardly reached the outer islands when we saw the *Mississippi* coming in—the ship we had been hoping for during the last week. As she drew near, we were not a little surprised to observe the marines on the hurricane deck, the big bow-gun pointed out of the port bulwarks, which were all down, and the entire crew at general quarters, it being yet hardly eight o'clock. When the ships had approach neared enough to hail, the wheels and steam prevented any communication; Capt. Nicholson therefore came aboard and explained the matter. He was direct from Hakodadi, where the latest news from the United States was by way of California, when the discussion respecting the conducting of British vessels firing into American ships was so strong that the captain was convinced that ere this, war must have been declared by Great Britain. In any event, he was determined not to be caught napping, and perhaps we might be an English cruiser simulating an American ship and waiting for any prey which might turn up. Nor when Capt. Du Pont had hoisted the *Minnesota's* number was he altogether convinced, but sheered round, so as not to expose his whole broadside to the possible enemy. Nicholson said that when he left Hakodadi, he was not sure that he ought to venture south, but go first rather to Paulowisky (as he called Petropaulowski) there to get provisions. It was a funny procedure, altogether, and will furnish the commodore and other officers matter for jokes galore."

TO HIS WIFE.

SHANGHAI, Oct. 15th.

The *Yangtsz'* has been reported outside for a day, and this afternoon I heard she was in. I had looked for tidings of your arrival in New York by the previous mail, but not hearing then, was sure that this would bring the pleasing intelligence. The first news was that the Atlantic telegraph cable had been successfully laid and was in working order, the President and Queen having sent the first message by it. Soon after I learned all this, a single letter from Talbot Olyphant came to me containing the sad tidings of dear Olyphant's death. It was a kind act in Mr. O. to write, terrible as the news is to me, and I have answered him by this mail. Toward evening came a note from Dwight telling me that you were in St. Albans when the child died. This is every thing; some accident has detained all the other home letters.

All this comes in conclusion to your long letters from Southhampton, detailing the occurrences of the voyage, the many sights you had been visiting in that neighborhood, and how happy and hearty and hopeful you and the children were. It is all well. It is all right, for I know that God hath done it. He doeth all things well, and at the best time; he doeth them, too, so that we may derive from them whatever proper benefits he wishes. I loved Olyphant very much; his sprightliness, his inquisitiveness, his obedience, his always genial, loving conduct, had knit him to me more and more—more, perhaps, than I ever knew till now. I shall now always love him as he was; he will ever to me be the same fair-haired, high-browed, laughing boy that I left on board of the *Imperador* last March, his great eyes beaming out every thing he felt. He will be fixed in my memory as I saw him then; he will never grow larger, never be disobedient, never be sick; there, inside the folding-doors of my heart, he is enshrined, where I, and I alone, shall see him, daguerreotyped in living lineaments of loving and distinct recollection. I shall not know, as you do, dear heart, how he pined and paled and passed away, how he looked in his sickness, his death, his shroud, his coffin, nor have the memory, as you will, of that last, longing look at him, when he was shut out of sight. You have no doubt told me all these details in the letters which do not come, and have in some measure relieved your heart by doing so. It is vain, perhaps wrong, for me to wish I had been there to support and relieve you during this severe trial, for the benefit God would have *you* derive from it may thereby have been much altered. As it now is, with only these two letters before me, I can commend you and the other children now left us to Him who has lent them. I know the barren fact that he is dead—no, not dead, but departed. The gift was reclaimed by the Giver and Redeemer, who has his perfect right to us and them, and Olyphant as well. We have had such continuous health and peace in our family that we had come to think, almost, there were no cloudy, sick, and evil days, when He draws near and recalls one of the loans, that in our pride and joy of them we might not altogether forget the Lender.

But ah, dear wife, how I mourn with you in this bereavement, your first as well as mine. We had begun to forget the responsibilities of parents in the pleasures our children gave us; and lest we should spoil Olyphant, letting his waywardness get the better of the unskilful discipline we exercised, God has taken him to complete the education we were marring. He wishes, too, to teach us to deal better with the others, to be more faithful with them, more instant in improving every day and hour, to teach them His ways, setting better examples of patience, firmness, and love before them.

JOURNAL.

"Oct. 26th.—The Chinese commissioners made a call on Mr. Reed to-day—the five from Peking, with the provincial treasurer and judge, attended by a train of lictors, servants, and guards, numbering some two hundred, the same rag-tag and canaille which followed them to Lord Elgin's. Kweiliang looked much better than at Tientsin; Hwashana was the same burly, hearty man; but the most interesting personage to us was Ho, the Governor-General, a sprightly man of forty-four, from Yunnan, whose abilities are likely to be taxed to the utmost to resist the advances of the rebels. Mingshen, who was hoppo at Canton in 1849, was one of the party, and I think his pride and Chinese conceit must have been touched to be obliged now to visit a foreign official at his private house when he remembered the bravado of Seu and Yeh and all the officials of that year. The interview took place at Hurd & Co.'s house, Mr. Comstock doing the honors of his table—the first American, undoubtedly, who ever entertained a prime minister of China. We shall, perhaps, get better acquainted with these high officials as years roll on, and I humbly hope to be able to do them good.

"In the evening I had the pleasure of giving the community of Shanghai a lecture on Japan; I say pleasure, for it enabled me to say a word or two in behalf of the benevolent enterprise of Mr. C. W. King in sending the *Morrison* to Japan, and in explanation of the objects and adequate results of Perry's expedition as a preliminary to the present successful negotiations with the Japanese rulers. There was a larger audience than any one present remembered to have seen assembled in the place, while everybody appears to have sat with contentment through a lecture nearly two hours long. At its end Lord Elgin and Bishop Smith moved a vote of thanks; Dr. Bridgman, who, as President of the Shanghai Literary Association, was on the platform with me, regards the experiment as a decidedly successful relief to the routine of dollars and dinners which so completely engross this community.

"October 28th.—To-day Mr. Reed returned the visit of Kweiliang. Our sixteen sedan-chairs and escort of marines passed into the Chinese city through the quietest crowd you ever saw. It was curious, as one peeped through the lattices of the chair, to watch the varying expressions of the people's faces, one quickly succeeding another as we hastened by. On the whole their putty-like faces have rather a dismal sameness, I must confess ; for candor forces the confession that there really has not been much beauty distributed among the Chinese. I was greatly struck with it to-day.

" Reaching their hotel precisely at one o'clock we found the commissioners at the door, while the music of their flageolets and kettle-drums sounded oddly amidst the deep tones of our booming bass-drums and other instruments : to intensify the international harmony a salute of three guns was fired as we entered. Kweiliang seated the minister between himself and Hwashana, while I sat next to Ho, the animated Governor-General. When I thought of the delegated power in this man's hands, having the direction and disposition over something like ninety millions of his fellow-men, among whom sedition, distress, and beggary are now making such awful ravages, he appeared to me invested and clothed with no little awe. What tremendous difficulties indeed must Daniel have experienced in holding fast to his fidelity when he was a chief president and associated with such men as these. I can understand this better now that I have become more acquainted with Oriental men of high degree. The Chinese nation is a wonder indeed, but the chief surprise is not that it gets on, but that it does not immediately tumble into ruins. God alone supports it, as He does all other nations, and we mistake when we look upon it apart from Him and His governance.

" The assembly was an imposing one, especially on their part, for the long robes and brilliant costumes of the mandarins surpass the close garments of the foreigners in elegance and appearance. The latter sat in line below me, while the Chinese officers, five only, were seated opposite, a mass of attendants, all standing like dummies, forming a background between them and the wall. Presently we were all conducted into an open sort of court, where a table was spread with a great assortment of ornamental dishes. The entertainment, however, was not a magnificent one, probably so as not to exceed that which Mr. Reed had set before them a day or two before. Our officers were told which were the birds'-nest soup, for of course they would have deemed their visit half lost if this dish had not been served. I need not detail our banquet, for you are already tired of our official interviews in this land. The Governor-General asked a multitude of questions, and we managed to have much conversation about small matters, such as his going to America at some unknown future time, how many children he had, and what sort of people the Japanese were. Our call was merely complimentary, so after discussing the collation and drinking the healths of the Emperor and President, and allowing the guard sufficient time to rest, we departed in the order of our coming.

"In the evening I dined at Mr. Comstock's, at a dinner given to Lord Elgin. He appeared to be in excellent humor, and entertained us very pleasantly, for he is a great talker, and with Americans has always enough to say about his visit to 'the States.'

"October 29th.—While I sat by the Governor-General yesterday, I told him that I had a box of Japanese tobacco which I would send him if he would accept the gift. This morning I forwarded it, with the following, which my teacher made me say in Chinese :

"'Allow me to state this : When yesterday I was at your honorable official-gate I had the honor to learn from you that you would not refuse what I verbally remarked in the pleasant conversation, and I have accurately borne the same in mind with entire respect. In my late visit to Japan, I brought away a box of tobacco, which your excellency may be pleased with, and I presume to send the trifle in order to reciprocate a little your kindness and favor, and show my thoughts, thinking, too, that you may then not altogether forget. I humbly hope that you may not smile at it, while I improve the occasion to wish you a joyful day.'

"To this he sent me a reply addressed on terms of equality,

using the same direction upon the envelope, so far as our positions allowed. Both of these notes are rendered so literally that you are sure to get much more of an impression of humility from their phraseology than the Chinese thinks of expressing; but the equivalents are not what I wish to give :

"'Allow me to reply this : Yesterday, in the suddenness and flurry of an interview, I was delighted at what you desired to say, and have now received the present of tobacco from Japan, a fragrant, odorous, beautiful thing. I think it is really an excellent article, and I am ashamed to receive it ; my countenance shows my embarrassment. But I must express my wishes, and therefore despatch this answer of thanks, while I avail myself of the occasion respectfully to wish you a joyful day.'

"Nov. 13th.—It has been a busy time since I last wrote you, and I am now on board the *Minnesota* bowling along the coast to Hongkong.

"On Monday Lord Elgin went to a small temple near the foreign settlement in Shanghai, and signed the supplementary treaty containing the tariff and regulations of trade which had been under discussion with the Imperial Commissioners. As soon as he left them Mr. Reed and his cortége of chairs started, I having sent Ateh to tell them that the American Minister was ready to sign the same document if they would wait. He had some ado to induce them to do so (probably because they had not yet taken breakfast), but we found them there, and signed in the same temple where Mr. Stevens and Dr. Medhurst met the district magistrate of Shanghai in October, 1835, in that curious interview, when Stevens burned the present of chickens. You will find the account of it in the *Chinese Repository*, and it is worth associating with our visit there of last week.

"By this tariff you will perhaps be surprised to learn that opium is legalized, and pays thirty taels per picul as duty. The Chinese government has yielded in its long resistance to permitting this drug to be entered through the custom-house ; so the opium war of 1840 has at length ended in an opium triumph, and the honorable English merchants and government can now exonerate themselves from the opprobrium of smuggling this article. Bad as the triumph is, I am convinced that it was the best disposition that could be made of the perplexing question; legalization is preferable to the evils attending the farce now played, and we shall be the better when the drug is openly landed, and opium hulks and bribed inspectors are no more.

"Besides the supplementary tariff treaty, Mr. Reed also signed a convention about the payment of claims for property destroyed at Canton and Whampoa belonging to United States citizens. The Chinese have agreed to pay the sum of 500,000 taels by deducting one fifth from the duties paid by American ships, commencing next Chinese new year. Of this sum three fifths is paid at Canton, one fifth at Fuhchau, and one fifth at Shanghai. There will be enough, when the whole has been paid, to satisfy all reasonable claims. I took leave of these high Chinese functionaries with a mixed feeling of respect and pity. They have had a struggle between their pride and their necessity, between their prejudices and their fear, on the one hand, and their consciousness of impotence on the other, which cannot be fully understood by us, and of course not appreciated. They have in the providence of God been called to stand in their country's breach, and take the risk, life or death, and that too with Kiying's fate just before them. I do sincerely pity them—coming thus in all conceit and ignorance to grapple with a vital question like that of foreigners residing in their capital, in sight of the Son of Heaven, and independent of His mighty authority. With these feelings it is exceedingly hard for the foreigner to sympathize, and perhaps it is best not to argue on questions like them, but to ride over such points, trusting to a further knowledge to show them that we know their interests better than they do. It is hard enough to give up old ideas and cherished prejudices when convinced by slow instruction, but to have them rudely blasted by power and arrogance, and obliged by force to yield, leaves a sort of moral soreness which time alone can heal. May God in mercy direct all to His own glory and the advancement of His kingdom among this multitude; and I am sure that He will do so."

TO REV. W. F. WILLIAMS.

U. S. S. *Minnesota*, HONKONG, Dec. 7, 1858.

I am writing on board this huge ship for the last time. She leaves to-morrow for Bombay on her way to Boston, carrying Mr. Reed and his suite. He has got through his work in China, and done it extremely well; and I have passed the time with him and his son very pleasantly. While they are not what one would honestly call religious people, they have none of the sharpness and criticism toward these which amiable worldly people sometimes exhibit as a sort of screen for their own shortcomings. I have never been expected or asked to do any thing which it was known I disliked, and I part from Mr. Reed with regret and respect. If I could have preferred some things different, they were trifling, and might have been replaced by others not as agreeable. I sincerely trust that he will reach his home in safety, for he is anxious about his family, and his own health is not strong. Few can understand the delicacy and difficulty of a position like his, aiding but not abetting, countenancing but not coöperating, with belligerents, in the presence of an ignorant people who cannot understand what war without conquest means. His conduct has been more severely criticized in England than I could have supposed possible, and no effort has been made by the writers to learn the truth as to their statements. Exposed as he was to sharp animadversion, and unable, through the closeness of their leaders, to learn what the other allies were doing, it is not surprising that his motives have been scandalized and his actions misrepresented. However, his honest course will be made clear by and by, though not perhaps to the same public.

That the respect and good feeling between these two men was as mutual as it was cordial appears from Mr. Reed's diary:

"Wednesday, Dec. 8th.—I awoke with a strange feeling of excitement and regret. This parting with friends whom you may never see again, and especially such a friend as Dr. Williams, does cause deep pain and I shall not attempt to disguise or deny it. We ate our breakfast cheerfully but rather silently, for the same thought was in each of our minds ; he then packed up his few things and about ten o'clock we went with him to the side of the ship and with an earnest 'God bless you' on either side we shook hands and parted. I have had with him now close and confidential intercourse—occupying the same room often—for more than a year (and perfect strangers before that), and we have never had other words or thoughts than those of kindness. He is the most learned man in his varied information I have ever met. He never obtrudes what he knows but is always ready with a precise answer. He is the most habitually religious man I have ever seen ; I do not believe the idea that he is all the time actually in the presence of his Creator, who watches every word, is ever absent from his mind. Withal he is very cheerful—and I have never seen him depressed ; if he shed tears for his little boy's death—and I doubt not he did—it was in secret. But I must stop these praises, or they will be thought exaggerated—yet there is one other merit in him (to me at least) : he is very fond of me."

Mr. Reed's successor, Hon. John E. Ward, had started from New York early in the year 1859, with instructions to deliver an autograph letter from the President to the Emperor in Peking.

HON. WM. B. REED TO MR. WILLIAMS.

LYONS, March 26, 1859.

MY DEAR SIR :—Your letter of the 21st January reached me in Rome, and I have deferred answering it till I should see and confer with Mr. Ward. We met here yesterday and he has been kindly and patiently listening to a long lecture on Chinese affairs, and I hope profiting by it. If you find him filled with preconceptions you must attribute not a few of them to me, and if they are wrong get him clear of them as soon as possible, for I have told him how implicity he may rely on your disinterested and generous friendship. I like him much and think you will—I like him the better because he seems anxious about a matter which at first startled me a little.

From economical considerations (for he is not a rich man) he followed the advice which was given to me and has had his brother made Secretary of Legation. He is now quite nervous lest this may give you pain and offence, and assures me nothing was further from his mind. I have told him to deal frankly with you and I was sure you would do him justice. It occurs to me—and to this I attach great moment—that it may very much facilitate what my heart is set upon, your leave of absence next winter which as I have told you I mean to ask as a personal favor.

Mr. Ward will tell you my general line of advice, which of course must be subject to the general course of the chapter of Chinese accidents. It begins by earnest urging that he go at once to Macao, see you, and avoiding Hongkong go as quickly as possible to Shanghai. All else he will tell you for himself. . . . I have said to Mr. Ward and I say to you that I shall look upon his success as necessary to my reputation as well as heightening his—I mean in getting to Peking, and I am confident you will be as anxious as either of us.

Believe me sincerely your friend,
W. B. REED.

In announcing the appointment of Mr. Wallace Ward as Secretary of Legation. Mr. Cass wrote to Mr. Williams from Washington hoping "that this appointment, which will relieve you of a part of your duties, will prove acceptable to you, inasmuch as your salary as interpreter to the mission will remain at the same rate."

On the way from Hongkong to Shanghai the frigate stopped at Ningpo, and Mr. Williams had the satisfaction of seeing the material result of perhaps the most prolonged effort of his life:

"I was at Ningpo a fortnight since [he writes to Mrs. Throop Martin] and was greatly gratified by seeing a font of the type which you and other friends in Utica did so much to obtain. I wrote the first letter respecting it to Berlin while I was in quarantine in Malta in July, 1845, and in June, 1859. I see the type made and in readiness for use. If it had not been my desire to accomplish the enterprise you so vigorously began, I might not have found reason enough for delivering as many lectures upon China as I did—over a hundred in all—to obtain the necessary money. These lectures moreover showed that the people of the U. S. might be better informed upon this empire if they had a reliable book to read, which was one reason for writing the volumes which I produced. Thus one thing leads to a second, if God does not blow on it; and now that this enterprise has proceeded so far that we have with our four thousand types enough to print all common works in this language, it is safe, is it not, to conclude that much good will come from our efforts?"

CHAPTER IX.

SHANGHAI, May 31, 1859.

Mr. Martin and I went to-day to see the Imperial Commissioners; they have been waiting a month the arrival of the foreign ministers, living in quarters which I suppose are mean enough compared with their proper official residences. Being received by the Treasurer we stated that the American Minister having sent us to acknowlege the request of the commissioners to appoint a day for calling upon them, we wished to deliver this message to their excellencies in person. It was evident that he did not like this proposition, but I observed that I had seen the commissioners last year under similar circumstances; whereupon he asked if he could see the American envoy under similar circumstances, to which a ready assent was given; and soon the reply came out that Kwei was prepared to receive me. The whole array of the Chinese Commission—the aged Kweiliang with the burly Hwashana, who might easily drink a pottle of sack, and the wiry, uneasy Ho Kwei-tsing—were spread out to receive us. It was evident that they had no objections to our going to Peking, and rather expected that the visit would be paid, but were not yet ready themselves to go. Having here awaited the foreigners they were prepared to either arrange with them the preparations for going to the capital, or indeed conclude the ratifications on the spot, as we might choose; but in their minds the date of exchanging was a minor matter—and the compact was no ways vitiated by delaying the ceremony. We offered them a passage on the *Mississippi* to Tientsin, but they said they could not go without the Emperor's permission. Nothing seemed further from their minds, as we took our leave, than the prospect or possibility of any trouble in our negotiations this year.

While in Shanghai at this time Mr. Williams' journal contains an entry relating to the American Minister to Japan, which supplies an interesting sequel to his own visits in that country.

"June 5th.—I have seen a good deal of Mr. Townsend Harris since he came up to Shanghai, and should judge from his conversation that he is a truly Christian man. His success is better explained if the fact be known that it was in answer to prayer. He has told me many new points in explanation of what took place when Commodore Perry was in Japan, and one of the oddest is that the old man who was brought forward in July, 1853, to receive President Fillmore's letter in such solemn state, was a corporal, or some such subordinate, who personated the Prince of Idzu for the occasion. The Japanese have laughed a great deal of their own good disposition over this performance, and the lies they enacted during that expedition—most of which they were ordered to do and say by their superiors, who, Harris thinks, are now learning that truth has many advantages over hypocrisy. They have had the greater part of Dr. Hawkes' Narrative [of Perry's Expedition] translated to them, and are not so very much surprised at it as one might suppose."

TO REV. W. F. WILLIAMS.

SHANGHAI, June 13, 1859.

The 15th will complete twenty-six years since I went aboard the *Morrison*—and she is here too, under Spanish colors and called the *Carmine*. I have my baggage now all ready to start again for Peking, the third time, and with every probability now of reaching it. The eighth U. S. envoy to China, John E. Ward, of Savannah, arrived about five weeks ago and during the past fortnight has been waiting here for the English and French Ministers, until whose arrival the Chinese plenipotentiaries would not leave for their Capital. They go off to-day and say they cannot reach it under two months—it certainly must be less than 1,000 miles—but I suspect that they will hurry a little when the English force appears off the Peiho.

The French this time are leaving the British to supply all the men, taking less even than the Americans. We have the *Powhatan* and a chartered steamer, the *Toeywan*, in which we manage to arrange ourselves. Mr. Aitcheson of the A. B. C. F. M. and Mr. Martin of the Presbyt. Board go with me to help talk, besides whom we have three Chinese for writers and purveyors, all of them professing Christians. Mr. Ward has three attachés, and Com. Tattnall fills up the party with as many of his naval corps as space allows. The English will be able to land nearly 4,000 men without crippling their ships, so that they will manage to keep their rear well guarded and open. I hope, judging from the temper of the Chinese plenos., that there will be no fighting on the way to the capital, for this would probably neutralize the English treaty, and perhaps all of them—reopening a conflict which no one can see the end of. But God has His plans in this part of Asia as elsewhere, breaking down barriers and furthering His truth by many agencies that missionary societies could hardly practise or afford.

HON. WM. B. REED TO MRS. WILLIAMS.

PHILADELPHIA, May 20, 1859.

MY DEAR MRS. WILLIAMS.—I meant to write you the moment I knew the President's decision as to Dr. Williams' furlough. He has very cheerfully granted him the leave of absence for a year and promises to enlarge it for another year if Mr. Williams desires. A despatch to this effect has already gone to China, and I think you may look for him early next winter. I am sure you will believe me when I say to you that I shall be delighted to have him back, for without flattery I can assure you I never knew any man for whom I entertained as strong an affection. . . .

Believe me very truly yours,
WILLIAM B. REED.

TO REV. W. F. WILLIAMS.

U. S. S. *Powhatan*, OFF PEIHO, July 5, 1859.

We arrived two weeks ago at this desolate-looking anchorage, where we found the French and English ships nearly twenty in number, but no sign of the Chinese officers or their greeting as had been promised us at Shanghai. The forts which were destroyed last year had been entirely rebuilt of the same material and with the addition of another in a commanding position; their vastly improved principles of fortification showed an advancement in this science, if not the direct result of foreign teaching. The port-holes were in the body instead of on top of the walls, turrets from whence shot could be fired at a better angle were erected at intervals, and ditches dug in front of the defences. As if the forts were not sufficient, a solid abattis of wood and iron spikes and beams had been placed across the river to hinder and destroy vessels, or keep them under fire until shot to pieces.

The English had been told that officers would be here to receive them and conduct their ministers and those of France and America to Peking; finding none, Admiral Hope was requested to open a way through the obstructions, and get the envoys of France and Great Britain to Tientsin. Before he began this difficult operation, we had likewise inquired at the forts whether any one had been sent to meet us; finding that though no high mandarin was here, the Governor-General of the province had that day reached a more northern entrance to the river at Pehtang, and was prepared to accompany the foreigners to the capital. It was but a low officer who came down to meet our boat, and he refused to become the bearer of any despatch or message from us; no sign of troops appeared about the forts, not even a flag, and we were told that there were only a few volunteers in them, but that these would fire upon any one attempting to remove the stakes or force a passage.

The next day this was tried by Admiral Hope, whereat instantly every wall was covered with men, while canon-balls flew from every port-hole, showing the preparedness of the Chinese. They had about eighty guns (but not all in action, I think) and the English not over thirty or thirty-five; in their forces there was a far greater disparity, the English having some 1,100 in action, the Chinese perhaps 5,000—but our information is deficient. The battle continued from 3 P.M. to midnight, with great disadvantage in position to the English, when they ceased and hauled off, completely defeated, with a loss of 452 killed, wounded, and drowned, three vessels destroyed, and three more ashore, and some 450 rifles in the enemies hands. Most of the loss incurred by the landing and storming party was in front of the battery, where the sticky mud and shallow water prevented the boats from reaching the shore; as the men ascended the glacis they were exposed all the while to a dreadful fire of small and large guns and (what could only happen in China) showers of arrows. The 600 brave fellows who landed suffered more than those in the ships; a single discharge knocked over forty men, some of whom were drowned before the boats could get them out from the rising tide. Had it been daylight, probably not one would have escaped, for the Chinese could have then seen them and picked them off leisurely at short range. Out of the Admiral's steamer, the *Plover*, only one man escaped unharmed from a crew of forty. After the battle was over the Chinese continued a safe fire for a whole week, doing little injury, however, and receiving hardly a shot in return. I never saw more bravery exhibited than in Admiral Hope, who remained when badly wounded in the thick of the fight, and has since been unceasing in his efforts to recover the gunboats which grounded under the forts; but his arrangements for the battle and his so completely undervaluing the enemy will be greatly criticized. The Manchus have shown much skill and valor in the defence of the passage, but the treachery of the government seems undoubted. Though I am convinced that Kweiliang was sincere in promising an entrance to Peking, the powers above him seem to have determined that no troops shall again reach Tientsin if they have power to stop them. I think that the present dynasty fear a repetition of the same trick which they played upon the Chinese in 1644,[*] if they allow even a thousand hostile soldiers to get footing so near the throne.

[*] The Manchus, being invited to Peking to assist in ousting an usurper to the throne of the Mings, declared themselves rulers of China by right of conquest, and established the reigning or Tsing dynasty. The fear of a possible repetition of this *coup* by the foreigners was an abiding one in the minds of the imperial family for many years.

The defeat is the most serious which the English have experienced in Asia since the march out of Cabul, and there the elements killed ten times more than their enemies. I was present during the whole contest, within range of the forts (but where there was no occasion for their firing) and saw it all without danger. It was a new experience for the British soldiers, who had always been victorious over the Chinese, and many of them ascribed the repulse to Russians, of whose presence there is not a particle of evidence.

The detailed description of this extraordinary encounter is given as follows in Mr. Williams' journal:

"At 2:50 P.M. the battle began; the Chinese fired three guns at the Admiral in the *Plover*, he having begun to remove the stakes across the river, and soon the forts and vessels were enveloped in smoke. The firing was very animated on both sides, and every thing was in readiness. Probably the Chinese were never better prepared. The forts on both sides of the river could reach some of the ships, but the latter could not so easily bring their guns to bear on two of the forts, most of them being anchored where they could not turn. I think these two forts were not injured much; they showed no outward signs of it, and kept up their fire to the last. The extreme southern fort was separated from the others by an open space and probably a ditch, but of their garrison, armament, and general effectiveness we could form no definite idea. It was plainly seen very soon that the Chinese had learned some branches of the art of war since last year, for the shots now hit the vessels, and did not fly all abroad as before; but we could only guess their execution. The Admiral was ahead, and his flag was the object of their aim, and received the fire of many guns. Just before the forts opened a boat was seen coming down to the heavy barrier of wooden stakes, the one beyond the row of iron spikes, containing a man holding up a letter in his hand; perhaps he had been sent by the Governor-General with it to the Admiral, but the latter would not now receive it. The first discharge of the forts made savage work with the boats engaged in removing the stakes, for the guns had been trained along their line, and the shot scoured through them, breaking the boats and killing the men. The fire of the ships silenced the guns of some of the forts, and especially those along the line of wall, but the guns from the turrets made havoc with them, as they were trained down upon their decks.

"The men in the junks behind us were eager observers of the fray, and erelong an officer came aboard of the *Toeywan* to have a better look. No orders had come to him to advance, but the progress of the action convinced him that he could not get there too soon; the force of the tide running out was such that if he tried to row up his men would be used up before he could get in. We were neutrals, and had no sufficient reason for forcing the barrier placed in the river, at least not until we were fired at. We did not yet know that the Chinese did not intend to let us go to Peking at all. He could not, and did not ask Com. Tattnall to give him a tow for the boats, but it was plain that he had put himself in the way to get an offer of this help, and doubtless went away disappointed that he had not heard one. Soon after dinner was served up, and while we were at table talking among ourselves and discussing the condition of things in hearing of the cannon, the impulses of the Commodore got the victory, and he sent his flag-lieutenant over to the junk to offer his assistance in towing up the boats where they would reach their ships. Mr. Trenchard had hardly left the *Toeywan* when a messenger arrived down from Admiral Hope to order these reserves to get ready to proceed up; he was, I think, passing by when he was told that we were going to lend this aid, and came on board to inform the Commodore of the progress of the engagement, and tell him how much the reinforcements were needed, and how much obliged the Admiral would be to get them. Steam was already got up, and we were not long in our preparations, nor were the junks far in the rear of the *Toeywan*, though it took a good while to get up to us against the tide.

"Meanwhile, in considering the matter, the Commodore concluded that the Minister ought not to be exposed to any danger, and had his barge manned to take him and his followers over to one of the junks until he returned to his anchorage. So the whole seven of us were obliged to get into it, and soon were standing on the highest part of the junk watching the action. It was one of those acts which shows a man's character in the boldest outline; looking at a few points, he makes a judgment of the case, and then acts on it; orders are given, with a few reasons for them, and we are all sent off before there is time to reargue the case. Probably the Commodore was right in making Mr. Ward leave the vessel, for the contingency of an accident to him was an important one, and the risk could be avoided. During the progress of the engagement our feelings and sympathies had become warmly excited, and it required only a breath to induce the Commodore to act. To afford this help seemed to him within his power, and at the same time enabled him to reciprocate the aid offered by the Admiral yesterday in getting off the *Toeywan*. Doubtless the procedure compromised the Americans with the Chinese, but it is impossible to say yet what they know of it or have inferred from it.

"The boats were fastened to the steamer, and she proceeded on her way and was soon in the midst of the battle; the shot flew past, but nothing was struck. After the boats in tow had left, the Commodore got out his barge, and with his flag-lieutenant went to visit Admiral Hope. He had gone into action with two gunboats near the barrier, but his flag had drawn the enemy's fire, and his own gun-boat had been so much crippled that he had left it and removed to the *Opossum* and then to the *Cormorant*, where the Commodore found him. The crew of the *Plover* gun-boat had been forty at the beginning of the action, and when Admiral Hope left her only three of them were untouched; he was on the bridge giving orders when a shot or a splinter struck his leg, and while supporting himself against the rope which runs along the bridge, another ball cut it in two, and he fell over on to the deck four feet or more, seriously bruising himself. The captain of the gun-boat, named Grayson was killed, and she was placed under the lee of the *Cormorant* utterly exhausted. The need of a reinforcement was therefore pretty strongly seen, and when it came, the guns began to reopen on the Chinese. As the Commodore's barge was coming alongside the *Cormorant,* a shot struck the after-starboard oar and broke the gunwale of the boat, and glancing in its progress upward by the two sitting in the stern, killed the coxswain. Mr. Trenchard jumped up, supposing himself to be struck, and he was perhaps paralyzed for a moment by the passing of the ball. The Commodore instantly told the crew to get over to the other side of the boat, and thus saved the whole from swamping, as she had already begun to fill. After the crew left her she filled and sank partly, and floated away altogether. The Admiral was still on the deck of the *Cormorant,* much exhausted, but keeping up the courage of his men by his example. The scene was a terrible one, and the dead and wounded were lying around, the former waiting to be thrown overboard, the latter to be carried to the hospital, for all the able men were busy with the guns. It was a singular visit, all its circumstances being taken into consideration, to have a friendly naval commander-in-chief come to see another of equal rank in his flagship during an action, there to learn the progress of the engagement and wish him success, but to be so situated that not much aid could be afforded. I have no doubt that the incident is almost unique, and it was only in China where such contrarieties are found that such an interview could have taken place.

"Some of the barge's crew, finding themselves on board without a boat of their own, carrying out their impulses, and, as they expressed it, 'in the way and nowhere to go,' joined the men at the guns and helped them to load. When a boat was found in which the Commodore could return on board the *Toeywan,* and his crew was told to get in also, some of them were so busy with the loading that they did not hear the call, and were left on board for a good part of the night; none of them were wounded, nor were they missed immediately by the Commodore.

"When he reached the *Toeywan* he returned to the former anchorage to assist in towing up the boats containing the landing party in reserve in the junks. Only two gun-boats could be spared for this service; these we saw coming down in advance of the *Toeywan*, and one of them was erelong fastened to the junk I was on board of, ready to receive the 120 marines armed for the landing. The position I was in was a novel one, and I watched the conduct of men on the point of going into a battle where so many of their countrymen had been injured and killed, as they learned from the crew of the *Opossum* as they got on her deck. The casualties to the men and injuries to the vessel were enough to show the nature of the struggle, and every thing tended to exaggerate what had actually happened, and to show that it was no parade fight they were entering. I helped one man standing near me to arrange his cartridges and get himself in readiness, but neither in him nor in those around could I see any thing like shrinking—no bravado, no enthusiasm, not much talking even, and that in a low voice. They went with determination to do what was told them, the result of discipline, doubtless, in a great degree, but the manner of their departure was perhaps as characteristic of the English as any thing I ever saw.

A boat was sent to take us back to the *Toeywan*, a four-oared boat that came easily enough with the tide, but it was evident she could not get back against it. Captain Wills, of the *Chesapeake*, gave Mr. Ward a passage to her, but Martin Aitchison and I were left on board the junk, and, as it turned out, for the whole night. I was not a little disappointed at this, but it was one of those things that could not be avoided, and the best thing was to be easy and make ourselves as comfortable as the deserted quarters we were in enabled us to be. The *Toeywan* anchored outside of the *Nosegay*, and the boats astern of her rowed towards the shore with the rest of the landing party. It was now sunset, the battle seemed to slacken on both sides, and we supposed many of the forts were silenced, by the irregular and distant manner of their firing. At the distance we lay only general conjectures could be formed of the result thus far; we heard of several persons, officers and privates, being wounded, among whom was Captain Vansittart, and the crews of the *Plover* and *Kestrel*. Soon after the sun went down behind the forts, and darkness began to show the flashes more distinctly, we were startled by a sudden resumption of the cannonading on both sides mixed with the rattling of musketry, the whole line of wall right in front of us being, as it were, alive with the vivid discharges. There was no doubt that the landing party was ashore, and had met with no little resistance. Occasionally fireworks were seen on the wall, which the sailors on the junk (three or four having been left in each to guard them) said were thrown up by the Chinese undoubtedly to show the position of their foe. The conviction was strong in my mind that the English had entered or clambered over the walls, and, as the musketry died away or changed its direction, I thought it was a sure sign that the English were driving the garrison farther and farther. Speculation at such a time was an exciting thing ; the fire of matchlocks, gingalls, large and small guns, and rockets, with the bright blaze of the fireworks still continued here and there until after midnight, but all was much too confused to decide. The ships seldom replied to all this discharge, whether to save them from being seen or to avoid injuring the shore party was all in doubt. We began to look about among the knapsacks to find something to lie upon and screen ourselves from the wind, for the night-breeze was fresh and cold. The Chinese sailors on board were much pleased to meet somebody who could talk with them, and were far more anxious to be allowed to let out more cable lest their vessel should override the second anchor and injure the bottom, than to speculate on the result of the engagement going on in our presence. They got up a few dishes for us, and were ready to communicate what they knew of the river and the obstructions in it. Which side gained the victory was to them apparently a matter of little interest, and they made no inquiries upon the merits of the contest. Perhaps they were a little afraid of showing their feelings, being themselves in the hands of one party, and not very sure of the intentions of those whom they could not understand, and by whom their vessel had been taken.

At last the suspense was at an end. We were lying on deck listening to the booming of the guns and talking over this and that feature of the contest when a cry from a boat was heard, and one was seen slowly toiling towards us against the tide, which had now turned. The boat was soon alongside, and two marines came up and four sailors—the former were covered with mud, wet and weary, and one of them said to me: "Well, you see me back again." The story was soon told. The English had been completely defeated, the landing party repulsed with dreadful slaughter, and not a man had entered the fort or climbed the wall. Such a result amazed us more than it will many who hear it from the papers, though the perplexing character of the firing had inclined one of the sailors who had been in the junk with us, and knew more than we did of such matters, to believe that some portion of the force had been unable to land and enter the works.

From this time till we left the junk, about nine o'clock, a period of eight hours, a succession of marines and sailors continued to arrive, and it was an exciting repetition of the same disastrous story to hear them detail their personal adventures and describe the death or disabling of their comrades. On some accounts I would much prefer to be at this end of a troop and hear the narrations of the men as they came back from the field, than to learn the same general facts from their officers. It was pleasant to hear their inquiries from each other of their missing comrades and the sympathy they expressed on learning of their death or injuries. The principal events were strikingly corroborated by the various men, and you may be sure there was no need of much questioning on our part.

The landing party, composed of marines, sailors, and the naval brigade, in all not quite 600 men, went up to the bank not far beyond where the *Toeywan* had grounded, and not at the jetty which I had visited. The water was high, and as the boats took the ground the men jumped over nearly up to their waists, thereby soaking their ammunition and wetting their guns. The number who got ashore dry was small, though a large part contrived to keep their ammunition out of the water. As soon as they got up the bank each man hastened towards the wall; no line was formed, and all ran to the attack, probably intending to reach the glacis and the shelter of the wall, there to re-form and ascend it on the scaling ladders. Instead of going up the river they all seem to have huddled together in one spot : some were actually drowned alongside the boats. As soon as the men had left their boats they found themselves sticking in the tenacious mud through* which they slowly marched up, many of them falling on their faces, tripped up by their clumsy shoes or slippery soles ; when they had got beyond the mud they found two ditches partly filled with halffluid mud and unable to bear a man's weight. This was a serious drawback and rendered more dangerous to pass by a great number of iron spikes sprinkled over the ground and through the mud. Beyond this ditch there was not a very wide place to stand, and but a small number could together climb the wall after the ladders had been placed in position. This was a difficult landing to effect in the gathering darkness, and it proved to be impossible under the terrible fire poured upon these men as they drew near the shore and left their boats. The Chinese had known probably from last year's experience that the English would land a storming-party, and had suspended their fire when they saw the boats approaching the ships, not because they were beaten off, but to prepare to receive the assailants. By the time the boats came up their guns and matchlock-men had been placed so as to direct their whole fire upon the English as they landed, and very deadly it proved. Some of the large guns seemed to have been fitted with slugs and pieces of iron, which swept away whole rows, while round shot, bullets, and arrows came down like a tempest. Nothing could resist such fatal discharges at so short a distance, and out of the 600 who landed, we hear that 200 at least were killed or disabled within a few moments. The Chinese, in order to see where their enemy was, had prepared fireworks at the end of long sticks which they held over the wall and burned ; the light was bright and illuminated the ground, and they could fire with certainty. The walls and embrasures were covered with men, some of them waving flags and daring the English to come on, others discharging their barbed arrows and, more dangerous than all, sending hundreds of balls among them. The English began to retreat, and then the casualties became more serious, for the wounded were often unable to help themselves into the boats and were drowned in the attempt; the shot struck some of the boats, and these were left on the beach injured and caught by the iron chevaux-de-frise on the bottom. Nobody could think of leaving the wounded there, and the boats went to and from the nearest ships, taking everybody who got in, and coming back as soon as possible. The party landed about half-past seven, and the boats continued to search the bank for wounded stragglers until two o'clock; their cries could be heard on board the ships and guided the Chinese too to fire at the boats searching for them. The dead were left, and in the morning the Chinese came down for their heads; but I heard no authentic case of a wounded man being decapitated by them. Some of the wounded soon died; all were taken to the *Coromandel*, where they filled the vessel in every part. Capt. Shadwell was hit in the foot, and Rev. Mr. Huleatt in the groin; both of them were among the first ashore. I heard a sailor, who jumped off the boat just after Mr. Huleatt, say that he offered to help him back into it, but he declined, saying: "No, you run on out of the fire; I can limp back somehow."

I cannot well describe my feelings and surprise as I heard all these details from the actors in the scenes described, from men who were asking each other where their comrades were and telling of their escape from the fate of many others. One lad from a boat belonging to the *Cruiser* cried out as he came alongside, to one of the men: "We left with ten this morning, and here are all who are saved; two are dead, one missing, three wounded in the *Coromandel*, and we are four." Others would tell how the shot went through the crowd, in one case making a complete swath so that they could see up the opening; and one dirty, mud-covered fellow who had fallen along the bank, exclaimed: "Talk of Balaclava! I was there, and this is much worse. I had rather go three times to Balaclava." Another said: "It was regular slaughter; we might as well have been sheep in a pen." Thus would the first surprise find expression in some curt phrase that exhibited the whole mind of the speaker and showed how unexpected this repulse was to men who had heretofore been uniformly successful in China. One of the marines said he had been grazed a little, and as he had had no chance to judge the extent of the scratch, we brought a lantern to let him see it. While he was feeling the wound, or rather bruise, the ball rolled out of his flannel shirt where it had lodged. This man was almost alone among the whole crowd in expressing his gratitude that he had providentially escaped injury. The others were using profane language just as was their wont, and nothing in their behavior indicated the least gratitude to God for sparing them, while they spoke of one who had had his head popped off for him, of another whose leg was dangling at the knee by the skin as he was hopping through the water to reach the boat, of a third who fell and was drowned just as he came near the boat, and of other such like casualties within their own observation. One boat returning with about ten wounded, was struck amidships by a shot which broke it, and all in it were drowned. None of them spoke of having fired at the Chinese, and many showed their rifles sodden with mud and water and unfit for use. It was a disastrous repulse indeed, but none of them cursed the Chinese nor seemed to be at all angry with them; all was fair fight, and they had been beaten. The impression was very general that a large body of Russians were in the fort directing the Chinese, who, the men were sure, never could have served their guns so well; and each one had some proof of this opinion, a foreign cap, or a uniform, or a rifle, or something else which he had seen on the walls. Several officers saw numbers of men dressed in caps of black fur; probably these were northerners who are used to such caps. Others saw men with bands across their breasts and trousers like ours, which may have been the straps holding the quivers of the bowmen, who had also bound their loose trousers closer. One man thought that fully five thousand arrows had been fired at them, which shows how numerous the Chinese were. To see bowmen resisting an enemy armed with revolvers and Minie rifles is another of the curious contrasts and incidents of this action.

I cannot learn the number of wounded or killed, and none

of these men tried to guess. The captain of the company had just begun to go over the roll for this purpose when we were leaving the junk; out of the one hundred and twenty who left it the previous evening, thirty were in the hospital, and perhaps more. The man whom I had helped to arrange his cartouch box was among the last who returned to the junk, and as he came up to the stern his face was radiant with pleasure and he really seemed to be very grateful for his preservation. "Are n't you glad to see me?" was his exclamation as he threw down his gun. Covered with mud as most of them were, one would have supposed that they would have washed, but those around me began first to clean their rifles and to wipe them dry. Some of the sailors were so beat that they went to sleep as soon as they reached the junk, while others asked for a bit of pork and a dram first. If there was no enthusiasm when they went away last evening, there was no sighing or cursing this morning; all were busy repairing damages or satisfying their hunger and speculating on the chances of renewing the attack. While we were waiting for a boat to come for us, the *Toeywan* went back towards the *Coromandel* to see what assistance she could render them before going out of port. The gunboat *Haughty* came slowly drifting down the stream in a sinking condition crowded with men, all of whom got off before she sunk. At this time the *Lee*, *Starling*, *Cormorant*, *Haughty*, and *Plover* were on shore, and the *Kestrel* sunk in deep water, truly a melancholy contrast to their gallant condition eighteen hours previous. Each of the gunboats had fired four hundred rounds of ammunition besides the probably greater expenditure of the larger vessels. "Let not him that putteth on his harness boast as him that putteth it off," was a sentence which came to mind in contemplation of this defeat of the English—a defeat likely to prove more disastrous to the Chinese than any beating they ever had.

We left the river about the same time as the *Coromandel*, and carried the news of the repulse to the fleet outside, none of which had heard the result of the engagement. Our friends in the *Powhatan* were eager to hear the tale and astounded at its tenor, for from that ship hardly any of the casualties to the attacking ships could be made out, the distance being just nine miles.

After the battle the American Minister sent the *Toeywan* to discover where and what Pehtang was:

"The water allowed the steamer to run within a long mile of the beach, and Mr. Martin, with two others, got into the gig to deliver a letter for the Governor-General and learn if possible where he was. The boat grounded half a mile from shore and the three had to jump out and toil on through the mud and water. The villagers fled in every direction as they waded ashore, but presently a few came back and were willing to talk. Governor King, it seems, is in this region, but now at one of the forts; these fellows did not know our flag nor could they read the address of the document, but they were becoming very friendly and learning all about us when suddenly one of them sung out, 'Hi, back to your boat, quick, the soldiers!' and others echoed, 'Be quick, quick, the horses are coming!' So Martin, getting a native to promise to deliver his note, took promptly to his heels, considering his errand done and knowing the danger of falling into the hands of a couple of hundred ruthless cavalrymen who would joyfully chop off his head and then ask who he was. His companions, not understanding a word, rather marvelled as they floundered after him, but all got back to the boat in safety and just in time to see the horsemen dash after them into the water."

The answer to Mr. Ward's message thus delivered was satisfactory, arriving some days later in a junk with the customary present, and declaring a readiness to conduct the Legation to Peking. By July 6th the English and French had entirely retired from these waters, refusing further communication with the Chinese. Two days later the Americans were transferred from their steamer in a junk especially decorated and prepared for them to meet the newly-appointed Governor-General, Hăngfuh, in Pehtang, "a squalid town, very suggestive of fleas, dirt, and beggary." The interview was a friendly one, and conducted with an almost ostentatious parade and elaborateness of preparation; the strangers were to be duly escorted to Peking, as soon as orders in detail could be received from the court, and the English and French would be treated with as much hospitality were they willing to come via Pehtang; meantime the *Powhatan* would receive supplies from shore during her stay here.

"The officials have exerted themselves more than I have ever known on a previous occasion to give éclat and parade to this reception. It appears to me that it would not have derogated in any respect from the honor of the English or French Ministers to have come or sent up to this place and examined it and found out what were its avenues and leadings before deciding to resort to arms. Mercy had no great weight in their councils, nor do they seem to have given much credit to the oft-repeated declarations of the Chinese that they were to go to Peking. These people are doomed, I fear, never to be allowed to make their own plans or carry out their own views."

Chief of the escort appointed to conduct the twenty Americans to the capital was Chunghow, afterwards well known to foreigners as Chinese Minister to Russia and the negotiator of the first Kuldja treaty—"a Manchu, a pleasant and lively person of 32, who seemed to be on springs, so uneasy and fidgetty was he." On June 20th the party started.

"The baggage and ourselves were landed by 7 o'clock, and all were under way by 9, but amid some delay which was not to be wondered at. Chunghow and Chang and the ever-present Pien, with other officials, met us in a hall near the landing-place, the path to which had been covered with straw and mats to protect us against a part of the mud. The carts, or carriages into which they put us for the journey, are commodious enough for a single person, but the want of springs renders them wretched conveyances to us, who are used to easy seats. The sides and backs are lined with cushions, while two also cover the bottom, and an awning is stretched over the horse. I believe that 32 of these vehicles were engaged for our use, besides the number required for the Chinese officials; about 25 coolies carry the glassware. The sun came out in all its July power, and what with the flies pestering us, the carts jolting us, the heat irritating us, and the monotony wearying us, we were heartily tired out at the end of two days, when we reached Pehtang on the Peiho, and were transferred to boats. The largest of these was very much like a flower-boat at Canton, but you will hardly imagine that it was very elegant when I tell you that the owner informed us that it was built 100 years ago and had been four generations in his family—or rather the four generations in it. Yet it proved a tight craft, accommodating six comfortably, besides the family and crew. I had the second boat, in which four others found room more conveniently even than those in the big craft. From the boatmen we learn that we are only five miles above Tientsin."

An amusing account, which was long seriously believed in Europe, appeared in a French illustrated journal this summer, describing this trip as being performed by the unsophisticated and timid Americans in a huge "box or travelling chamber, drawn overland by oxen and then put upon a raft to be towed up the river and Imperial Canal as far as the gate of the capital. They were well treated, and were taken back to the coast in the same manner."

The party reached Tungchau, the river-port of Peking, on the 26th, and exchanging their boats for carts and horses, were conducted to the capital the following day.

"Upon entering the city gate the wretched stone road without was exchanged for an equally wretched mud road within, both of them of 'unutterable depravity,' as our chaplain in his anguish remarked. The interior of this Manchu city is disappointing; not that I expected much of show or neatness, elegance or grandeur, knowing the nation, but I hardly looked for beggary, decay, and dirt to the degree now seen. It took us about an hour to go from the gate to our lodgings in the *Shih-san-tiau*, or Thirteenth Row, for through the vast crowds assembled the progress was as slow as a walk could well be. Our escorts, Chunghow and Chang, were already in the hall to salute the Minister upon his arrival, who after sincerely thanking them for the unaffected kindness and care they had shown during the week of our journey, asked them to inform the Imperial Commissioners of his presence in the city. Two officers were designated in the crowd of attending officials who should provide for our wants and watch our movements while here. This place is a summer palace, one of five establishments which belonged to Saishanga, the Prime Minister in 1850, who was degraded for want of success against the Taiping rebels, and whose property of course escheated to the Emperor. The woodwork and roofing are in good order, and the satin cushions and aprons on the chairs and tables make all the rooms appear showy, but to our notions nothing about this habitation is substantial or comfortable. We were served with a bountiful Chinese dinner the first two evenings of our stay, but hereafter we are to be furnished with provisions and cook them after our own fashion. On paying our caterer we learned that dignity had required about twenty cooks and coolies to get three meals, but he and his attachés were well satisfied with three dollars for them all.

"July 30th.—To-day took place our first interview with the Prime Minister.

"The Judge, Sieh, had asked yesterday, in a call upon Martin and myself, that no parade should be made in going to this visit, and that only the Legation proper should attend. Mr. Ward, his brother, and Martin were therefore the three besides your humble servant who rode out at ten o'clock this morning to the Kiahing sz' monastery.

"The interview was opened by a few inquiries respecting

their health since our last meeting, and the Prime Minister spoke of his journey of 36 days hither from Shanghai. These remarks were abruptly finished by his breaking out in a tone of unusual asperity that the English had broken their treaty, that it was now null, and they must bear the blame for they had begun the conflict on the Peiho. The imperial government had the same right to control its ports and rivers as had other nations; there was no insult intended to the English in doing so at Taku. The way by Pehtang was still open. It was a singular proceeding on the part of the English to bring so large a force when they came ostensibly to exchange a treaty; such a course led him to doubt their peaceful professions. The Americans in coming on the same errand with no force gave them better proof of their friendliness. It was evident that Kweiliang was still exceedingly sore at the slight received from the British Minister at Shanghai. The remainder of our call was taken up in discussing the terms of an audience with the Emperor, which, we were told, his Majesty personally desired."

The well-known audience question, here opened for the first time since Lord Amherst's embassy to Peking in 1816, remained a burning and agitating topic between the Chinese officials and foreign representatives until its final settlement in 1873. Enough has been said and written on the subject to make any long explanation unnecessary here; but it has never been easy to impress upon Western minds the genuine apprehensions which agitated the imperial counsellors as to the disturbing effect which a concession of audience without prostration would produce upon a people educated to regard its ruler as a divinity. It is hardly too much, indeed, to say that a slight to a Roman Augustus, or to a Pope in the middle ages, might have been allowed with less danger to the dignity of the potentate than this act of approach without low obeisance to the "Dragon Throne." Either from motives of curiosity or from a real desire to retain by gracious condescension the friendship of the Americans, Hienfung had evidently a strong wish to see the strangers now at his capital, and in order to do so had consented to waive all but the mere semblance of a prostration; the *kotow*, or kneeling and knocking the head upon the ground, was to be turned into a bow which should be ostensibly interrupted by the attendant official. A concession so considerable had never before been suggested by any Chinese dignitary or noble. In the debate which occupied this and several following interviews, Mr. Ward enjoyed the decided advantage of never having demanded an audience with the Emperor, and of being in Peking not from treaty right, but upon invitation of the Commissioners to exchange ratifications there. The argument became more animated as the desire of the Emperor increased, and it was not a trifling matter to his officials that his expressed wish should remain ungratified; the religious nature of the *kotow*, however, was confessed when one of the Commissioners declared that it was the same reverence which must be shown the gods—adding: "Why, I would offer incense or sacrifice before the President in your country, if required to do so; on the same principle you ought to conform to the usages at our court." When it was pointed out that a refusal to kneel indicated no want of respect to his Majesty, but was persisted in because no Christian could possibly render this form of homage to any but his God, Kweiliang could hardly contain his amazement at the rejection of so high a favor.

"The real nature of the *kotow* was never more fully stated

than it had been to-day, and my previous notions respecting it were confirmed, that every Chinese regarded the ceremony as a religious one. What, then, becomes of the quibble of the Jesuits,* who declared that it was merely a form, and upon whose dictum the Dutch Minister, Titsingh, performed the obeisance scores of times when in Peking, in 1796? There is, really, not the least difference between the reverence paid by their subjects to the Pope and the Emperor; both demand it, on the ground that they are vicegerents of heaven, and sitting in the seat of God, they claim the honor due to gods. Knowing what these Chinese functionaries said to-day, no Christian man should ever again discuss the question of performing the *kotow*. It would be an idolatrous act. . . .

"While at dinner, after the meeting, Mr. Ward asked that four or five horses might be furnished to the Legation for our rides about the city; but Kweiliang said that etiquette required us to wait until we had seen the Emperor, when he would be happy to show us every thing of interest. This was taken as the finale, but I should have been inclined to argue the point a little, for it really confines us in our yamun until the issue of the discussion; and should this not be satisfactory, we run a risk of seeing nothing. . . . We have not been allowed to exchange calls with the Russians who are in the capital, and find that a note from Gen. Ignatieff, the Minister here, was delayed six days before delivery; this seems to indicate a fear, on the part of the Chinese, of our collusion with other foreigners against the government. Yesterday Mr. Martin and I made an application to the guard for a map of Peking, and Ateh, who delivered the message, tells me that their dismay and apprehension at receiving this request was something so ludicrous and unexpected, and withal, so serious, that he both laughed and wondered, but came back empty-handed.

"July 31st. Sunday.—Chaplain Wood preached this morning, and was listened to by seventeen persons with much interest—two of our number being sick; it was the first Protes-

---

* Jesuit priests were in high favor at the imperial court in the sixteenth and seventeenth centuries, and submitted readily to this obeisance at every audience.

tant service, I suppose, ever held in this capital. As we raised our few voices in praise, we heard, near by, the loud matins of some lama priests reciting their liturgy—sounding for all the world like a Romish service. In the afternoon I had a pleasant time with Martin and Aitchison, in reading and talking over the first epistle to Timothy in the Greek. The Sabbath has passed to us as quietly in this city of millions of idolaters as if we had all been in South Hadley, which is the stillest village I ever was in.

"August 3d.—In order to prepare for the visit of Kweiliang and Hwashana to-day, Judge Sieh came in at nine o'clock, privately, as it were, and before we knew of his presence, had arranged a table and seven chairs in the reception-room. When we told him that we were perfectly competent to attend to this matter ourselves, and showed him the board already laid in the dining-room, he immediately proceeded to divide the long table into two portions, saying that as the Commissioners were closely watched in the capital, it would not do for them to allow more foreigners to sit at the feast with them here than they had entertained last week, but that if the continuity was broken, no fault would be found!"

The interview was a tedious one, lasting five hours, and entirely devoted to the discussion of an audience. It was followed by other meetings and a constant interchange of correspondence, but all to the same end. Kweiliang finally sent a note, as though in despair, asking: "As an audience is necessarily involved in the visit of an envoy to the capital, and as he refuses to see the Emperor, why, then, had Mr. Ward come?" It should be stated to the credit of the Chinese, that at no time did they drop a word of menace, or hint that the Americans, in their helpless position, would consult their own safety by complying with the obeisance proposed. The Commissioners' disappointment at being unable to bend the republican knees was unfeigned; the more so, perhaps, because the court had resolved to bring about some compromise of the ceremony, and establish thereby a useful precedent for other treaty powers. They consented, at length, to accept the President's letter to the Emperor, which was delivered and received with the usual ceremonies at the last interview with Kwei and Hwa, on August 10th. Pehtang was agreed upon as the place where an exchange of ratifications should take place. The following day the Legation left Peking, making the journey to the coast under the same escort, and in the same conveyances as before. A mournful and touching incident of the return was the increasing illness of Mr. Aitchison, followed by his death before reaching the sea. The journal describes his rather desolate end:

"At last the morning dawned and Brother Aitchison's sands of life were fast running out. Through the livelong night he had been talking wildly, interrupted now and then by a moment of clear thought and an expression of his hope, but at no time in his most excited moments uttering a word which he could possibly regret. Who of us could bear to have the cover taken off his mind, so to speak, and let another look in and see the inmost habit of his thought, his desires, envies, impurities? and which of us would come out of the ordeal as well as Aitchison? During the early part of the night Martin learned something of his wishes and feelings, but when I came to watch, his weakness triumphed and he could not answer connectedly. At one time heaven seemed to open to his vision, and he looked up in the clear star-light and cried: 'I see Jesus and the saints; I see my wife and child!' At dawn, when I lifted him from the boat to the litter, he exclaimed: 'Am I dead? Why not wait until I die?' So we left the river-banks, each in his own cart as before; when we reached Si-ti-tau, about noon the first news was that Aitchison had died in his litter an hour before. No one was with him at the moment, but it made no difference to him now. I went to see him lying in the litter, pale, thin, and careworn. It was not such an end as one would choose, but his happiness is not measured by his unkempt remains. He came here in great hopes of remaining at Peking, and commencing missionary work by himself, but the fond hope is now changed to the fruition of immortal joys on high.

"The only interruption of the pleasant weather experienced during this whole expedition of four weeks occurred the evening before reaching the coast, when it rained violently and flooded the roads. In the alluvial soil of this plain the highways are soon cut up by carts, and when the Embassy reached Pehtang about 2 o'clock on Tuesday, its streets were already ankle-deep with mud. The Governor-General and Treasurer of Chihli, Hăng-fuh and Wan-hiuh, were already in waiting, surrounded by a large retinue of officers, whose numbers were now increased by our escort, and they desired us to waive all ceremony of preparation and exchange the ratified treaties at once, before our going on board ship. This was accordingly done, and certificates of the exchange signed before evening. This ceremony over, the Chinese proposed to deliver to the Minister one of the two prisoners taken from the English in the recent battle, who had declared himself to be an American, and brought him forward for that purpose. He proved to be a Canadian by birth, and confessed to us that he had lied in hopes of getting free; it required some time to explain to the Chinese the political difference between Canada and the United States, the more so as no maps were accessible. After a full elucidation of all the points of the case they concluded to surrender the man to Mr. Ward entirely on grounds of humanity, and he was thus received. In the hands of a more impetuous people his falsehoods might have easily been the death of all our party.

"The next day, Aug. 17th, the *Toeywan* took us to the outer anchorage where lay the *Powhatan* with the Admiral. On the 18th, we were forced to bury Aitchison in the sea, having hoped to carry the body to Shanghai; in the evening we set sail for that port, arriving on the 22d.

"The newspapers at Hongkong have generally thrown discredit on the visit of the American Minister to Peking, ridiculing some things, doubting what they pleased, and showing their proficiency in vituperation. It is sad to see the bitterness of these papers against the Chinese. The *Hongkong Register* goes on in a strain of imprecation upon the Chinese, denouncing their treachery, and hoping that 'they will erelong get such a thrashing as they never had before'; it is quite dreadful, especially since the writers profess to be Christians, and they are venting this savage malediction against pagans, of whose motives and conduct they can, of course, have but the most imperfect knowledge. We hear but little of the opinions of the people in this region respecting the battle of last June. Trade goes on at Shanghai as if nothing had happened. At Canton, where they are under the guard and guns of the Allies, there seems to be no desire after a disturbance, and trade goes on slowly—a sad contrast commercially to the activity of three or four years ago, and not very encouraging for future prosperity."

His sense of the injustice of these contemptuous and wanton attacks on the part of a sordid and selfish press impelled him to devote the first moments after his arrival in Shanghai to writing a sober and careful account of the visit to Peking for the *North China Herald*, in order that a fair report of the expedition might do what it could to counteract the malignity of the journals. A fuller and more elaborate "Narrative of the American Embassy to Peking," drawn up with his usual scrupulous care as to facts, was read before the North China Branch of the Royal Asiatic Society in Shanghai on the 25th of October, and published subsequently in its Journal. This remains the only printed record of this mission, excepting the more popular resumé of the same account published over his name in Bidwell's *Eclectic Magazine* two years later.

During his stay in Shanghai, and while Mr. Ward went upon a visit to Japan, Mr. Williams, in company with one of the English missionaries, visited Kiaking and Hangchau, making the journey upon the Grand Canal and remaining away a fortnight. It was one of those excursions which his busy habitude and the sedentary nature of his occupations had made extremely rare pleasures in his life, since such trips into the interior of China had become possible to foreigners. When the Legation again assembled at Shanghai its last formal act in connection with the treaty negotiations brought the Minister and his party to Suchau.

"Oct. 31st.—Arrangements have been made to pay Ho, the Governor-General of this region, a visit, at which I sincerely hope that the details still unarranged for publishing the treaty may all be settled. I am glad to take this first step toward our getting off to the south, for when this call is paid we shall soon be away. To live in this dawdling manner is eminently unsatisfactory to me, and the practice I 've had of following admirals and plenipotentiaries to Yedo and Peking during the past six years has not tended to enamour me of the calling at all, at all ; so I look forward to a release, and the prospect of a visit to Utica cheers me on."

TO REV. W. F. WILLIAMS.

MACAO, December 28, 1859.

I am gathering up the ravelled ends of my affairs and committing such interests as I can to friends here, preparatory to my departure next month. The chief thing which has detained me has been the details and management of the money received from the Chinese to pay U. S. citizens for losses, and as we are likely to pay a dividend next month, and as this will furnish a guide for all future payments, I shall afterwards be able to start. If there are ships going to California I shall select one to take me to San Francisco, from which a few days will carry me to New York. Mr. Brown has returned from America, bringing three of his children with him, and they are now at Kanagawa, I hope, all lodged and beginning the good tidings of salvation to the Japanese. My labors in that language will also aid a little in his, and he will find some facilities I prepared many years ago now of service. The way that access has been opened to the Japanese since my voyage in the *Morrison*, in 1837, excites my gratitude to God, whose purposes of mercy to all lands seem to rapidly develop. Last year I wrote three letters to the directors of three mission societies in New York, urging them to establish missions in Japan, and now each society has a mission there, and the prospects are good for continuance. I don't know that better men could be found to begin missionary efforts than Brown, Hepburn, and Liggins.

I never, I think, felt such a disappointment as when I saw the English defeated last June, but the confidence in its final good results which came over me after a while has not yet left my mind. I am sure that the Chinese need harsh measures to bring them out of their ignorance, conceit, and idolatry ; why then deplore the means used to accomplish this end, so much as to blind our minds to the result which God seems to be advancing by methods whose inherent wrong he can punish at his own time.

With the return of the Legation to the south of China the management of the indemnity was put in charge of two commissioners, who audited and paid the claims during the following year. The Chinese had good reason to be grateful to Mr. Williams for the last few weeks of his stay in Macao. It was found that American ships had recently been participating in the coolie trade and carried off kidnapped men to Peru. Indignant at an outrage by his countrymen, over whom he had now some control, Mr. Williams caused the arrest of one vessel charged with having such unwilling freight on board, and presided at the examination of more than three hundred men, all of whom were released and sent home.*

By February he was at length able to enter upon his leave of absence, and with the ratified treaty to return once more to America, while the British and French forces were preparing their advance against Peking to avenge the disgrace and slaughter of Taku. His journal of the two years thus concluded ends with the familiar strain :

"I cannot close better than by commending you and yours to God, who has so far watched over us, and whose promises are still as sure as ever, praying that He will fit us for all His holy will, whether here or there, till He bring us safe to Himself."

* His only Chinese tract was written in this connection in 1859. It was entitled "Words to Startle Those Who are Selling Their Bodies [to go] Abroad," being an exposé of the means employed by the Portuguese to beguile natives into accepting contracts for coolie labor. "I get six of these tracts printed," he writes at this time, "and covers put on for a cent, and have had about 6,000 circulated within the past fortnight. The Chinese have been dreadfully misused by these coolie dealers ; in Macao the Portuguese are not able to get workmen to come either to their houses or ships, so great a dread have the natives of being stolen and packed off to the barracoons. Over ten thousand Chinamen have been sent away in 1858, and half this number are already gone this year from here. The Portuguese are ruthless and reckless, and they get hold of natives ten times more the children of hell than themselves, and make these act for them."

CHAPTER X.

THE second visit to America was uneventful. A renewal of friendships half lost in the lapse of time; a few lectures delivered in Washington, New York, Utica, and other places where the interest or occasion seemed to demand some recent information about China; a call (we may be sure) at the mission rooms in Boston, where he was warmly welcomed and consulted to-day who had been instructed of old—these were the employments and enjoyments of the year of rest at home. It was a period of awful commotion in America, when the storm which had for many years been gathering in the South broke fiercely and suddenly upon the country. To Mr. Williams this was, perhaps, a more startling catastrophe than to those who had been able to gauge the increasing intensity of political feeling by the index of the daily press. But although his residence abroad had tended, as is usually the case, to free his mind from the bias of local considerations, to fix it more intently upon great issues, neither absence nor distance had abated a particle of his generous and enthusiastic love for his country which is the essence of patriotism.

Nothing, he thought, could exceed the danger to our political institutions, as well as the infamy of tolerating slavery; nothing but war was likely to stop this evil, which was from the first the real issue of the rebellion. "The affliction which has come on our formerly united country," he writes soon after returning again to China, "is a judgment and a remedy together—a judgment because of our boasting and forgetfulness of the mercies we had received, sinning against the sovereignty of God, which He alone can punish as He did Nebuchadnezzar's self-laudation; a remedy for the awful blight and wrongs of the system of slavery. Somehow I am almost sure that slavery will never henceforth raise its head as it has done in the past. Our attention is so excited toward the United States, that when we meet with persons on the walks, the steamers, the country-houses, we can do nothing else but talk of the war and learn details of the battles. It is a harrowing subject, and gradually disables one from all continuous study. A missionary lady from Mississippi is staying with her sick children in my house now, and her feelings are greatly aroused, though she is as strong for the Union as I am. One's feelings carry off one's patriotism in many cases."

His interest, as usual when fully quickened, became severely personal, prompting him not only to pay for a substitute throughout the war, but to seriously debate the propriety of his leaving home at all in such a crisis. The repeated suggestion of returning to serve in some capacity in the army, occurring in many letters written from China during the Rebellion, indicates the feeling continually uppermost in his mind. Contributions to the Sanitary Commission, to hospitals, and for the relief of poor negroes were frequently sent back from China; but nothing was so characteristic of the man in his sober and practical patriotism as his refusal, when United States currency was below one half of its face value, to draw his salary (paid abroad in gold) until the rate of exchange had fallen.

"I leave this country," he writes upon the eve of departure," only in the hope of doing still a little for the good of China's ignorant people. I should like to help in the struggle now begun here, but that contest is in another line from mine. I am glad to have seen the commencement of such a defense of this free government as the last month has exhibited; I trust the issue will strengthen it as the Revolution established it. God's hand will guide and uphold His own ark and forward His own purpose, for He sees the end from the beginning."

In June, 1861, Mrs. Williams and his youngest daughter set sail with him to reach China for the last time by ship. The two older children, who with his brother Frederic were the last to wave adieu from the wharf at New York, were left in America for their education. It is one of the inevitable sorrows of life in the far East, however agreeable or successful it may prove, that a residence there cannot long continue without separation from one's family as well as home. Seldom, however, does it happen that the worst fears of affectionate parents in parting from their children should be realized with such melancholy suddenness. The ship reached Hongkong in September, and by the first mail from home came the news of the loss of their oldest son, Walworth. During the months when they were on their outward voyage the lad sickened and died in Utica. The sorrowful father had builded up more hopes than he was aware of upon the promising boy so lately left, and the disappointment of a thousand cherished dreams for his future made this affliction perhaps the most severe that ever befell him. It is with no desire to reveal the depths of a parent's grief, but to add one more illustration of his self-control in moments of the keenest suffering, that a few sentences are taken from a letter to the brother who was with the boy during his last hours.

MACAO, Oct., 1861.—A fortnight has now elapsed since we learned what was then more than two months old, and I can see many things which were ordered in great mercy in the dispensation, that did not appear so brightly then. Like a photograph which when first taken is so dim as hardly to show an outline, but which with more light erelong brings out its lineaments to the perfection of a clear picture, so do the dealings of God's grace act on us—though in this, unlike the picture, the reason for the dimness is the wickedness of our heart and understanding. How shall we learn the lesson He teaches, how make the improvement of His chastenings which shall appear in the fruit we bring forth, how glorify Him in the fire, so that like silver in the crucible we shall reflect His image? We can indeed do nothing for ourselves in these various paths unless His strength and guidance come to our aid.

MACAO, Oct. 19, 1861.

MY DEAR BRIDGMAN :—You may have wondered why no letter has come from me since my arrival ; the news of the death of my boy Wally has however drawn my thoughts away from every thing save what is associated with him. It has come to dampen and frustrate all the plans we had framed in connection with him and mission work, leading us to look to the Master and Friend we have above—who has better plans in view than ours, and who comes thus near to us that we may be drawn nearer to him. As we sailed down New York harbor last June we left Wally standing on the wharf with Kate and my brother Frederic, the three being among my dearest earthly friends. The two children had been allowed to come to the city to see us off, and were to rejoin their schools, Wally being with Rev. Mr. Dwight in Clinton, who had taken much interest in him and was fully prepared to turn his ideas toward mission work and people. His teacher writes me that evidences of his preparation for death were apparent in the way in which he attended to all his religious duties. His temper was pleasant and he was evidently a favorite with his playfellows. . . . Ah, how one recalls every little incident connected with the dear boy ! while memory brightens her tablets to reproduce his looks, his words, his acts, his plans. I know you 'll understand my thus referring to him. It is a severe loss to us both, and chiefly to his mother, who has thought and spoken of hardly any thing else since hearing of it. We know, indeed, who has thus taken away our first-born and transplanted this flower from our garden to His, but the severance is none the less grievous.

By the mail in which he looked to receive the sympathy and consolation of his warm-hearted colleague, there came instead to Mr. Williams the unexpected and distressing intelligence of his death, at Shanghai. More like an elder brother than a friend, the loss of Dr. Bridgman in the full prime of his usefulness brought upon him a sense of desolation such as their close and uninterrupted companionship from the period of early manhood alone could explain. His first note to Mrs. Bridgman seems to carry to the widow a burden of personal sorrow almost as keen as her own :

" If I had at my command all the sources of consolation which the whole world could afford, they would be of no worth, compared with those you have already at your command in the promises and hopes of the Gospel ; and by these we have both, I humbly hope, been abundantly encouraged, through the great mercy of God. I can sympathize much with you, my dear friend, for I feel the departure of your husband to his rest beyond the toils and anxieties of the world, as the absence of a dear brother—of one closer to me through many years of pleasant labor, counsel, and joy, than almost any other person in the world. You know of this intercourse—how cordial and free it was. From the day I reached Canton, in 1833, to the day—so sad a one—when I learned of his death, there was no interruption to our friendship. I cannot relate the kindly acts, the friendly suggestions, the timely counsel, the patient forbearance and assistance which came from him during the eight-and-twenty years of our acquaintance, for they were continual. I love to recur to them, now that I shall see him no more; they serve to brighten my memory, though memory increases my sorrow at the loss. But as for him, what wonderful things he has already learned, what glorious ideas, vaguely imagined here, have been filled out far beyond earthly conception, and what a vision he now has of the Saviour in all perfection ! . . . Since my dear boy, Wally, has gone, that other world draws nearer; and the departure of my best friend in the mission work adds another strand to the bridge over the chasm, by which my thoughts travel to the unseen. God draws us thus away from time into eternity, loosening our hold here, strengthening it there."

TO MRS. BRIDGMAN.

MACAO, January 24, 1862.

The perusal of your letters, with the notes taken by Dr. Brown, respecting the last days of Dr. Bridgman, has revived, more than ever, the records and remembrances of past years, and I have daily had him, and you, too, in mind. He was a dear friend to me—one for whom I've much reason to bless God, and with him I hope to enjoy God forever. His last hours encourage our faith in the promises on which we trust, for they supported, cheered, and guided him during the hours when earthly friends can only stand and look on. The remembrance of his persevering patience and uniform kindness is continually inciting me to follow him.

Mrs. Williams and I both thank you heartily for sending

these notices of his sickness; they have gone through the hands of the friends here and at Canton who knew him. It was a merciful provision in God's providence which led Brown and Boone to his bedside, to help you and comfort him; they and we will enjoy the same kindness from others before many years, and my daily prayer is to have grace to employ my time and energies in God's service continually until He calls me away.

I have been collecting the Doctor's letters to me during the the last five years, for nearly every one received before that, amounting to a portfolio, was burned in the Factories, together with a collection of J. R. Morrison's, and extracts for the *Repository*, which he had sent me for perusal. Those which I have I will take to Shanghai when I come; they are chiefly on business, and probably contain only short extracts which would enrich a memoir with any thing worth reading. Yet these every-day details make up everybody's life, and we can and must glorify God in fulfilling the duties of every day. The death of Wally came upon me as a messenger, guiding me to a better understanding and devotion to this work; and the departure of my yoke-fellow so soon after—within the same month —engages me to renewed zeal. Both my dear boys sometimes appear to my visions, calling to me from over the walls of the New Jerusalem; they are seldom far off from my thoughts. I bless God for their loan, and think that I was quite resigned by His grace to give them up; they continually draw my desires after them, and cheer my heart by the records of the past in which they were spared to us.

A month after the arrival of Mr. Williams in Macao the Hon. Anson Burlingame, who had been appointed to succeed Mr. Ward as Minister to China, reached Shanghai. The successful termination of the attack of the French and English allies upon Peking the year before had broken down forever the high wall of exclusion by which the Emperor in his capital was surrounded, and inaugurated the new era of foreign residence within its gates. An attempt was made by the Americans to establish their Legation there as soon as the other treaty powers, but the death of Hienfung, in August, 1861,* and the closing of navigation on the Peiho soon after Mr. Burlingame's arrival, detained its members in the south through the winter of that year. These months were profitably employed by Mr. Williams in re-writing his "Commercial Guide" for its fifth edition, which was completed early in 1862, though not published until 1863. The book when issued was a sturdy octavo of some 670 pages, containing the recent treaties and new political and commercial changes dependent upon them, as well as the trade regulations of neighboring countries. This fresh matter, together with its greatly enlarged sailing tables and descriptions of the leading articles of commerce, made it practically a new book; it still remains as the most valuable aid to the foreign merchant in these details. The work, though in the line of much of his earlier labor in China, proved to be a more difficult task than he had anticipated, involving far more drudgery than the previous editions. "This," he observes in the Preface, "is partly caused by the distribution of the foreign trade in China among many ports, whose extremes are nearly two thousand miles apart, and partly in collecting the details respecting the articles and management of the trade, and other points of information usually sought for in a work of this nature. When Canton and Shanghai engrossed four-fifths of the foreign trade, the details and regulations relating to it at those two ports supplied pretty much all that was necessary for

---

* The Emperor, whether from illness or fear, never returned from Jeh-ho, in Manchuria, whither he had fled upon the approach of the allies to Peking.

China; but when further research showed that every port in the country has its local usages, careful investigation at each was necessary to entire accuracy."

While preparing the "Guide" Mr. Williams also made a compilation, for convenient and authoritative reference, of all the treaties between these Eastern countries and the United States, "with the various decrees, regulations, and notifications based thereon," as well as the Chinese text of the treaty of Tientsin. This was printed at the London Mission Press, Hongkong, in March, 1862, an octavo of 190 pages.

With the opening of the rivers in the north Mr. Burlingame and Mr. Williams made their way to Shanghai, visiting the intervening treaty ports. The Taiping rebellion, which had now for nine years been raging through all the central provinces, was become a source of danger even to foreigners.

"The country is everywhere open," writes Mr. Williams from Shanghai, "but it's not over-safe to travel. The vicinage is a scene of rapine and bloodshed and suffering beyond description. What we now see and hear forms a commentary of the liveliest sort on the descriptions given by the prophets of the carnage of ancient armies. The insurgents are not so easily caught, and the heat is too great for foreign troops to go forth and try to enclose them. They may soon beleaguer this settlement and stop the provisioning, in which case the distress among the natives who have fled hither for protection would compel some sharp remedy on the part of the foreigners. Shanghai is now a foreign town to all intents; the French seem to be trying to appropriate most of it to themselves.

Their objects in China are rather suspicious, and through the priests they will soon wield a powerful opposition to Protestants."

TO HIS WIFE.

SHANGHAI, May 15, 1862.

I have taken a ride on horseback this P.M., and am now more inclined to sleep than to write, but my time is narrowing down. I have received your letter written from Hongkong, which tells me you are all well. How thankful I am! . . . When I reached Ningpo on our way up here on the 1st, I found that the allies had concluded to pick a quarrel with the rebels who held the city, by making something out of firing a gun at the *Ringdove*, for their conduct was too atrocious to be longer endured. It was sickening to hear the tales of murder, rapine, burning, and destruction everywhere following in the trail of the Taipings, most of whose troops and many of whose leaders are mere boys, under eighteen, that have been caught and trained to deeds of infamy and blood, in which they soon become reckless. The city was attacked by the foreigners on Friday last, and soon cleared of these miscreants, who probably felt a little uncertain of their position. It has not suffered much. While there I slept one night at Mr. Mangum's and saw all the missionary friends. Rankin speaks of great interest in the Gospel among some of the villagers not far from the city, and says that the rebels have put no hindrance in the way of his work.

May 29th.—We had a call yesterday from Sieh, the Commissioner of Commerce, and Wu, the Tautai. They were received at Russel & Co.'s in the most unpretending manner by Mr. Burlingame and myself, and spent two hours talking on various matters in a quiet way and apparently without much interest on their part. The civil war in the U. S. has evidently drawn their attention, and they had some questions upon it. This Sieh, you know, I suppose, was our evil genius at Peking three years ago. . . . I lose a good deal of time here in one way and another, but there seems no remedy but patience. The nearer the end of life draws, the more do I see that Christian faith and holiness shown in a godly life is all the pure gold there is left out of all our doings. But if we were put in the crucible, how much would remain?

TIENTSIN, July 9th.—I suppose you have just received my letter of last week from Shanghai, sent off the day after I left that place in the *Contest*. I have, I think, spent more days there than I wish to henceforth, and know few regrets now upon leaving it. The absence of Bridgman, and the remembrances recalled by his place and works when living where he spent so many years, has perhaps increased the tinge which attaches to it; but the bustle and novelty of the whole community, together with the unsettled feeling which a newcomer experiences who recollects the Shanghai of former years, distasted me of the place. Mrs. Bridgman keeps on with her daily rounds and maintains her useful school of girls, but her support has gone and she feels the loneliness and the lack of cheerful companionship. Tientsin is for the moment rather dull, but a piece of land has been bought for a settlement, fifty foreigners are already living here, and the trade is likely to grow yearly. I attended a prayer-meeting with the missionaries stationed in the town,—a strong contrast to the condition of things when Reed and I set up housekeeping here in 1858. Thus God gradually opens the way for his work-people.

We are to leave this for Peking on Monday, the 14th, three years, just, after my former visit. The trip on the river will occupy four or five days, and will perhaps be the pleasantest part of the journey, dependent on the weather. We are to go first to the French Legation, Mr. Burlingame having seen Mme. Kleczkowski at Shanghai, and her husband urging it. Having no Legation of our own, we must abide in some place before we can get one; I don't know what luck we shall have in so doing. As to the details of life and duties, I can tell you nothing of interest save that I look to the day of my return south with hope, and humbly trust that we shall again meet, not soon to part voluntarily, for I've had enough of it.

PEKING, July 24th.—You think I ought to tell you something about Peking, but descriptions fail wofully when there is so little in common with what you 've seen. From the top of the city wall, which is perhaps fifty feet wide and about seventy high, one sees a vast array of houses stretching away out of sight, or until they come to their limits indicated by the high towers on the walls. The view is everywhere obstructed by the numerous high trees, locust, ailanthus, elm, etc., which overtop the low houses, and allow only glimpses of the higher buildings. Rooks, crows, and swallows of large size fly and scream among these trees and find food around the streets and houses. But the noisome streets, stinking pits, dusty ways, and loathsome beggars, seen when one descends from the walls and goes through their enceinte, take away a great portion of the pleasant impression and bring one back to the reality of heathenism. The walls of the city are monuments of labor, huge piles of earth covered with bricks of great size, and at every gateway surmounted with five-storied towers. The labor of heaping up such mounds is conformable to one's notions of Chinese ant-like toil. The English artillerymen, when here last year, were disappointed that they had not the chance of knocking holes in this mass with their shot, and convincing the spectators how useless it was for defence.

The public buildings are generally in a most dilapidated condition, indicative of the poverty and carelessness of the government. The decay of public care and forethought in the rulers of a despotism like this involves the neglect of every thing under the guard of lower officers. Really the progress of the nation turns on the energy of the Emperor; it has no forward principle in its own civilization, though it does not seem to retrograde very fast. In their relations with us personally, the officials are friendly in most things, and when they can't hold out longer in an argument, and have not particular fears for themselves, they yield to what is proposed and retire to their quiet. ·The two with whom foreigners have most to do are old men; but after all one can tell them of far-off nations and their own position toward us, they have still the vaguest ideas and narrowest notions. They are grown-up children and I fear quite beyond teaching. Our old negotiator, Kweiliang, has gone; he died last week of apoplexy, in a moment as it were, full of years and honors, at the top of the roll of officers, and before any thing had occurred to distress or degrade him. Hwashana, as you know, died two years ago; Kiying in '58; now the whole trio are gone.

Travel discomposes me more than it used to, I think, and I have had to think of many things since arriving here, especially with reference to a place to live in. The houses here are universally of one story, which renders them dark, as one's room is lighted chiefly by doors. There is the utmost liberty in going about and one can roam over town and country without let. Many discommodities doubtless exist as to a residence here, which will slowly decrease; rich people only can now live here comfortably, owing to the expense of getting furniture, clothing, and many eatables from Shanghai. The natives are miserably poor in the capital, and every thing in the way of carpentry, smithwork, and building is immeasurably inferior to that in the southern cities. I am busy with overseeing the repairs of a house intended for Mr. Burlingame, and find that it requires much more attention and thought than I expected. There are 120 workmen employed, ten per cent. of whom are always looking on most industriously.

Oct. 13th. The autumn is beginning to appear in every lineament of nature, the changing verdure, the falling leaves, the fickle weather, the dry and crispy grass, the ripening fruits,—all tell me that I am staying here a great deal longer than I had expected. Mr. Burlingame, who went last month to Shanghai for his family, is now on his way from Tientsin (I suppose), and will soon be here with wife, child, and nurse, to take possession of his house. Then I shall be away as soon as I can, hoping to reach you before the fall at Macao has passed into winter.

I have been induced, through the strong representations of Blodget, to buy a mission house in Tientsin; it is a house which the English occupied, and will, he says, serve the mission very well, and, if I purchase it, can be improved by degrees without fear of school, family, or congregation being turned out because of a greedy landlord's wanting a higher rent. So I have paid for it without having seen it, because there could be no delay if it was to be secured. I hope it will prove a help to the mission and long be occupied by faithful men. It is rather odd that the first house I ever owned should be one I have never seen, in a town where I shall probably never live. . . . I hope this will be my last to you from Peking.

This busy visit to Peking and Mr. Williams' relations towards his countrymen and the whole body of missionaries there, are described by the Rev. Dr. Blodget, who was with him at that time:

"Manifold interests centred in him when he came to his new home. The American Minister in the first place had need to be provided with a residence at the capital, and was almost helpless in this matter without him; the affairs of the Legation required his constant care, even to clerical duties; his literary labors could not be remitted, for a book was in the press in Hongkong; different mission societies were desirous of locating in Peking, and all looked to him as a steadfast friend and counsellor.

"With Dr. Williams there went to Peking Rev. S. J. J. Schereschewesky and Rev. J. S. Burdon,* both afterwards esteemed and successful missionaries in that city, both dependent at first upon him for shelter in a house which he had bought for his family use. For myself, with whom he had been previously connected in the mission, he purchased land and buildings for a mission compound, paying the money down and offering to retain them at his own risk if the Society did not wish to buy them when advised of the transaction. Later the missionaries of the American Methodist Church pitched their tent in houses owned by him until they had secured a permanent home in the city; while the missionaries of the Woman's Union Mission, upon their arrival in Peking, found him equally helpful in forwarding their plans and endeavors. Continued kindly offices and judicious gifts indicated his per-

* Both afterwards bishops, the former of the American Episcopal Mission in North China, the latter of Hongkong.

manent love for the mission work, and his regard for that portion of it which was carried on immediately around him."

TO W. F. WILLIAMS.

ON BOARD *Shanghai*, OFF TAKU, Nov. 16, 1862.

I am now on my way home to Macao, on board a steamer and surrounded by garrulous, disputant Chinese passengers, bound down to the sunny south. I turn to you with pen to beguile the time and please my thoughts by sending them far hence to Mesopotamia. . . . My visit to Peking has somewhat altered my views respecting the influence of my position in the United States Legation, and I am seriously thinking of moving there with Sarah next year, if the path opens clearly. When I tell you that among other means of usefulness there I have free access to the members of the Great Council of the empire (who are detailed to attend to foreign affairs) and lately persuaded one of them not to allow an American general, who has just been killed while in command of some native troops near Ningpo, to be worshipped as a deified hero, you will admit that an influence for good can be exerted from such an office. Moreover, there is no one just ready to take the post, whom I should like to see in it, and I can retain the position as long as I please. In Peking I have been able to get a house under such circumstances that the two missionaries whom I left in it are secure of a residence at least, and can invite any one to meet them there and explain to them the things of the Kingdom of Heaven.

SHANGHAI, Nov. 27th (being Thanksgiving Day).—Since the above was written I have had a trial of patience in the slow progress southward, the unhappy Chinaman who has chartered this vessel having failed of getting a price for his cargo of northern fruits here, and after much bartering and hesitation resolved to take his perishable freight to the south. . . . The civil and political condition of China now affords a subject of much speculation, and I know not whither the changes will tend. France, England, and Russia are likely ultimately to divide the huge carcass between them, though neither now wishes to commence slicing near the vitals. Russia has already appropriated some of the outer parings along the valley of the Amoor, and can make more use than the others of the Tarim basin and of Gobi down to the Great Wall. France is sending all the priests and nuns who will come, and does much to support them; their passages out are paid, and their missions form the chief object of diplomatic interference at Peking. England, more powerful in commerce and more open in meddling, brings ships and takes charge of navigation on the Yangtsz, employs cajolery, manages the imperial custom-houses, and puts her feelers through the fabric of Chinese society to test its strength and find customers. The indomitable industry of this people would render the country a richer booty to its conquerors than any other Asiatic nation, but an industrious people need to be treated tenderly before they will work for owners. Yet we all are more or less disposed to rejoice over the humiliation of the Chinese for their ridiculous conceit and overbearing distant treatment of Occidentals who have come with friendly intent.

TO DR. P. PARKER.

CANTON, Jan. 13, 1863.—I am now in Canton, spending a few days, a sort of farewell visit, as it were, and have found that it has not altered much during the last year. The houses along the river are gradually filling the vacant lots, the old Factory site is still unoccupied, and Shameen still open in most parts of its area. The city recovers slowly and its old prosperity is not likely soon to return.

I expect to go north again as soon after the beginning of spring as I can arrange to do so, and give up my residence here to make the best sort of one I can in Peking. The change is not so agreeable as in going from north to south, but this appears to be what I ought to do. . . . We look forward with some anxiety to hear what Congress is about, whether supporting or thwarting the President and his policy. The issue of a subdued country must be accepted by one part of the country, or the other, and if the South get the best of the contest, we at the North must expect to be their servants forever. It is now a struggle for free institutions, and slavery will go over the land in form or spirit unless it now dies.

TO MRS. H. C. WOOD.

SHANGHAI, May 25, 1863.—Here I am on my way to Peking with wife, children, box, bundle, and bag, all in a heap, like the big wagons that used to go through Utica on their way beyond and westward; that was going into the wilderness of nature to improve and adorn it, and make the waste places habitable, but this is going into the wilderness of sin—as bad morally as ever the one of Hagar's distress was physically. However, if God goes with me, and strengthens me, I shall not fail.

TO REV. W. F. WILLIAMS.

PEKING, July 23, 1863.—It was hard to make up my mind to leave the southern cities, the charming home at Macao, and begin anew in this region, but I could see no reasonable excuse for remaining there without shirking duty, leaving to others what I should in honor do myself, and then be mortified to find it badly done. We were eminently unlucky in our plans, chiefly from going on wrong premises, for we took a large steamer at Hongkong for Taku, and found great difficulty in transshipping there for Tientsin; it would have been better to have taken a smaller steamer at Shanghai for Tientsin. I packed up books, beds, and chinaware in the greatest hurry, sold off all my furniture that could not be carried, and cleared out from Macao in six days with sixty packages; I ought to have given myself a fortnight, and packed them deliberately. However, Providence brought us at length to Peking on the 16th June, in the brighest of weather, 34 days after leaving Hongkong. I have a dread of looking into the baggage, which is not yet opened, lest all within be in ruins. The house I am to occupy is undergoing some alterations, and we remain meanwhile with Mr. Burlingame, in the same house that I had made over for him last year, thus reaping a reward of a certain sort for my labor then. I entertain no doubt that Peking is the place for our Legation, if we are to exert an adequate influence on China. The experience of two years proves the power of reasonable counsels upon the rulers of this empire, especially assisted as ours have been by the satisfactory results in collecting the customs duties through foreigners. They are beginning to see now that our plans do bring with them some benefits to China, and that we do not take advantage of residence in the capital to browbeat or threaten them. Poor fellows, indeed, for they are sensitive and proud, dreaming that all sorts of fancies actuate us, perplexing themselves with solving riddles of their own creation, while they are ignorant of the plainest points of statesmanship. Little by little the work goes on, however, and God uses the tools and the men which are likely to carry it further, as they are at hand. The Chinese are greatly to be pitied, among other misfortunes, in having such a miserable language through which to obtain ideas and knowledge of foreign countries.

I think you would have fits at seeing the way in which the Pekingese build or repair houses. The timber is all of it the old poles and beams of still older houses, cut and sawed and trimmed for the new position. What was the original size of these beams one can only speculate upon; they seem to have come down from huge pillars and passed through a dozen edifices before they reached my humble house; their decayed spots are plugged like rotten teeth, and where the ends are defective they are spliced, and so eked out. The bricks come from old walls and are gradually triturated to a pebbly size. Mud and lime are mixed in various proportions, and when you are not watching the lime varies incontinently, and nothing but mud holds the bricks in their places. Mortar as we make it, is unknown, for sand is not procurable near the city. If the roof did not rest on the pillared frame, the house would soon crush in from the mass of timber and tiles that form the roof. Of course such fashioned houses do not exceed a story, and most are not above fifteen feet to the ridge-pole. The floors are tiled, the fireplaces and beds made of masonwork warmed underneath, and the windows of latticework covered with paper. When we propose improvements upon these things, the lethargic people look agape at our notions.

TO PROFESSOR J. D. DANA.

PEKING, Aug. 10, 1863.—I see that your "Geology" has been recently issued, from which I reasonably infer that rest has gradually effected a cure, and now it is not unsafe for you to resume your studies. I hope you have still, by the goodness of God, a long service in which to vindicate His works and show that the works and words of God do not and cannot dispute or neutralize each other. With men like Huxley, Colenso, or Oken, who bring up all their attainments to lower or overthrow the truths of revelation and show their malice against them and their Author, it will be necessary to go far and deep in order to show the fallacies of their arguments. I am glad that you have taken up this line of research or argument, and are not disposed to let underhand attacks on the SS. pass unnoticed ; for the number who can prove that man is not a monkey and did not evolve from a monad is not very large.

I reached this city about two months since with my family, and have so far been unable to get the repairs upon my house done. I don't much wonder that China is such an old country, for her inhabitants think less of time than any I have ever seen, and spend it without conscience. It is not a pleasant city to live in compared with those on the coast, and owing to the example set by the Legations in spending a good deal and keeping up large establishments, we are all compelled to pay enormously for living, in comparison with the natives. Nothing foreign has thus far penetrated from the coast, excepting the fancy articles, like glassware, watches, etc. If those Frenchmen who discoursed so learnedly and conclusively to each other about a century ago on the perfection attained by the pagan but moral Confucianists could live here a month and see the actual misery, dirt, and strife, they would willingly go back to Christian countries and keep quiet. Yet we are surprised that society gets on as well as it does, and that poverty is not goaded by suffering to throw the land into anarchy in order to relieve or destroy itself. The restraints must be powerful to sufficiently resist the disintegrating effects of ignorance and discontent which ferment around us.

Once settled in Peking, Mr. Williams commenced his long-cherished design of revising his " Tonic Dictionary," and introducing the Mandarin dialect sounds with the characters. He found himself well placed for such a work, with sufficient leisure outside of business hours to carry it on continuously, if slowly. As happened more than once in his literary labors, revision was attended by expansion, and this by change of plan, until his project insensibly had launched him into a new work. It was found that something more was required among foreigners than a vocabulary of common terms, and Mr. Williams could not fail to acknowledge the justice of the general demand that he should produce a successor to Morrison's Lexicon. The fact that he was repeatedly prevented from going to Shanghai to superintend its printing served, probably, more than other causes to enlarge the scope and contents of his dictionary until it had developed into a volume of large proportions. For ten years it formed the constant occupation of his working hours whenever Legation business permitted, and opposite to him at his desk there sat always his Chinese writer, or native scholar, whose time was employed in defining terms and idioms, and searching the range of his literature for illustrative sentences and authorities.

TO REV. W. F. WILLIAMS.

Sept. 27, '63.—I have just returned from a trip of four days into the country to visit a coal quarry and a cave.* The weather is charming and invites us abroad to see what we can of the land. The people are everywhere civil and peaceful, and the environs of the capital present an exceptional picture of industry, quiet, and thrift. The secret of the permanence of Chinese institutions is much in the industry to which all are trained. We never saw a single gun, sword, or other weapon

* A cavern near Fangshan, about fifty miles southwest from Peking.

during our journey; bill-hooks, goads, plough, flails or other farmer's instruments filled the hands of the people; the harvest this year being unusual, the peasants have no complaint. Jogging along on our horses we rode for the better part of our excursion upon the highway to the far west, which Marco Polo describes; in many places the large blocks of granite with which it is paved are worn so smooth that one would have to dismount and crawl on hands and knees to travel in safety. Arrived at the mountains we were hospitably entertained by the inmates of a monastery and allowed to cook our own provisions in what might be called the refectory kitchen, and slept as comfortably within sound of the prayer drum and chanting priests as ever we did at home. The cave, which we visited at the end of a brisk walk in the morning, was well worth the trouble of our getting there; it is very large and filled with beautiful incrustations, the results of the action and percolation of water. No traces of former life here have been discovered, though I think that researches under the stalagmites would disclose some fossil bones. The Chinese have carved a caryatid of Buddha about fifteen feet high, near the entrance of the side of the cave, and the many pilgrims here offer things to it —iron cash, incense-sticks, etc. The entire cavern has not yet been explored, and the remoter chambers of it are walled up lest visitors be lost in them. A small monastery has been built at the entrance, in which was one priest all shaven and shorn, about seventy years old, the picture of senility and dotage. In the region of the cave are about forty different monasteries, served by eighty priests, who derive their support from glebe lands confirmed to them in 1490. They have terraced the hillsides, in places nearly eight hundred feet high, and turned the barren-looking slopes into fertile fields; the Fourierist principle prevails in the management of these farms. The ravine or gorge where most of the temples stand, is a wild scene and attracts many (native) visitors to see the cliffs, the steeps, and the winding paths among the hills. The autumnal flora was in its glory and I am sure I must have noticed two hundred species, mostly in bloom, making the trip up and down to the cave a walk through a flower garden. The preponderance of leguminous plants over syngenesious is a feature in the flora here in contrast to our New York autumn plants, owing possibly to the limestone soil. Mr. Blodget, of the Tientsin mission, accompanied a Mr. Raphael Pompelly, of Owego, New York, and myself, and rendered it altogether a most pleasant jaunt. I find that my legs don't carry me quite as they used to up hill and down, and especially fail in their duty when told to take me down one thousand rungs of a ladder into a coal mine.

Oct. 21, '63.—I have moved into my new house since I wrote you last and I am gradually finding its ins and outs, infits and refits, lights and shades, etc. There are eight little rooms or houses, two of which communicate; the others are isolated. Two small paved courtyards furnish the only open spaces within the lot, to which add a gateway and side-alley. The Chinese know nothing of yards surrounding their houses, but build them either directly upon the street or enclosed by a high blank wall; gardens and plots for culture are thus protected and concealed from view, for thieves would carry off every thing exposed. These eight small rooms are all just above the ground, three of them having boarded floors and the others being tiled. The bedroom, which is the highest and most comfortable of all, is in the extreme rear. We keep a door-keeper, a cook, two coolies, a groom, and one waiter, all under the butler or major-domo; besides these there is a nurse (the only female domestic), our laundrying is done abroad, and drinking and washing water all brought into the house by water-carriers; with these retainers we employ less than others here, and get along not so well as some. Every thing in the habits of the Chinese here tends to laziness and poverty, and a man had rather serve for four or five dollars a month—finding himself—than to work harder and earn eight or ten. Our servants have no idea of exerting themselves beyond their own limited range of duties, and the cook would perhaps leave if asked to carry a note. One of the annoyances here is the custom servants have of demanding perquisites out of purchases made; they seem to consider their wages of small account, but are on the look-out for every chance at what is called a "squeeze." It is almost unknown in Canton, but is in vigor here owing to the numerous official establishments, the assembly halls, and the various boards or depots, whose attendants and lictors look to these perquisites for their living, and sponge from every man who draws near for favor, demand of justice or employment, or aught else besides. The vexatious effects upon the temper of such a system of musketo-biting on one's funds are not small, and your patience is put to the perfect work which is necessary to its growth.

Nov. 24th.—I send you two cards of high functionaries who called last week upon our Minister to thank him for his aid and counsel in getting them out of a curious and dangerous complication into which they had brought themselves. I suppose you 've heard of the flotilla which was fitted out in England for the Chinese government, and left this year under command of Osborn, a captain in the British navy of credit and renown. On reaching Peking, Mr. Lay (the agent and paid official of the Chinese in England) and Capt. Osborn made known the engagements they had entered into as to the control of these war steamers, when it was perceived by the Chinese that their agent had greatly exceeded his instructions, and contrived to make himself the Secretary of a really formidable navy without their leave. They naturally declined the engagement, but the disposition of the steamers and their officers was not so easily settled, as the prospect of eight men-of-war, armed and equipped, turned against them, or turned adrift, or turned back, was on every hand surrounded with difficulties. Capt. Osborn, however, who appreciated their perplexity, acted most honorably and proposed to take the vessels back to England, sell them, and refund the surplus to the Chinese. The American and French Ministers both aided the English in inducing a peaceful arrangement, and the fleet is to be disbanded in England. Mr. Lay has been dismissed from Chinese employ, and returns whence he came. I think he has been better treated than he would have been by any Western nation—but neither would he have acted so toward any other government. It has taught these officials two or three things in international law, and also bettered our relations with them, since our course has proved that foreign ministers desire their progress only as they are able to advance profitably to themselves. . . .

Three [missionary] societies have their agencies at Peking, and at each place their efforts are rather frittered away in inefficient plans which often end in a cul-de-sac. It is not easy to manage independent Protestants in their evangelical labors; I have known men so decided in their opinions as to a scheme of preaching or the like, that almost all of their time was consumed in combating their fellows, and in the end they would hardly consent to do as they had a mind to.

From which it may be seen without saying that the contretemps of life are not wanting even among missionaries. Mr. Williams was more than once sorely tried as an unwilling and helpless spectator of some hopeful plan which failed for lack of coöperation. That his sympathy in their labors was not, however, in the least abated, appears from the following defence of missions in answer to certain criticisms in English periodicals.

[From the *Observer*, N. Y., April 7, 1864.]

[Last summer we copied from British periodicals a wanton attack upon Christian missionaries, and we attempted to show how shallow is the philosophy that makes civilization an indispensable requisite to the introduction of Christianity. Our paper with those extracts goes to Peking and there comes to one of the most learned and accomplished of our missionaries. S. Wells Williams, LL.D., author of "The Middle Kingdom," is now secretary of the American Legation, and we do not exaggerate in saying that no man in China is better qualified than he to expose the fallacy of that logic by which the enemies of Christ's kingdom would resist the efforts of Christians to plant the Gospel in the unbroken wilds of barbarous paganism. In the midst of his absorbing duties he finds time to indite the following masterly and philosophical argument, which he sends to the *New York Observer,* in answer to the sophistry and error of the *Westminster Review* and the *London Times*. It will command the interested attention of every intelligent Christian reader.]

PEKING, January 11, 1864.

TO THE EDITORS OF THE NEW YORK OBSERVER :—In your paper of Sept. 3, 1863, which has only lately reached this city, there is an article headed " The Gospel and Civilization—Which is to Go First?" containing extracts from the *English Churchman* and the *London Times*, the drift of which is to prove that missionaries have begun wrong in their efforts, and that instead of teaching the heathen the truths of the Gospel first, they ought to teach them the arts of civilized life as a stepping-stone to the truths of revelation. A train of argument deduced from the practice of the Apostles is applied to enforce this mode of reasoning, which apparently has for its end chiefly to find fault with what others are doing to evangelize the world, and thereby get a complacent excuse for the writers' doing nothing themselves. You very plainly expose the fallacy of the whole argument by showing that the Bible and facts are both against its reasonings and conclusions, and in truth every one who has candidly examined the subject is fully convinced that the only way to elevate and civilize any pagan people is to preach the Gospel to them in all its fulness of precept and exemplify it by every form of benevolent action.

But there is a reason for preaching the Gospel first as a means of introducing civilization, which lies in the nature of the human mind, and to overthrow the argument of such writers. It would meet them with a power they now have little idea of, if they would for once try honestly to carry out their own scheme. It is tersely expressed in the words of Christ : " And the truth shall make you free." The reason why civilization cannot precede Christianity in this great work is because it never teaches the truth to the people ; it never presents to the mind those sanctions for upholding and reverencing the truth which are alone found in the Word of God. Until the mind of man feels that its inmost sins and thoughts are known to an All-Seeing Eye, there is no restraint upon them: for no god in the pantheon of any heathen people was ever endowed with the attribute of omniscience; it is altogether beyond the ideas, as it is against the wishes, of sinful man. Until the sanctions of the Bible come to aid the missionary in his teachings, by the Holy Spirit impressing upon the soul its accountability for its violation of God's law, he knows that his teachings have no power to alter their conduct. But the effects of the truth upon the mass of a people as a means of elevating them in the scale of humanity are seen as soon as individuals begin to live up to the requirements of Christianity, and a small community of Christians, shining forth amid their heathen countrymen, the light that has newly sprung up in their hearts, becomes a centre of improvement. Even among a people like the Chinese, who are possessed of the conveniences of life and held together by an organized government founded on the consent of all classes, the want of truth and integrity weakens every part of the social fabric. Moral ethics, enforcing the social relations, the rights and duties of the rulers and ruled, and the inculcation of the five constant virtues, have been taught in China for twenty-five centuries, and yet have failed to teach the people to be truthful. They never can do it, for they have no sanctions calculated to influence the mind and strengthen it to resist temptation. The Chinese race has, perhaps, risen as high as it is possible in the two great objects of human government—security of life and property to the governed, and freedom of action under the individual restraints of law,—and it presents now a subject worthy of study to the philosopher in tracing out the reasons why unaided human teachings have been so much more useful and durable here than they were in the lands of Zoroaster, Seneca, Socrates, or Longinus. But until truth becomes even here the basis of society, so that a man sinks in the estimation of his fellows if caught in a falsehood, and is afraid to lie because he will be despised, the Chinese must remain far below any Christian nation. They cannot progress in civilization until they become truthful. No corporate bodies formed among them for the purpose of carrying out great plans of improvement can cohere in consequence of this inherent weakness, because no subscribers will trust their money to such a company. No insurance company can obtain the confidence of the community ; no trust company can succeed, let it promise ever so much. If the government issues coin it is taken for its intrinsic worth, like bullion, because it is so soon tampered with as to lose its nominal value ; and the case is still worse with its bonds,—so that China alone, of all the nations of the earth, has even now no national silver or gold coin and no bank bills, the only currency being a miserable copper-iron coin, so debased as not to pay counterfeiters to imitate it.

The writers in the *Times* and other papers would, I suppose, teach these things among their first lessons of civilization, though perhaps they regard the Chinese, Japanese, Siamese, and other Orientals as sufficiently civilized, and needing no further instruction. But missions must precede civilization : for they alone furnish sufficient stimulus to improve a man's social condition, by giving him adequate reasons for changing his life and religion. When he is taught that he is an immortal and accountable soul, he then begins to feel that he must use the talents and bounties God has given him to their highest and best ends. Compare the Haiwaiians and Maoris, among whom the truths of Christianity have been plainly preached by Protestant missionaries, with the Annamese and Tangalos in Luconia, among whom only the forms of Christianity, confessional and baptismal rites, adoration of saints, bowing to the cross, reciting of rosaries, and such like, have alone been introduced : and we see that the different results are owing to the neglect, in the latter cases, of teaching that truth which makes men free from superstition, error, vice, lying, and indolence. Truth alone is the proper aliment for the mind ; on it alone can all the faculties acquire their full development ; and until they receive it the conscience will feel no sense of weakness or wickedness such as the Bible describes, and no efforts will be made to come to the light, and expand under its genial rays. Consequently, there will be no progress in civilization, though taught its most approved and useful features.

It seems almost useless to refer to such puerile objections to the plan of missions on the part of those who probably never aided them with their bounty, and could never have carefully inquired into their operations, successes, or principles. Civilization, even as seen in the most civilized countries, is only the exhibition of the principles of Christianity ; and how unwise it is to propose to elevate the heathen by introducing among them the results of those principles before giving them the foundation on which they rest ; beginning the social structure with the coping and not at the corner-stone ! But their plan, if practicable in its conception, would fail in its ends ; for without a regard for the truth in all its forms no nation can rise to the highest style of civilization ; and nothing but the Gospel, blessed to the heart by the Holy Spirit, can implant this regard, and sustain the mind to its full development.

We have, even in China, plenty of those emissaries of evil, who, having had their minds strengthened by the sublime truths of revelation taught in their youth in Christian lands, but their hearts untouched with a sense of sin, come among this people and teach them even a worse style of depravity—so to speak. These have the power to do wickedness with a persistence of energy which the pagan does not often reach. Christian nations should in equity maintain Gospel missions everywhere to save the pagan nations from the destruction this pseudo-civilization, as set forth by these runagates, is bringing upon them.

S. W. W.

TO REV. W. F. WILLIAMS.

PEKING, June 10, 1864.—Since my last to you, I have been quietly going on with the revision of my dictionary and attending to official duties ; so that I have enough to keep me busy. Just now we have a curious instance of the efforts people will make to obtain riches and deem their labors nothing. You may have ere this heard of an American named Ward, who entered the Chinese employ and became the leader and life of a band of natives, whom he drilled in Western discipline. He succeeded in obtaining the confidence of the officials and of his own men, and began the successful repulse of the Taiping rebels, which is likely during the present year to end in their dispersion. He was killed in September, 1862, in an assault on Tsz'ki, not far from Ningpo, and when dying declared that the Chinese owed him 140,000 taels ($200,000), though proof was wanting otherwise than his own assertion and the confession of Chinese officers. The latter, however, were unable to pay his executor when he demanded the liquidation of the claim, and they have not yet done so. Now the father of Gen. Ward, hearing of the windfall in China, leaves the United States to recover it; and in this effort he has been zealous and persevering, in a way to shame us missionaries; and here he is in Peking to get Mr Burlingame to intercede for him with the officials. They are, indeed, favorably inclined to him on his son's account (to whom they have voted a tablet and shrine for the peace of his spirit), and they give him hope of pay. The old man, who esteems his son as equal to any general or strategist on record, has become quite one-sided in mind through this engrossing pursuit; his earnestness and sacrifices are instructive. I have done almost nothing during two weeks but prepare and translate his papers for him.

TO THE SAME.

CHANG-NGAN-SZ, OR MONASTERY OF PERPETUAL QUIET, a temple west of Peking, Aug. 12, 1864.—We are spending a month or two of the hot weather at this place—fourteen miles from the city,—at the base of the hills which command a view of the plateau of central Asia. It forms one of a group of eight separate monasteries cared for by twenty or more priests —the Russian, American, French, and other ministers occupying the remainder,—higher up the hill, and embosomed in groves of trees, from which they look out upon a magnificent prospect of teeming fields stretching onwards toward Peking. The one we occupy is spacious and clean, but not so new as some of the others; it contains three terraces within the high enclosing wall, and has eight or ten different buildings, altogether, arranged around two court-yards that are planted with many trees; in all, with its cattle-yard and two cemeteries, the entire enclosure may occupy some five acres. The idols are of many sizes, all of them belonging to the Buddhist pantheon, and are daily attended by acolytes, who rap the bell and tap the drum to arouse the gods, when prayers are said, sacrifices presented, candles lighted, incense burned, and heads knocked before them. For sacrifice, a little boiled rice, a plate of fruit, and a libation of whiskey serves the purpose ; the images are of clay and wood, gilded, and dressed in long mantles, which pretty much hide them. Among the trees in the yard, or "compound," are six specimens of the white pine, one of which is, I am told, over five hundred years old ; it is covered nearly to the outmost branches with a bark as white as if the whole trunk had been whitewashed—this bark flaking off when old, like shell-bark hickory, and thus keeping the tree forever white and fresh. It is truly a fine tree, and has been introduced by some admirers into England and France, where, however, I am inclined to think it will not show so splendid a trunk, because of their comparatively humid climate. With the trees and fruits and flowers and fishes in pots, the temple courts are always attractive and shady ; it is a pleasant retreat from the dust and smells of Peking, and we have rejoiced in clambering the hill-sides and breathing fresh air for these six weeks.

Since last I wrote, the rebellion in China, which has been gnawing at her vitals since 1849, has received its death-blow by the capture of Nanking and the death of its leader, Hung. It is the culminating stroke of the successes begun in 1861 by the American adventurer, Ward, of Salem, who had organized and drilled a force of natives, and of whom I have spoken before. After his death the work was continued by an Englishman named Gordon, who showed great skill, and was successful in leading the little band from one victory to another, until Suchau and other strongholds were captured from the insurgents. I had no faith in this rebellion from the first, as likely to prove a means of promoting the truth, for there was no adequate cause for insuring such a result, while the conduct of the rebels during the last five years has shown a ruthlessness and fanaticism enormously greater than when they began their career of slaughter in 1850.

Bishop Boone, of the American Episcopal Mission, is dead,

after a service of twenty-eight years in Java and China. He leaves a clear example as a Christian pastor and energetic worker in the foreign community at Shanghai—which lately subscribed $7,000 to give him as a sort of amende for his losses in South Carolina investments. Though a Southerner, he was rather for the old Union and decidedly opposed to slavery as a political institution, but upheld it as consonant with the SS.

TO DR. PETER PARKER.

PEKING, Sept. 1, 1864.—It seems as if I would like above all things to spend half a day with you, and learn more of the events happening around you than I can get from the papers that come here. I have been so much excited by the details of battles during last May and June—our last dates—that I think and dream of them all the time. And yet when you get this they will have been veiled by later and not less important events. What a drama of agony and grandeur and deep importance to live and see! God's hand of judgment and mercy is everywhere, mingling the two to our country that it may learn righteousness and love peace. Truly we know now better than ever the meaning of the phrase, "terrible things in righteousness."

Since the capture of Nanking, which has much elated the government here, the drilling of troops is continually practised in the city, whence when once taught they are dispersed to various places where they can instruct others. The perfection of the movements of some of these regiments is remarkable, no foreigner having been near them except to drill their officers. Your former friend, Tsunglun,* whom you met at Taku in 1854, has charge of their drilling, and takes much pride in its success. The Russians furnish the arms.

By the beginning of winter he writes to his brother

---

* One of four Chinese officers whom Dr. Parker met on the Peiho in October, 1854, when sent as Secretary of Legation by U. S. Commissioner McLane to negotiate for his reception at the capital or by a high commissioner.

Frederic of Mr. Burlingame, who was then contemplating an early return to America with the intention of resigning:

" . . . He is one of the most enthusiastic of men, and looks cheerfully upon home affairs, assured that this sad war will purge out the leaven of slavery from our institutions and reunite the North and South more closely in future than ever before. His influence here upon the Chinese has been considerable, and still greater upon the other ministers. Accordingly we hope all the more that he will remain longer than any of his predecessors have done. He wants very much, however, to go home, whether Lincoln is elected or not, and see for himself the condition of affairs."

The minister obtained leave of absence and returned with his family to the United States in the spring of 1865. After the re-election of President Lincoln Mr. Burlingame was earnestly urged by William H. Seward, Secretary of State, to return and carry to a conclusion the important projects he had begun in China. This he wisely and fortunately consented to do, abandoning in the determination flattering prospects of political distinction at home. As member of Congress, Mr. Burlingame's career before his appointment to China had been a brilliant one, his rare eloquence and manly defence of his cause—notably his resolute conduct in the Brooks affair in the House—combining with the singular strength and charm of his personality to make him one of the most popular public men in America. After his arrival in Peking his course toward the Chinese developed into a line of policy entirely characteristic of his kindly and sincere nature ; this diplomacy, which soon became known as the " coöperative policy," heartily seconded by his warm personal friend, Sir Frederick Bruce, the British Minister, guaranteed to China her autonomy and treatment on the same terms as any other independent power.* Despite the opposition of the foreign trading communities along the coast (the bitterness and arrogance of whose bearing towards the natives can be measured and understood only by those who are familiar with the principles and conduct of foreign adventurers in the East), the Burlingame policy succeeded before long in establishing an equitable friendship with the leading statesmen in China, and in preserving their country from the inevitable effects of a doctrine which if persisted in would have resulted in the disruption of the empire.

Into such plans, as may readily be imagined, Mr. Williams entered fully and cordially, and it was a severe disappointment to him when Mr. Burlingame declared his intention of resigning his office upon reaching America. Their relations, both private and official, had, since their first acquaintance, been of the pleasantest kind; in summer living upon the same hill-side, sharing alike in the contents of country life and the relief from the city's heat and intolerable dust; in winter joining in the social or diplomatic duties of their station, hardly did a day pass without bringing them together, or a despatch arrive without the Minister's appeal to the advice and experience of the Secretary.

* As defined by Mr. Burlingame, "That policy is briefly this: An agreement on the part of the Treaty Powers to act together upon all material questions; to stand together in defence of their treaty rights, but determined at the same time to give those treaties a generous construction; determined to maintain the foreign system of customs, and to support it in a pure administration and upon a cosmopolitan basis; an agreement to take no cession of territory at the treaty ports, and never to menace the territorial integrity of China." It was a policy substituting fair diplomatic action for violence, and has been pursued since its inauguration by all the great powers.

TO REV. W. F. WILLIAMS.

PEKING, October 25, 1865.

I have entire charge of the Legation, and find it thus far easy enough. Sarah helps me with the copying, and I can write all that is requisite. I have lately been the topic of newspaper tirade for my course respecting an American once in the employ of the Chinese, who turned traitor, was taken prisoner, and delivered up, and again joined the rebels to be again captured by the government troops. While in their custody the second time he was drowned by a boat's capsizing in a rapid down which he was being conveyed, and thus ended his miserable life. The United States authorities in China are invested with more authority than power, but if the fleet which has just been stationed in these waters remains, these miscreants can be checked. Some of them have acted like fiends towards the natives; of those who were condemned in American consular courts, one was hung, one cut his throat the day before he was to have been executed, and one broke jail while under sentence of death. Thus some efforts have been made on our part to restrain evil-doers, and we are educating the Chinese gradually up to a higher plane—I should rather say, God is employing His agents to make Himself known in one way and another in this land. It is thirty-two years this day since I landed in Canton, and how rapid has been the change during that part of China's history! . . . .

I am still busy on my dictionary, and am now on the syllable *shan*. This work reminds me much of my camel ride from Cairo to Gaza, a monotonous travel through a dreary sameness, relieved by a few shrubs, and sometimes a flower. Such is Chinese literature, for it is (to our taste) destitute of imagination, and making a dictionary to elucidate it is indeed a drudgery. But so is laying a cobble pavement, and both are useful in their ways to help the traveller. The printing is likely to demand much time, but I do the work of the hour, and let next year take care of itself.

TO REV. RUFUS ANDERSON, D.D., BOSTON.

PEKING, September 6, 1865.

MY DEAR SIR :—I have had the pleasure of reading your letter to Mr. Blodget respecting the extension of missionary work in Peking, and your proposal to establish a new mission of the Board in central China, in Kiukiang, if that port should be found eligible. Now that the rebellion is ended, thanks to the arm of the Lord which has supported us through the dreadful struggle, it is to be hoped that mission work will receive a new impulse, and the world be the better for our victory over slavery.

I have a special interest in Kiukiang—on the banks of the Great River, as the Chinese usually call the Yangtsz' River—from having had my attention directed to it soon after coming to Canton. In one of the volumes of the *Missionary Herald* you will find an extract from one of my letters in which a mission at or near the Poyang Lake is mentioned as one of the things I hoped to see. I have not the letter to refer to, but I remember the feelings I had when writing it, and the unbelieving hope whether it would ever come to pass in my day. God has spared me to write you another letter about a mission to that same lake, and I do so in the believing hope, now that the breaker has gone up before the missionary, that he will soon go there. One would have thought that all the places that could be reached in China would have been occupied by missionaries immediately upon their being opened, judging by the expressions of earnest longing that were uttered years ago when they remained closed to their efforts, but such has not been the case. Of all the unoccupied posts, I think Kiukiang to be the most desirable for occupation. It stands, as you will see by the map, near the head of the Poyang Lake, into which flows the Kan River, whose basin drains and unites the whole province of Kiangsi. This province is a little larger than New England, and, according to the census, contains over twenty millions of people, so that its claims are neither unimportant nor unseemly to the attention of those who are seeking new fields for Christian labors. I have no doubt that a missionary settling at Kiukiang, which is the commercial capital of the province, will find a rapidly increasing population drawn thither by the trade, and as soon as he had acquired something of the language, would be able to carry on all the branches of labor he had strength for. The climate is regarded as salubrious, more so than some other parts of the valley of the Yangtsz', but at present no specific data are accessible to verify this point. The country in its vicinity can be no doubt occupied as soon as the city is well worked; but what a meagre plan is this to send one or two missionaries to labor in a large city, and to influence the whole of a region as large as Virginia. If my representations can encourage you to open a fourth mission in China, I know of no place so desirable as Kiukiang, yet I pray you not to abandon Canton, where the laborers are few and the harvest great, where the long years of unfruitful toil are now followed by much that promises good to the people and joy to the church, and where one of the most energetic of Chinese races live.

This should be a time of much encouragement to lay large plans of Gospel work in China. The devastations of the Taiping rebellion. have ceased, and the people are inclined to listen to foreigners when they find them friendly. The Romish Church is enlarging itself in every direction, and its three hundred priests are exerting themselves in every province and increasing their adherents by thousands every year. When I look back and see how the way for preaching the truth has gradually opened up in China, and how very inadequately the Church has sent its messengers into these waste places during the last twenty years, I begin to think that we shall not have to ourselves the honor of establishing the Gospel in China, but that this in future will be the work of natives more than ever it has been in the past. However, to do any thing in such a cause is a privilege. I trust that erelong you will soon find the men and means to enlarge and hasten a thousand-fold its achievement.

Mr. Burlingame, upon leaving Peking had sold his house, and his return made it necessary for Mr. Williams to secure premises where the United States representative could be properly accommodated. The purchase and re-arrangement of Chinese dwelling-houses having proved unsatisfactory in many respects, he determined to build a suitable house for the Legation, and having charge as

American representative in China, of the unexpended remainder of the indemnity fund of 1859, he invested a portion of the accrued interest in carrying out his plan. Unlike other capitals of great nations, Peking offered no inducement to foreigners to reside there, and, owing to the exclusion by treaty of Western merchants, had, besides its diplomatic and missionary community, no foreigners whatever, occasional visitors being entertained at the various Legations. The house occupied by the American Minister was so small, indeed, that he was not only unable always to extend this expected hospitality to countrymen, but could not even admit the sedan-chairs of the Chinese Ministers within his humble portal, forcing the Prime Minister to alight in the street and make his way within on foot.

But his enterprise proved for Mr. Williams a more serious personal responsibility than he anticipated. In the language of a subsequent Minister:

"He thought that a part of it [the indemnity fund] could be made to earn a better interest in this way than it was doing, and that this business-like step—so rare in government officials—would be approved. After setting forth with clearness the necessity that existed for such buildings, and showing that the interest only of the surplus had been touched, Mr. Williams voluntarily offered, if this division should not be approved, to assume the responsibility by taking the buildings himself and refunding the money.

"The Secretary of State, while admitting the necessity for a permanent Legation, and approving the motives which actuated Mr. Williams, disapproved of his thus diverting the funds, and ordered him to return the money to the Surplus Fund. This order was promptly obeyed." *

* Mr. F. F. Low to Hamilton Fish, Secretary of State, No. 20, Aug. 5, 1870.

Whatever he thought of this action of his government, there was no question in Mr. Williams' mind of the need for accommodations which should render the United States respectable in the eyes of the Chinese, and no one appreciated better than he the importance of a degree of ceremony and dignity in presenting a distant and almost unknown nation to the notice of an Oriental sovereign. He carried out his plans for a Minister's residence, therefore, choosing a site opposite the Russian Embassy, and completing the work in time to receive Mr. Burlingame upon his arrival in October, 1866. The building was the first attempt to introduce in Peking certain elementary Western ideas of construction, and cost the amateur architect a vast expenditure of his time and patience; his reward came when Prince Kung, arriving in a sedan borne by eight men to the inner door of Mr. Burlingame's house, exclaimed " This is at least decent!"

TO PROFESSOR J. D. DANA.

PEKING, February 11, 1867.

I am sure that you owe it to yourself not to exert yourself to the limits of endurance, for you have I hope much work yet. I am surprised to learn that you have been able to get a new edition of the " Mineralogy " ready so soon after the " Geology " is published ; method and perseverance have enabled you to accomplish so much, and it is the habit of application which is the cause of much of the difficulty you find, I suppose, to keep still long enough to keep well. But when our bodies are laid with their fellow dust, there will be none of this restraint from disabled or worn-out machinery in the mental operations. What an euthanasia was the departure of Professor Silliman that Thanksgiving morning, thus gently to be bowed out of one room of God's universe into another, and find himself giving thanks to Jesus Himself !

I am still at work at my dictionary, a plodding and uninteresting, but useful job; I hope to begin to print in Peking, but there are more than 3,000 characters yet to examine, and six or eight is a good day's work. None of my previous books on this language are extant, all having been sold or burned up. They did some good, however, in their day, and are still in service to some extent, I hear. This dictionary will be about the last performance I shall undertake, though I have a MS. of a Chronology and Gazetteer so far ready for the press that a few weeks or months would finish them.

I have been busy these last two summers in collecting plants in this vicinity, which I send to Dr. Hance, a German at Whampoa, who has more knowledge of Chinese plants than any one else. I have found four new ones for him, and many others of great rarity and interest. The grasses hereabouts are rather numerous for so dry and rocky a region, and present many singular features ; but the flora altogether is scanty. I have in three summers, aided by others, found only 300 +, but the locality having been imperfectly explored, there is room for further discoveries. I collect these plants as well to teach my children how to look at things, and now one of them has begun to imitate me in pressing. When I used to wander about Utica and Troy, I certainly could not have supposed those tramps would stimulate me to equal them again on the Si Shan, near Peking. If there were any petrifactions about here I should rather hammer away at them than seek for plants ; I have half a mind to send for some pins and other apparatus for collecting insects. The works of God delight one everywhere.

Such fragments and bits of reference to his continued delight in the favorite pursuits of his school-days occur in scattered plenty throughout all the letters of his later life. It would be difficult to exaggerate the enthusiasm with which he entered upon the quest of a new plant or fern, or the infectious quality of his eagerness in collecting and examining specimens when abroad in the fields with others. Many who met him first in this way, upon such rides and excursions in the country as often brought out a good assemblage of the foreigners in Peking, would return to beg the favor of other walks and talks in company with Dr. Williams, an evidence of his influence which always greatly touched and pleased him. Indeed it was impossible for the most indifferent not to share in some degree the pleasure of the little group, which, led by him, wandered with tireless feet over those bleak hills, or climbed their uncertain paths upon deft and heedful donkeys, ever intent on securing one more specimen which should be deemed worthy "to send to Dr. Hance." And when upon rare occasions that experienced botanist wrote that the fern or weed was hitherto unknown, or that a new species had been named by European scientists the *Asplenium Pekinense*, or finally that another had received the title of *Adiantum Guilielmi*, the grateful news was a cause of common rejoicing in the community. In this way some four or five species were first brought to notice by Mr. Williams during his residence in Peking, one of these being an elder which is still known to those living there by his name (*Sambucus Williamsii*).

The passion for collecting, which, as Darwin says, "leads a man to be a systematic naturalist, a virtuoso, or a miser," was strongly developed in him. The same impulse which induced him to accumulate phrases and characters in conversation with the Chinese, impelled him while amongst the river folk near Canton to get together all the varieties of fish native to that region, an unfamiliar study for him, but one which he turned to some account afterwards in the Natural History chapter of "The Middle

Kingdom."* " He was a delightful companion in walking," writes his friend Dr. Blodget, " and on this very account: his conversation not only drew upon his stores of knowledge in history, science, and religion, but would as often descend to topics of common life or dilate upon the things in nature spread out before him. Flowers were his especial delight. His fondness for botany became almost a passion, the beauty and wonder of growing things being ever a joy to him. Often on an evening's ramble he would gather a bouquet to adorn the table, and was never weary in pointing out their beauty and interest—often, it must be confessed, to dull and forgetful listeners; or he would describe the cereals and grasses which filled the fields or grew along the roads near his summer retreat, the ' Tremont Temple,' and these impromptu and unconventional lectures were often the choicest intellectual treats.

" And if we followed him with his flowers to his cheerful home, he seemed in inviting us to his table to possess the happy art of making these visits appear as favors conferred upon himself, rather than as obligations imposed upon his guests. Nor was he unobservant of the simple country people whom he met in the streets or country lanes. He loved to give them kindly salutations, adding at times some question as to the welfare of those whom he knew, and a bit of friendly help to those in need. His

---

* " I sent some two hundred and more specimens of fish to the U. S. in 1836, to be put in the Museum of the Smithsonian Institute, and heard nothing of them until James Dana wrote me a score of years later that Agassiz was making good use of them; Agassiz himself told me in 1860 that they had been of essential service to him in some of his examinations."
—Letter to W. F. Williams.

name and those of his children became in time well known to these poor peasants, and to this day its fragrance lingers in their comfortless homes."

TO ROBERT S. WILLIAMS.

PEKING, Oct. 25, 1867.—Your letter came to hand just after our return from a jaunt to Kalgan and the Mongolian plateau, where we went after finishing our usual summer sojourn at the hills. We were gone twenty-five days, and saw many new places and sights, among which the Mongols in their felt tents, with flocks and ponies and dogs about them, were not less quaint than singular. The journey to Kalgan took five days, and was performed in mule litters—a sort of palanquin hung between two mules, and large enough to contain two persons, their bedding, dishes, conveniences, etc., without difficulty. When once you are mounted and off it does not give you much chance to get out again and walk, for the litter is four feet from the ground; but for ladies it is preferable to a cart. In some parts of the way the road lies through a gorge of the mountains, where a creek (or a torrent, according to the weather and season) flows aside of the road between high cliffs or copses, with farm houses and patches of millet, sorghum, or wheat to alternate and vary the series of natural pictures. The principal pass* of this kind takes one up a thousand feet to the first stage of the table-land, and is crossed by a spur of the Great Wall, which runs up the steep ascent and over the highest ridges, where one wonders what enemy except a flock of goats or monkeys could be expected to approach. This part of the wall is only forty miles from Peking, and is often visited, but nature's picturesqueness here is as fully worth seeing as man's curious handiwork; beyond the pass the road is less romantic, but no road among hills can lack a certain charm after living in a flat like the Peking plain.

At Kalgan we found the two mission families, Mr. Gulick and Mr. M. Williams, comfortably settled in two dwellings,

* The Nankau Pass.

where we were most kindly entertained. Taking carts here for the ascent to the plateau we reached a little hamlet of inns and sheep-folds, some twenty miles distant, by nightfall. You may think twenty miles no long stretch for a day's ride, but we ascended in this time some 2,000 feet and more, and seldom could go faster than a walk. The contrast between the lowlands and uplands was very curious, for irrespective of the difference in height, the nature of the country was not less diverse. Below, the surface was hilly and mountainous, cast up to abrupt peaks and cut down to deep gulches—as rough a region as you can imagine, destitute generally of trees, but cultivated here and there in terraces built in a wonderful way along the slopes. Above us, over the ridge at the watershed, rose the prospect of a vast rolling plain, green with the close-cropped grass, but without a house or a field or a tree, and but here and there a tent with its straggling flocks of sheep and camels. The village we reached looked at a distance like a parcel of card houses set up on a huge stretch of baize, so dwarfed did it appear in the clear air in the midst of this vast expanse of green. From the edge of the ridge the prospect over the mountains behind and below with their naked sierras, suggested a tremendous deluge that had poured down the slope, washing the flesh all off the ribs of mother earth, while above us her decent sides remained covered and softly rounded. I can hardly bear to leave this magnificent view, its ruggedness only made human by rare patches of growing grain on the terraces, or more often the white spots of grazing sheep, but never a village to see amidst the congeries of rocks and ridges. Far in the smoky distance was the Great Wall, surmounting an impossible summit, but it was only a line, lost in nature's vaster markings and plains.

We remained two nights at the hamlet, not uncomfortably housed, visiting the Mongols in their felt tents, drinking quantities of fresh and boiled milk from various animals, and seeing how the better sort of them lived. They make a tent of eighteen feet diameter and a dozen feet high—a more comfortable abode than you would suppose, and on a cheerful day it seemed pleasant; but I think in rain, snow, and cold the tent must be a dreary place. No high attainments in civilization could be made while people preferred these to houses—even if Abraham and Isaac did live in them.

In a letter to Professor Dana, he adds to a brief account of this trip:

"We visited a chief or beg's establishment, and saw princesses and dames in their best condition. They looked for all the world like North American Indian squaws; but I wish I could describe their head-dress, so covered with coral, turquoise, rubies, and other stones, that in order to keep in place the two tresses which fell in platted ropes on either side, they fastened the structure to the ear-lobes by a back-stay. This arrangement kept the tresses from falling forward when the wearer stooped; it also placed the face in a frame of parti-colored gauds that drew off the gaze from the round and dumpy sleepy-looking face within. These people are in the same state, I suppose, as when Herodotus described them, and will remain so until some self-sacrificing missionary goes to live with them."

Soon after his return from this little trip Mr. Williams was called upon by the resignation of Mr. Burlingame to take charge of the affairs of the Legation for the sixth time, while his former chief accepted the leading place in the first mission from China to all the treaty powers, since known under his name. The appointment of such a mission, and still more his selection as its head, was as much a surprise to Mr. Burlingame as to other foreigners, and appears to have first suggested itself to the Chinese goverment when the American Minister announced his retirement. A step made so suddenly as this in the direction of claiming her share of friendly recognition at foreign courts, by a country that had been content for centuries to sit apart enveloped in ignorance and pride, was of course hailed abroad with rhetorical flourishes, the echo of which has endured to this day. The scope and idea of the embassy was at that time undoubtedly exaggerated; what was designed in the minds of a few enlightened officials as a precursor of a future diplomatic service was heralded alike by ignorant and interested foreigners as an immediate advance to the methods and ideals of Western civilization. In the selection of Mr. Burlingame for the initiation of their experiment the Chinese displayed an astuteness which has more than once characterized their perception. "The envoy, Anson Burlingame," runs the Emperor's rescript, communicated by Prince Kung to Mr. Williams, "manages affairs in a friendly and peaceful manner, and is fully acquainted with the general relations between this and other countries; let him, therefore, now be sent to all the treaty powers as high minister." It was a recognition in the author and defender of the "coöperative policy" of a sincere friend, in whose perfect honesty they could rely, while profiting by his tact and eloquence as their representative. It was a selection by means of which the Chinese testified to the great ascendancy he had gained in their councils and conferred upon the United States perhaps the greatest compliment ever paid by one great nation to another.

Mr. James G. Blaine sums up the man and his peculiar position in words of more than passing interest: "As an example of the influence of a single man attained over an alien race, whose civilization is widely different, whose religious belief is totally opposite, whose language he could not read nor write nor speak, Mr. Burlingame's career in China will always be regarded as an extraordinary event, not to be accounted for except by conceding to him a peculiar power of influencing those with whom he came in contact; a power growing out of a mysterious gift, partly intellectual, partly spiritual, largely physical; a power whose laws are unknown, whose origin cannot be traced, and whose limits cannot be assigned; a power which, for the want of a more comprehensive and significant term recurring to our postulate, we designate as magnetism."

CHAPTER XI.

TO MRS. H. C. WOOD, UTICA.

SAN SHAN NGAN, *i. e.*, Tremont Temple,
a Buddhist Monastery, fourteen miles
from Peking, June 29, 1868,

Where I have taken it in hand to reply to your heartsome letter, dear cousin, and tell you how it has refreshed me to get such. Your epistle is indeed written upon very thin paper, too attenuated for easy reading, but the sentiments supported the tissue and brought it out here safely. You wrote on a cold, blowy, snowy (March 4) winter's day; I answer on a genial, breezy summer afternoon, sitting in the guest-room of an ancient pagan fane, and looking out over the vast expanse of this plain, whose limits, like the sea's, are bounded only by the horizon. In its midst rise the walls and towers of the city, with its dagobas and palace roofs peeping from the elms and locusts and presenting a gay relief to the monotony of fields and groves in the wide expanse between us. In Peking we are situated just on the edge of the plateau of central Asia, and these hills where my old temple lies are part of the buttress which upholds the great table-land that stretches westward and rises at last into the Himalaya and Bayankara. All down their slopes they are scarred and gullied with torrent tracks, but are bare of trees and mostly even of grass; so for lack of a screen of foliage to prevent the rains from at once evaporating, the heat parches their weather-worn sides, and this very parching in its turn prevents the vegetation from growing, and perpetual barrenness results from violating the natural laws of fertility. If you good people in the United States don't reflect in time, your hill-sides will become as denuded as these are, and the conditions of the soil will alter; you can see in this region all the steps which have resulted from stripping the mountains of their forests.

You wonder if I *feel* that I am fifty-six years old, and understand my position, as the politicians say; really, I fancy that I don't yet feel as I supposed folks at this stage must in other bodies than mine. I am as well able to study and write as ever, and can walk and ride and even climb pretty well yet. Altogether I hope to be spared to do a little more and live to see my Chinese dictionary through the press. I find that the one which was issued twelve years ago has helped many to learn this language, and by this time copies of it have got to be scarce and in great demand. The job of making another is a long one, to be sure, but the end seems worthy of even a long job, and I've come now to within some 1,200 characters of the end, and in case I should be taken off the work can be finished by some one else. Just now I'm hindered by building a house in town; and when you learn that this means that I must give directions as to the size of every door, show how to put in the bolts, make the workmen lay their walls straight, direct them how to mix the mortar, regulate the nailing of the floors, point out the mode of fixing a door-latch, supply every size of screw and nail, change all the bad glass and coping stones, and so on, and so on, you may conclude with me that at the moment dictionaries cannot prosper rapidly.

Mr. Burlingame's departure has made a great vacancy in our small circle (for his family formed an important part of this community), besides throwing some extra work on me. I hope that his mission to the Treaty Powers will be of service to this people and its government, who have paid so much for their first lesson in diplomacy. His place is not an easy one to fill, and how our new Minister will supply it will test his qualifications more severely than writing articles for *Harper's Monthly*. Dr. and Mrs. Martin, of the Presbyterian Mission, have also recently left for the United States, with their two boys; thus our friends about us change, and at present only three or four foreigners are living in Peking who came here before I did. It has been, on the whole, a pleasant life, more so I am sure than those of the merchants whom I have known, —less care, less uncertainty, less luxury, less temptation, less to get between the soul and heaven, less, perhaps, to regret afterwards. There are no more trials in common life here than with you, and according as one takes these so is their effect. It is not so much the hard work as the misdirected effort which occasions loss in mission work; dearly earned experience is well enough for the missionary—for he can't learn otherwise,—but it is bad for the cause by reason of its waste and delay. As an instance, we once had in Canton a most pious Carolinian who was so eager to diffuse the truth that he composed and published a small tract which he actually could not read himself; imagine the kind of benefit it did! But God perhaps employs these inadequate and imperfect means that we may see it to be His work throughout.

The millennium will come in good time, but ever since I re-read in Jerusalem Christ's declaration that that city must be trodden down till the times of the Gentiles are fulfilled, I gave over the hope of seeing it and am content to work for it. The Gospel must first be preached to all nations, as I told Walter King once in 1847,—preached intelligently and clearly that the race for whom Christ died may know why he died, and this work has not yet been done. It is going on, however, and Corea is now the only land where it cannot be freely preached. In 1833 I found two missionaries in Canton, Morrison and Bridgman, and with them was one convert—the result of twenty-odd years' of labor among the Cantonese; the other day a Scotchman from Amoy told me of thirteen hundred (Protestant) converts in that city, and Amoy is but one of many stations in China. So as I look backward I am refreshed for looking forward, and the more willing to bide God's time in this undertaking which seems immense only to our little selves.

During the early months of this year (1868) Mr. Williams carried to completion his plan of building a legation by erecting a Secretary's house upon premises immediately adjoining the Minister's residence and within the same enclosure.

"I am again in the dust and discomfort of house-building, and even the former experience of it in 1866 does not appear to have accustomed me to the trials of patience and difficulties of explanation, in a language not very familiar, which are required in managing the workmen. They are so disposed to slight their work and scrimp the pattern when one is not looking, that I must perforce spend time over them which I had rather use in some other way. My dictionary lags at such periods, and now by Mr. Burlingame's departure I am left with the usual allowance of double work and care,—to which you may add that the children have no other schoolmasters than their parents,—so I have a daily exercise of all the virtues."

TO R. S. WILLIAMS.

TREMONT TEMPLE, August 24, 1868.

The pleasure you derived from talking with Mr. Burlingame has been reflected to us, and we have been particularly glad that you were able to see him so long. I suspect that he and his associates will be hauled and pulled till they are quite tired out. Mr. Burlingame is one of those men who have great kindness of heart, and this *bonhomie* brings him into favor with most who have personal acquaintance with him. He is the best man the Chinese could have found in Peking for the mission to foreign countries, and if any one could give the leading men of those countries a favorable view of this empire, he is likely to do so. But while from a distance China possesses much to interest those of other countries, they soon find upon examination that she is really a pagan, half-civilized land, and infinite allowance must be made for what we could never approve. She is trying to understand what are her rights among mankind, and to advance in the maintenance of those rights, as well also as to grant to others the privilege she is bound to accord. But the lesson is hard, the road to political wisdom long, the obstacles numerous, and she finds, like the slaves down South, that she comes in for one kind of treatment as an equal and for quite another as an inferior. It is the advance of missions and their attendant instruction that assures us most clearly of her real advance in whatever shall fit her for her high station.

Whether or no I should have taken the post of Minister to China or from China is a question I am never likely to be called upon to answer practically, and its hypothetical answer comes to nothing. I desire chiefly to do daily the things I am called on to attend to, and let the others wait till they come up. Just now I should like to see my way clear to issue a new edition of the "Middle Kingdom," but it is not so easy, and perchance may never be. My dictionary must be attended to first, as I have an idea it will be most useful. As for the "Middle Kingdom," it hardly sells fast enough to pay many people for keeping it on hand, and the sale of a book is something of a test of its fitness.

Mr. Burlingame's successor, J. Ross Browne, remained in China less than a year, and by July, 1869, the post was again vacant. On the subject of his appointment to the position of United States Minister, which was at this time much urged by friends at home and in China, Mr. Williams writes to Mr. Nye, in Canton:

PEKING, March 12, 1869.—I hardly know whether you would have found many to accord with you if your recommendation to W. H. Seward had succeeded, for I cannot think that the most of our countrymen desire a man who has been so long in this country to be their representative. While I most fully appreciate your friendship in making this effort, it is not probable that there will be any change in the policy of the government at Washington, which has only these foreign appointments for its partisans. If Mr. Jencke's bill ever passes, even in a modified form, there may be less of this miscellaneous distribution of places to people who have no special claim for filling them. What is most wanted in China is consuls who can read and speak Chinese, for the detail of work in its most important points comes to them. We have not a single consul (except the one in Tientsin) who can speak an idiomatic sentence in Chinese, and our government has no idea of educating any, or of paying aught for bringing forward students of the language. I suspect I have as much opportunity for doing both China and United States good service in my present position as if I were Minister, but perhaps the total of that service is much less than I suppose. I myself think that the work on my dictionary may be more enduring than that found in the State Department since 1855 ; but here too others can judge much better than I. One thing is certain, that the elevation, instruction, reformation, and strengthening of this empire, and fitting its people for the duties and privileges of a civilized nation, is a greater work than any one can understand until he tries it. Happy is he whom God employs to promote it.

Mrs. Throop Martin, in a note written the preceding year, affords in this connection an interesting side view of one of the hidden springs in American diplomacy:

"Mr. Seward, when we dined with him one day last summer [1868], expressed himself very warmly in Dr. Williams' behalf, and said that the reason he had not received the appointment of Minister was because he was '*altogether too good a man, too highly endowed*, and in all respects too unexceptionable to receive the appointment.' A pressure was made on the President on Mr. Burlingame's resignation, which Mr. Seward could not control. The Secretary seemed much chagrined by his disappointment."

TO R. S. WILLIAMS.

TREMONT TEMPLE, Aug. 2, 1869.—Your letter found us all in good health, as has indeed been almost always the case, and enjoying the summer at our usual retreat from home. I am again in charge of the Legation by the sudden departure of Mr. Browne—who, I suppose, left Yokohama yesterday with his large family, after a twelvemonth's experience of a Minister's life and labors. He would not remain to see his successor, any more than his predecessors, none of whom have been willing to turn over their work properly, throwing it, instead, into my hands and starting off. If you have any influence whatever, exert it in behalf of Mr. Jencke's plan of a civil service to save our country from the ruin now apparently threatening its integrity. It is an object worthy of every good man's energy to see that the unseemly scramble for office, which paralyzes all the energies of those who occupy one, should be in some measure stopped or abated. The clamor of newspapers would be less if there was any kind of examination into the fitness of candidates for a post so important as some which are given away to the first applicant. Few Americans in China can feel much interest in their consular authorities, for they never remain long enough to become much acquainted with them, nor they with their duties. . . .

I place the compliment of J. Watson Williams in his historical lecture about the Academy in Utica—placing me with Dana, Dwight, and Horatio Seymour—as the highest one I ever had, for I cannot say that I regard my LL.D. from Union as so very high. Yet what is it that makes men honorable but the carrying out the answer to the first question in the Catechism?

We are soon to go down to Shanghai, from whence Sarah and the children proceed to Canton, and so on through Europe homeward by January next, while I return here to manage the Legation and work at my dictionary. . . .

SHANGHAI, Oct. 21st.—We have all come down here, and I am made glad by your letters which I found upon arrival. I go back to Peking in a fortnight, the others leaving me here. We may not see each other soon again, but that is all in God's hands. We do the best we can under the circumstances.

TO G. TALBOT OLYPHANT, ESQ.

SHANGHAI, November 6, 1869.

MY DEAR MR. OLYPHANT.—It is now six years since last I was here, and there has been a great increase in the size and change in the looks of the settlement in that time. It is doubtless destined to be a very large emporium in the coming centuries, and to exert a vast influence on both sides of the Pacific upon the populations ere long to line their shores. The

Chinese are showing that they are fully able and inclined to keep their own trade in their own hands, and its gradual enlargement will depend upon their wants and industry—unless the deleterious effects of opium upon both neutralize all progress.

I am not very bright just now, owing to the departure of wife and bairns, with whom I shall probably never have much more regular life such as we have had. Justice to the latter demanded that mother should go with them and see after their education and growth in goodness and manners, leaving me here to work on in my post. I had planned to spend the coming year here in the publication of my Chinese Dictionary, but the sudden departure of J. Ross Browne has thrown the charge of the Legation upon me for the eighth time since I received it from Wm. Marcy fourteen years ago; so I'm compelled to return and look after things in Peking, and do what I can single-handed. I am left quite alone, and cannot even get a copyist, unless I ask some of the missionaries to do a few sheets for me amid their higher duties. However, as my day is, so, I hope, strength will be, but after thirty-six years' residence in China I must begin to look down hill in respect to vigor and perseverance

He accepted thus, for the second time in his life, the hard necessity of sending away his family, after an inward struggle, the severity of which no one who observed the composure of his parting could have measured or even guessed. How keenly he felt the separation from his wife and the two remaining children is indicated by nothing more clearly than by the tone which this and other letters show:

TO R. S. WILLIAMS.

PEKING, Dec. 22, 1869.—I am getting on in my rather empty house, where I find that there is more to do than the day serves to finish. Dr. Martin furnishes much pleasant talk to pass away the hours at eventime, and we have events enough to furnish topics, though there are neither evening papers, railroads, telegraphs, elections, riots, shipwrecks, anniversary meetings, woman's rights conventions, or stock-brokers to engage our attention and make us civilized. I spend most of my day in the office across the yard, where I have a snug place with a look-out to see whoever comes into the compound. I need not go out from Sunday to Sunday, unless I like, but I could not get along that way, so I take walks or rides. My two horses and all the house servants cost me much more than food and clothes together, which is the case nearly all over Asia. But being a high mandarin, I am, of course, required by propriety to have a retinue, and so whenever I go to ride my one groom follows on another horse, to hold mine when I get off, take in my card, hold the stirrup when I mount, and such like antics, which would, I guess, have somewhat surprised my dear mother if she had known I was ever coming to such an end.

TO THE SAME.

Feb. 24, 1870.—As you speak of a complimentary notice of me in the New York *World* (wretched paper), I will cap the quotation by referring you to a different one in a Shanghai news-sheet, complaining that I am so old, so fogy, so much of a twaddler, that Uncle Sam should make me a bishop—fancy Uncle Sam's *making a bishop!*—and thus put me on the shelf out of the way, as I am neither handsome nor profitable where I am. On the whole, for piquancy and interest, I like the Shanghai squib the best—better than the medal, indeed, which I don't deserve.*

* By means of his good offices with the officials, Mr. Williams had assisted the envoy from Sweden in negotiating a treaty with China during the previous year. He was rather surprised by the receipt of a gold medal with the following:

"STOCKHOLM, MINISTÈRE DES AFFAIRES
"ETRANGÈRES, le 3 Janvier, 1870.

"MONSIEUR :—S. M. le Roi, mon Auguste Soverain, désirant vous donner une marque de sa bienveillance vient de vous conférer une médaille à Son effigie portant l'inscription : ' *Litteris et Artibus.*'
"En vous transmettant ci-près cette médaille, je profite de l'occasion pour vous offrir, Monsieur, les assurances de ma considération très distinguée.
"Le Ministre d'Etat et des Affaires Etrangères,
"LE CTE. WACHTMEISTER."

His acknowledgment frankly expresses his surprise : "This unexpected mark of his regard is received by me with many thanks, though I hardly know what I have done to deserve it."

March 24th.—The sad and terrible news of Mr. Burlingame's sudden death in Russia, which has just reached us, turns my thoughts first of all to his bereaved widow, one of the dearest of our friends, and her children, and adds another instance of hopes extinguished in the midst of life while its great work was hardly begun.

If his hopes for the welfare of China, which had now become for him a second country, were dashed by the disaster at Taku, the disappointment of his higher expectations for the great end of her advancement, which this sudden death involved, was simply overwhelming. To him, whose sorrow went forth first to the mourning family, it was more than a personal loss, it was the deprivation of China's great friend, the interests of whose newly awakened empire he represented with abounding enthusiasm and ability.

TO MRS. ANSON BURLINGAME.

PEKING, May 26, 1870.

MY DEAR MRS. BURLINGAME :—How sad I 've been since hearing of the great loss you have so suddenly been called to mourn. We got the news here about twenty-five days after your day of anguish and desolation, and a few days later it was announced to us officially. The event has been talked about a good deal among the Chinese, but the utter unexpectedness of this end of the services of Mr. Burlingame to all those who had known or commissioned him seems to be the uppermost feeling. They regret his loss as weakening, if not neutralizing, the leading position of the Mission in the eyes of the nations to whom it is sent, and they feel that the others cannot take his place, or receive the confidence he had from them.

I have thought of the death of your husband in many points of view : his position in the Chinese service as the representative of this pagan government before Christendom, his fitness for urging their claims to kind treatment, the loss they have sustained, the long intercourse we have had during our residence here, and our accord on every important point,—these have all brought their reminiscences to increase the sadness on hearing of his departure never to return. But your own bereavement has been the leading idea, and I pray that you may have been sustained during those hours when the world and the things of life could give you no support. I remember your tender sympathy when my dear girl Kitty died, and the wish, the strongest wish is now that you may feel, truly and lovingly, that God has done it, and His way is the best, the tenderest, the kindest that can be. The little time we have to spend here is so full of duties and work, and yet how vast their results to each of us! I have perhaps thought of them more since I have been alone, but they are constantly present to my mind, and, I have no doubt, to yours also.

TO R. S. WILLIAMS.

PEKING, May 26, 1870.

I have not complete copies of *all* the books which I have published, nor indeed of all which I have written. The "English-Chinese Vocabulary" and "Easy Lessons" have both been long out of print, the few remaining unsold in 1856 having gone with the Factories, and the "Tonic Dictionary" will bring fifteen dollars any day in China; I fear there is not much chance for you to complete your shelf of books of and by the Williams' family. I have no great conceit of my mental children, I can tell you—which is the reason perhaps why they did n't grow very large, for if I had thought more of them I might have taken more pains with them. If all that I have ever written and printed were brought together into one room, I should no doubt gaze and gasp in wonder at the pile, but I think I should not re-read it. . . .

The Chinese government has given $14,000 to Mr. Burlingame's family, besides spending nearly $10,000 for his obsequies; and have issued an imperial proclamation praising him highly. I think they have done handsomely enough to satisfy reasonable men. He deserves well of them, for the whole world might have been searched in vain to find another man who combined just those qualities which fitted Anson Burlingame for his peculiar mission to introduce China into the family of nations. His death deprives the officers here of the benefits of his experience and earnest urging to go on in the way of improvement in such a manner as not to upset old institutions until the new ones can take their places. I think they were looking forward to his return to get an idea of their position in the family of nations, and would have listened to his suggestions with respect. The Chinese government is so poor that it cannot do much yet in the direction of improvement, even if it had the desire; and its officers are so dishonest that money is wasted and work is slighted far worse than it is with us. From all accounts, however, we seem to be rapidly getting down to the level of the Chinese in the abuse of public money.

Before the date of this letter Governor Low of California had come to Peking as United States Minister, and the prospect for printing the dictionary at Shanghai became again an encouraging one, again to be vexatiously delayed. The sudden outbreak of a mob at Tientsin against the Roman Catholic missionaries there, and the massacre of some twenty foreigners (June 21, 1870), spread consternation among the foreign residents in all China and demanded the prompt and vigorous action of their representatives in Peking. Fortunately the riot proved to be a mere local uprising brought about by exaggerated rumors concerning the French Sisters of Charity. Europeans and Americans elsewhere were undisturbed, though possessed for many months by distorted apprehensions of a Chinese Indian mutiny, when the unknown element of Chinese malignity should rush forth and sweep them all from the land. The diplomatic corps at Peking immediately united in demanding reparation and assurances of safety from the government, the French Minister, M. Rochechouart, being naturally chiefly concerned and most importunate. The timely outbreak of the Franco-German war by its abasement of France contributed to a peaceful settlement of the question, if it was not indeed the sole preventing cause of a war with China.

TO R. S. WILLIAMS.

PEKING, October 26, 1870.

The Chinese government is sending an envoy to Paris to try and explain and apologize for the riot and massacre at Tientsin, and I hope he will succeed. A war between China and France would be no honor to the latter, and do much damage to China at present, for it would exasperate the people at large against the introduction of all foreign knowledge and teaching. At Tientsin twenty men have been executed and twenty-six banished, besides the two chief officials, but the people of that town are malignant, and the twenty men are regarded rather as martyrs than as criminals. The best part of the community really believe that the stories about plucking out children's eyes, etc., are entirely true, and you can easily imagine the deeds and feelings likely to arise amongst a population with such ideas. Moreover, behind and more powerful than these are the literati who are just as inimical to us as the Scribes and Pharisees were against new truths brought in to supplant what their position depended on. The struggle is likely to test the utmost strength of the government, which may yet succumb amid the unequal strife. In consequence of this Tientsin trouble the chances are that I must defer my dictionary a little longer, but it is receiving additions.

TO THE SAME.

PEKING, Nov. 24, 1870.—Wm. H. Seward has paid us a long visit together with a large party, including Admiral Rodgers and officers, musicians and marines, in all fifty-six people. We managed to house them, for I had an empty house where the musicians and marines could be huddled together and take care of themselves. The marines, twenty-one in all, were soon sent back to the ship, much to the relief of every one, for it would have raised the city to have marched this guard and band through the streets—where processions are never allowed, —even if the cortège could have made way through the curious crowd. The party thus agreeably diminished remained here nearly three weeks, visited the Great Wall and other points of interest, saw Prince Kung and the high officials, and were, on the whole, gratified with their excursion. The music, which we heard twice a day, was a rare and wonderful treat to us poor folk here, where a band has never been since the capture. The Secretary is bodily almost a wreck, for the paralysis of both arms renders him helpless, but his mind is clear, memory good, and physical exercise does not tire him easily, for he walked more than five miles with me one afternoon. His adopted daughter, Miss Olive Risley, who waits on him as amanuensis, is kept pen in hand most of the time, and is fully equal in alertness and intelligence to her exacting position. I had many conversations with him, some of them most interesting to me, about former politicians, Clay, Stanton, Lincoln, and others, but his own importance continually eclipsed theirs, and diminished somewhat my enjoyment. I have much respect for what he did at his post during the Rebellion, but I am sorry to find how low his mark is in regard to society and the progress of truth and purity in the world. He is more of a politician and less of a statesman than I had supposed, takes extremely prejudiced views of religious enterprises (of which, indeed, he cannot properly judge, because he cannot sympathize with their motives), and is dogmatic to excess. I have not much more criticism to make on him, except that he is not adding to his fame by this journey. Mr. Low thinks that he is rather failing in all his powers.

The Tientsin affair has been settled, the Chinese think; the French Chargé has received 460,000 Tls. ($657,000), of which 250,000 Tls. are for the families of the victims and the rest for the buildings destroyed. The acceptance of this sum seems to me to close all warlike action on the part of France, but I hear that Rochechouart says that he has left his country free either to fight or make up. The American mission chapels are paid for—4,500 taels,—and the English soon will be. . . . What a pest France is in this world! She never learns to treat others justly, nor is she content to mind her own affairs, while the mass of people are almost as ignorant as heathen, and quite as superstitious. She has made more wars, more trouble, more tyranny, more persecution, than any other Christian (so-called) nation. They are a strange mixture; I'm glad I was n't born one—or a Chinaman either.

TO THE SAME.

PEKING, May 25, 1871.—Another dear one has gone before us, and brother Fred will send us no more of his loving letters, no more of those hearty thin sheets, worth more than their weight in gold, or their cost in postage—which is saying much from this corner of the earth. Dr. Raynolds wrote me from Mardin the day after the funeral about his last illness and peaceful end. We could not have hoped for better care than he had at the last, and God supported his heart, as flesh and blood failed, till he was over the river and out of our sight. Dear Fred! How thankful should we be for his example, his work, his end; it is a precious legacy to all, especially to the Syrian Church, where his works and influence will long endure. I prefer to remember him as buried amongst his chosen people, a testimony of his labors to the end.

In the death of this brother Mr. Williams sustained a loss more grievous in its way than any he had ever known. It was the sudden removal of an influence which inspired him to nobler efforts, as well as of a favorite brother whose heart had been joined to his own by a bond of peculiar sympathy since the day when a devoted mother had given them both to God. Rev. Frederic Williams succumbed to the exhausting climate of Mesopotamia after a service of twenty-two years among its cities, during which time he had founded churches and trained many converted natives to become teachers of their people with rare and gratifying success. Withal, as to his own ability, he was modest and distrustful in the extreme. No better instance of that quality of demure yet decided sense of duty which was common to both the brothers can be found than his characteristic letter proposing himself as a missionary to the American Board: "I am induced to offer myself [he says] simply because, as there is a great call for men and those qualified do not go, others must, or the fields must remain uncultivated. . . . I judge it to be my duty to offer myself. As for that enthusiastic ardor for the work of which many speak, I have not one bit of it."

TO GEO. TALBOT OLYPHANT, ESQ., NEW YORK.

PEKING, April 27, 1871.

The Coreans form now the last secluded nationality of importance in the world which shuts out its fellow-men, and I have some expectation that the present effort of our Minister, Mr. Low, will result in the beginning of intercourse with these people. But what a contemptible figure our own nation cuts in carrying out treaties after they are signed—making no provision for consular officers, buildings, or interpreters for the government which it attempts to set up in an Eastern country. No United States consul in China, unless he has been a missionary, knows or expects to learn a word of the language, caring only to keep and work his post for a little while, on the average perhaps less than five and twenty months. Sometimes Englishmen are our consuls, sometimes Dutchmen, and these often are preferable to the ignorant Americans who would disgrace the posts if they had them. I do not, however, see the smallest prospect of an improvement until the consular system is made an organized service, at least in these Asiatic lands where we are under our own laws.

The reference to Corea may be explained by the departure of Mr. Low in a war vessel to that country upon an errand somewhat similar to that made by Commodore Perry's to Japan in 1853, hoping by a show of force and exercise of persuasion to secure protection to Americans wrecked upon those shores. The expedition, was a failure so far as this result was concerned, and the Minister's absence kept Mr. Williams another summer in Peking, again delaying his departure to Shanghai.

TO R. S. WILLIAMS.

PEKING, Oct. 26, 1871.—I expect to go to Shanghai next month to begin the printing of my dictionary, long deferred, and if it is done so that I can get back here next winter it will be all I can desire and perhaps more than I can accomplish. . . . It sometimes seems rather pleasant to look forward to having an easy time of it, visiting or sitting at leisure at home, but when I begin to dissect such a life I shrink from the vacuity and objectless condition of mind it would beget. So, as long as I can, I prefer working on here where things seem natural to me and the cause is one of the very best. This job of printing will, however, leave me little else to think of for many months to come ; meantime I leave my official work here to two men, at the cost of half my salary. Mr. Low will therefore be well enough supplied with aids for his writing, translating, and copying.

"This dictionary," he writes to another at this time, "is a tedious work, without any refreshing passages—mere waste and barrenness, as if you were forced to read through a directory, with a photograph of every individual in the list, and knew none of them. There will be adequate returns, no doubt, if the job is well done, but the future rewards and usufruct do not exhilarate the one who collects the significations. However, it seemed to me to be a work that I could do, and which was needed; if God bless the design, the labor, and the accomplishment, I sha'n't need to look higher than His approving blessing."

TO HIS WIFE.

PEKING, Nov. 8, 1871.—I am not going to tell all my struggles and sinking of heart at leaving the dear home, for you 've been through it all and know what it is to me. . . .

SHANGHAI, Nov. 26th.—I have been here five days and have already begun my printing; the first page was proven yesterday. I left Peking on the 9th, a beautiful and mild morning, but one in which I hardly knew what to do first, so much disturbed was I at the near prospect of leaving the home where you had warmed the look of each room, and where your and the children's faces cheered each corner. I am not much given to tell my feelings—and perhaps some of my friends think that there are not many to tell about—but 't was a wrench to the heart to leave the old house which I may perhaps never see again. Mr. and Mrs. Wade, Dr. Martin, Holcombe, and others rode with me out of the city gate, and more came to the house to bid me good-bye. Blodget rode down to Tungchau, and we had long converse during the pleasant ride; it is a blessing to have such a friend as he is. I slept at Tungchau, for the baggage was delayed till morning, and started from the same river bank where I first landed in July, 1859, amid a crowd like an ant-hill for multitude. . . .

I am settled at the Mission Printing House, where I have a tolerably good room, and for company Wherry, J. Mateer, and Gordon, the head-printer, Dr. Hepburn taking dinner with us every day; so I 'm started at last on my big job, hoping that God will grant health and mind to finish it. My eyes are reasonably good and serviceable.

TO THE SAME.

YOKOHAMA, August 2, 1872.

The heat had become so oppressive in Shanghai that many of the printers fell sick, and Mateer was induced to give them a vacation; so I have been persuaded to run over here and see how Japan looks after eighteen years. I reached this place last Saturday, and am staying with Dr. Syle. I had Yung Wing for a companion from Shanghai, and with him plenty of pleasant intercourse. He goes directly to New Haven to confer with his friends there respecting the disposition of the Chinese students whom he is taking to America for study, thirty of whom Laisun conducts to San Francisco next steamer.

I have hardly time to tell you what a curious operation of memory it has been to recall the former and present look of this country, and try to record the impressions then left. Digging and building have completely altered the natural landmarks, and only the bluffs and hills behind the town remain the same. But however much the physical aspect has changed, its mental and moral condition has modified a thousand times more, the fermentation and new growth attracting every part of this and other lands to watch its development. I attended a service in Japanese, and partook of the communion with the young church to which Dr. S. R. Brown introduced his teacher to baptism; about twenty members were present, two of whom were women, and one of the audience was a Buddhist priest who came to see the mode of worship and hear what doctrines were taught. I told the assembly about my previous visits to the Bay of Yedo and of their countrymen who prayed in my house many years ago for the conversion of their friends at home whom they never again expected to see. It was translated by Mr. Thomson, for I should make poor work now with a speech in Japanese in my rusty old age. It is not often that one can visit the same place thrice in a lifetime under such remarkable differences of reception.

SHANGHAI, Aug. 24th.—I passed a third of my three weeks in Japan at Yedo, in a kind of dreamland existence—past, present, and future all mingled together in a way very difficult to explain, but highly enjoyable. I visited the tombs of the Siogouns, but they are trifling and poor compared with the Ming Mausolea, near Peking, yet hardly less worth seeing in their way. The carving and cleanliness please one extremely. With one of the teachers in the college, I rode to a hill-top, whence we had a wide view of all the plain about the capital, teeming with its parks and fields and villages, a pretty sight. After all that I had heard about the city, and the tantalizing glimpse I had of its trees in 1854, it was a gratification to roam through it in this joyful summer weather, while the queer feeling of being dragged through its streets by two strong fellows at a gait of five miles an hour did not at all lessen the novelty. But to me the most interesting sight of the visit was the baptism of an educated scholar who had accepted Christianity and all of its responsibilities, and joined the Church of Christ. As I joined in their services I thought of the prayers of those countrymen of his in my house in Macao, and what God hath wrought in these five-and-thirty years. Hepburn told me that I was well known in Yokohama by the nickname of Mr. Tadoshi, or "Mr. But," because I often used that particle in talking, which, being an unusual word, attracted their notice.

TO PROFESSOR J. D. DANA.

SHANGHAI, September 21, 1872.

DEAR JAMES :—I cannot deny myself the pleasure of letting you know how glad I am to hear that you have been honored by receiving the Wollaston Medal, and I am pretty sure that the notice is likely to be true. To say that you have well earned it is from me quite needless, and though others will be ready to congratulate you, who can better appreciate your position in the scientific world; yet none, I am sure, can do so more cordially than the one who tramped around Utica with you after Trilliums and Cypripedieæ forty years ago. I rejoice at all your fame and influence, and hope you will become the Nestor of your college.

I am plodding on in a different line, one not so interesting or instructive as yours, perhaps; but as you are rather megasthenic, so I am content to be microsthenic (to use your own terms), and help my brethren acquire this language, to the end of their speedier ability to speak their message to the heathen.

I am almost half through the body of the work on my dictionary—say over five hundred quarto pages. I think you've seen a page, which is about as interesting as the celebrated brick the scholastics took around as a specimen of the house he had for sale. But of course I take great interest in getting my bricks out as fast as possible, and without flaws in them.

I can hardly realize that I am now sixty years old, and that you will be in February next, D. V., but I don't know what state of mind I must get into to realize this condition of things, and when I am sixty myriads of years old, I suppose it will be no easier to do so. I do know, however, that we have both of us very much to be devoutly thankful to God for, and the feeling of His loving-kindness and presence grows on me every day.

TO HIS WIFE.

SHANGHAI, Jan. 13, 1873.—You can see by the proof-sheet enclosed how the dictionary crawls on; it is not as thrilling as a page of Dickens' "Little Dorrit," and yet I think that you for one take as much interest in these sheets which I send you one after another. The labor and care do not at all diminish as it goes on, but I fear there will be many mistakes notwithstanding all my oversight and proof-reading, for I find that the printers sometimes show their spite against my repeated alterations by changing the types after I have dismissed the page as correct. I am sure that if I had only the ambition of doing this dictionary for literary fame, I should have long ago collapsed and given it up; but I see in every page the hope that it is likely to help in the good work of evangelizing China. I am troubled somewhat with giddiness, as if the brain was rather strained, but I have always had a weakness this way and never could do things which other boys did, owing to this symptom of vertigo; matters of this sort don't grow better as one grows older, but with care the organ will be able to do more work. Somehow I feel as though sixty were a turning-point in one's days, and the sense of having reached that age solemnizes me often and makes the end seem nearer.

But the few weeks which followed showed him that the strain of his unremitting work was more than he could bear. A brief flight to Ningpo for rest among its azalea-clad hills did not restore the tired brain. For the first time in his life he felt himself unequal to his daily task. In March he telegraphed for Mrs. Williams to join him, and she arrived in time to take him to Peking, just as the body of his dictionary was printed and before the fierce heat of summer commenced. His work had almost cost him his life.

TO H. DWIGHT WILLIAMS.

TREMONT TEMPLE, August 15, 1873.—Things are quiet enough here, and the people have not gone into fits because the Emperor saw some foreigners face to face and in an upright position the other day. Strange rumors, however, as to the effects upon the foreign ministers are about—that Wade died soon after; that Rehfues [the German Minister] was so badly scared as to run away; that Low left for parts unknown instantly; and Ferguson had likewise to decamp from fear, so that the Russian plenipotentiary is the only survivor. But these rumors soon give way to others, and the affair is forgotten as soon as discussed. The audience was nevertheless a great step ahead, and as the practice of receiving foreign ministers becomes more frequent, the Emperor will be allowed to take a greater share in treating with them, and become less of a puppet in the hands of his officials. The *vis inertiæ* of this fossilized body which rules China seems sometimes to me to be the only obstacle to the advance of this country towards a high condition of civilization.

Owing to Mr. Low's return to America soon after Mr. Williams reached Peking, the Secretary of Legation did not witness an audience at the palace until the arrival of the Minister's successor the following year. The interest and importance of the ceremony are discussed in a subsequent letter. A far more personal concern was attached to the concluding labors on his dictionary, the introduction and index to which occupied during the autumn and winter of this year every moment saved from official duties. His health had in some degree been restored by a return to the familiar temple among the hills; and in this restful spot, with the help of his daughter, who had come from America with her mother, he was able to compile the index to the 12,527 characters of his work. The apparent anomaly of an index at the end of a dictionary arises of course from the peculiar nature of the Chinese language, which renders it impossible to arrange its words both by sound and composition, as in alphabetical languages. Thus while the character belonging to any given sound can be found in this lexicon by turning to its alphabetical place (in its romanized form), the sound and meaning of a written word-character must be obtained by analyzing its construction, determining its radical or root, and searching for it in the index of the 214 radicals under its proper group; when found here the page number refers the student to its place in the body of the book. It would be difficult to make clear this *modus operandi* and the necessity for such a complex arrangement, without introducing here a treatise on the Chinese language; but a few words must suffice to point out some of the stumbling-blocks in the way of the Chinese lexicographer. Added to the inherent embarrassments attending any attempt to collocate a non-alphabetical language, come the further obstacles of the numerous dialects in China, in each of which the common symbol represents a totally different sound, not unfrequently with a different initial, to the despair of those in search for the meaning of a word; then the paucity of sounds (less than 550 in the court dialect,) which brings together a great number of words under each; then the strangeness of having a different modulation (*tone*) for every word, which, as the author says, is "as if one were made to talk up and down the gamut and apply *do, re, mi, fa, sol, la* to all his words"; then the aspirates, which again alter sounds nearly identical to the Western ear, *pa* and *p'a*, for example, representing wholly different things; then the varying forms often found for the same character; and again the apparently illogical diversity of significations belonging to the same word;— all these perplexities, and many more, attend the study of this monstrous tongue.

The technical features of the language are discussed in the introduction to his dictionary, a treatise of some seventy pages, which the author divides into eight sections on the Mandarin (or court) language, his system of orthography, the aspirates, the tones, the ancient and obsolete sounds, the dialects, the radicals, and the primitives. In the case of a language, the dictionary of which cannot be handled without considerable previous knowledge, the preliminary explanation of its constitution and the author's method of dealing with its peculiarities comprise an important part of the work; upon this Mr. Williams was employed during the whole of the following winter and spring in Peking. It was printed, and the entire work put through the press at Shanghai during the early summer.

TO R. S. WILLIAMS.

THE HILLS, August 1, 1874.

Nothing in the way of news, excepting one item of some interest to me—the arrival of the first copy of the dictionary, which completes the long-prolonged labor of eleven years. It makes a quarto volume of 1,356 pages, and is printed evenly and nicely. It will form a convenient help to those who try to get hold of this language, but as to its real worth I shall have to wait till the students have tried it and can tell me. By and by I shall send some copies to the United States, where, however, I expect little or no sale. Once I tried selling some of my own books in New York, and received in payment for all sales o. I was not encouraged to try again.

The appearance of the Syllabic Dictionary was regarded among foreign students of Chinese as one of the noteworthy events of the century. Its first copies were eagerly passed from hand to hand, and the leading features of its arrangement, mechanical finish, illustrative translations,—even its size, weight, and price,—were discussed by students of the language with an earnestness which indicated the high expectations and prepossessions of the whole body of those who were in any way brought into contact with Chinese literature. The fullest praise came from those best qualified by their scholarship to pass upon its merits, and though critics were by no means agreed on many controversial questions in the difficult and obscure points of Chinese philology, their verdict was abundantly in favor of the performance. The sentiment of many as voiced by one was to the effect that the real value of the dictionary lay in "that department of it, which far exceeds all the others in importance, the quality of its explanations and definitions; and here, we conceive, is the best test of the skill of a lexicographer to be found, *in giving the fullest meaning in the fewest words.* It is possible for almost any one, by means of a long paraphrase, to describe the import of a Chinese phrase; but an exact and full equivalent in English, comprised within the limits of a few words, is often not to be arrived at without patient and careful searching, and sometimes not even then. The *genius* of the two languages, the modes of thought and expression, are so diverse that in many instances it is almost impossible to convey the force of a brief Chinese phrase in a proportionately brief English sentence, and this difficulty is aggravated by the frequent use in Chinese of short proverbial expressions, involving an allusion to some historical event or popular legend, an exact translation of which into English would generally be unintelligible. As an instance of this use of proverbs, and at the same time to illustrate the appropriateness which characterizes the definitions of the new Dictionary, we select a single phrase, *ki hu chi shi,* the meaning of which will perhaps be best understood by applying it to the present position of the Japanese in their Formosan enterprise. The phrase is thus defined in Morrison's Dictionary: ' The state of a person who rides on a tiger, it is more dangerous to dismount than to remain on its back; to be so involved in a bad cause that retreat is certain ruin.' Dr. Williams' definition is in these words: '[in for it,] as when one rides a tiger; there 's no backing down.' Dr. Morrison uses thirty-five words, Dr. Williams thirteen. Every one must recognize the superior aptness, point, and brevity which mark the latter translation." *

* Mr. E. C. Taintor, Commissioner of Customs, in the *North China Herald.*

Nor was there a dissenting voice heard against the conclusion (by Dr. Blodget) that "this Dictionary, as a whole, is a treasury of knowledge in regard to China and Chinese affairs, a treasury accumulated by many years of study both of Protestant and Roman Catholic missionaries. Well may its author, now the oldest resident in China of those from Western nations, as he looks back upon his past course, and especially upon the eleven years of toil in the completion of this dictionary (in which even every Chinese character has been written by his own pen, although at the same time he was discharging the onerous duties of his official position, in which frequently the combined functions of Minister, Secretary, Interpreter, and general business agent have devolved upon himself alone), take a high degree of satisfaction in his completed work, and render humble thanks to the good Lord who has enabled him to bring it to a close. He now makes this new offering to promote every good interest of China in her intercourse with Western nations, and signifies his unabated love to the missionary work by placing the Dictionary within the reach of those engaged in it at but little more than one third of its original cost."
—*New York Observer*, November, 1874.

The allusion in the last sentence is explained in the following letter. Though published at his own expense, and sold at a figure slightly above the actual cost of printing, the work was to its author a thank-offering rather than a possible source of gain.

"The stimulus to past effort [runs the preface], and the hope that it would not be in vain, both sprang from the desire to aid the labors of those who are imparting truth in any branch to the sons of Han, especially those religious and scientific truths whose acquisition and practice can alone Christianize and elevate them. At the end of the forty years spent in this country in these pursuits, I humbly thank the good Lord for all the progress I have been permitted to see in this direction, and implore His blessing upon this effort to aid their greater extension."

TO R. S. WILLIAMS

PEKING, December 9, 1874.

DEAR BROTHER :—Your short letter containing the items of the dividend granted by the Pipe Co. was instructive in its way, and had a lesson to me which the managers of that company knew nothing of. When the dictionary was nearing the day of its publication I began to think how I could in some way help the mission work for which I had made it. The missionaries would not have been willing to receive copies free, as they could afford to buy it, but many of them are poor, and I think none of them could look to their societies in such a matter. Counting only the Protestant missionaries actually in China, including unmarried ladies, I ascertained that about 120 persons would be entitled to receive the book, and to these I offered it for $9 a copy, which was a donation on my part of just $9 each. They appear to have all understood the matter as given in this way, and on my part I make this offering to mission work as a token of thankfulness for having been prospered to the completion of the book. Now comes your note about the dividend on this stock, as if all my donation had been repaid with interest before I had made it—though by this time I believe that every person has received his copy. I put these two things together as being set one over the other for the instruction of those who are interested.

As I write the planet Venus is crossing the sun, but I fear that the hazy clouds have prevented our astronomers from being able to mark the ingress as accurately as they wished. They have worked early and late to get ready, and it is hard that the coy goddess should go and veil herself in illusion as she kisses Apollo, while so many persons the world over have been anxious to see the unusual meeting. This letter goes before the transit is over, so I cannot tell you the result. There are three parties here observing it.

The following account of his audience with the Emperor of China marks the climax of that great change which in the forty years of his residence had brought the Grand Khan from his attitude of universal assumption and absolute exclusion to the acknowledgment and reception of foreign ministers as equals. The magnitude and importance of this innovation do not need to be pointed out to those who have followed Mr. Williams' career from the day when he was reported to the Hong merchant Kingqua as a "foreign devil" who had come to Canton to live under his tutelage.

TO R. S. WILLIAMS.

PEKING, November 30, 1874.

The American Minister, Mr. Avery, had an audience yesterday to present his letter of credence to the Emperor, and I went with him as his interpreter. I was not in Peking last year when Mr. Low had his audience; and if I had been, other arrangements were made by the five Ministers who then had the first collective audience given in China, which would have prevented my being present on that occasion.

Much against my wishes and the repeated requests I had made, the court appointed Sunday morning for the audience; but probably my request made at the Foreign Office had never been thought of out of its precincts, and the day was selected in the palace more from its being a lucky day than for any other reason. It was a beautiful crisp morning as we left the American Legation at eight o'clock in our sedan chairs, and together with the Japanese Minister who passed on his way to the same place, we made with our attendants a procession of more than fifty people. . . .

A guard of honor was placed at one of the inner (palace)

gateways, and another just by the *Fu-hwa* entrance, leading into the enclosure. Four or five high officials were waiting to receive us, and a large company of other officers civil and military stood in order on each side. Outside of the gate, in the street, a crowd of about a thousand people had gathered to see the show, all of them as silent and decorous, even in their curiosity, as if they had been drilled for the occasion. The officials led us into a small room where we found a table spread with many scores of plates filled with fruits and sweet-meats, prettily arranged in small pyramids. Here we were to wait until the Emperor arrived and was ready to receive us. He doubtless knew at what hour our arrival was to take place, and perhaps may have already come over from his palace, but I was told he would arrive erelong. All Orientals deem it due to their position to keep those whom they regard as inferiors waiting for their appearance. In this hall were many of our official acquaintances, so that the time passed pleasantly enough. One of them told us that he had risen to go to court at four o'clock and was a little tired now; while another, an old man of 83, was nodding half the time. As the Chinese learn something more of our customs, perhaps they will not hold their courts and councils before sunrise. . . .

While waiting for the hour of audience, I had time to think of the singular contrasts this meeting presented with some previous ones I had assisted at in China, and with some former experiences with our colleagues, the Japanese. The retrospect was suggestive, from my own life, of the great changes which are taking place among both these peoples. . . .

It had been arranged that the Japanese Minister should be received first, as he was the senior in office and had applied first. The *Tsz-Kwang-Koh*, or Pavilion of Purplish Brightness where the Emperor awaited us, was distant about three furlongs, and the many people scattered along the way, and the escort walking with us, rendered the scene very animated and showy, but one used to Western ways missed the bustle. All was decorous, elegant, and clean, but it was still, and like a show of mummers too. As if contrasts were the order of the day, another appeared in the dresses worn by the two envoys. Mr. Avery was attired in a plain black suit, while Yanagiwara, the Japanese, glittered in the sunlight as his profusely embroidered coat reflected its rays, his white trousers and dapper sword adding to a splendor which was capped and completed by a white ostrich feather in a big chapeau. His secretary was not quite so brilliant, but the two were the observed of all observers, and I suppose to our disadvantage, for the Chinese think much of show and colors. The hall where the Emperor sat was in a pretty pavilion, raised on a marble plinth, with an open front to the south and a large platform before it, on which were ranged his attendants. None of them stood directly in front of him, for to intercept his free and unobstructed view in that direction would, in their opinion, seriously injure the paternal influence of his government throughout the vast domains over which his sway extends. Most of the servitors remained below the terrace, near a tent which had been erected for our accommodation, and into which we all four passed before going up. This tent was a real convenience, for here we took off our overcoats, and thus were not exposed long to the chilly air of a November morning.

As the Japanese came down the terrace Mr. Avery and I ascended. In order to see as well as possible, I had provided myself with stronger glasses, but Chunghow, the officer who accompanied us, was so urgent and repeated in his request that I would take them off, that I did so, knowing the curious dislike which the Chinese have to being addressed by a person wearing spectacles. I was by this prevented, however, from seeing much of the sight which I had hoped to see.

The distance up to the yellow table on which the President's letter was to be laid was not more than eight or ten feet from the threshold. We entered a little at one side, bowing three times as we approached, and at the last bow were close up and immediately in front of the table. The Emperor's throne of state was a high-backed gilded chair, standing on a dais, about four feet above the floor. He sat cross-legged, while on either side stood two noblemen of high rank, called High Ministers of the Presence ; one of these was his own uncle and another his father's brother-in-law. Farther in the rear was a large screen of black marble, on which was an inscription, but this, as well as the throne and attendants, was very obscurely seen, as no light shone in from behind. The pillars which supported the hall were gilt, and altogether it had a very fine appearance.

Mr. Avery having read a short address in English, I followed by reading its translation in Chinese, standing a little behind and aside, perhaps two feet from the table on which the Minister's letter of credence was laid alongside of the Japanese. What added to the style of the audience were two rows of uniformly dressed officers, standing in diverging lines from the throne to the entrance, so as to enclose, as it were, the table and those before it. They numbered about twenty on a side and stood as motionless as statues. His Majesty, I am told, is rather under size, of a light complexion, and bears a family resemblance to his uncle. He has lately shown some desire to cast aside a few of the trammels of etiquette which imprison him, and every one must wish for him wise counsellors in the conduct of affairs which are coming upon him.

As soon as I had finished reading, Prince Kung fell on his knees before the Emperor, who had only acknowledged the President's letter by a slight nod, to receive his orders. I could not hear a word spoken, but he got up in a moment, slipped down the inclined plane upon the floor, and came forward to tell me that his Majesty wished the Minister good health and had received his credentials. He did this in a hurried manner, and did not look particularly charmed with the duty, but as he is very near-sighted, the effort to see distinctly has turned his usual expression into a scowl, so I would not judge of his feelings by his face; for my own part I should prefer not to get down on my knees before my nephew in the presence of two foreigners who stood upright because they could not be made to kneel.

As we retired, inclining our heads again three times, there came to my mind remembrance of the long argument which Minister Ward had conducted on just this point in 1859. To-day I was so placed as to carry out in some degree in my own person the principles of that discussion, and I felt more than ever that we then should have done both ourselves and the

Chinese a wrong if we had made even a curtsey before the sovereign of China. The one great idea associated with him and his position in the minds of his subjects, is his rank above all other monarchs on earth, and that he is officially the Vicegerent, the Son of Heaven, of whom only one can of course exist in this world. This assumption is like that of the Pope to be the Vicar of Christ, and towards both these high personages it is regarded as an acknowledgment of their demands to bend the knee or knock the head when coming before them. The court of Peking is desirous of concealing the fact as much as possible, that foreign ministers when presenting their credentials do not bend the knee at all; but inasmuch as more than two hundred officials are witnesses to this fact at every audience, the truth must eventually creep abroad.

The reception lasted only five minutes or so, and the Japanese awaited our return to the tent, whence we all went together to the waiting-hall. I thought that the Chinese showed some taste in having their audience thus in the open air, even if not actually out-of-doors; for the glorious sunlight and the fresh air, with the grove of fir trees around us, each added its own special charm to the scene. It was peculiarly Chinese, which is as different from our usual notions of Oriental grandeur and ceremony—Persia and India, for example—as it is from European style. There was no music or noise of any kind, no cavalry guard or files of halberdiers, no rows of chamberlains lining the way up to the throne; and, I may add, no speech from the throne in reply to the addresses. Some of these things may be altered as years run on and the audiences of foreign ministers become more common, but they may lose thereby some of the present features without gaining others as good.

On reaching the waiting-hall we all four, on the repeated request of the officers, sat down at the table to partake of the refreshments. I rather complained of having been deprived of my expected sight of his Majesty, but they pleasantly said that I had made it up in respect to him in not wearing my glasses. They earnestly invited us to go to the Foreign Office with them and partake of a feast which would be sent there from the imperial table, as is usual in such cases, but the Americans decidedly declined this expression of imperial condescension and hospitality, while their colleagues accepted. I think the invitation will by and by be dropped, for it is somewhat of an impertinence, and when the Dutch Envoy accepted it in 1798, the Son of Heaven, then styled Kienlung, actually sent him some half-eaten bones from his table. . . .

Thus ended this audience with the Emperor of China. The day is one in my experience which strikingly marks the progress and changes which have begun in this land, and leads me to hope that even more may be introduced without disturbance. Some foreigners are urgent that their ministers be received within the forbidden city, but if all future audiences happen on such cheerful days as this, I would prefer to have them in the Kiosk of Purple Brightness. Others complain because the representatives of Western powers have their audiences in the same place as the Coreans and Lewchewans, who there hand up their tribute and knock their heads, but this again to my view is a petty scruple, while the contrast between the two has its own lesson.

TO HIS SON.

PEKING, January 26, 1875.

We have had considerable news here since last mail—the demise of one Emperor and the accession of another, both of them not much more than boys, and of themselves quite unfit to rule nations. The deceased Emperor gave no promise of any fitness for the scenes and issues coming upon him, nor did his position offer much opportunity of learning what was necessary. His cousin who succeeds him is not four years old, and was selected, it is said, because they are cousins on both sides, the Empress-mother thus getting additional reasons for holding on to her power. Well, if she will reign well the change may be for the best. As soon as it was seen that Tungchi would not recover, there was some discussion as to the proper person to succeed, the choice being from a dozen cousins of the same generation, some of them being nearly grown men. But the Empress-mother is said to have got ahead of them all by bringing in her own nephew, just taken out of his warm bed, and telling the four Princes, uncles of the dead Emperor, that his successor was before them. I am told that his father is not well pleased with the turn affairs have taken, for as the father of the reigning sovereign it will be impossible for him to make or receive the kotow—an awkward position, since without this no dutiful son ought to approach his father, or dutiful subject his ruler. He is a passionate man, this seventh prince and unwilling sire, and is desirous now of going to Manchuria a while to cool off. But amid all the stories current we cannot of course tell the exact truth ; yet it seems that a change of monarchs has been made under a doubtful law of succession, without any disturbance.

Meantime the people of the land are obliged to mourn a hundred days for the Emperor who has "taken the long journey," during which time they are not to shave their heads, wear any thing red, fire off crackers, open theatres, ring bells, strike drums, or get married. Even the red sentences pasted on door-posts and lintles are to be taken off, while blue cloths cover the shop signs. Last Saturday the Emperor's coffin was taken to a temple near the Coal Hill, escorted by hundreds of officers, all in white lamb's-wool robes, the bearers alone having frocks of red and green striped. Had the death happened in summer, or indeed at any other season, the people would not have minded much, but the period of mourning now is a great damper to the New Year's festivities, and will doubtless send hosts of fire-cracker- and gala-mongers, as well as barbers, into bankruptcy.

With the opening of the river, in the spring of this year, Mr. Williams entered upon his second leave of absence and commenced the home journey by way of Europe with his family. This trip was intended rather as a means of restoring his health than for pleasure. The drain upon his vital energy during the past three years had left his nervous system in a state of prostration and almost of collapse, which for the first time in his life made him seriously concerned about his health. This becomes apparent in his letters to near relatives, where he now often drops a reference as to his condition, who had never before alluded to his own ailments; and especially noticeable in contrast to his former buoyancy and self-reliance was his dread of any new undertaking however trivial. The tonic of change and travel appears to have been the necessary remedy for this nervous debility, which largely wore away during six months of leisurely travel through Austria and Central Europe to England. But the effects of recent overwork were visible in his indifference to most of the intellectual and artistic attractions in the great cities, many of which, indeed, his near-sightedness quite debarred him from enjoying. However, he marched bravely enough through museums and galleries which he thought gave pleasure to those with him, and got his own distraction from the objects contained in these collections. The following letter indicates the wide gulf between him and the purely æsthetic side of Christian worship cultivated in many places on the Continent.

TO R. S. WILLIAMS.

PARIS, July 10, 1875.

The effect upon one's mind after looking at all the statues, pictures, carvings, and ornaments found in the churches in Europe is not conducive to spirituality. The power of sense over spirit reveals itself in the condition of the people who worship in these churches; but that is an old story. I am more interested in the effect upon my own mind, and the service and communion last Sabbath at the American chapel here brought out the contrast between the two forms of Christian worship more distinctly even than I could have imagined. I am thankful, more than ever thankful, that I was not trained to worship God in a church like the cathedral at Antwerp, where Rubens' two paintings of the Cross are more thought of than the sermon or the Bible. I have read lately with renewed interest the command given beforehand to Moses, that the pictures found in Canaan were to be altogether destroyed, as well as the images, lest the Israelites be led into idolatry. One who has lived in China, where the idolatry is effete, unartistic, ungraceful, feels that it has no power over the soul; for who cares for Kwanyin, Ma-tsu-pu, or Kin-hwa, or who sympathizes with their worshippers? But when the associations of a pure faith are combined with statues and paintings of consummate art, spiritual things become to us degraded to the level of worldly things, carnal and sensuous.

Nothing in his whole life so pleased and moved him as the spontaneous welcome from his friends upon his arrival in Utica. There was an exultation mingled with the surprise of these unexpected greetings which nerved him to a healthier mood, adding a necessary stimulus to the previous benefits of travel and change. To one whose most precious memories still clung to the village of his birth, it was a refresment merely to be recognized by old-time friends. " My reception here [he writes] among old friends has been an ovation, and I much wonder at the manner in which I have been greeted. Many more of my old acquaintances are living than I had supposed, from not having heard one word from them during the fourteen years of absence; the reviving of the past in sight of the present forms a curious kind of dissolving view of much interest." And again, in reply to a note of welcome from Professor Dana:

"Since I came here I've had so many greetings from old friends, schoolmates and relatives, that I have lived in a kind of exhilarating gas, the past and the present forming a curious mixture for the memory and affections to revive old times in. It is only once or twice in a man's life that such excitement can be experienced, and it surprises me that I should have been remembered to such a degree during so many years of absence. I think that much of it is owing to the cause in which these friends take an interest.

"If I continue as well as I am now, and other things remain favorable, I expect to return to Peking in the summer of next year. I have left things there so that it would be difficult for another person to attend to them; moreover I have all along had the intention of going back if my head recovered from its overwork, which it seems to have done. Yet I know that once weakened in any way, there is great aptness on the slightest strain to show that it refuses work. How joyous it will be, when this frail tabernacle has been laid aside, to do the work and service God gives us in that world where He dwells in glory and power!"

An abiding dread of the return of his ailment prevented him at this time from making many appearances in public, and forbade those favorite and familiar pulpit talks on the condition of China which had been his chief occupation in previous visits to America. With Mrs. Williams he moved from place to place where relatives and friends most urgently called them, a pleasant progress that could hardly fail to rest and restore the jaded mind. His eyesight gave him very serious anxiety, and was the cause more than his failing health of his resolve to retire from the Legation in Peking before infirmity made him helpless. It is surprising, in view of his own doubts and the fears of his friends at this time, how much he yet lived to accomplish; but the extreme near-sightedness and diminished power of vision which had slowly come upon him during the past few years never again permitted the same intensity and continuance of work that heretofore had marked his career. With the intention, then, of concluding his affairs as quickly as possible he returned to China by way of San Francisco in March, 1876, being delayed a few weeks in Utica on account of a fall on an icy walk which dislocated his wrist.

Arrived in Peking he made arrangements with the Department of State for the rental of the Legation property to the government, and forwarded the following to the Secretary:

LEGATION OF THE UNITED STATES,
PEKING, June 20, 1876.

Hon. HAMILTON FISH, Secretary of State:

SIR :—Since my arrival in Peking last month, the conviction has forced itself more and more upon my mind that my eyesight is failing—it may be slowly, but apparently surely. This, with other reasons, has brought me to the conclusion that the best thing I can do under the circumstances is to retire from the position which I hold as Secretary and Interpreter in this Legation. In an interview which I had with you last January I mentioned the condition of my eyesight to be such as to give me anxiety, and it has not since grown any better.

I therefore respectfully request that some person may be appointed to fill the place, and I will remain here until he arrives, or his commission is received, and then turn over to him whatever pertains to it. This course seems to me to best meet the exigencies of the case, with due regard to all the interests involved ; and it provides for contingencies by proposing the change in time. I am not, I think, in immediate danger of failure, but am even now crippled at times in using my eyes. I hope that there is no informality in the manner of this request which will prevent its being acted upon immediately.

I have the honor, etc., etc.

As one of the instances, not too frequently met with in our civil service, where private and official sentiment seem to go heartily together, Mr. Fish's reply is appended:

DEPT. OF STATE, WASHINGTON,
August 7, 1876.

S. WELLS WILLIAMS, Esq., Peking, China :

DEAR SIR :—It is with great regret that I receive your resignation of the office of Secretary and Interpreter of the Legation in China.

Your official letter of resignation will be officially acknowledged, but I must in acknowledging your letter addressed to myself say that I feel that the service is losing one of its most trusted officers, one whose name and reputation have ever reflected credit upon the position, and upon the country whose officer he was, and whose high personal character will long be remembered with respect and with admiration.

I am, my dear sir, truly and respectfully yours,

HAMILTON FISH.

The formal notification of release from the State Department contained, in addition to some other words of praise, the following allusion to Mr. Williams' most noteworthy achievements, which affected and gratified him "the more" (as he frankly avows in his reply), because "it has not been very often that my official action received the special approval of the Department."

" . . . Your knowledge of the character and habits of the Chinese and of the wants and necessities of the people and the government, and your familiarity with their language, added to your devotion to the cause of Christianity and the advancement of civilization, have made for you a record of which you have every reason to be proud. Your unrivalled Dictionary of the Chinese Language and various works on China have gained for you a deservedly high position in scientific and literary circles. Above all the Christian world will not forget that to you more than to any other man is due the insertion in our treaty with China of the liberal provision for the toleration of the Christian religion."

The resignation sent, Mr. Williams resumed the routine

of Legation work at Peking until the reply should authorize a transfer to his successor. The duties of the office were light, the Minister, Mr. G. F. Seward, having brought from his former post of Consul-General at Shanghai an experience and ability which required no especial assistance from the Secretary.* In lieu of the old dictionary work he employed himself out of office hours in compiling an index to the Legation archives, a necessary and tedious task which for lack of clerical assistance fell to his care. "The record [he says] is a review not wholly uninteresting to me, recalling many things which had already gone into forgetfulness and bringing back to me discussions now seen to be all fruitless; some things I should like to alter, some emphasize, some erase; but I can now only index as they stand. It is a little as though I were looking into the books to be opened at the last great assize."

The weakness and failure of his eyesight frequently interrupted this as well as all other pen-work, and he was glad in the summer to escape its heat and dust in the old hill temple. Here he invited a number of friends, mostly American missionaries to keep him company, a pleasant few who shared his hospitality with mingled relish and regret, because it was the last he could offer them in China. The American Centennial was celebrated with as much enthusiasm (if not éclat) in Peking as in places where many could gather to do the occasion justice. Twenty-six met the Minister at the Fourth-of-July dinner in his Legation, and it is related that four of the gentlemen—

* Mr. Seward was the only U. S. Minister ever appointed to China whose qualifications for the office consisted in any acquaintance with its duties before appointment.

among whom was Mr. Williams—committed the imprudence of attempting some verses in additional glorification of the event, but so far as is known their offences never appeared in print.

It was during this year that the first of the disgraceful and inconsiderate attempts at legislation prohibiting the immigration of Chinese to America was hurried through Congress through the influence of demagogues and sand-lot orators, in defiance of well-defined treaty rights. The news was of course humiliating in the extreme to Americans living in China, but more from dishonor of their country before other foreigners than before the Chinese.

"The Chinese here [writes Mr. Williams in August] care nothing for the ridiculous resolution passed about them in Congress last June, and are in blissful ignorance as to its results forbidding them to go to the Beautiful Land—as America is called in their language. If our law-givers knew how singular they made themselves (to mention details only) by calling this people 'Mongolians,' in their platforms, resolutions, editorials, and bills, they would fain stop it, for it only illustrates and makes clear their ignorance and spleen. As well call the Portuguese Iberians, or the English Celts, as the Chinese Mongols; they have almost nothing in common, did not come, within historical times. from the same ancestors, and in the language, manners, civilization, and government are as unlike as any two nations on the earth. We see too many of both races in this city to feel pleased at seeing our legislators and speakers stoop to such a piece of ignorant folly to curry favor with a few thousand discontented Irishmen on the Pacific coast. But this reflection bears rather upon the stupidity than the sin of what has been done."

The hope of influencing his deluded countrymen by temperate protests and plain statements in regard to the Chinese did perhaps more than any thing else in reconciling him to leave China. He foresaw a means of continued usefulness in returning to America and raising his voice in behalf of the maligned Chinese immigrants to this hospitable land.

His resignation accepted and his successor in the Legation appointed, it only remained for him to slip away from the busy scene of his life's work. By a coincidence in itself rather striking, he left Peking for the last time on the forty-third anniversary of his first arrival in Canton. His own account of the parting is worth giving for the insight which it supplies in the conduct of his feelings at this solemn turning-point of a career.

PEIHO RIVER, October 26, 1876.

MY DEAR WIFE :—Yesterday was one of the eventful days of my life, one which can never be repeated, which contained its own history in concentrated lines of enduring record upon my mind, and will be remembered in just as enduring pictures of impressive groups and faces. Let me tell you about it as I glide down the White River on this clear autumn day, the like of which in this delicious climate you know so well.

A week ago all the missionaries assembled at Dr. Martin's house and spent an hour or two in praising me and recounting my valorous deeds in a way I was neither accustomed to nor wholly easy under ; and I was of course obliged to reply. Aside from this feature, the reunion was very pleasant—one which does n't happen often in a life, and, I think, will be remembered by all who were there.

I had sent all my boxes and carts down to the boats the day

before yesterday, and had made all my parting calls, beginning with Palladius and ending with Butzow,* so that I arose yesterday in our old room with the feelings you understand who have done things and seen faces for the last time, and know the regrets involved. The last trunk was locked, the last bag strapped, the last bundle tied, and all were ready for the cart, when I was called over to breakfast by Mrs. Seward's servant, but not before I had family worship with Abé, a Ningpo Chinese who had been in the United States with McCartee. He had been in the habit of doing this, and now no one remains to do it with him. The house has been empty of furniture since the auction, though enough was left to make me comfortable during the last few days. The people and scenes of past few years crowded my mind as I went through the empty rooms, until I was glad to escape from them to breakfast. I am not, as you can bear witness, much given to sentiment and its expression, but yesterday morning I could have easily been caught in tears if I had given way to my feelings.

Soon the friends began to come down from up-town, and with them we lounged about until ten o'clock, when I left the group which you can picture standing in the courtyard of the *Mei-kwoh fu*, waving and bidding their farewells—October 25, 1876, forty-three years to a day since I was rowed up the river to Canton in the *Morrison's* gig, and first met and knew American missionaries in China. A few walked with me out of the city gate, and, as I looked back through that dusty, bustling thoroughfare, I was not sorry that there were no more. The parting shake and all was over; I had done with Peking, which I first entered seventeen years ago, and which has seen many sweet, eventful scenes of my life.

The ride to Tungchau with our dear friend Blodget was one of those charming passages in life which long and loving friendship alone can produce. The day was immaculate, and on the way we discoursed about God's glorious work among the Chinese, the approaching Missionary Conference, and other matters, until the walls of Tungchau appeared long be-

* The Russian Archimandrite and Russian Minister.

fore we had half finished. It was a ride which both of us, I think, will long remember.

So the parting from all these good people was made. But I might tell you many more incidents, were not my heart just now almost too full. On the diplomatic side two special dinners were given me before leaving, by Wade on Saturday and by Seward on Monday, at both of which I met all the society of Peking, receiving from them the highest marks of courtesy. Then, as though to represent the other side, Martin, Edkins, and Whiting had me to dine. I met all the missionaries at Martin's, as I have told you—a memorable reunion. The evening before I left I went to the weekly prayer-meeting, preferring rather to pass the last evening there than elsewhere, and that room where I said farewell to so many will be like a Mizpah, I am sure, a token that God will watch over us when we are separated.

I received a long succession of farewell visits, and, among them, three or four from members of the Foreign Office, the highest officials in the city having come to bid me good-bye. I met them all together (except the Prince) at the office, and we parted on the best of terms. Each of the nine mandarins has sent me a fan as a souvenir, full of Chinese protestations of kindness; I really think they all entertain as genuinely friendly sentiments as I could wish. Tung and Pao have grown aged and achy since I came to Peking, and they are not much older than I am.

What more can I say? They were not heartless and formal farewells that I received, but the expressions of genuine regard. How different does Peking look now from the Peking which I left in July, 1859, with the dying Aitcheson, and how many tender associations nestle in its dusty streets!

Mr. Williams' reference to his adieus to the Tsung-li Yamun recalls an incident of his regard for one of them, which he related in an address given in New York.

"One of the members of the Foreign Office, now dead, was the governor, in 1849, of the province of Fuhkien, and published a geographical and historical account of other lands, the matter for which he had collected mostly from personal inquiries of Rev. David Abeel and of the son of Dr. Morrison. Being too favorable in his remarks on foreign lands, he was degraded for its publication' and returned to his native village, about 1851, where he engaged in school-teaching. Fourteen years afterward, this man, Seu Ki-yu, was recalled to the service of his sovereign for the same reason which had wrought his degradation, viz., his superior knowledge of foreigners, then more than ever needed in dealing with them at the capital. Our own government, at my suggestion, sent him a fine portrait of Washington, whom he had eulogized in his *Ying Wan Chi Lioh*, or 'Survey of What is within the Islands and Seas.' The last act of Mr. Burlingame as Minister to China was to present it to him in Peking. His infirmities erelong compelled him to resign and return home, where he lingered a few years."

In Shanghai, where he remained a few days before taking steamer for America, he received from the large company of his friends commendations and testimonials of esteem which told him that his work had been well done. The career of most of those who go to the far East is brief. Before he had fairly reached the threshold of old age, Mr. Williams was called the Nestor of foreigners in China, not one being now left who was there when he arrived, while a greater part of the missionaries then in the country had been born since he landed in Canton. On the whole it was a retrospect of great progress made in promoting plans for the instruction and welfare of a government and people—one which, in spite of wars and suffering, he could not but thank God for having witnessed. The Protestant missionaries in Peking sent after him a farewell letter, expressing their friendship and appreciation, which, after touching upon his services and experience in China, concludes:

"In your departure from China, we lose the society of a personal friend, whose hospitable home has ever invited our presence and opened its doors to our monthly meetings for prayer. Our sympathies will follow you as you exchange the heat and dust of Peking for the shady walks beneath the elms of New Haven. We shall not cease also to remember her whose cheerful presence adorned your home in China, and contributed so much to the success of your labors, and we shall follow with lively interest each member of your family.

"It is not often that the Providence of God allots to any one man so long and so distinguished a term of service. We thankfully recognize in it His good hand, and pray that your later years may be crowned with His abundant blessing."

Some portion of a similar letter addressed to him by the missionaries in Shanghai will fittingly terminate the record of his life in China:

"Your kindly cheerfulness and patient industry and Christian consistency have won our hearts, commanded our admiration, and given us an example full of instruction and encouragement.

"Your labors as editor, author, and lexicographer have laid us and all students of Chinese history and the Chinese language under great and lasting obligations to your extensive and accurate knowledge and to your painstaking and generous efforts in giving it to others.

"The high official position which you have so long occupied as United States Secretary of Legation and Interpreter, and nine several times as United States Chargé d'Affaires, has given you many and important opportunities of turning your knowledge and experience to valuable account for the benefit of the Chinese, the good of your own country, and above all, for the advancement of the cause of Christianity in China. And we would express out grateful sense of the conscientious faithfulness with which you have discharged the duties of this responsible post.

"But especially shall we delight to remember that in all your relations, literary, diplomatic, and social, towards natives and foreigners in China, for the unprecedented term of forty-three years, you have faithfully and consistently stood by your colors as a Christian man and missionary."

"I was rejoiced indeed by these tokens of approval," writes Mr. Williams from Japan, "especially by their address signed by all the missionaries in Shanghai, for I regard them as expressions of their approbation of my course during all my life in China, and that to me is a good and great point. It was also quite unexpected, and I knew nothing of the latter till just as I was leaving. It sounded after they had all gone ashore like the requiem of departing days, and at this last moment I began to doubt if I had done right in leaving China. It has been like rooting up an old tree, and the sap may refuse to run when nourished by an unaccustomed soil. Time can only decide its wisdom. However, those scenes and partings cannot be recalled, and I've no desire to do them over. Whatever good or evil I've performed in my time in China must now remain. God can make their effects a part of His blessed plan for the glory of His name in the country and the fulfilment of His promise. I've been greatly blessed in my experience in my associates in mission work, in my personal health, and in the places I've occupied; for all these privileges I must sincerely praise and bless the Giver of all."

In this day of parting and farewell, it was the missionary, not the scholar or diplomatist, who was leaving his chosen field.

CHAPTER XII.

VARIOUS motives induced him to fix upon New Haven as his residence in America. In the restful seclusion of a university town he was able to satisfy his taste for calm and orderly living, while in its intellectual atmosphere he could follow the conditions of his temperament better than in the place he had called home during childhood; moreover, the presence of his family, who were now living there, and his acquaintances among the professors of Yale College—notably with Professor Dana, the oldest of his friends—had already established ties which made him feel less strange in New Haven than elsewhere. The creation of a chair of Chinese Language and Literature had long been mooted by certain of his friends with a view to connecting his work and influence with the university curriculum; but fortunately for his impaired health, the endowment for such a professorship was not immediately forthcoming, and while just escaping from the pressing routine of a busy lifetime he could for a few months after his home-coming give head and hand an entire rest. His life and the home which he made in New Haven was the golden sunset of a long and busy day. It happened mercifully for him that the years which passed between his work-time and his wages were for the most part pleasant and useful, not, as too often comes to those like him, years of ennui, sorrow, or gloom. Yet he was no idler. He was too nervously and actively constituted to be content with idleness, and this habit of diligence would have rendered him unhappy in complete inactivity. Though the alteration in his surroundings was as complete as can be imagined, and his feelings must have suffered many a wrench in turning away from the old life to accustom himself to the new, he tried simply and absolutely to forget the part left behind, being fully possessed by the apostolic exhortation to stretch forward to the things which are before in order to reach the mark of his high calling.

He came naturally and at once into the circle of cultivated men and women, for which the seat of Yale University is distinguished, and his delight in a society of lofty aims and undimmed ideals was as keen as their appreciation of his own abilities was spontaneous. His was the truly catholic temperament, which was fully alive to whatever men think and do, and he was as ready to impart as to receive information on subjects which came before him, either from books or from friends. While his aptitudes and tastes classed him among fellow professors, his varied life and abundant experience of men had freed him from that narrowness of vision which too often characterizes clever men of science or letters inadequately disciplined by contact with affairs. The common inference that because his days had been spent in China his information was confined to Chinese subjects, used rather to chagrin him, "as if," he once complained, " I never read English books nor spoke the English language in the East!" But the extent and accuracy of his general information was a surprise to those who first met and exchanged views with him upon matters not connected with his own special pursuits. Before a social and literary club (of which he became a member in April, 1877), which met some half-dozen times a year, he prepared papers on subjects of his own choosing at nine reunions within four years, some of these being on " The Exodus of Negroes from the Southern States " (1881), " The Sovereignty of the Lew Chew Islands," " Extra-Territorial Jurisdiction," " Nihilism," and " Mormonism," besides others, of course, on Asiatic topics. His letters at this time disclose, amid fond remembrances of his former home, his alertness and concern for questions of current interest.

TO REV. J. THOMAS, SHANGHAI.

NEW HAVEN, February 19, 1877.

MY DEAR MR. THOMAS :—The life in China is beginning, like a dissolving view, to pass into the indistinct past, and be merged in the new scenes and people which surround me ; it does not lose its distinctness so much as its responsibilities ; I have no further interest there in what is going on, and feel that henceforth my duties cannot be there, but here. The review of those forty-three years, like most reviews of one's conduct, sometimes catches hold of the neglected, the undone, the misdone, and the shortcomings ; but I pass over on the single plank to the other side of the subject, and say : " If the Master enabled me to do any thing, He knew beforehand all my plans and hopes, and which of them formed parts of His own plans," and rest there. The importance of mission work increases as I regard it from this end of my life, and I am sure that it will seem more glorious after I get where I can look into it more fully.

When I entered my state-room [on the steamer upon leaving Shanghai] I was much pleased to find an envelope containing a most friendly farewell in verse, expressing the writer's kind feelings. As it had no signature, I could guess only by the penmanship whose it was, and either yourself or Mr. Muirhead was the alternative. My thanks go out to whichever it may have been; you may be sure that I am obliged, deeply so, for all the loving words and tokens of those I esteem so highly.

I have been in the United States about two months, and have seen with the greatest interest the moderation of the people respecting the decision as to our next President. The question will be decided, and you will have heard the decision long before you get this, but you cannot easily appreciate the deep interest felt in it by all parties, nor the issues which hang upon it. The popular majority was large for Tilden, and the Democrats were the more strenuous to get their side uppermost, but I think they will fail; they are going to take it gracefully, awaiting the next election in 1880. I am glad for the sake of the negroes that Hayes' majority of one vote in the electoral college assures them of a certain kind of protection against the wrath of the poor whites, who cannot bear to have them vote anyway, and hate them for voting the Republican ticket. Threats of rising in case Tilden was ruled out have been uttered as feelers by men who felt his incoming to be their only chance of an office, but the general voice was for waiting and putting no such question to the trial of another war. This test to our form of government has been a much more crucial one than you would imagine from the newspapers, and thoughtful men are here and everywhere divided as to the policy (aside from parties) demanded by the best interest of the country.

I have got into my own house at last, and shall gradually come to a sense of what this position involves, and learn what I can best do. My expectations are not high. There is some religious interest in this part of the country; Moody and Sankey are working in Boston, and a general tone of thankfulness pervades society at the settlement of the political dispute.

Most affectionately yours,
S. WELLS WILLIAMS.

TO MRS. THROOP MARTIN, AUBURN.

NEW HAVEN, July 11, 1877.

MY DEAR FRIEND:—The Chinese proverb, "The life of an old person is like a candle between two doors, easily blown out," often recurs to me as I see in myself the approaches of old age, and the rapid growth of children into activity, pushing me on just as I pushed on others some years ago.

The faculty of Yale College made the appointment to the professorship of Chinese at the last commencement, as I suppose Professor Dana has already written to you. I believe that the opinion prevailed that the best argument they could use to obtain the requisite funds for the chair would be the fact that the chair existed and had no cushion. I hear that the matter was discussed among the members of the corporation, and the conclusion reached was probably a good one. When the September term opens, I shall know better what are the duties, prospects, and capabilities of the post. I am sure that it will be a gratification to you to learn that your plan of ten years ago has come to its completion, and that the ancient people and tongue of China have received an acknowledgment in Yale. If a respectable salary can be secured for its maintenance, I think that coming years will prove that the field thus opened will repay cultivation. I doubt whether this point would have been reached so soon if you had not stirred in the matter.

It was at this Commencement that the college bestowed upon Mr. Williams the honorary degree of Master of Arts. He describes some impressions obtained on this occasion to Dr. Blodget:

"This Commencement is the first which I ever attended, and I have been interested and gratified by what I've seen and heard. The gathering was larger than usual, eight hundred covers being laid in the hall, and still a hundred and fifty or so were crowded out. Among those who came were J. T. Dickenson, formerly a member of the Singapore mission, and Dr. Parker; the latter's visit here I enjoyed very much. It is pleasant to see with what respect Woolsey was greeted and applauded by the graduates, after so many years of separation. One alumnus told me that if a deputation should come here from the planet Venus to find a model man to take back with them from earth, Woolsey would be his choice. Perhaps many would agree with him, though I think the journey thither might be rather a hard one for their delegate."

Although the question of establishing a chair of Chinese Language and Literature was not a new one in Yale College, the action of the corporation in electing its first incumbent was a surprise to the professor thus suddenly installed. "The corporation are heartily sorry," writes the secretary in his announcement, "that at present no endowment is in their hands from which a salary can be provided; but they have taken some measures which, as they hope, may soon remove this reproach. And they will congratulate themselves on the great good-fortune of the college if it is able on any conditions to add to its corps of professors a scholar whose special attainments are so universally recognized and esteemed." The college was successful a year later in obtaining a fund, the interest of which furnished a nominal stipend for this professorship and placed the chair on a permanent foundation. Some reason for its prompt action in this matter may have existed in the fact that the University of California had already offered a similar position, with the additional comfort of an assured salary, to Mr. Williams, and this was understood to remain open. His regard for the college in New Haven was, however, already very great when he came to that town to live, and it hardly needed his formal enrolment among the faculty to bring him into sympathy with their aims and ministration. Though never actually called upon for instruction in his department, he made his influence hardly less felt as a factor in the intellectual life of the university. By means of occasional lectures delivered before a great variety of audiences, by notes and articles in newspapers and magazines, more than all, perhaps, by the genial manner in which he encouraged and received the undergraduates who came to his house, his presence and example became an incentive to all who were brought within the broad range of his culture.

First among the matters which claimed his attention after reaching home was the infamous maltreatment of Chinese on the Pacific coast. In order to overcome the indifference with which this disgraceful hostility was contemplated in the Eastern States he set himself at once to the task of bringing it before the public mind. Intensely loyal to his convictions, he not unfrequently called down upon himself most unsavory vituperations for his persistency in attacking the injustices of a brutal and unchristian persecution. Many of the foolish fears regarding this threatened bugbear of Chinese immigration are already forgotten, but a quotation from a letter written in February, 1878, will convey a notion of their influence in the national legislature :

" The ill-will exhibited in California and Nevada against the Chinese has found expression in Congress by a dozen of the most partisan bills which were ever brought up. One, presented by Mr. Shelley, from Alabama, wants to have the 125,000 Chinese in the United States all penned up in a waste region, ' as far as possible from all white settlements,' where each man is to be furnished with forty acres, and prohibited ever to leave the corral, and no Americans, except preachers and missionaries, are to enter the 'outer boundaries' of this inclosed area (7,800 square miles) under penalty of disfranchisement and imprisonment for not less than five years, without hope of pardon. So we have at last found out what is the unpardonable sin—for an American, at least. This bill is one of several of similar character, each being a disgraceful effort to drive out the Chinese. They have increased only 6co in eighteen months, and you would think each Chinese in the Union was a Chev. Bayard for prowess, a Samson for strength, an Attila for fury, from the way in which these Sinophobists go on." *

Mr. Williams' most elaborate production in behalf of this miserable and maligned people was a paper on "Chinese Immigration," read before the Social Science Association at Saratoga, in September, 1879, and afterwards published in a brochure by Messrs. Scribner's Sons. In it he describes "the origin, kind, and prospects of this immigration, the conduct and the rights of the immigrants, with notices of their treatment, so as to come to an intelligent idea of the question." Like all his literary work this was rather characterized by a cautious judgment and thoroughness than by impassioned or highly imaginative writing, but it is hard to see how this important subject could have received more impartial and comprehensive discussion, or its opponents more effectual discomfiture than in this temperate pamphlet of less than fifty pages. One passage from it is worth quoting as an illustration of his manner in treating a wrong which provoked most profound emotions:

"The summary manner in which the courts of California converted the Chinese into Indians, when it was desired

* Letter to Gideon Nye, Esq.

to bring a law to bear against them, has a spice of the grotesque in it. The physiologist, Charles Pickering, includes Chinese and Indians among the members of the Mongolian race; but the Supreme Court there held 'that the term Indian included the Chinese or Mongolian race.' It thus upheld a wrong, while it enunciated a misconception. It placed the subjects of the oldest government now existing upon a parity with a race that has never risen above tribal relations. It included under one term a people whose literature dates its beginning before the Psalms or the Exodus, written in a language which the judge would not have called Indian if he had tried to learn it, and containing authors whose words have influenced more human beings than any other writings, with men whose highest attainments in writings have been a few pictures and tokens drawn on a buffalo robe. It equalized all the qualities of industry, prudence, skill, learning, invention, and whatever gives security to life and property among mankind, with the instincts and habits of a hunter and a nomad. It stigmatized a people which has taught us how to make porcelain, silk, and gunpowder, given us the compass, shown us the use of tea, and offers us their system of selecting officials by competitive examination, by classing them with a race which has despised labor, has had no arts, schools, or trade, and in the midst of the Californians themselves is content to dig roots for a living."

Appeals of this sensible and tolerant nature do not leave an immediate mark upon the multitude who read, but among the smaller company of thinking men, to whom such a paper is especially addressed, its influence in directing honest opinions could hardly be overestimated. A more direct effort to stem the tide of popular prejudice, now in full possession of Congress, was the petition written by Mr. Williams and signed by the entire faculty of Yale College, urging the President to veto the Chinese Immigration Bill of 1879.

"I have been as pushed as I can be this morning," he writes, February 19th, "to get ready a remonstrance to President Hayes, urging a dozen reasons why he should veto the Bill; it is to be signed by the faculty and sent off as soon as it can be. I shall have it printed if only to show my sentiments. The needlessness, the unwisdom, the ridiculousness, and the dishonor of the Bill are all about equal. I wonder that Blaine should have lent himself to it, and told all the nonsense and errors the papers ascribe to him. It is all a bid for votes from the lowest strata on the Pacific coast."

The petition is framed with the cogency of reasoning and precision of statement which characterized all of his official and documentary writings, and is as forceful to-day as when first drawn up. One clause, relating to the reflex action of such a measure upon Americans in China, contains the germ of much of his public career there, and demands repetition in this place :

"If this Bill becomes an Act some results may ensue which should be considered. The privilege of self-government depends at present upon the sanctity and stipulations of the treaty of 1858. The Chinese Government has never shown any intention to abrogate those treaties forced from it by Western nations, though its authorities chafe under the confessed disabilities it places them in regard to complete jurisdiction on their own soil. Therefore, if the first step be taken by our government in changing treaty stipulations, we furnish the other party with all the example and argument needed, according to the uses of international law, to justify it in abrogating this principle of extra-territoriality. To do so will throw out our countrymen living in China from the protection of our laws, and neutralize consular interference in upholding them, thereby turning the residents over to the provisions of

Chinese law, and the usages of Chinese courts administered by ignorant or prejudiced officials.

"We do not refer to other reasons for this request, derived from the repeated declarations of the American people respecting the freedom of our shores to all nationalities. We will not discuss the well-known laws of supply and demand, influencing labor and wages, which have already begun to show their power to restrain the inflow of laborers. Nor will we bring forward the adverse effects such a Bill may have upon the great and growing commerce and intercourse still to arise between the nations on the shores of the Pacific Ocean, for these points must in some measure be all familiar to you. But we do, in conclusion, adduce the highest considerations, drawn from the value of a nation's honor and good faith, and from the relative power, knowledge, and civilization of the two countries now in question, giving the preponderance to the United States in all possible contingencies, for your thought in deciding the question."

President Hayes' veto of the bill in question saved the nation from the disgrace of this irrational and unnecessary legislation, and a commission sent to Peking in 1880 to arrange a modification of the treaty accomplished the end of restricting Chinese immigration to the United States in a legitimate manner.

The great famine of 1878 in Northern China enlisted his keenest sympathies and aroused, as may be supposed in a case where suffering was involved, all the energies at his command for its alleviation. Whatever public notices and private appeals could effect in stimulating the pity of those about him, Mr. Williams tried eagerly and often. His knowledge of the afflicted provinces and his personal acquaintance with the missionaries of all denominations who were engaged upon the spot in organizing methods of relief, combined to make him a useful co-operator in circulating information and receiving contributions in America. A letter written to Dr. Blodget, who was actively employed in the work of mercy at Peking, affords a glimpse of the subject nearest his heart.

NEW HAVEN, May 18, 1878.—I have your two letters with the list of villages in Shansi where drought is doing its gaunt work so fearfully. The choice of evils set before David, of pestilence, war, and famine, the last being the most dreadful, must have been the bitterest of all experiences to him; you now have a better realization of the slow, increasing suffering involved in that last infliction than any commentary could give you.

I have done what I could in making known here the dreadful state of things in your region, and send slips herewith to show you how I have condensed the details. I have no idea what success has followed my appeal in the papers at Chicago, Mobile, Utica, Amherst, New York, New Haven, and Columbus, but they cannot all have failed to draw forth some charitable mite of relief. The scenes of suffering described in papers from China, of mothers burying their moaning children, of others eating their dead or dying relatives, of every kind of privation, suffering, and death, have haunted me till I can scarcely think of any other form of life in Northern China than that of people like spectres hovering over the ashes of their burnt houses, and making pyres for themselves out of the ruins of their temples.

I have already written to Olyphant & Co. to send you $100 to help you in supporting some of your people in their misery till God sends rain on the earth and revives life and work to His creatures. You will know what is the best use to put the money to in selecting those who are needy.

The information given of the twenty-two villages wherein so many have died, fled, or sickened is not easily made effective, for people get a better idea of the crying need for aid from more typical and individual cases, where they are encouraged to give because it is likely to really save life. It seems to be nearly impossible to rescue those in Shansi, for they are far beyond our reach ; but the famishing in and around Tsinan, Schan chău, Teh chau, and Westerly can and ought to be accessible. Human efforts, if limited to those near each person dispensing food, would be more efficient.

The response to such appeals for succor in America was characteristic of the genuine kindliness of our countrymen, and a comfort to those who feared lest their treatment of the Chinese on this side had dulled their sense of Christian charity. An attempt was made by Mr. Williams and others to induce Congress to return a portion of the indemnity surplus of 1859 (which had by this time reached a total of $600,000), in order to relieve the famine district, but the prejudice against the Chinese was too strong; Senator Hamlin reported the bill unfavorably, alleging that the starving would all be dead before the money could reach them in China! The same surplus continues accumulating to this day.

These were a few of the interests and occupations to which he gave these first years of retirement. Occasionally a suggestion for work in a new direction would reach him from his friends in China, and engage or stimulate him to some new effort. One of these may be mentioned as resulting in his essay on the translation of God and Spirit into Chinese, already referred to. Though excluded by general consent from the discussions in the Missionary Conference at Shanghai (1877), the Term warfare revived about this time with all its former earnestness and acrimony, and with as little prospect of settlement as in 1849, while the increasing number of native converts trained in the use of the different terms gave the subject a greater importance every year. Mr. Williams, though he had never entered publicly into the discussion while in China, was sufficiently cognizant of its scope and issues to state the question broadly, and alive to its importance to realize that he could win the intellectual confidence of unbiased readers only by recounting the arguments on both sides. Those who know the warmth and irritation which seem to be an almost necessary feature of this controversy among pious men in the East can best appreciate the candor and liberality of this article by one whose own convictions were final. His position consequently occasioned comments from certain persons on the side of *Shin*, which he notices in a letter to Dr. Blodget (1879):

"You say that some surprise is expressed in China that I should have written so mildly about using *Shangti* for God in my pamphlet, when I talked so hardly against it in China; but the listeners here and there are quite unlike. The readers of the "Bibliotheca Sacra" wished to know (I thought) only the arguments used on both sides of the question, and in stating them I would have weakened my presentation if I had gone into any of the polemics we have become used to in China. I have no desire to decry or scold those who employ that term, convinced as I am that they are doing the cause of pure religion great wrong by using it. They will do much greater wrong by trying to harmonize the tenets of Christ and Confucius, or to show how much of the worship of the Tien-tan can safely be adopted by the Yésu tang (Protestants). Our new wine will not bear the adulteration of what is in those old bottles—but Wisdom will be justified of her children."

Touching his honesty in argument, it is significant that a sturdy member of the opposing ranks, in seeking fresh polemic ammunition for this dispute, went to the "Syllabic Dictionary" for evidence supplied by translations of the terms at issue wherever they happened to occur in the illustrative examples, observing that "Dr. Williams would never think of concealing what appeared to him to be the true meaning of a phrase which it was necessary for him to translate. . . . Indeed Dr. Williams' is the most distinguished name among the advocates of these views; and yet in his great dictionary he bears testimony to the fact that one meaning of *shin* is spirit"; and in his research the critic finds many examples to his mind.

Those who were near him and best appreciated his capacity for new literary work could not but regard his many benevolent and accommodating labors with regret. The promise long since made, that with continued health he would devote his time seriously to revising "The Middle Kingdom," seemed in the full tide of his various interests and occupations further than ever from fulfilment. He was eager always to accomplish a present good, letting schemes of future advantage bide. The prompt answer of a letter, however brief or unimportant, he considered as much a duty of common courtesy as replying to a question asked in conversation; and for this reason he used to contemplate the heavy mail brought to him every morning with a consternation that was almost ludicrous. The evil of this wasting correspondence was greater in his case, because his eyesight allowed him each day only a limited number of hours at his desk, and he seldom permitted another to help him. In the case of his friends he maintained frequent and regular correspondence, usually upon the large letter-sheets more common in the first half of this century than now.

Like most broad-minded men he was ever as willing to

impart from, as on the alert to increase, his stock of knowledge. The calls for lectures and informal addresses, in a community accustomed to look to the church, or college, or lyceum platform as a regular and legitimate source of information upon all current topics, consumed a still greater portion of his time, but these he seldom had the heart to refuse. " I have spoken several times on China within the past few weeks," he writes soon after coming to New Haven, " and always tried to give my words a tendency to its spiritual advancement. At this distance this feature seems to me of greater importance than ever." And as an instance (among many) of the real delight this service of his Master gave him, " I made," —he says in 1879—" a pleasant visit to the house of Mr. McCall, in East Haddam, and talked on missions twice to a small house full. One old man took me by the hand as the congregation separated and said : ' I *am so* happy to have heard all you 've told us ! ' and I came away perfectly refreshed. Mr. McCall is one of God's hidden one's—a country pastor worthy of all love ; I never had seen or heard of him before this Sunday. . . . But I fear I am becoming rather too widely known in the way of lectures for my own quiet, and am a kind of refuge for ministers temporarily laid up with colds and influenzas."

Mr. Williams had come away from Peking with some design of revising or rewriting " The Middle Kingdom," of which a resident in China well competent to judge had remarked : " Though printed nearly thirty years ago it has still a value in the full and accurate instruction it contains on all subjects relating to China that no book of later date has taken from it." On the other hand, of course, much of its information was incomplete and many statements from the standpoint of subsequent events had become inaccurate. It had been written with the view of supplying the cardinal facts about China from such sources as were at hand, and with the expectation that some profounder student with more leisure would erelong supersede it with a fuller account. The book had, however, held its own for a generation, and was become a standard for reference among Chinese students, being even used as a text-book in some Anglo-Chinese educational institutions. In view of the credit earned during these years of use,* of the long experience of its author with the people and country of China, and of his own part in recent events there, it seemed well worth while to review the whole work in the light of the recent knowledge obtained by special students. The sheets remained upon his desk from the time of his coming to New Haven until its completion—or until ill-health compelled him to turn its final accomplishment over to another hand—nearly six years later, a reminder, as the dictionary had been before, of that "something which will last, which will be found worth putting into the foundation (out of sight, perhaps, but not out of use) in God's temple of life."

To Dr. Blodget he explains some of the obstacles and checks in the way of this achievement:

"My crippled wrist hinders my penmanship in rapidity as well as in looks, and sometimes I am obliged to entirely stop my writing. It will never be any better, I fear, for five years have now passed since the dislocated joint was restored. I feel the advances of age in many ways, and am perhaps disposed to overdraw on my strength in order to answer the vari-

* The greater portion had also been translated into German and Spanish.

ous demands made on mind and body—and here less mercy is shown to the infirm than in China. There people can learn the condition you are in, and do not expect too much, but here my position is supposed to involve ability. I hope to be able to finish what I have begun on 'The Middle Kingdom,' but sometimes I doubt the possibility of accomplishing it. God's promises and truth preserve me from failing and falling, and his presence grows more and more vitalizing."

The decreptitude of years had not indeed fallen upon him so severely as to debar him from performances which humbled and surprised younger men who watched him, but after a life of almost unbroken health and incessant activity he chafed under the necessity of slower and restricted labors.

In February of this year (1879) he writes to a brother:

"I have been pretty busy of late trying to work away at the revision of 'The Middle Kingdom,' doing a little at each sitting, if so be I may be allowed to live long enough to finish it. I cannot tell you how my time is frittered away by letters from everywhere and on all sorts of topics, which I am supposed to know and learnedly discourse upon. . . . In Hartford last Sunday, at the anniversary of the Tract Society, I made the acquaintance of Governor Jewell, who tells me that a Japanese admiral, whom he met in St. Petersburg, spoke of knowing me in Japan. An odd triangle that—Nagasaki, Petersburg, and Hartford—for me and my fame to occupy!"

And again, some months later, to his son, who was in Europe:

"I am writing at your desk, having moved my papers in here, but taken nothing off it, not even your tobacco. My correspondence seems to increase in every direction, so that you must not expect many letters from me. I have no leisure even to do what I wish on 'The Middle Kingdom,' but I see God's hand in all these unexpectednesses and do what comes first. I must confess, however, that I am discouraged at the prospect of ever finishing the job. The subject has grown immensely during these thirty years, and I shall be expected to know it all through. I shall, though only trying to be accurate, not exhaustive, often enough fail even at this. After all, one cannot do much in such a line of research that will endure, for it is constantly changing and developing and needs frequent delineation.

"As I write this a man comes all the way from Chicago and wishes me to look over a genealogical register of his planning, printed in blanks to fill in with all my ancestors and successors to the end of time and borders of eternity too. He stays seventy minutes, but has to suspend his talking while I answer the questions of the census-taker on his rounds. As soon as both of these are gone, and I have written a little more, the mail comes in from China and Japan, and the letters from Purdon, Blodget, Hepburn, Yates, and Martin all have to be read 'and contents noted.' Then in come two of the Chinese boys in college and prevent my going over to see Collin Wells' mother and take her to the Art School as I had promised. By the time I get down to my sheet again my thoughts are thoroughly scattered—and besides these things are the drawbacks of my hand and head and eyes."

The revision of twelve hundred pages, nearly every one of which must be submitted to considerable correction or enlargement, involving references to hundreds of volumes, was a feat of sufficient magnitude to engross the whole attention of a much stronger man. As in the case of his dictionary, Mr. Williams hardly realized the labor involved when he began his undertaking, but was content to plod on towards its completion with the solemn conviction that if the thing were worth doing he would be spared to accomplish it. "This job of work," he characteristically writes to a friend, "seems to be about as useful as any I can undertake," and in this expression lies the clue to an understanding of all his life work: To be up and about his Master's business, constantly employed upon some subject which came well within the range of his abilities, content with that measure of excellence which would serve his supreme end of usefulness. In the seven years' task of revision, though often sadly interrupted during long periods when sun and dust had time to fade and soil the well-worn manuscript on his desk, he spent probably twice as many hours as the preparation of the entire work had cost him in 1846. The labor of condensing a pamphlet into a paragraph, of gathering the facts from many volumes to supplement a statement, or of compressing the old information in order to accommodate the new, was often greater than that of composing fresh matter.

An event had occurred in 1879 which caused Mr. Williams an unexpected annoyance and expense, besides involving him in another interruption to his present work. Thieves had broken into the Mission House at Shanghai and stolen two hundred and fifty stereotype plates of the dictionary stored there. The total gain to the ignorant wretches who performed the burglary probably amounted to less than three dollars, the worth of the copper, but to the author, who was contemplating a new issue of the work, the loss was a serious one, and involved as many thousands. By taking advantage of this opportunity he was able, however, to amend this portion of the dictionary before the pages were reset; the corrections of critics and improvements or additions noted in his own copy were embodied in the revised pages and printed two years later in a new edition.

Little is said in the record of these years of his domestic life, for if the spirit of the character portrayed in these pages has been set forth aright no formal description is needed to suggest his mighty attachment to the close and gracious intimacies implied in the word *home*. How abundantly indeed its relish gladdened and cheered him, each year adding to the fulness of its blessing, this meagre record is altogether unable to express. But dearly as he loved and warmly as he appreciated the society of his family circle, its importance and influence upon himself were probably never quite realized until the light of the household went out in Mrs. Williams' death, January 26, 1881. She had sensibly declined in strength during the few preceding months, and seems herself to have long had that singular premonition by which brave women often bide in secret the time when death draws near; but to those about her the end came suddenly, her illness lasting only a month after it had drawn their attention. For obvious reasons this is not the place to describe a disposition whose charm and beauty consisted in her perfect fitness as a wife and a mother, but without some mention of the operation of her character upon that of her husband this memoir would be incomplete. Her enthusiasm and cheerfulness, joined to a practical wisdom of daily affairs as great as his own, made her precisely that type of womanly excellence best adapted to supplement and sustain her husband's nature and position. There was an energy and forethought in her conduct, often called into service during the vicissitudes of their married life, which by its courage seemed to lend strength and heart to his own action; and in the control of his family and household she added to his wise principles and sagacity the tenderness of one who sympathized as well as controlled.

Her loss was the removal of an influence which had illuminated every joy and trial of his maturer years. By it his intellectual efficiency and vital energy were alike profoundly affected; his hold on life visibly weakened from the moment her sustaining companionship was removed, for at his age the severing of a union so close and sympathetic as theirs must have shocked and penetrated every part of the system. The overwhelming effect of this great catastrophe in the life of so sensitive and undemonstrative a man as Mr. Williams may be indicated in some degree by a few jottings in his wife's unfinished diary, which he took up on the day of her death and carried to the end of the year,—the single instance of his recording his daily happenings and experiences while living at home.

Wednesday, January 26, 1881.—My Sarah died at 5.30 A.M. to-day. This is the whole story; it is the end of her probation, her discipline, her conjugal life, her motherly care, her sisterly love, and her Christian course. During the night her mind was too weak to understand any thing or express herself. Last evening I asked her if she had any hymn in mind which she wished to hear read; she replied: "Lover—Jesus." So it was Wesley who furnished her with the last breathings before she saw Him, whom not having seen she loved. Dear wife of my life, mine for one third of a century, adieu till we meet on the Sea of Glass.

"I read to her many hymns," he writes to one of his children, "in which she found food for thought as she lay quietly on her bed. The ailment left her mind weak at times, and it was easier for her to listen than to talk.

One night she turned to me saying: 'Wells, give me some promises.' So I told her all I could think of for half an hour, beginning with 'When thou goest through the deep waters, I shall be with thee'; 'Comfort ye, comfort ye my people, say unto them that their warfare is accomplished'; 'I will never leave thee nor forsake thee.' She fell asleep while this pleasant effort of memory was going on, and I was refreshed for my slumber too. I would not have given much for words from any other book in the darkness and sadness of that night, nor do I think any sayings of priests or philosophers would have cheered her as these did."

After the burial in Utica Mr. Williams returned to the empty house. In the diary he notes:

February 5th.—This morning was the first of my experience in my own bedroom of having no one to talk with while dressing; the blankness was relieved by the recollection of her sweet words and experiences during the month of sickness.

I have been answering some of the two dozen letters of condolence received from dear relatives and friends, whose sympathy and love call forth my own as I tell them the story of Sarah's peaceful end. Yet these friends, with all their kindness, are somewhat like the postman who leaves their letters at the door: they cannot enter the heart where I live in God's care.

February 9th.—Wrote a critique about the treaties with China for the *Congregationalist;* it is a needless compact on the whole, and some of its provisions cannot be executed. No laws can be effectual over the Chinese in their own country so long as opium is legalized.

TO REV. WM. MUIRHEAD, SHANGHAI.

NEW HAVEN, April 16, 1881.

MY DEAR FRIEND:—I have two notes from you lying before me, both of them bearing witness to your sympathy and remembrance. We have both been called to go down into the valley whose sides are so closed in that we must gaze upward and look for the Father of Lights to cheer and show us our way onward. Happy are we then to be acquainted and to hear the same word which he spake to his disciples, " Ye know the way." That mysterious expression of Paul's, that he was to fill up what remained behind of the sufferings of Christ, has often recurred to me of late, bringing new sensations of the oneness that ought to exist with him, exalted though he be.

In your case you were unable to be with your wife, while I was allowed to watch in mine the gradual trimming of her lamp, her preparing of her garments, until the dawn of a morning brought the Bridegroom, and he found her waiting. Her entire illness was mercifully without a pang of pain, and her mind was clear throughout. The night before she fell asleep for the last time I repeated Wesley's hymn, and when I came to the line " Thou, O Christ, art all I want," she murmured, " How sweet that is," ending her life with this confession. What better could she have ?

" They twain shall be one flesh."—We know better than any commentators what this means now ; the distress proves the strength of the bond ; the many sources of consolation found in God's word shows as well that he knew the need we are in when such grief comes. But the blankness of heart for those who know nothing of his presence and the peace thereof, how awful must it be !

The people around me here have been wonderfully kind, for Sarah made many attached friends. She is buried, besides two of her sons, near my own parents, and there I shall by and by be gathered too. The spot is a beautiful one on a hill-side in my native city, so that I am in some degree like the Chinese, thinking so much of *kwei hiang*. The rest of the journey does n't seem to me to be very long, now that she is at the end. If I live eighteen months more I shall be 70 years old, and all after that is borrowed time. How thankful we should be to have been co-workers with God in the evangelization of China.

The diary may be trusted to record events in this year of his life :

February 11th.—A surprising proposal was made to me to-day by Dr. E. W. Gilman to accept the position of President of the American Bible Society. It was suggested, it seems, by Winston and Tracy, and is intended more as an acknowledgment of the dignity of missionary work than any thing else. I pleaded my very poor eyesight as disabling me from properly fulfilling its demands as a presiding officer, but he described them as not like those of a debating body and as soon learned. I told him that I must consult with friends, for it is plain to me that I am unsuitable; perhaps others will not think so.

February 14th.—Thinking all the time of Mr. Gilman's proposition. I can't compass its requirements at once. I went to see Dr. Woolsey this P.M. in order to learn more respecting the details of the Bible Society presidency, and whether my defective vision will unfit me for fulfilling it properly; he is troubled in the same way and knows what is expected. I have been guided by his advice (and George Day's too) to give consent to Dr. Gilman's proposal. The Lord will give me needed aid when the time comes; the post was not sought for.

March 7th.—The official notice of my election to the post of President of the Bible Society came to me this morning, signed by a special committee for the purpose. I hardly know what to do with the honor so unexpectedly put upon me, or in the post so singularly opened for me. Dear Sarah is not to know it—perhaps she does; I am constantly connecting her with all my position and doings. I am happy in the thought that as I did not seek the place I shall be aided to fill it to God's glory. I receive it as an honor done to the mission work of the American churches of every denomination.

March 9th.—A driving rain has kept me and most people indoors to-day; but I have finished the revision of the printed portion of "The Middle Kingdom." It remains now to continue the history of events since the old edition was issued. China is too big a subject to put into two octavo volumes, and I see no use in trying to get all its headings into my book. References must suffice. I find some difficulty in digesting my materials in my mind so as to make a readable narrative of this period. The past thirty years form too long a vista to be all taken in at one retrospect.

March 12th.—I have at last been able to resume the revision and have begun the account of the Taiping Rebellion. The more I learn about that terrible visitation, the more perplexed am I to understand what was God's purpose in permitting it.

Spent the evening with Prof. Fisher, who read to me the account of St. Francis of Assisi preaching to the birds, and their responses to his exhortation, out of the Acta Sanctorum. The number of unexplored continents of learning in this world are quite beyond my reckoning, and this is one of them.

March 24th.—Living alone involves so many different relations to one's self and the activities of the mind, that I find it to be a rather interesting study. No one to talk to before rising or when dressing, and nothing to read, it throws my thoughts over creation, leads them to speculate on the character of God, estimate life in relation to it, and desire more than ever to be like it. Nothing gives me so much comfort as the feeling of the truths of Revelation and my safety in trusting to them.

I met a gentleman this evening, an inquiring man, who has been studying the Rig Veda in order to learn Hindu notions about God. He places that people higher than he would if he had lived among them. He has also been looking into the Chinese classics, and quoted Confucius largely but not very accurately. This man is not a bad specimen of the results of such researches, and shows how false a conception of moral views of pagan minds can be honestly derived from translations in which an English word conveys more than its derived original term.

April 5th.—I was sitting at my desk in the library about two this P.M., when the stone slab containing the petrified Orthoceratite shell fell out of its wooden frame, toppled over the cornice of the book-case, and struck the corner of the writing-desk within three inches of my arm, breaking off a corner of the stone as it fell to the floor, doing no further damage. For an instant I knew not where the crash came from, and when I realized the hazard I had escaped in a broken arm, or instant death from a blow on the head, my gratitude and wonder were too great for utterance. The stone weighs twelve pounds, and had been four years in the place. It was a great mercy.

April 7th.—I went to New York this morning, reaching the Bible House at about two o'clock, when I went into the Managers' Room for the first time. A large elderly man, looking at Governor Bradish's portrait, was the only person in the room. He said: "I do not know you, sir"; to which I replied: "Nor I, you; my name is Williams." "Then I am your predecessor," said he, taking my hand cordially, and I knew then that it was President Allen, of Girard College, who had come up to attend my inauguration, evidently with a good deal of effort. At about 4 P.M., the Board of Managers having met and read the letter announcing its action for filling the presidency and my acceptance, Mr. Wolcott came into Secretary Gilman's room to inform me that they were waiting to receive me. Taking his arm I went in and was conducted to the chair on the dais, the members rising meanwhile. Mr. Winston then made a short speech, referring to my life in China, the missionary and diplomatic positions I had filled, and my doings, closing with a pleasant expression of the gratification of the Board in my becoming its president. I replied in such terms as came to my mind, chiefly dwelling on the reason which I supposed had influenced their choice, in the close connection between teaching, translating, and distributing the SS. in pagan lands.

In the evening there was a reception held in the same room, there being present eighty or more gentlemen, one of whom was General O. O. Howard, the officer at West Point.

May 6th.—The prayer-meeting this evening was too thin, owing to the rain, to make any one warm up; rainy weather discourages this duty exceedingly, but suppose all its members had a toothache which could only be cured by going there to pray for it, as Tyndall proposed—would our faith grow more than it does now by such an operation? I wonder why people turn away from gathering in such groups, if they ever had the satisfaction I've had all my life in going to them. A prayer-meeting is in itself the most honorable meeting it is possible to think of or attend, if it is rightly considered. For a company of human beings to draw near God, and make known their requests, offer their praises, and unite their confessions and homage, is either a most awful impudence or a most responsible worship. Nothing shows the induration of sin on the heart more than the disregard of this great privilege, or the lightness with which it is heeded.

May 23d.—The idea that I shall never see the revised edition of "The Middle Kingdom" sometimes comes into my mind in a most disturbing manner. In many ways I can observe the gradual approaches of age, weakness, and decay, and these signs are suggestive of such thoughts, I suppose. The work lags through their influence, and thus looms up larger than ever—a mountain too high for me to climb.

These extracts are valuable as illustrating in a high degree the strength in resignation of a man whose soul was attuned to perfect accord with the Divine will. However painful the experience or heart-searching the visitation, he saw God's goodness around and within him. "New and untrodden gullies among the hills by Peking," he writes in this year of trial, "always contained new plants when I was on their search; so new walks in life reveal new sources of instruction and profitable reflection. . . . It is noticeable how much and often the Bible calls on us to rejoice, be glad, praise, sing, make merry, even loud noises, as if the Spirit knew the temptation of sin always to suggest fear of retribution." But for all the courage of his moral nature that sustained him in affliction, his physical energy began to succumb under the stress of an unaccustomed strain. This was apparent now in various ways, most notably, perhaps, in a growing willingness to submit to bodily comforts and the solicitude of others about his health—usually the last indication of surrender on the part of one who has exulted in many years of independent vigor. Still more in his literary work were signs of failing evident to those who knew his former habits; the effort of composition which had before cost him singularly little pains became now a slow and troublesome task, often interrupted by weariness, though resolutely continued as remedy and easement of sorrow. When the writer of these lines returned from a long absence, in the fall of this year, he found the surest witness to his father's prostration in the supplementary chapters of "The Middle Kingdom" that had occupied the past six months, a confused and prolix narrative; but the patience which he displayed in submitting his manuscript to suggestions and corrections, finally allowing the whole of this concluding portion to be rewritten, marked a thoroughly sanctified spirit. His humility, indeed, in regard to both critics and detractors was at all times remarkable; though a man of decision and mettle he was ready to listen without a murmur to the most fractious and unreasonable censors of his style and opinions, nor was he ever goaded into making an intemperate reply.

A last quotation from the diary will show something of the real solemnity with which he approached the life limit set by the Psalmist:

September 22d.—To-day I enter my seventieth year, a day I have long looked forward to, and sometimes never expected to reach. It is a serious day, and seems to mark the dividing line between active and inactive life, giving me the few remaining days of life to consider the coming eternity. My record cannot be altered; I now regret so many things and acts which years might have buried in forgetfulness, that nothing I ever did seems to be worth any thing. It will always be so, I suppose, while life lasts, for sins and their results cannot be forgotten to a mind conscious of their nature. Dear Lord, keep with me to the end.

A second honor was conferred upon him this year in his election to the presidency of the American Oriental Society, of which he had been a member since 1846. His only contribution to its Journal was made in 1880, an article on Ma Twan-lin's notices of Fu-sang and countries east of China. The question as to whether Fu-sang stands for some part of the American continent, which was discovered and peopled by Chinese in the fifth century, is still a matter of controversy, but the testimony thus far brought forward in its favor is perilously contradictory. Mr. Williams' argument was against such a supposition. His interest in the society, at all times a real one, was naturally much increased by the new dignity of his office; he outlined a paper on the Miao-tsz, a tribe of aborigines in China, for a meeting held in his house October, 1881, but his expectation of enlarging this for publication in the Journal was frustrated by ill-health.

An account of this year ought not to conclude without some mention of a characteristic and amusing Christmas salutation received from the Chinese professor at Harvard, Mr. Ko Kun-hua. It will be remembered that in 1879 a sum of money was subscribed to support an educated native as instructor in Chinese at Harvard University for three years, in order to test the demand for that language in America. Professor Ko, a genial and cultivated gentleman, whose eminently kindly nature and personal qualities are not yet forgotten in Cambridge, exchanged visits with Mr. Williams during the first year of his brief residence in this country, and in the course of their further acquaintance seemed to have cherished a warm attachment to Mr. Williams. Soon after a call made in New Haven, this December, there arrived a tiny book, with the following characteristic measures written in Chinese character, with metrical and literal translations attached, and explanatory notes added:

> "*Ping ping ping tso tso,*
> *Ping tso tso ping ping.*
> *Tso tso ping ping tso,*
> *Ping ping tso tso ping.*"

Which was versified by the author into English:

> " In the light of the spring sun far over the sea,
> The city imperial shines in my view,
> But fairer and dearer than this is to me,
> Are the clouds and the water of your land to you.
> The teacher's red curtain once used by Ma Yung,
> At Yale and at Harvard for us has been hung,
> And thanks to the hole which your learning has drilled
> In the wall of your language, with light I am filled."

The scholarly and exhaustive notes to these lines inform us that "the 'Annals of Han' says: 'Ma Yung had high talents and great learning. In his time he was a thorough scholar. He sat elevated in the hall; putting up a red gauze curtain across it, he taught his pupils before the curtain.' You are in Yale College and I in Harvard College, both of us teaching Chinese. Therefore I use this quotation. Ma Yung lived 1700 years ago.

"DRILLED, WALL, LIGHT. 'Annals of Han' says: 'Kwang Hang was poor, but fond of study. He drilled a hole in the wall to read by his neighbor's light.' You have written a 'Syllabic Dictionary of Chinese and English," which has helped me very much in translating. I am the same as Kwang Hang, being aided by your light. Kwang Hang lived 1900 years ago."

This experiment of introducing the study of Chinese as a means of promoting our commercial interests with China was brought to a melancholy termination by the rather sudden death of Professor Ko, in the following February. His verses and his urbanity deserve to survive him.

An event which made a deep impression upon Mr. Williams was the death of Dr. Leonard Bacon in December, 1881. The friendship which existed between them was singularly intimate, considering the time of life at which it commenced. "Everybody here [writes Mr. Williams] laments the master in Israel who has been taken away, like Elijah out of the midst of the sons of the prophets, as in a chariot. What a glorious life and translation his was! The effulgence of it will last for many years in this region. I have seen much of him for the past five years, never without admiration and gratitude."

On the last day of the month in which this was written (January, 1882) he met with a severe accident in a fall on the icy pavement, which broke his left arm and dislocated the shoulder. His action after the occurrence was extremely characteristic: without waiting for assistance or indeed letting any passer-by know of the injury he had received, he walked home—a distance of half a mile,—let himself into the house, and then crying to his son upstairs: "I've broken my arm, will you get a doctor while I lie here?" calmly placed himself upon his study lounge to await the arrival of the surgeon. The fracture healed quickly and well, a proof of the advantage of temperate living, which pleased him greatly. His chief solicitude and annoyance arose from the fact that this mischance prevented him from delivering a series of lectures which he purposed to begin on the day following at Princeton College. It was evident, moreover, and not surprising that the nervous system had received a palpable shock. Not indeed that he worried over his own condition, but that he chafed at all in a matter which was beyond human control—this seemed to indicate more than any thing the decline of his natural self-mastery.

This casualty did not, however, keep him long away from his desk, where he continued at work on "The Middle Kingdom" and his correspondence. Among letters written at this time was his reply to an invitation issued by the Utica Semi-Centenary Committee, of which his brother was chairman. It shows a lively interest in his birthplace that he was willing to contribute to the record of this celebration three printed pages of recollections and expressions of regard. "Few of the citizens of Utica," he says, in concluding this message, "who will join in this half-century commemoration have gone farther than I have, or stayed away longer ; yet my love for the old homestead seems to grow with increasing years. . . . Allow me in conclusion to thank you for this opportunity of joining in your civic celebration. As I cannot tell you any thing about Utica, I am constrained to say what I do about the land of my adoption—speaking with pleasure of the wonderful advances it has made within the past five decades ; and I believe that during the next five the Governor of the nations, whose wisdom and power are now seen, as his promises to the land of Sinim are fulfilling, will show even greater things for the ancient race of Han."

With this letter went the following to his brother:

NEW HAVEN, February 27, 1882.—I send you my letter for the Symposium, and doubt whether I should have succeeded, if you had not been chairman, for my desire to please you stimulated and strengthened my powers. You must remember how little I could write about your city, who had lived so long at its antipodes.

I am getting on as slowly as an eight-day clock on a summer afternoon, but I think surely. It is four weeks to-day since I fell, and my appetite and sleep are both good—better than my penmanship by a great deal. My cup runneth over with my mercies, for I am content with the dispensation of our Heavenly Father. I had learned before to be content with all kinds of dispensations for other people, and now I am learning what these mean for Wells Williams. The change from the third to the first person has some serious features, and I am sure is well ordered. He has made all my bed in my sickness, through and during which I have had a great degree of freedom from pain. I cannot tell you of the varied and multiplied kindnesses I 've received from New Haven friends during the last four weeks. The record shames me, and should incite me to do likewise to others when I get abroad.

A few days after this letter had gone, while leading family prayers in the morning, he suddenly lost the power of utterance. With the exception of a slight bewilderment, which passed away shortly, there was no indication of any accompanying intellectual derangement; it was natural to account for an instantaneous deprivation of this sort on the basis of paralysis, and this he himself believed to be his malady, but it appears rather to have been that unusual one known as aphasia, or the suffusion of blood in the brain lobe which controls the faculty of speech. Several days elapsed before he could pronounce *yes* and *no*, but as the process of absorption slowly went on other words came to his lips, and still later short sentences. Except for the ready comprehension of whatever was said to him, it was much like a child's effort and experience in learning to talk. A curious phase of his trouble was the fact that Chinese words and phrases were the first to come back to him,—to the bewilderment of those who tried to discover his wishes—and even scraps of French and Italian (imperfectly as he knew these languages) seemed to recur to him more readily than English. By the end of three months he could endure the presence of a visitor, or write a brief message, but any excitement or over-exertion was sure to bring on symptoms of distress in his head, which plainly showed how serious his complaint was. Three months spent at Litchfield, in the hilly country of Connecticut, where he had an abundance of invigorating air and was in no danger of undue agitation, proved extremely beneficial. When he returned home in the fall he found it possible to look over the proof-sheets of "The Middle Kingdom," which by this time was about half printed. The limit of his working capacity was, however, soon reached and not unfrequently over-stepped, a sore and continual trial to the man whose thinking faculty remained unimpaired and whose lifelong habits called for some occupation. A slow decrease in physical vigor, the result of anæmia, was manifest as cold weather returned, and the length of his walks sensibly diminished; but though frequently thrown upon his own limited resources for amusement and occupation he never lost his cheerfulness or expressed any impatience. He discovered in the task of cutting the pages of new books in the University Library an employment for many empty hours, and insisted upon finishing his daily modicum of volumes, which he carried to and from the library with almost comical earnestness. In July, 1883, he went to the White Mountains with his brother, Mr. Dwight Williams, whose care and nursing through his long illness had greatly aided in his convalescence, and in the company of a few congenial friends who came to the same spot for its fine air he passed an active and pleasant vacation. The following note to Dr. Blodget is written with a sprightliness which hardly indicated that it was to be his last to this dear friend.

HOLDERNESS, N. H., August 9, 1883.

It is a good while since I got your welcome letter, but I have left it behind in New Haven, and whatever there is in it which wants an answer must wait. I have come to this place in quest of health, and this note perhaps shows an improvement on former ones. It is a surpassingly beautiful place; the hotel is perched upon a hill, from whence four lakes are visible, and over the adjoining height Lake Winnipiseogee offers still more scenery. Mr. Whittier [the poet] was here for three weeks, and I got as much acquainted with him as I dared for my own head's sake. Like all men who use their faculties in God's service, he has a storehouse of experiences which are worth hearing. His deafness is distressing to him, and with his age and strength I should not think him able to live very much longer—according to my diagnosis. My friends from New Haven say that I have improved in health since my arrival; my power of reading is certainly greater, but the speech does not come at my calling. I can't attend the meeting of the Board at Detroit, but I hope I can assist at the American Oriental Society at New Haven in October.

I am glad to say that the last proof-sheet of " The Middle Kingdom " went last week to the printers; if this has the blessing which the first edition has, I shall be content. I had a regular siege to write the preface, and could hardly have done it after all if I had not had the aid of my son. It cost me, I think, more pains than the preface and introduction to the dictionary. I did not realize before how weak my brain was; the recovery of my powers of speech and writing seems yet a long way off. 'I must decrease; others must increase'; and God be praised that the work in which He has promised that the kingdoms of this world will be given to His Son will never lack His ministers and servants. We can rejoice together when we see all the sons of Han that attain that blest abode through our instrumentality.

The effort to draft his preface gave him more trouble indeed than he confesses to in this letter; he submitted it with much diffidence to several acquaintances, and listened with patience to their suggestions, but was sorely tried when the publishers urged him to add a few bolder statements in reference to the improvements in the book. This he thought would sound like an advertisement, and he refused to modify for such a purpose. It stands, therefore, with few alterations, much as he wrote it, the criticism which in other places had amended ruthlessly enough being stayed upon these few last words touching the land of his adoption:

"I have endeavored to show the better traits of their national character, and that they have had up to this time no opportunity of learning many things with which they are now rapidly becoming acquainted. The time is speedily passing away when the people of the Flowery Land can fairly be classed among uncivilized nations. The stimulus which in this labor of my earlier and later years has been ever present to my mind is the hope that the cause of missions may be promoted. In the success of this cause lies the salvation of China as a people, both in its moral and political aspects."

In spite of some halting phrases and solecisms, none of which were spared by the few hostile reviewers who exercised themselves upon the book, there seems to be in this final message a fragrance of benediction on the people of China which might have been lost in the correcter sentences of another. It would perhaps be hard to find in any tongue a book that can show a more honorable achievement, or that has exerted a wider and weightier influence for the good of an alien race, than "The Middle Kingdom." "A wise man," says the sage Mencius, "is the teacher of a hundred generations"; the honesty and charity which characterize these volumes will tell future readers that their author loved as well as studied this people, and inform many generations of his hope for them.

Since "The Middle Kingdom" had become, much to its compiler's surprise, the current authority upon its topic, he was resolved in this revision to make the work worthy of the influence it exerted. The constant and determined demand for such a compendium may be inferred from the fact that after its publishers had made due announcement of the immediate issue of the improved work, a few purchasers continued to buy the antiquated edition up to the day of publication. What his experience as editor had taught Mr. Williams of the value of judicious discrimination in such summaries had not been forgotten during his subsequent career. His literary taste was decidedly better now than in his early manhood. His sources of information had increased in proportion to the increase of knowledge and the multitude of events to be noted. His position among Sinologues had altered from that of an obscure student to one of reputation and authority. His share in the events of a generation's space was such as to enable him to discuss them from a close personal acquaintance. All these were advantages peculiarly his own. On the other hand, he perfectly realized how a minute inventory of this wealth of added familiarity with his subject would have swelled the volumes to enormous proportions and defeated his object of making them readily serviceable; but while lamenting the necessity (always a sad one to an author) of discarding so much garnered learning and condensing the rest into a narrow space, he resolutely adhered to his sensible plan. Many themes were touched upon only to point out their magnitude, while others were purposely dismissed with a reference to some accessible authority. In spite of discrepancies arising from this necessity, and of occasional incongruities when old citations differed from new, this comprehensive synopsis of a country and its people has been accepted as trustworthy and just by the vast body of those in search of information on China. Its success is probably due to Mr. Williams' intellectual organization; his mind was not only active, but retentive; patient as well as truthful; inclined to distort no facts to fit his theories. In the language of one of those who best knew his mental calibre, " he took a sensible, comprehensive view of subjects brought before him, and adhered to it consistently. What he saw, he saw clearly and at once. He did not dwell too long in elaborating his views or in modifying what he had written. Content with that degree of excellence which he was able easily and naturally to attain, he passed on to other subjects and fresh labors."

The book was issued from the press in October, 1883, a few days before he celebrated the half-century anniversary of his first landing at Canton. "Well, I thank God for this," he said, briefly, when the first bound copy was put into his hand; but the eager eyes that lighted up his pale face as he turned over the pages of his final performance showed a more than common joy within. He made no pretence of concealing his interest in the press notices of his work which were read to him as they appeared. It pleased him especially that the English reviews were generally favorable, though these rarely failed to condemn his so-called "opium intolerance"—his settled conviction that England, by reason of her opium policy, was at the bottom of much of the present misery in China. When one bitter criticism from the pen of a British resident in China was shown him, "You had better keep this carefully," he observed; "some of the fault he finds is real, and the mistakes he points out may serve to correct a future reprint."

It seemed as though his life had been spared to see the consummation of this important endeavor, after which he faded gradually away, and was no more. His anæmia appeared to lessen during the summer, but it returned with the cold weather and rapidly reduced his strength and energy. Early in February the signs of decreasing vitality indicated that the end was near, and to none more clearly than the patient himself, who calmly discussed his mortal ailment with those who came to watch and serve by his couch. He lingered thus for two weeks, praising God as ever for his goodness during a long life, and for his mercy in visiting him with a painless disease. None who saw him in these last days can ever forget the calm and chastened countenance which seemed already to have taken on the sereneness of another world. On Friday evening, February 16th, after a day of unconsciousness, he suddenly arose in his bed, made a fruitless effort to speak, then falling back on his pillow, ceased to breathe. It was the euthanasia, the departure in perfect peace, which he had often longed for; the fit ending to a singularly peaceful life.

> " So may'st thou live, till like ripe fruit thou drop
> Into thy mother's lap, or be with ease
> Gathered, not harshly plucked, for death mature."

The funeral took place on Tuesday, February 19th, in the chapel of Yale College, where his body was carried, after brief prayers at the house. The public services were conducted by Dr. Barbour, the college pastor, and addresses were made by President Porter, Dr. Clark, Secretary of the American Board, and others. On the following day a private religious service was held at the house of his brother, R. S. Williams, in Utica, and the interment made in Evergreen Cemetery, by the side of his father and his wife, near many relatives and friends who had preceded him by a little.

The leading characteristics of my father's heart and mind have been abundantly revealed in the record just concluded, and little should be needed on this subject to complete the mental portrait of the man. A few reminiscences from the more familiar standpoint of family and friends may serve, however, to set forth his personal appearance, and add, perhaps, some impressions of his social traits which are not so readily inferred from his own words and actions.

Physically he was a man somewhat above medium height, fairly well-proportioned, active and wiry rather than strong, and, up to the period of his last illness, entirely confident in his movements and muscles. I remember him as not only never ill, but as always well and quite free from trifling ailments such as often interrupt the working lives of healthy men. His only serious physical defect was myopia, which grew upon him after middle life so rapidly as to render him almost blind without his spectacles. He first noticed his nearsightedness while at school, but from ignorance and the want of proper glasses the trouble was increased until it became a serious affliction. He began to use spectacles at Canton, where with a pair of the enormous discs worn by the Chinese he played the melodion at weekly prayer-meetings, presenting such an appearance, it is said, as to at first seriously impair the gravity of his friends assembled at the service. Perhaps the most noticeable feature of his face was the nose, which was broken in childhood and afterwards assumed rather extravagantly Roman proportions. My father who was the last man in the world to resent any reflections upon his physiognomy, used to amuse himself with those who on the strength of his proboscis questioned him about his Hebrew ancestry, observing dryly that he and Adam seemed to be taken for Jews as a matter of course.

He walked quickly and lightly, and with evident pleasure, always preferring to walk, rather than drive or ride, and in the country often stopping to investigate some stone or flower, or to admire the landscape. He seldom omitted an exchange of greetings with passers-by, a habit which may be traced to his conviction that foreigners in China, especially those who spoke the language, ought to lose no opportunity of showing their good-will to natives. In this way he secured many acquaintances among the country folk about Peking, and was remembered by many hucksters and beggars in the city; and the practice led, moreover, to his picking up many colloquial expressions and stray bits of information, kept in mind for an astonishing time, to be brought finally to some appropriate service.

If his feet always served him, his hands, however, were not so reliable. A sort of trembling palsy increasing with his years rendered them very unsteady, and occasionally—as after wood-sawing or riding—quite useless even for writing. He used to laugh at his own ineffectual attempts to write his name or pass a full cup at table. One day he came back full of glee from the wood-shed to tell us how he had been taken for an old toper by a guest of the Minister's, who found him putting up his saw with trembling hand and proceeded to lecture him upon the vice of intemperance. As to the habit of drinking it may be said briefly that he had a horror of it, and was glad to be of use in the cause of temperance in this country. There was in him, however, none of the bigotry which prohibits wine in the household or refuses to use tonics. This may have been due partly to the fact that drunkenness is a vice almost unknown (except among foreigners) in China, but it came more likely from a catholicity of temperament which appreciated the varying needs of individuals and recognized the insufficiency of heading off a great evil by petty restrictions.

His manner was a union of reverence and reality. No one could look into his face without being struck by the fact that he was at once a praying and a practical man; the most casual intercourse with him brought out these two predominant qualities which became indeed a part of his nature. He prayed for what he wanted as simply and hopefully as a child, and received the mercies and crosses which came to him in the same trusting spirit. But he was the last man one would think of as ever shrinking from a plain duty or from a decided action when his own exertion was necessary to accomplish his desire. This combination of qualities, and the fact that he never trusted to the glow of inspiration in the performance of work, gave him the air of being essentially prosaic. It is true that though instinctively cultivated in his friendships and tastes he was little spoken to by works of art. The confession of his insensibility to these things occurs more than once in his letters written from Europe, and many times he would declare that in their more complicated expression neither music nor painting gave him any pleasure. He was not, however, altogether wanting in imagination of a refined and delicate quality, and this was notably instanced in his occasional use of striking and appropriate figures in conversation or in public addresses, where they were introduced without effort or affectation, the spontaneous outcome of his fancy.

And in this connection those who knew him were often taught how a man without much æsthetic endowment may in simply seeking God attain to elevated conceptions of great artistic beauty. When he studied or explained the incidents of our Lord's life he seemed to realize them with a distinctness of mental vision that made these scenes as interesting and vivid as any in his personal experience. Sacred history was to him not only the most momentous but the most picturesque record ever written. He once asked a party of gentlemen at his table what event chronicled in ancient and modern history they would have chosen to witness; and after each one had bethought himself of some favorite battle or parade, he declared his own choice to be the drowning of Pharaoh's army, and thereupon began, from his own acquaintance with the country and from recorded facts, to paint so glowing a word-picture of the scene—Moses, the greatest of heroes, standing god-like over the impotent Egyptians, his joyous host crowding the height, while Miriam led the triumphant chorus, their colored garments illuminating the desert sand, their pæan rising above the angry roar of the sea—that his guests listened astonished while the naked outline of the Exodus was transformed by this quiet man into the stirring description of a mighty pageant.

My father was not disposed to consider truth as a treasure to be discreetly hidden in a napkin, and was apt sometimes to bring out the actual facts of a case with a plumpness that admitted of no further finessing. This was done, however, with a sincerity that rarely caused offence, but on occasions where he thought he had spoken too harshly I have seen him go, even to servants and little children, to say in a few hesitating words how sorry he was to have distressed them. These were the infrequent crises when the quick temper with which he was born attained a momentary ascendancy, and they left upon the mind a strong impression of the sweetness and good sense which were the result of his long practice of stern self control. Generally he felt none of that mere joy of combat which plunges many into the warfare of controversy. His taste for polemics was so small, in fact, that he preferred many times to keep silence, even to the point of being misunderstood, rather than join in a discussion where men's feelings were involved; but when once fully aroused to the necessity of defining his position or upholding a fundamental belief, he proved himself to be no mean adversary.

His mind was never greatly troubled by entertaining or encountering doubts; not that like Montaigne he could slumber comfortably upon them, content to leave certain questions standing forever open, but rather because of the prevailing singleness and simplicity of his faith, which, founded upon a few great essentials, presented no loophole for distrust and uncertainty to enter. "In counsel," Bacon said, "it is good to see dangers, and in execution not to see them, except they be very great"; when once he had come to terms with himself as to a course of action, apprehension and timorous half-thoughts no longer disturbed the composure and steady movement of his performance. And this it is which accounts in a great measure for his high and constant sense of duty in his life-work, which in all occupations was fixed upon the single end of helping to save the heathen. Nothing but a consecration that possessed his whole soul, and an abiding faith in the final triumph of God's righteousness and love, will explain the earnestness and persistence of his devotion to missionary labors.

He impressed children with a peculiar feeling of reverence, which must have been instinctive on their part, for it was sometimes apparent before they had even heard him speak. This little tinge of awe made them shy of approach, but those who finally gave him their confidence were amply repaid. He was a famous friend, never tired of explaining to them the wonders of nature, and answering their questions with a clearness of definition that made him very popular. He would go to almost any trouble in his efforts to please them. The only serious accident that ever befell him in China was the result of climbing a cherry tree, when he was nearly sixty, in order to get the blossoms for a little girl; a branch giving way he fell to the ground, and was picked up partly insensible and with a broken collar-bone, but he insisted upon presenting the flowers before being taken to his room. With his own family he was affectionate but strict, having, in the case of his older children, many theories which, I think, he must have allowed my mother gradually to laugh him out of, for I noticed that with the others he was more severe in sentiment than in practice, indulging us in many things which he would not permit himself. He made us commit to memory quantities of Bible verses, a certain number each morning, without which neither he nor we could have our breakfasts; and with our religious training, as may readily be supposed, he was unremitting. But I obtained more moral instruction—as I did general information—from his conversation than from his direct teaching.

Within the small circle of his household his experience and knowledge were looked upon as conclusive and exhaustive. It seemed incredible to his children that there was any really important human experience which he had not enjoyed or endured. I well remember my own astonishment, after reading the "Prisoner of Chillon"—surreptitiously, of course, for Byron was not allowed in his house,—when I learned that my father had never languished in prison! Not that he made himself into a hero before us—indeed he had a horror of exciting childish fancies by any tales of adventure,—but rather because this was an intuitive inference from the fulness of his wisdom.

Enough has been said in the foregoing pages of his manner of working. He had no moods dependent on health or whim, but was always able to write on the subject in hand. He was exceedingly regular in his habits, and liked uninterrupted hours of work quite as well as most studious men, but these he rarely enjoyed owing to the varied nature of his occupations. A chief secret of his long activity may be found in the fact that he never forced himself in any way by excessive hours or night work to do more than his strength allowed. Though a voracious reader he seldom (within my own memory) read long at a time, for leisure and eyesight were both usually wanting. His extensive information came more from his rare power of observation, wide interests, and his habit of fixing new facts by immediate reference to some authority, than from any extraordinary familiarity with books. In terms of modern life his stock and quality of knowledge would be classed rather as that of a journalist than of a librarian.

My sister writes of him :

"My earliest recollections go back to those sunny days in Macao, before we moved to Peking [in 1863], when oftentimes he used to call us 'small fry' out for a walk—always a great joy,—and try to make us use our eyes on plants or stones or insects along the way, and how he puzzled us with the long names, each of which he insisted upon our learning. He was rare company for a tramp, even to us unappreciative youngsters ; in later years we had often reason enough to bless him for the health and pleasure that came from this habit of walking and seeing with both eyes. It was something of a trial to him, I believe, to give up his home in Southern China, and often I heard him sigh for 'the good old Canton days.' It must be remembered that in those years it required a good degree of courage to face the discomfort of life in Peking, its crude and cheerless native houses, the dust and rigor of its climate, its shiftless workmen and servants, its remoteness from Shanghai and civilization, and the frozen river in winter which cut off all our supplies. But in spite of these drawbacks and the hardships of pioneer life, I never heard a murmur of any kind from him. He was not only always contented himself but was sure before long to make others about him contented, and this by sheer force of his natural serenity, for he was not hilarious or witty or one to make you laugh.

"When I joined him with mother in Shanghai (May, 1874), we lived with him for several weeks at the Presbyterian Mission House until the dictionary was done. It was a mighty struggle, for body and brain were giving out fast owing to the tedium of his task, but he plodded steadily on through weary yards of proof-sheets and tiresome directions to the printers.

We were alarmed for his health at the time, but I think we never sufficiently realized the strain and effort this must have been upon his nervous system; for months he hardly slept at all, though often he walked miles in order to catch a bit of sleep through weariness, and with each morning returned his old enemy the headache and his old trouble of failing eyes. How he longed then to be back again at the temple on the Peking hills, and how pathetically he would comfort himself after a bad night with the reflection that in a little while we would all be at peace there! The change came for him not a moment too soon, and I can see now his look of supreme content when, after some vicissitudes, we were finally settled in the temple for the summer, and his joy at resuming the old restful life there—going over the same rambles in search of flowers, rejoicing in the beauty of the views, greeting his friends, the donkey-drivers and peasants, with warm interest, and questioning each as to his welfare since last they had met. He was usually off for a scramble up one of the ravines before breakfast, coming home with a handful of flowers for the table, saying that these and the blessing always gave him a better appetite.

"Others can testify with better grace than I how good and wise he was. It was not so much his store of knowledge as the fact that his information was forever accessible, his facts never hazy, that chiefly impressed me. An instance of the extraordinary retentiveness of his memory occurs to me in illustration of this. I was reading Grote's 'History of Greece' aloud to him one evening, and for some reason was interrupted a moment; just as I was beginning again he said: 'Let me see if I can give you the rest of that without being told,' and went on to recite page after page of the narrative in substantially the order of the book, to the end of the long chapter. It must have been more than ten years since he had looked into the history. His knowledge of the Bible was quite as astonishing; its history was more familiar to him than any other, all the dates of his chronology being reckoned from events in Jewish annals. Its study was an unfailing source of joy to him, and he was never so happy or so inspiring as when giving his Sunday Bible Lessons. It was during these that one realized what an extraordinary storehouse his mind was; though his verbal memory was not remarkable (and I never heard him make a very long quotation) he hardly ever failed to give precisely the reference or explanation that was necessary.

"His life was a very methodical one: by nine o'clock every morning he was in his office, by four he was ready for his walk. I can see now the almost boyish delight in his face as he came running across the yard from his study to see if any one was ready to tramp with him—for walk he must every afternoon and in all weathers. Almost the only other form of exercise he could tolerate (except riding) was sawing wood, an accomplishment upon which he rather prided himself, always insisting that if there were any logs in the wood-shed they should be reserved for his manipulation. I don't think the mandarins, or foreign officials either, ever quite accustomed themselves to this monstrous lapse of dignity; but wood-fires were rare luxuries in Peking, so he was not often caught with his saw-horse.

"And of the beauty of his thoroughly Christian character what shall I say? Nothing, of course, that can more than give an idea of its perfect consistency, for one had to live with him to realize how entirely in thought, word, and deed the word of God was the rule of his life. Day by day and year by year that word seemed to become more real to him, and his faith to grow stronger and more beautiful in it. But the memory of this is rather a precious legacy to us than a subject of comment to lay before others. I may mention, however, his peculiar leniency in judging the conduct of others; though as severe as a Puritan in his own standard of right and wrong, he was always ready with excuses for the shortcomings of another. Nothing troubled him more than our thoughtless comments on a neighbor's actions, or any harsh criticisms of conduct, however strange or unkind it might appear; 'if you can't say pleasant things,' he would observe, 'you had better not say any thing,' and he lived up to his precept."

"He possessed a remarkable memory [writes his brother,

Mr. R. S. Williams, of Utica], and his close, critical observation of every subject with which he came in contact, coupled with rare powers of explanation, rendered him a charming conversationalist and of course a most welcome guest in any circle. Few could spend even a moment in his company, when he was in the talking mood, and not derive some lasting pleasure or benefit from his inexhaustible fund of general information. Instances of this far-reaching and absorbing quality of his mind will occur to every one who knew him well ; it comes back to me now how often in wandering with him over the scenes of his boyhood I 've been amazed at the readiness with which he was able to re-people every familiar locality with his early associates, relating their various haps and mishaps, often following out the history of their later lives with various incidents of failure or success, as the case might be, showing how the boy was the father of the man.

"His long residence in foreign lands abated in no degree his affection for his own country, and her institutions were ever near his heart. His life may be said to have covered the complete succession of our war-time memories, from the revolutionary heroes, who figured in every Fourth-of-July procession of his childhood, and stories of the war of 1812, which were as household words in our family, to the rebellion, when his whole soul was stirred and his patriotism found expression in large contributions to the welfare of our soldiers on the field. The appeals of the Sanitary and Christian Commissions found in him a liberal response, and in spite of his distance from the field of action their reports of aid and comfort rendered to the army reached, I am sure, few more interested readers anywhere. But while his charities were world-wide, their central object was naturally missions at home and abroad, and to these he was always giving. Most of these donations were very secret, and bestowed in such a way as not to be easily traced to their source, and often he would purposely keep the knowledge of the sums given from himself, directing me to forward 'about such an amount, and make it more if you deem it best.' I think it must be more than twenty years ago that he wrote me, when directing a contribution to the American Board: 'This (with what I've previously given) will make rather more than I have ever received for salary and expenses from the treasury of the Board since I came to China in 1833, principal and interest together—what a blessed privilege it is to me to be able to return it!' Often he made contributions to the same object through different channels, 'that the total might not seem too large, and so flatter my pride.' Again, as illustrating the modesty of his offerings, I find in a letter of 1865 : ' I don't care to reckon up how much you have given to the Board in my behalf, or to tell what an advantage it was to the mission in Peking to be able to go into a home of its own ; for all this charity is not a scintilla of credit to me, as I worked not to get it, and am only a sort of tunnel to dispose of it.'

"He was particularly fond of aiding the American Sunday-School Union in its work among the freedmen at the South during reconstruction times. 'There is a huge debt we owe to these poor blacks just made free,' he wrote once, 'for our fathers held their fathers in unrequited bondage, and how can we pay what we owe better than to give their ignorant children the blessed freedom of the Gospel. Send some money for me to support a S.-S. missionary among them, as I want to do my share toward liquidating this debt.' In this manner he supported this missionary in whole or in part for several years, and received some amusing and interesting letters from the school-teachers in response to his contributions. And in this connection it may be noticed that he was one of the first to appreciate the work of Dwight Moody, and sent him a liberal contribution to aid the beginnings of his labors in Chicago ; his interest in the evangelist ceased only with his life. I could give numerous other instances of his benevolence, of which I knew much from my having charge of his funds in this country, but enough has been said to indicate what a large part charity played in the conduct of his life—charity not of deed alone but of thought and word."

A few words from friends as to my father's character will properly define and illustrate the impression he produced on others; and first from one to whom he was most sincerely attached in China, Rev. Henry Blodget, D.D., of the American Board Mission at Peking:

"My personal acquaintance with Dr. Williams commenced in Hongkong, in 1854. At that time he had been twenty-one years in China, and was just returned from Japan with Commodore Perry's expedition. Naturally he was filled with joy at its success, a peculiarly grateful result to him as being in marked contrast to the rude repulse he had suffered when, seventeen years before, he and his associates had been driven from the shores of that same country. He was then, as I first saw him, in the vigor of manhood, full of good cheer and kindliness, quick-witted, intellectual, and zealously devoted, as ever afterwards, to the interests of missionary work.

"In Peking, where we lived many years in close intimacy, he took an active part in all that was going on in the community. His place in the Missionary Association or monthly meeting for prayer was seldom vacant; at his own request the latter meeting was for a time held regularly at his house, and his doors were often thrown open for the gatherings of other religious associations, at which he was sure to have something of interest or value to contribute. He loved also to join in a little weekly prayer-meeting, and for some years repaired regularly for this purpose every Tuesday evening to the house of a friend who lived nearly two miles away; there his voice was often heard in lowly manner entreating the Lord 'to hear these our humble breathings at His throne of grace.'

"He held through life with a childlike faith the truths taught him in his early years, nor was he ever tossed upon the sea of doubt in regard to the fundamental facts of Christian belief. The facts of science he was also willing to believe, but over all, in all, and through all, he saw God, the God of his fathers and of our common creed. While he was farthest from any affected sanctity of manner or tone of voice, there was always something reverent in his bearing when he spoke of the great things of Christian faith which were central in his heart.

"He was, moreover, eminently social in feelings and habits.

Always a welcome visitor in the circles in which he moved, he was alike agreeable and at ease in foreign legations, merchants' houses, or in the houses of his friends the missionaries. And it was upon these latter that he most eagerly and oftenest called, and in his own house they were by him and Mrs. Williams most cordially entertained.

"His name will remain in the permanent history of the early efforts of Protestant missions in China, as well as in the record of the establishment of our present political relations with this empire. And this represents also the almost equal division of his long life here, the first half of which was wholly and intimately connected with Christian missionary labors, the second half with treaty-making and diplomacy. A second and hardly less important part of his life-work—the whole of which was so fruitful in literary performance—lies in the faithful records he has left us of these important events, which not only have the value of being those of an eye-witness, but of one who was also a careful observer as well as participant, possessing a well-balanced judgment of those wants which were occurring in his own day.

" Thus he lived and died in the serene and blessed hope of a future happiness which he should enjoy. When beloved children were taken away by sudden death, the hope that they were saved to him by Christ was his strong support. He was submissive and cheerful. A like grace sustained him in the loss of his wife, with whom he had the fruition of many years of great domestic prosperity and joy ; and when his own frame began to weaken and give way, he evinced the same cheerful hope and trust that had sustained him in every affliction. More than twenty years ago, when walking with me in a crowded street in Tientsin, he broke out with strong emphasis in the words, 'I shall be satisfied when I awake with Thy likeness !' As I remember, he then added : ' I should like to have these words inscribed on my tombstone.' It was the definite prospect of awaking some day to this glorious satisfaction that sustained him in the sinkings of nature, in partings with friends, and finally in his own solemn and beautiful passing away from these earthly scenes."

The following extracts from two letters of Sir Thomas Wade, late British Minister to China, afford an estimate of equal interest:

"Our acquaintance began in 1849, soon after his marriage, and in the years 1850-51 it became much more than an acquaintance; for being myself in circumstances of great grief, I corresponded with him as I have never corresponded with any other man, and it was then that I formed the opinion of him which I have never seen cause to change—I mean my opinion of him as a Christian. I have not always agreed with him; indeed in some matters of opinion or policy I have altogether disagreed with him; but he always seemed to me to be striving to be a Christian, seeking ever to do God's will as it is taught in the Bible, and resigned to God's decrees; more, even *thankful* for his crosses. I forget what ailment in particular was affecting him some eight or nine years ago (long before his paralysis) when in answer to some remark of mine he observed 'I would not be without it for worlds.'

"Dr. Arnold says in one of his letters or sermons, 'Depend upon it, unless your life be part of your religion, your religion can be no part of your life,' and it was recognition of this principle that made your father's life really great in the greatest sense. He was one of the very few whom I have known whose mind seemed *never* to lose sight of the precept 'Seek ye *first* the kingdom of God.' This was what he did throughout all the work, literary or other, into which he threw himself with an energy perfectly phenomenal; and on this earth he had his reward in the peace of mind which he derived from his perfect trust in God. 'There is such repose in Williams,' said Lord Elgin.

"Another of his characteristics was his self-restraint in censure of others whose opinions or proceedings must have shocked him. I mean his censure of individuals. As a writer he has been, I think, unduly severe upon us, the English, as a nation or government; but he looked on opium as the curse of China, and assisting as he did at the beginning of the first war, he could not but regard us as guilty of high-handed actions in a bad quarrel and for the furtherance of selfish interests. But for a man whose views on the most serious subjects made him uncompromising even to sternness as to what was right or even allowable, I never knew any one who so bridled his own tongue, or who so consistently opposed a contrary tendency in others. His life was, as you say, a grand life and yet so simple and quiet."

Out of a large number of letters with cordial estimates which have reached me from China, here is one which may be taken as a type. Mr. E. B. Drew, of the Chinese Imperial Customs Service, writes:

"I regard Dr. Williams as a rare and most remarkable instance of a man possessed of amazing industry and perseverance, and in whom these qualities were stimulated by piety and a burning love of God and mankind. It was this combination of the strongest working qualities with the most powerful stimulus possible to man that kept him steadily laboring—not for years alone but for decades and quarter-centuries—on vast and comprehensive tasks, and enabled him to bring them to a grand and triumphant end. His are two *monumenta ære perennia* (if my Latin plurals are not forgotten), and I often cite his career to my younger acquaintances in China to show what immense results steady aims inspired by religious love to God and man are capable of accomplishing."

No review of the character of Mr. Williams has been more justly drawn or admirably expressed than that of President Porter's written for the *Missionary Herald*. His conclusion is worth quoting:

"Like Franklin, beginning as a printer, he was called to stand before kings; but he never forgot his Master in heaven, nor the greater than any earthly kingdom which He is establishing on the earth. When on one occasion he spoke to the students of Yale College of the certain triumphs of this kingdom, it was with the enthusiasm of youthful consecration and the confidence of life-long service.

"Few men were better fitted in temperament, in intellectual tastes and habits, in moral energy, and in spiritual self-consecration, for the constant and unsparing drudgery involved in such a life. Few men, it is believed, have put their powers and gifts to a more constant and productive use. His elastic spirits, his wakeful curiosity, his minute observation, his loving sympathy with man, and his affectionate trust in his Divine Master, seem never to have failed. . . . The buoyant and cheerful temper which made sunlight for others whenever he was present also reflected unbroken sunshine into his own soul. The Christ, who dwelt ever in his thoughts as the Hope of Glory, enabled him to find indications of hope in the social and spiritual movements which he had watched so closely for more than a generation, and oftentimes from points of view which gave him almost the outlook of a prophet. He was not the man to exaggerate under the impulses of an excited fancy, but whether it was in fancy or in fact, it is a fact that toward the end of his life he spoke with glowing and almost prophetic confidence concerning the changes which were to befall China and Japan within the next generation. He was by himself and in his words a living and speaking witness of the dignity and inspiration of the missionary calling and the missionary spirit when it becomes an inspiration.

"There was much in the closing years of his life to admire and almost to envy. The sweetness and simplicity of his character made friends for him with all who met him. It is no exaggeration to say that every casual acquaintance was illumined and inspired by the briefest interview. Though feeble in body and with impaired eyesight, he maintained his habits of close and constant literary occupation. . . . He sought employment with his hands almost to the hour of his death, and in the quiet but unspoken triumph, nay rather in the unspeakable serenity of the peace which Christ gives to those who are eminently His, he breathed out his life."

"During the years of his residence in New Haven [writes his physician and near neighbor, Dr. S. G. Hubbard] I enjoyed the rare privilege of almost daily intercourse with Dr. Williams. He impressed me, in common with those who knew him, as a man of the most lovely character and exalted sentiments of Christian life and patriotism. He possessed in a remarkable degree those qualities of a great teacher which enabled him to impart to others in a most attractive manner the fullest information, not only respecting the country and people among which he had spent so large a portion of his life, but of the political, social, and religious histories of all Eastern nations.

"His knowledge of physical geography, particularly of those countries, was surprising, in view of the nature of his professional pursuits and the almost narrow limits of the field within which the great labors of his life were conducted. His wide intelligence in general science, and his familiarity with those questions which in his time occupied the minds of public men, indicated the liberal breadth of his culture, as well as the minute exactness of his knowledge. In whatever society he was found he was the centre of a delighted circle of listeners. His brilliant conversational powers, the force, clearness, and terseness of his style of speech were excelled only by his modesty and candor. Truly he was a great teacher.

"Of such a many-sided man I would not attempt an analysis; but any estimate of his character must be inadequate which does not include as first and foremost and best of all those traits which most adorn the highest types of Christian manhood."

Rev. R. A. Sawyer, D.D., published a number of reminiscences in the *Evangelist* soon after his death, among which we read:

"On a certain occasion he stood before the University and spoke of the missionary work in his quiet way from an experience of forty-seven years, and the impressions made may be inferred from the remark of a student on retiring: 'Did you mark Dr. Williams' face? He looked like St. John and St. Paul in one—the most eloquent face conceivable!' The instincts of youth are seldom truer than in this judgment. No one could look into Dr. William's eye as it lit with thought, glowed with fervid conviction, and twinkled with controlled humor all at once, without the feeling that he was in the presence of something as rare as it was unique. The fulness of mind and heart were fused into a crystalline manliness, which won affection and exacted reverence; and when by a fall on the slippery sidewalk the shock was given which for nearly two years assaulted and at length terminated his life, the serene strength of his character came out like a mighty fortress from which obscuring forests had been cut away. To have heard him speak in terms of Scripture as he pointed to that disabled arm, was to learn something new, both of faith in God and of the meaning of His word. To be led by him in prayer was to go literally upward to the "secret place," when in solemn quiet one of the greatest men spoke in childlike terms, as he breathed his confidences into the ear of the Father Almighty.

"Dr. Williams sympathized with the late Dr. Bacon in his oft-expressed opinion that 'public prayer was fast becoming a lost art.' A distinguished minister once used the following expressions in pulpit prayer: 'We thank Thee that all men are Thy children, and that when we love men, we love Thee; when we think highly of human powers, we praise Thee; when we worship human genius, we are not idolaters, as our fathers thought.' Coming out of the church a Western man went swinging by, saying to his comrade: 'Great Scott, what praying!' 'He probably means,' said Dr. Williams, 'John the Scot, who taught that every man was a theophany; and that is the way the new theology prays. Let us go in here,' he added as we passed an Episcopal church, 'and follow one of Cranmer's prayers, to get the taste out of the mouth.'

"The scholarship of Dr. Williams was exact and searching, yet it covered a wide territory. His resources of information were as ready and sure as they were ample. His spirit was catholic and tolerant, yet he was zealous for 'the ancient faith,' and dealt vigorously with any thing that tended to throw discredit on the work or belief of the great authorities of the reformed faith. Leaving the College chapel once, he exclaimed, 'Long life to our preacher! He does not hold up our fathers in the faith to be laughed at.'"

It would be hard to find within the limit of a single sentence a truer estimate of his qualities than that which Mr. Trevelyan applies to Zachary Macaulay—between whom and my father there were points of resemblance so significant as to attract the notice of very many—when he says that "The secret of his character and of his actions lay in perfect humility and an absolute faith."

INDEX.

ABEEL, Rev. D., 61, 106
Aitcheson, Rev. Wm., 299, 306; his death, 321, 322
Allen, Rev. D. O., 132
Amaral, Governor, assassination of, 171
American, merchants assist the English to trade, 115; undisturbed in Macao, 117; relations with Lewchew, 187; shipwrecks on Japan, 184, 213; frigates destroy the Bogue Forts, 241; diplomacy at Taku Forts, 256-262; relations to other allies at Tientsin, 277; aid to British at Taku Forts, 304; Legation reaches Peking, 316; treaty ratifications exchanged, 322; coolie traders, 325; policy in China, 359; immigration laws, 414, 427
American Bible Society, presidency, 445, 447
American Board of Missions, printing-press in Canton, 39; first missionaries in China, 61; liberality of Olyphant towards, 78; its China branch returns to Canton, 144; meeting in New Haven, 149; allowance to Canton mission, 164; proposes to give up mission press, 234; Mr. Williams resigns, 245; a mission in Central China, 361
American Oriental Society, 151; presidency, 450
Anderson, Rev. Rufus, 43, 75, 158, 159, 180, 245
"Anglo-Chinese Calendar," 168, 172
Arabs in the desert, 135
Audience question, discussed at Peking, 317-320; first granted to foreigners, 394; description of, 401-406

BAGG, Dr. M. M., 6
Bartlett, Charles, his school, 27-29

Bartlett, J. Russell, 151, 163
Bazin, A. P. L., 141
Bettleheim, Dr. B. J., 227
Beyerhaus, type-founder in Berlin, 143, 146
Bible, cheapness of Chinese, 64; revision of Morrison's version, 75; partly translated into Japanese, 99; term for God in, 166; revision progressing, 175
Blodget, Rev. H., 339, 340, 348, 367, 390, 399, 416, 432; estimate of Mr. Williams, 474
Bogue Forts, destruction of opium at, 103; Dr. Bridgman and Commissioner Lin at, 115; destroyed by American frigates, 241
Bombay, visit to, 132
Bonin Islands, 189-192
Bonney, Rev. S. W., 186, 206
Borrow, George, 143
Bridgman, E. C., 60; his labors and character, 61, 62, 63; prepares the "Chrestomathy," 105; and Commissioner Lin, 115, 120; interpreter to Cushing, 127; revises Bible translation, 165; 186, 274, 281, 282, 288; his death, 331, 337
British, merchants surrender opium, 103; trade through Americans in China, 115; expelled from Macao, 116; fleet arrives in China, 118; second rupture with China, 241; plenipotentiary arrives, 250; characteristics at Tientsin, 277, 280; force at Taku in 1859, 299; defeat at Taku, 301-312
Brown, Rev. S. R., arrival in Macao, 111, 165; in Japan, 285, 325, 332, 391
Browne, J. Ross, 377, 378
Bruce, Sir Fredk., 259, 358
Burchard, Rev. Ely, his school, 25-27
Burlingame, A., arrival in China, 333; goes to Peking, 335; 337, 339, 343; his influence, 358; and policy, 359;

483

return to China, 364; becomes Chinese envoy, 370; his peculiar fitness, 371, 374, 376; his death, 382

CANTON, life in, 48, 54–61; risk to foreigners in, 68; survey of, 74; river scenes near, 84; Lin's treatment of foreigners in, 102; trade closed at, 113; mission returns to, 144; arrival at, in 1849, 163; temper of the natives, 168; insurrection and mission work in, 237; evacuated by the British, 248; capture of, 250, 323; farewell visit to, 342

China, accounts of, 48; new era opens for, 123; in "The Middle Kingdom," 160, 163; toleration of Christianity in, 165, 275; political position in 1862, 341; and the Burlingame mission, 370, 376; and the U. S. immigration bill, 430; famine of 1878, 431

Chinese, treatment of foreigners, 68; sailors and the missionaries, 80; peasantry near Macao, 89; contempt for foreigners, 113; soldiers, 120; emigration to California commences, 170, 177; and English, 279, 280; officials, 289, 292; civilization and Christianity, 352; embassy to foreign powers, 370; and the American immigration laws, 414; maltreated in America, 427

"Chinese Chrestomathy," 105

"Chinese Commercial Guide," 125, 240, 243; its fifth edition, 334

Chinese language, difficulties in procuring teachers, 58; interruptions in learning, 81; text-book and dictionary published, 124, 125; studied in Paris, 142; idioms, 181; understood in Japan, 212; samples of epistolary style, 290; obstacles in arranging, 395; chair of, in Yale College, 421, 425

Chinese Repository, founded, 62; 67, 78, 126; loses on Dyer's types, 132; 165, 172, 174; brought to a close, 178, 180; remaining copies burned with the factories, 242, 244

"Chinese Topography," published, 126

Cholera, in Troy, 41; in Utica, 45

Christianity, in China, toleration edict of 1845, 165; toleration clause in treaty of Tientsin, 273; its effect, 275, 281; Japanese fear of, 284; and civilization in China, 351

Chunghow, 314, 316, 403

Chusan, captured by the British, 118

Clarke, Thos. Allen, 17

Cleveland, lectures in, 147

Clinton, Gov. DeWitt, in Utica, 14, 32

Cochinchinese officials, visit from, 86

Co-hong, Canton, 55–57; and Gov.-Gen. Lin, 103; its downfall, 123

Cushing, Caleb, in China, 126

DANA, James D., 20, 173, 344, 367, 392, 421

Dana, Miss Susan, 11

Davis, John W., in China, 175

Dictionary, printing Medhurst's Hokkëén, 81; its cost and completion, 93; Vocabulary issued, 125; Tonic, begun, 172, 179; completed, 239; a third, begun, 345, 360, 365; Syllabic, published, 397

Dutch, merchants in Japan, 184, 213; used in interpreting, 195; in Desima, 283

Dwight, Rev. H. G. O., 25, 139

Dyer, Samuel, his Chinese types, 128; his death, 129; his work discontinued, 132

EAST India Co., factory of, 58; withdrawal from China, 73, 101

"Easy Lessons in Chinese," 124, 158, 383

Eaton, Amos, his school, 32–36, 46

Egypt, visit to, 133, 134

El Arisch, 135

Elgin, Lord, 183, 223, 249, 257, 264, 267, 277, 280, 288, 290, 291

Elliot, Capt. Charles, 102; his character, 103; withdraws on board ship, 116, 121

Erie Canal, opening of, 13

Elucidator, anti-masonic paper, 4, 29

"English and Chinese Vocabulary," published, 125, 383

FACTORIES, Canton, 55–60; foreigners confined in, by Lin, 102; mob before, 109 and 112; residence in, 164, 170; destroyed, 242

Foreigners, in China, 48, 54; treat-

ment of, 68 ; confined in the factories by Lin, 102 ; organize Morrison Educational Society, 111 ; and a Chinese mob, 112 ; anomalous position of, 114 ; changes after 1842, 123 ; and the Tai-pings, 203 ; unite in claims against China, 249
Formosa, its southern end, 206
Framingham, Mass., 2
French, allied with English against China, 249 ; soldiers in Canton, 250 ; troops not present in 1859, 299 ; retire from Taku, 313 ; objects in China, 335

GALLATIN, Albert, 151
Garritt, James, 10
Gaza, visit to, 136
Gorihama, landing at, 195
Gray, Asa, 28, 218
Griffis, Rev. W. E., 183, 213, 215
Gros, Baron, 249, 259, 277
Gutzlaff, Rev. Charles, 59, 66, 75, 83, 86, 93 ; goes with the *Morrison* to Japan, 95

HAKODADI, as an open port, 212 ; visit to, 218, 229
Harris, Townsend, 283, 298
Hastings, Thomas, in Utica, 3
Hienfung, Emperor, his accession, 176 ; and the Tai-pings, 200 ; instructions to Commissioners at Tientsin, 279 ; and the Americans, 318 ; his death, 334
Ho, Governor, 252, 288, 289, 290, 297, 324
Hongkong, surrendered to the British, 123 ; American Board Mission in, 144 ; arrival at, 163 ; murders at, 169
Hope, Admiral, 300, 301, 304
Hospital, established in Canton, 77 ; closed, 122 ; preaching at, 172 ; its success, 180
Howqua, hong-merchant, 57, 77, 113
Hwashana, Imperial Commissioner, 264, 265, 276, 282, 288, 297, 339

INDIA, visit to, 133
Ivison, Henry, apprentice of Wm. Williams, 6 ; in Sunday-school, 22

JAPAN, control in Lewchew, 95 ; visit of the *Morrison* to, 96-99 ; Perry's expedition to, 183, 193, 203 ; a book on, 204 ; treaty concluded with, 214 ; third visit to, 283 ; lecture on, 288 ; in 1872, 391
Japanese, first impressions of, 196 ; sentiments of officials and people, 209, 221, 224 ; shops and people at Nagasaki, 283 ; trickery, 298 ; minister in Peking, 403
Japanese language, spoken in Lewchew, 94 ; study of, 99, 108, 185 ; usefulness at Hakodadi, 219, 220 ; proposal to compile a vocabulary, 231, 232
Japanese sailors, in Macao, 83 ; taken to Japan in the *Morrison*, 93-99 ; employed in printing-office, 100, 108 ; seven, at Macao, 122 ; picked up and returned, 184 ; Sam Patch, 226
Jerusalem, visit to, 136
Julien, Stanislas, 141
Junks, mission work among the, 80
Juvenile Society for Learning and Doing Good, 23

KAGOSIMA, Japan, the *Morrison* driven from, 96, 97
King, Charles W., 94
Kinqua, hong-merchant, 54
Kishen, Peace Commissioner, 118
Kiying, signs treaty of Wanghia, 127; obtains toleration of Christianity, 165 ; appearance at Tientsin, 267 ; his fate, 269, 277
Ko Kun-hua, Chinese professor, 450, 452.
Kweiliang, Commissioner, 264 ; his appearance, 265 ; signs the American treaty, 276 ; 278, 282 ; at Shanghai, 288 ; 297, 301, 317, 318, 320 ; his death, 338

LA FAYETTE, General, visits Utica, 13
Lay, G. Tradescant, 80 ; distributing tracts with, 87-91, 105 ; leaves China, 109
Lay, Horatio Nelson, 267, 349
Leang Afa, 60, 65, 76, 199
Lewchew Islands, visited by the *Morrison*, 94 ; by Perry's expedition, 187, 192 ; return to, 207 ; and Japanese govt., 213 ; American compact with, 227
"Lieh Kwoh Chi," a Chinese novel, 228

Lin, Gov.-Gen. of Kwangtung, 101; appointed special commissioner, 114; his character, 115; degraded and recalled, 118
Lin, or Hayashi, Japanese Commissioner, 208, 210, 224, 225
Lo, Chinese writer, 206, 212, 218, 219
London, first visit to, 142
Low, F. F., 363, 584, 386, 389, 394

MACAO, 59; removal of printing-office to, 80; life in, 83–91; British Superintendent in, 101; establishment in, 107; English expelled from, 116; barrier fort captured, 119; C. Cushing in, 126; in summer, 170; departure from, 343
McLean, Wm., printer, 3
Macy, Rev. Wm. A., 240
Malta, quarantine at, 139
Mandarins, petty tyranny of, 58
"Map of China," in Chinese, 157; its publication, 161; presented to a Chinese, 261
Martin, Mrs. E. T. T., 128, 146, 162, 295, 425
Martin, Rev. W. A. P., 258, 260, 263, 264, 267, 272, 274, 276, 297, 299, 306, 313, 319, 374, 390, 415, 417
Matsmai, Japan, 213, 219, 220
Medhurst, W. H., Sen., 75, 81, 291
Medical Missionary Society in China, 77
"Middle Kingdom," 61; its conception, 149, 155; its publication, 160, 163; translated in German, 282; revision of, 435, 436, 445; its preface, 457; the revised edition published, 458
Minnesota, steam frigate, 249, 281, 283, 285, 291, 293
Missions, foreign, and Mrs. Sophia Williams, 10; and printing in China, 39; kind of work in, 62; early hindrances to, 76; before the Opium War, 104; enlarged after treaty of Nanking, 123; in India, 132; transferred from Hongkong to Canton, 144; and "The Middle Kingdom," 161; unsettled state of, 173; in Lewchew, 227; Mr. Reed's testimony for, 274; started in Japan, 284, 325; in Peking, 340; defence of, in the *N. Y. Observer*, 350; in Central China, 361; and missionaries, 375; farewells in Peking and Shanghai, 416, 419; Mr. Williams' liberality towards, 472
Mississippi, steam frigate, 197, 221, 225, 254, 260, 285, 297
Mongolia, trip to, 368–370
Morrison, John R., 59, 84, 103, 125, 168, 269
Morrison, Rev. Robert, 60, 61; his career, 69; his death, 71; 73, 93, 102
Morrison Education Society, 111, 165
Morrison, ship, 49, 51, 93, 94, 116, 181, 196, 298
Morrow, Dr. James, 217, 222

NAGASAKI, 184; visit to, 283; harbor of, 285
Napa-kiang, Lewchew, visited by the *Morrison*, 94; by Perry's expedition, 187; arrangements at, 192, 198; inhabitants, 207; squadron returns to, 226
Napier, Lord, arrival and death in China, 101
Nazareth, visit to, 138
New Hartford, N. Y., home of Thomas Williams, 2. 3; Mrs. Samuel Wells' farm, 12
New Haven, American Board meeting in, 149; home and society in, 142
New York, parting experiences in, 50; return to, 144, 148
Nile, trip upon, 134
Ningpo, visits to, 228, 295, 336, 394
Nye, Gideon, sends Mr. Williams through Europe, 131, 139; buys Manchu type, 143; and "The Middle Kingdom," 163; recommendation to Secretary Seward, 377

OHO-SIMA, the *Mississippi* at, 225
Olyphant, D. W. C., 43, 49, 51, 61, 77, 93, 111, 145, 157
Opium, surrendered and destroyed at Canton, 103; smuggling resumed, 118, 123, 175; and England, a Chinese official on, 261; Japanese fear of, 284; legalized by treaty, 291
Opium War with China, causes of, 114; commencement of, 118; its conclusion, 123

INDEX. 487

Osborn, Amos O., 27
Ouragawa, Japan, 96

PALESTINE, journey in, 134–139
Paris, visit to, in 1845, 140 ; in 1875, 408
Paris Hill, N. Y., school in, 25
Parker, Peter, M.D., arrival in Canton, 76, 84 ; goes to Japan, 94 ; forced to leave Canton, 104, 106 ; returns to America, 122 ; interpreter to Cushing, 127 ; 164 ; made chargé, 175 ; 203 ; appointed U. S. Commissioner to China, 234 ; 236, 242 ; retires, 249 ; 269, 357, 425
Pehtang, Americans at, 313, 314, 321 ; treaty ratification at, 322
Peiho, allied fleet meet at mouth of, 254, 299 ; defeat of the British, 301–312 ; travelling on, 315, 415
Peking, question of foreigners entering, 259, 260, 297, 301 ; Americans arrive at, 315 ; leave, 321 ; capture of, 333 ; described, 338 ; houses in, 344, 348 ; temples near, 355 ; parting from, 416.
Perry, Commodore M. C., 18, 181, 183 ; his character, 193 ; in China, 199, 205 ; transfers pennant, 208 ; treaty-making at Yokohama, 211 ; fails to reach Yedo, 216 ; his qualities, 223, 229 ; correspondence, 230, 231, 235, 298
Pompelly, Prof. R., 348
Portuguese, in printing-office, 110 ; assist the English in Macao, 117 ; governor assassinated, 171 ; captain at Ningpo, 228 ; and the coolie trade, 326
Poutiatine, Count, 249, 255, 263, 267, 277, 280
Powhatan, steam frigate, 208, 221, 223, 227, 228, 238, 299, 312, 314, 322
Printing, by Seward & Williams in Utica, 3 ; press sent to Canton, 39, 78 ; learning, 44, 47, 49 ; in Canton, 63, 65 ; hindrances to, in Canton, 104 ; office in Macao, 110 ; at Bombay, 132 ; Imprimerie Royale in Paris, 141, 142 ; in Canton, 174 ; determination to stop, 180, 234 ; office burned with the factories, 242 ; list of works printed, 244

QUANSHINGQUA'S dinner, 68

REED, William B., arrives in China, 249 ; 251, 252, 258, 259, 262, 264, 266, 273 ; signs treaty, 276 ; 278, 282, 288, 291 ; his departure, 293, 294 ; letter from, 299
Rensselaer Institute, Troy, 31–36
Russian, plenipotentiary joins Allies in China, 249 ; dinner on a man-of-war, 255 ; and American course at Tientsin, 277, 279 ; interference at Taku suspected, 311 ; Legation in Peking, 319

SERVANTS, necessity of, in Canton, 114 ; removed from the English in Macao, 117 ; checks upon, 181 ; in Peking, 348
Seu, Gov.-General, 172, 175
Seu Ki-yu, 417
Seward, Asahel, partner of Wm. Williams, 3
Seward, Geo. F., 413, 416
Seward, T. W., 19, 23, 53
Seward, Wm. H., 378 ; visits Peking, 385
Seymour, Horatio, 27
Shanghai, Bridgman in, 165 ; foreign settlement, 202 ; visit to, 238 ; address to missionaries at, on toleration clauses, 281 ; tariff treaty signed at, 291 ; with Ward in, 297 ; and the Tai-pings, 335 ; changes in, 379 ; printing dictionary in, 390 ; farewell to, 418
Shepard, R. B., apprentice, 7, 40
Shui, capital of Lewchew, 183 ; visit to, 207
Sieh, Chinese writer, 187 ; his death, 190
Simoda, as an open port of Japan, 212, 214 ; visit to, 217, 220–222 ; destroyed, 283
Stanton, Vincent, his capture, 119
Stevens, Edwin, 60 ; his Bethel at Whampoa, 78 ; death, 91 ; 106, 291
Sunday, in Paris, 140 ; in Perry's squadron, 216 ; on the *Mississippi*, 254 ; in Peking, 319
Sunday-school, Mrs. Wm. Williams' interest in, 10 ; character and influence of the Utica, 20–22 ; in New York, 156

Susquehanna, flag-ship, 187, 197, 206, 208
"Syllabic Dictionary," begun, 345, 360, 365; its printing, 389, 393; introduction and index, 395; published, 397; criticisms, 398, 399, 434; plates stolen, 440

TAI-PING rebellion, 199, 201, 202, 335, 356
Taku Forts, the Allies at, 254–262; capture of, 263; rebuilt, 300; battle and repulse at, 301–312
Tan, Commissioner, 256, 257, 261, 264
Tattnall, Commodore, 299, 303, 305
Term controversy, 166, 175, 433
Tientsin, Allies proceed to, 263; treaties signed at, 276; return to, 337; mission house bought in, 339; mob at, 384, 386
Toleration of Christianity, in treaty, 261; obtained at Tientsin, 270–273; subsequent influence, 275, 281
"Tonic Dictionary," begun, 172; resumed, 198, 232; published, 238–240; saved from destruction in the factories, 243; a revision commenced, 345; price in 1870, 383
Tracts, attempt to print, 60; cheapness of, 64; and Chinese sailors, 80; distributing, near Macao, 87–91; distribution hindered, 104
Tracy, Rev. Ira, 49, 52, 106
Tracy, Wm., 45
Treaty, of Nanking, in 1842, 123; of Wanghia, 127; of Kanagawa, 211, 212; signed, 214; negotiations at Taku Forts, 260–262; at Tientsin, 265–277; signed by English and French, 280; second American, with Japan, 283; supplementary tariff, signed, 291; ratifications exchanged at Pehtang, 322; compendium of U. S. treaties with Asiatic countries, 335; of 1880, 443
Troy, N. Y., Rensselaer Institute in, 31; cholera plague of 1832, 41, 42
Types, metallic Chinese, efforts to procure, for mission press, 128; Manchu, 139, 143; made in Berlin, 144; lectures to procure, 146; destroyed in burning of the factories, 242; account of, 244; in Ningpo, 295

UNITED STATES, first treaty with China, 126; expedition to Japan, 183 and *sqq.*; Legation removed to Macao, 241; and the Allies in China, 249; and China in 1858, 259, 265; joins the Allies again in 1859, 299; Legation house built in Peking, 362; consular service in China, 377, 388; legislation against Chinese immigration, 414
Uraga, Perry's expedition at, 193; refusal to stop at, 208
Utica, N. Y., Wm. Williams moves to, 3; fire department in, 5; appearance in 1820, 12; its rivalry with Whitestown, 13; High School, 27; the cholera plague in, 45; efforts to raise a type fund in, 128, 146; 160; second visit to, 327; welcome in 1875, 409

WADE, Sir T. F., 417; estimate of Mr. Williams, 476
Walworth, Miss, 152
Wanghia, treaty of, 127
Ward, Gen. F. G., 354, 356
Ward, John E., 294, 298, 304, 313, 320, 322, 324
Weed, Thurlow, on Wm. Williams, 4; as apprentice, 6
Wells, Samuel, 7; his widow, 12
Whampoa, 54; Stevens' work at, 79; ships detained at, 115
Whittlesey, Mrs., on Mrs. Sophia Williams, 8
Williams, Mrs. Catherine Huntington, 47, 130
Williams, H. Dwight, 5, 34; in New York, 149; his care of his brother, 456
Williams, John P., 243; his death, 249
Williams, Olyphant, birth, 182; his death, 286
Williams, Robert, of Roxbury, Mass., 1
Williams, S. Wells, on Utica fire company roll, 5; birth and boyhood, 11–15; fondness for reading, 16; T. A. Clarke's reminiscences of, 17, 18; shyness, 20, 36; recollections of Utica Sunday-school, 21; first journal, 23; schooling, 24–28; joins church, 29; goes to school at Troy, 31; accepts proposal from A. B. C. F. M., 39; leaves

INDEX. 489

Rensselaer Institute, 46 ; learning printing, 44, 47, 49 ; departure for China, 50 ; arrival in Canton, 54 ; first impressions, 58–61 ; literary attempts, 63 ; robbed near Canton, 68 ; removal to Macao, 80 ; life in, 81–91 ; first visit to Japan, 94–99 ; proposal to ordain, 104 ; prepares the Chrestomathy, 105 ; his health, 106 ; publishes his "Easy Lessons, 124 ; tries to start a type fund, 127 ; returns to America *via* Europe, etc., 132–145 ; lectures in the United States, 146 ; social tastes, 151 ; engagement, 152 ; marriage, 159 ; receives the degree of LL.D., 162 ; return to China, 163 ; pleasure in Macao, 170 ; at work in Canton, 174 ; his work in the *Repository*, 179 ; goes with the Japan expedition, 185 ; his enthusiasm as a naturalist, 190, 217 ; sentiments regarding the expedition, 192 ; illness, 203 ; returns with expedition to Japan, 206 ; has most-favored-nation clause inserted in treaty of Kanagawa, 214 ; strictures on Perry, 216 ; reflections on the expedition, 223 ; translates a Chinese novel, 228 ; Perry urges him to write a history of Japan, 231 ; presented with a Perry medal by Boston Board of Trade, 232 ; appointed United States Secretary and Interpreter to China, 234 ; finishes the "Tonic Dictionary," 239 ; his loss from destruction of the factories, 243 ; resigns from the A. B. C. F. M., 245 ; political prescience, 248 ; family sent to the United States, 252 ; at Taku Forts with the Allies, 254–262 ; delegated to discuss the treaty at Tientsin, 265 ; obtains the insertion of a Toleration Clause, 270–273 ; explains it in Shanghai, 281 ; Mr. Reed's opinion of, 293 ; goes with Ward to the Peiho, 298 ; arrives at Peking, 316 ; account of the visit to Peking, 323 ; exertions to stop the coolie trade, 325 ; sentiments on slavery, 328 ; re-writes "Commercial Guide," 334 ; goes to the north with Mr. Burlingame, 336 ; assists missions, 340 ; settles in Peking, 343 ; begins a third dictionary, 346 ; defence of missions in the *N. Y. Observer*, 350 ; letter to Dr. Anderson on a mission to Kiukiang, 361 ; builds Legation in Peking, 363 ; botanizing near Peking, 365, 366 ; trip to Mongolia, 368 ; conducts his family to Shanghai, 379 ; receives a medal from the king of Sweden, 381 ; goes to Shanghai to publish his dictionary, 389 ; trip to Japan, 391 ; illness, 394 ; his "Syllabic Dictionary" published, 397 ; audience with the emperor, 401 ; return to America, 407 ; welcome in Utica, 409 ; returns to Peking and resigns his post, 411 ; farewell to Peking, 415 ; leaves China, 420 ; surroundings in New Haven, 422 ; appointed professor of Chinese at Yale, 425 ; efforts in behalf of Chinese in America, 427 ; pamphlet on the Term Question, 434 ; begins to revise "The Middle Kingdom," 437 ; effect of Mrs. Williams' death, 442 ; elected president of American Bible Society, 445 ; of the Oriental Society, 450 ; breaks his arm, 452 ; illness, 455 ; the new "Middle Kingdom" published, 458 ; his death, 461 ; reminiscences and characteristics, 462 *ad fin.*

Williams, Mrs. Sarah Walworth, 152, 170, 185, 204, 379 ; her death, 441

Williams, Mrs. Sophia, her character, 7–9 ; interest in Sunday-school and foreign missions, 10, 14 ; death, 30

Williams, Stephen, of Roxbury, 2

Williams, Thomas, 2

Williams, Walworth, 164, 181, 238 ; his death, 329

Williams, William, printer in Utica, 3 ; service in War of 1812, 4 ; character, 6 ; suggests his son as missionary printer, 39 ; during cholera plague, 45 ; marries again, 47 ; removal from Utica and illness, 130, 146 ; death, 176

Williams, Wm. Frederick, 29, 163, 329 ; his death, 387

Wilson, Geo. S., apprentice, 7 ; his influence on boys, 23.

YALE College, 421, 422 ; Chinese professorship in, 425, 426 ; remonstrance against Chinese Bill of 1879, 429

Yedo, Bay of, the *Morrison's* visit to, 95, 96; Perry's expedition in, 193, 197; return to, 208; trip up, within sight of the city, 215; visit to, in 1872, 391

Yeh, Gov.-Gen. of Canton, 241, 243; refuses to meet Reed, 250; incidents of his capture, 251

Yokohama, interview at, 210; Simoda exchanged for, 283; in 1872, 391

THE END.